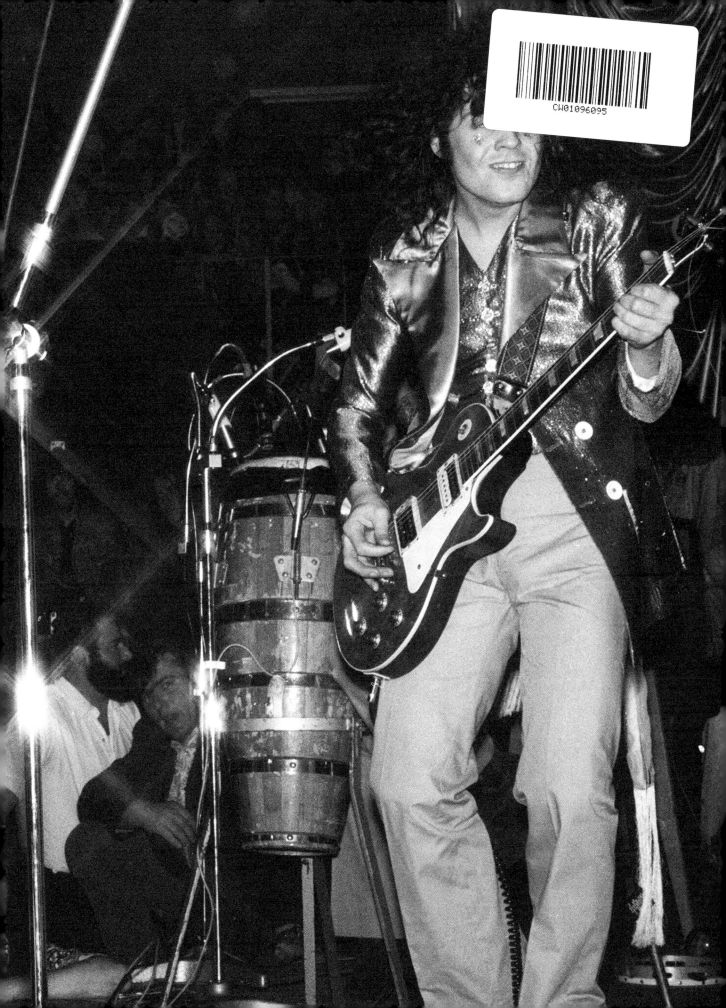

GLAM!

When Superstars Rocked the World 1970–74

To Cristiana of the Eternal City

Copyright © 2022 Omnibus Press
(A division of the Wise Music Group
14–15 Berners Street, London, W1T 3LJ)

Cover and book design by Amazing15
Picture research by the author

ISBN 978-1-913172-28-2

Printed in the Czech Republic.

www.omnibuspress.com

GLAM!

When Superstars Rocked the World 1970–74

Mark Paytress

OMNIBUS PRESS

London / New York / Paris / Sydney / Copenhagen / Berlin / Madrid / Tokyo

Four Steps to Glam Rock Heaven...

'I never lost that feel for pop. It was always there. There was the quiet period, flowers and peaceful. But I didn't feel that way anymore. It's not a very peaceful world. I want to boogie – but with good words as well.'

Marc Bolan, 1971

'I like the showbiz in showbiz yet everyone was getting so crazy they were all trying to deny it. But whatever you want to think, it is showbiz. When we get up there on stage, we're just the same as Hedy Lamarr.'

Ringo Starr, ex-Beatle, director of *Born To Boogie*, 1972

'C'mon, it is the Permissive Society, right? The Swinging Seventies. I mean, Andy Warhol, *Flesh*, *Trash*, you name it. Anything goes today, doesn't it. Can you just turn around while I put my trousers on?'

Robin Tripp (Richard O'Sullivan) to Jo (Sally Thomsett) in 'Three's A Crowd', *Man About The House*, ITV 1973

'If I've been at all responsible for people finding more characters in themselves than they originally thought they had, then I'm pleased because that's something I feel very strongly about – that one isn't totally what one has been conditioned to think one is.'

David Bowie, 1974

Cockney Rebel

Contents

Introduction

Are You Ready, Steve?

This is a book about pop in the early 1970s. It's about surviving the sixties and finding strategies to re-energise and flourish in its aftermath. About how a young man with the most maligned voice on the underground rock scene became the face that launched the new decade. How a struggling, jack-of-all-trades performer turned his eclecticism on its head to create a whole new way of becoming a pop artist(e). How the one-time 'worst band in the world' reinvented itself as a Grand Guignol rock'n'roll horror show.

But mostly it's about how a generation of try-hards and nobodies seized their moment in the first flush of a new decade – with a little help from a new wardrobe and the fear of remaining eternally obscure. Between 1970 and 1974, there was no time for subtlety or shyness – the intro was everything.

And here, in roughly chronological order, are twenty-five of the best from the glitter/glam era (or indeed, from any era, including three that go daringly against the grain). Stick 'em on – there's no better way to prepare for the story about to unfold…

Love Grows (Where My Rosemary Goes) – *Edison Lighthouse*
Spirit In The Sky – *Norman Greenbaum*
Groovin' With Mr Bloe – *Mr Bloe*
Hot Love – *T. Rex*
Stay With Me – *The Faces*
Son Of My Father – *Chicory Tip*
Back Off Boogaloo – *Ringo Starr*
Metal Guru – *T. Rex*

School's Out – *Alice Cooper*
All The Young Dudes – *Mott The Hoople*
Blockbuster! – *The Sweet*
Desperate Dan – *Lieutenant Pigeon*
Cum On Feel The Noize – *Slade*
20th Century Boy – *T. Rex*
Pyjamarama – *Roxy Music*
Drive-In Saturday – *David Bowie*
See My Baby Jive – *Wizzard*
Can The Can – *Suzi Quatro*
Saturday Night's Alright For Fighting – *Elton John*
I'm The Leader Of The Gang (I Am!) – *Gary Glitter*
Teenage Rampage – *The Sweet*
Jealous Mind – *Alvin Stardust*
Rebel Rebel – *Bowie*
This Town Ain't Big Enough For Both Of Us – *Sparks*
Just For You – *The Glitter Band*

Another time, another place – wasn't it ace…?

Mark Paytress, 2022

Prologue
The Death of Rocktopia

In a large field on a small island off the coast of southern England, Jimi Hendrix was fighting to save his career.

For four years, the guitarist had been the figurehead of the rock revolution; the poster boy for the psychedelic experience, and the love, peace and harmony that would surely follow.

But at the 1970 Isle Of Wight Festival, held over the August Bank Holiday weekend, Hendrix was tired, erratic, restive. So too the crowd, a noisy minority of whom had outmanoeuvred the aggressive security guards and their dogs. They tore down the corrugated iron fences in the hope of seeing their heroes for free.

Arriving on stage late to a muted welcome, Hendrix made peace offerings of his arrangements of 'God Save The Queen' and the overture from The Beatles' *Sgt Pepper* album. But 'All Along The Watchtower' was perfunctory, lacking all the strange grace of the single.

The guitarist had little energy for his old songs, just as he'd grown tired of the old tricks that had made him the sensation of '67: the kitschy feather boas, the thrusting sexuality, playing the guitar with his teeth, or behind his back, before burning it. They had served him well. But these were serious times for the rock revolution – or what remained of it.

Hendrix, his former wild-man hairstyle now trimmed in solidarity with the civil-rights struggle, had also been taming his sound. He wanted to be more inclusive; to spread the power of love, the power of soul; to embrace the funk sounds emanating from America's cities. He even spoke of making big-band music.

But the rock machine that turns you on also does you in. By 1970 rock had become big business. And, locked in a cycle of big-money tours by management and challenged by his search to create new music, Jimi Hendrix was no longer at his best.

The explosive opening of 'Machine Gun', at seven minutes long, was a desperate last gasp. The epic piece then limped on for another fifteen minutes, during

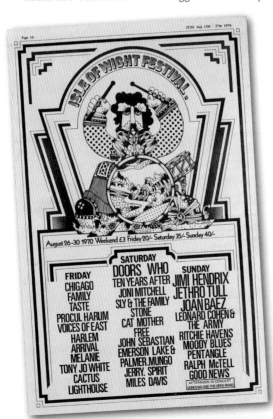

RIGHT: By August 1970, Isle Of Wight Festival headliner Jimi Hendrix had become a superstar in retreat. Less than three weeks after his erratic performance, rock culture's leading light was dead.

Everybody at the festival went home with 'Ride A White Swan' in their heads.

JIMI HENDRIX
1942-1970

DRUG OVERDOSE KILLS ROCK IDOL HENDRIX

which time he briefly walked off stage. The reluctant superstar was spent. The crowd, many disappointed by Hendrix's first gig in Britain in eighteen months, packed up and went home.

Weeks later, *The Daily Telegraph Magazine* featured a cover story on the festival entitled 'Was This The End Of Rocktopia?'. Rock's utopian dream was over. Within three weeks of the festival, Jimi Hendrix was gone too, dying in the early hours of September 18 as he lay beside a casual girlfriend, empty wine bottles and vials of pills.

Yet something more positive had also taken place back on the island. DJ and MC Jeff Dexter – who introduced Hendrix on stage, having hastily sewn up a tear in the guitarist's trousers – had slipped an advance copy of a new single into his DJ box before leaving London.

It was the latest from Tyrannosaurus Rex, a mostly acoustic duo who were regulars on the underground and festival circuit. They'd even played the first Isle Of Wight festival in 1968, headlined by The Crazy World of Arthur Brown and San Francisco acid-rockers

Jefferson Airplane. This time around, though, they were away gigging in the northeast.

Dexter had known Rex frontman Marc Bolan since the early sixties, when both were short-arsed, sharply dressed East End Mods. Once, after seeing the British film *Summer Holiday*, 15-year-old Bolan – then known by his birthname Mark Feld – announced he wanted to be the next Cliff Richard and asked Dexter to manage him. The request went unheeded.

Seven summers later, Dexter – now an underground DJ of some standing – was able to make amends. 'I played 'Ride A White Swan' continuously for the five days I was there,' he says. 'Everybody at the festival went home with it in their heads.'

The new song sounded like Tyrannosaurus Rex gone pop. But Tyrannosaurus Rex were now gone forever. In the shops on October 9, 'Ride A White Swan' bore a new credit: 'T. Rex'.

Chapter 1
Light Emanated from Him

Twinkle, twinkle, little star,
how I wonder what you are!
Up above the world so high,
like a diamond in the sky.
– English lullaby derived from 'The Star',
a poem by Ann and Jane Taylor, published 1806.

On January 30, 1970, Marc Bolan of Tyrannosaurus Rex married long-time girlfriend June Child at the registry office in Chelsea Old Town Hall, along the King's Road. June wore a twenties-style cloche hat; Bolan's mop of hair was flecked with confetti; DJ Jeff Dexter wore a woman's fur coat. It was a small, happy, hippie gathering. Afterwards, everyone went to Lorenzo's in South Kensington.

The couple had been inseparable since late spring 1968. They shared a flat in Blenheim Crescent, on the bohemian borders of Notting Hill and Ladbroke Grove. June drove the car and handled unofficial management chores for Marc. He came up with the songs – or 'spells', as he liked to call them.

Amidst their tapestries and antique-shop treasures stood a small statue of Pan, the pipe-playing pagan god. To Bolan, who had a habit of renaming everything, the figure was 'Poon', and Poon was his higher power. Whenever guidance was needed, he scrawled a note in his distinctive runic hand and placed it beside the statue.

Weeks into the new decade, Bolan was busy feeding notes to his lucky charm. His career had reached a crossroads. What, pray Poon, had fate in store for a porcelain-faced, softly-spoken aesthete wrapped in silk scarves and neckerchiefs? An androgynous exquisite with a fondness for green,

strap-fastened Mary Jane shoes from high-society cobblers Anello and Davide?

Alone at home on a spring day in this new era, the words came quickly for Marc. They usually did, in flashes of inspiration spiced up with nuggets plucked randomly from esoteric books, William Blake's *Complete Writings* being a favourite.

Bolan's lyrics were too fantastical for most. 'It was more Donovan than Dylan,' says producer

BLAKE
COMPLETE
WRITINGS

OXFORD STANDARD AUTHORS

Tony Visconti, who had discovered Bolan in an underground club in autumn 1967. 'Mythological imagery, Avalon, Guinevere.'

In that respect his new song was little different. But this time the lines came out pop-shaped, guided by a simple repeated hook – 'Ride it on out' – with no chorus required. 'Ride A White Swan' scanned like a nursery rhyme. Twinkle, twinkle, little star.

Marc took off to his practice room, the informally named Toadstool Studios.

'It was a broom cupboard with a snare on a stand, percussion equipment and an acoustic guitar!' Mickey Finn, Bolan's bongo-playing bandmate, later remembered.

But this was a day for the electric, probably the white Strat he'd been playing for several months. 'Ride A White Swan' would be nothing without the amplified notes that kicked the song into action and kept it swinging.

> The stuff that half the haddocks are wearing, I was wearing years ago.

★

Marc Bolan had always commanded attention. Back in 1962, young photojournalist Don McCullin found three clobber-mad, upwardly mobile youths on the streets of Hackney, northeast London, and featured them in a photo-essay for gentleman's magazine *Town*.

'You got to be different from the other kids,' 14-year-old Mark Feld told writer Peter Barnsley. 'I mean, you got to be two steps ahead. The stuff that half the haddocks you see around are wearing I was wearing years ago.'

He was a 'Face' then, in the days before young, individualistic Modernists mutated into off-the-peg Mods.

LEFT: Marc and June Bolan on their wedding day, January 30, 1970. 'He always looked to her for guidance,' says friend and producer Tony Visconti.

ABOVE: Profiled in a photo-essay on street style for the September 1962 edition of *Town* magazine, 14-year-old Stamford Hill 'Ace Face' Feld (right) mocked the imitators as 'haddocks'. 'You've got to be two steps ahead,' he insisted.

My people were fair and had sky in their hair...
But now they're content to wear stars on their brows

EMI REGAL ZONOPHONE

ABOVE: Artist George Underwood was introduced to Bolan by school pal David Jones, later Bowie. 'While we were talking, suddenly Marc sat cross-legged on the floor opposite June, also cross-legged, and they stared silently into each other's eyes for what seemed like ages. No chemical assistance was used [for the illustration] – just my imagination and some Gustave Doré engravings for inspiration.'

By the late sixties, Bolan had transformed himself. Now a poetry-spouting romantic with Pre-Raphaelite ringlets and a mystic aura, he was everyone's idea of the archetypal hippie.

'He wasn't,' says Tony Visconti. 'He abhorred drugs and he wasn't into free love. He was playing at it.'

But Marc had a quality that endeared him to the flower-power crowd. 'Light emanated from him,' Visconti adds. 'He had the most charisma of all the stars I've met or worked with.'

By the end of the decade, the 'anything goes' hippie scene – with its fuzzy philosophising and flamboyant, multicoloured fashions – was becoming

old hat. A more macho rock culture, happy to slouch around in jeans and T-shirt while listening to far more robust and marketable rock acts, had eclipsed the 'freaks'.

It wasn't Bolan's scene. 'I wear chicks' shoes,' he said, 'because they look nice, and because you can't get men's in green and silver and purple. And I wear chicks' sweaters because I like tight clothes.'

Bolan had anticipated change the previous summer, plugging in an electric guitar for a peace-shattering, production peasouper he called 'King Of The Rumbling Spires'. Bizarrely, *Melody Maker* predicted great things for it: 'Electrified teenybop! Could easily crack their chart problem.'

The only thing it cracked was Tyrannosaurus Rex, bringing Bolan's battle of wills with original partner Steve Peregrin Took to a head. Took, who fully embraced the stoner lifestyle, made his way to the distant end of Ladbroke Grove where his acid-biker mates hung out.

The Took-era Tyrannosaurus Rex had enjoyed some success. Two albums charted; two early singles skirted the top thirty. But it was always going to be difficult to live down the title of that first Rex album, released in the post-psychedelic summer of '68: *My People Were Fair And Had Sky In Their Hair… But Now They're Content To Wear Stars On Their Brows*.

'Tyrannosaurus Rex, with [Radio 1 DJ] John Peel at the wand, conducted us on a tour of a land of rattles, plinks, plonks and poetry, and the applause was rapturous,' wrote *Melody Maker*'s Chris Welch of a 1969 gig.

Took's departure prompted Bolan to make a clean break. His replacement was Mickey Finn, a painter of psychedelic interiors with a face fit for Italian cinema. His handiwork featured on the walls of The Beatles' Apple Boutique and at Granny Takes A Trip on King's Road. His abilities as a percussionist were of less certain pedigree.

TYRANNOSAURUS REX: most commercial pr...

Electrified teenybop!

accompaniment on a non-blues ditty, that owes more to Cowpoking Jim Hornswoggle, than Blind Black Fi... ...and his ...it's

sumptuous, almost Orientally splendid reviewing chamber, and seized my typewriter. They wrote a few insulting lines, then fled through the library window, pausing only t...

pop group. Airy young men in white trousers, with packets of Menthol cigarettes stuffed in their shirt pockets, writing for ...w Underground

SHELLEY PAUL: "The Clowns Are Coming In" (Jay Boy). Shelley is just sixteen years old. Long legs, short-bobbed hair and a mor...

award for th... numbingly pueri... lar single reco... the week, I we... hesitatingly this for...

'I used to knock the shit out of somebody's chests at the bottom of a bed,' Finn recalled. 'But Marc and June bought me a pair of clay bongos and I got on with it.'

That suited Bolan's needs. Rex's pixieland sound needed de-cluttering, but 'The Look' also mattered. Marc and June agreed that Finn's finely sculpted features would complement Bolan's soft visual image. It also helped that the painter-turned-timekeeper was a cheery fella with no delusions of grandeur.

The new pairing recorded a fourth Rex album, *A Beard Of Stars*, in November 1969. Its gentler songs gazed towards the mystic margins of the singer-songwriter market, but guitar-heavy set closer 'Elemental Child' ventured off somewhere else entirely – more Jimi Hendrix than Tim Buckley.

One song, 'By The Light Of A Magical Moon' – a tip to Little Richard's 'By The Light Of The Silvery Moon', a top-twenty hit in 1959 – was selected for release in January. It was a new Rex for new times. Bolan had toned down his distinctive vocal style (often lampooned as 'Larry the Lamb' in the letters pages of the rock press); the lyrics were intelligible; the sound crisp and airy; the groove upbeat, almost funky.

He'd also smuggled in a sonic good-luck charm, a soundburst of pop-fan hysteria lifted from The Byrds' 'So You Want To Be A Rock 'N' Roll Star'. Back in 1967, the song had been a joke at the expense of all-conquering manufactured group The Monkees. ('Cardboard pop stars,' Bolan wrote in his 1967 diary after seeing them on a freebie at the Empire Pool, Wembley. 'An impossible drag.') Bolan's intent was guided by wish-fulfilment.

Those talismanic screams fell on deaf ears and 'Magical Moon' flopped. *A Beard Of Stars* fared better, briefly peaking at No. 21; Tyrannosaurus Rex were still an album act.

Reviews were the usual mix of faint praise – *Melody Maker*'s 'jolly, poetic [Rex] appeal' – and put-down. 'Maddeningly monotonous; pop at its most pretentious,' declared the *Evening Standard*'s Ray Connolly.

When Trevor Brice of harmony poppers Vanity Fare complained, 'I think it's horrible. It's like an old age pensioner singing,' Bolan could wear the criticism as a badge of pride. But hearing DJ Tommy Vance slate the album on BBC Radio 1's *Top Gear* – where John Peel had been conducting Rex love-ins for two years – infuriated him.

'[Vance] became totally horrific and paranoic,'

ABOVE LEFT: *Top Pops* magazine, October 1968. 'We never take long to record,' said Bolan, pictured here with Rex percussionist Steve Peregrin Took

ABOVE: Bolan's chain-mail style top and electric Stratocaster hinted at a heavier sound for Rex's first album of the new decade, *A Beard Of Stars*.

OPPOSITE BELOW: Tyrannosaurus Rex's summer '69 single, the darkly uncommercial 'King Of The Rumbling Spires', seemed an unlikely candidate for *Melody Maker*'s 'Electrified Teenybop!' headline. The magazine's resident Rex enthusiast Chris Welch was clearly onto something.

ABOVE TOP: Tyrannosaurus Rex's
first single of 1970, 'By The Light
Of A Magical Moon', included
a hopeful burst of screaming
teenage fans apparently lifted
from an old Byrds hit.

ABOVE: Resurrecting Eddie
Cochran's 'Summertime Blues'
early in 1970 was evidence
that Bolan was moving on from
Tyrannosaurus Rex's distinctive
offbeat style. The Who released
a full band version on 45 in July,
though Rex's two-man take
was more faithful to Cochran's
unembellished original.

ABOVE RIGHT: The tenth
anniversary of Cochran's death
prompted a wave of rock'n'roll
reissues during 1970. Bolan,
who claimed he once carried
Cochran's guitar outside the
Hackney Empire, stained his
Gibson Les Paul orange in
homage to the rocker's famous
Gretsch.

Marc told Chris Welch. 'He said he couldn't understand any of the lyrics. Why can't they understand me?' he grumbled.

The interview concluded with a veiled threat. 'We're thinking of going on at the Festival Hall with 400 watts each and freak 'em all out! All the kids will come to see freaky Bolan quietly doing his thing – then *NEAGH!*'

There was no Festival Hall gig, only a St Patrick's Night knees-up at Exeter University the following week. Also in the diary were a string of third-on-the-bill dates supporting Deep Purple, Chicken Shack, Colosseum, the Edgar Broughton Band and the recently launched Faces.

Bolan's hurt was inadvertently revealed in a March '70 interview with underground rock mag *Zigzag*. While discussing the latest album, conversation suddenly switched to Nijinsky, inspiration for a song on Rex's 1969 set *Unicorn*. Marc compared the innovative dancer/choreographer to Pink Floyd's original madcap, Syd Barrett.

'[Nijinsky] was so into what he was doing. Then he freaked partially and everybody kicked him in the face… said he was mad. He died about four years later.' Marc Bolan had grown tired of being misunderstood.

On February 26, 1970, rock'n'roll revivalism – sparked by Bill Haley & His Comets' 1968 tour of Britain – breached the hallowed, patchouli-scented walls of London's premier underground venue. Among those 'Rocking The Roundhouse' were gold-lamé legends Marty Wilde and Joe Brown, hotly tipped revivalists The Wild Angels and Bert Weedon, whose *Play In a Day* guidebooks inspired a generation of British guitarists.

The night brought out an unlikely mix of teds, bikers, hairies and nostalgists. Bolan, wearing his old school blazer, also came to pay homage.

'Quartets of big blokes in leather jackets danced together, energetic steps like physical training exercises,' observed Chris Welch later. 'That's the Chicken Slop,' Bolan explained.

Welch, who had declared Bert Weedon a 'superstar' in his review of the gig, observed the depths of Bolan's passion for vintage rock'n'roll during a visit to his Ladbroke Grove flat, days later.

'It's nice to get back to the originals,' Bolan told him over cheese, wine and Brussels sprouts. On the turntable was an anthology of Johnny Burnette and the Rock 'n Roll Trio's recordings, one of a glut of recent releases plundering the rock'n'roll era.

Rock musicians were now sufficiently of age

to celebrate the music of their youth without embarrassment. The MC5 kicked off the new decade with *Back In The USA*, topped and tailed with Little Richard and Chuck Berry covers. Closer to home – perhaps too close, given the involvement of Steve Took – Ladbroke Grove's underground king, Mick Farren, had slung a version of Eddie Cochran's 'Summertime Blues' onto his otherwise collage-style *Mona – The Carnivorous Circus* album.

'What we really need is a band that everyone can go and fall about to,' Farren told *Melody Maker*'s Richard Williams, 'rather than having heavy intellectual exercises all the time.'

With progressive and hard rock acts dominating the universities and breaking into the concert-hall circuit, the last remnants of the underground seemed to be crying out for a revival of active, stand-up engagement.

On May 14, 1970, Tyrannosaurus Rex returned to the recording studio for the first time in almost six

months. Much of the time was spent on a new song called 'Jewel'; Bolan made every syllable shine, every consonant count. His guitar lines, which were super-distorted, followed the Hendrix trail.

But 'Jewel' was all about the riff, a mean and nasty rumble. To anyone with a copy of that Johnny Burnette collection, whose opener, 'Honey Hush', was probably the best side of baseball bat-swinging rock'n'roll ever recorded, it was also strangely familiar. Bolan had chosen well and interpreted freely. 'Jewel' sounded dynamic and commercial, along the lines of recent rock hits like Juicy Lucy's cover of Bo Diddley's 'Who Do You Love?'.

The change in pace suited Marc. Returning to the studio soon afterwards, he recorded a version of Eddie Cochran's 'Summertime Blues'.

The original was deceptively threadbare – guitar, bass, handclaps, minimal drums and Cochran's don't-bug-me voice. Eddie was newsworthy too. There had

ABOVE: Tyrannosaurus Rex were often photographed in natural settings. 'One day, they found a little dead bird which distressed them to no end,' Visconti recalls. 'They buried the bird and said an earth prayer for it. I could see that one day he'd like to see fire spring from his hands.'

RIGHT: Bolan named Tyrannosaurus Rex in 1967 after a line in *A Sound Of Thunder*, a science fiction short story by Ray Bradbury dating from the early fifties.

BELOW: *The Girl Can't Help It* was revived in 1970 to mark the anniversary of Cochran's death. One of the stars of the 1956 film was Little Richard, the rock'n'roll era's most daring, extravagant star and an inspiration to many seventies stars-in-waiting, including Noddy Holder, Ian Hunter and David Bowie.

OPP PAGE BELOW: The original 'Ride A White Swan' tape box reveals that 'Jewel', an electrifying Hendrix-style number based on an old Johnny Burnette Trio riff, was initially slated for inclusion on the maxi-single.

been a flurry of anniversary records commemorating his death in April 1960. On the day of the 'Jewel' session, BBC TV screened rock'n'roll musical *The Girl Can't Help It* in Eddie Cochran's memory.

The original 'Summertime Blues', a top-twenty hit in Britain in 1958, had been a huge favourite with that era's skiffle groups. Friends recall the pre-teen Mark Feld having a crack at it. But only the young enthusiast himself could vouch for his alleged encounter with Cochran at the stage door of the Hackney Empire, with his insistence that he'd carried the 21-year-old's Gretsch 6120 to a waiting taxi.

A light goes on in Bolan's head. He calls back. 'I want that sound!'

TYRANNOSAURUS REX
MAGICAL MOON
Stereo Single

THE GIRL CAN'T HELP IT !

TOM EWELL
JAYNE MANSFIELD
EDMOND O'BRIEN
JULIE LONDON
RAY ANTHONY
BARRY GORDON

CinemaScope

Ride a White Swan

Words and Music by MARC BOLAN

Recorded by **T. REX** on FLY RECORDS

ESSEX MUSIC INTERNATIONAL LIMITED 20p

MUNGO JERRY, the four young men who experienced extraordinary "overnight" success during the recent "Hollywood" open-air festival, have certainly not let their new-found fame go to their heads.

"We don't feel like stars. In fact, we really don't want to be classed as POP stars in the accepted sense," they say frankly. "Of course, becoming a hit group is great. But we're not on an ego trip as a result. We just want people to enjoy listening to our music in the same way as we do playing it."

And if you were lucky enough to be among the 35,000 who watched them work the other weekend—seated onstage in a line, stamping their feet with great fervour as they banged out their jug-band brand of sounds—you'll appreciate that what they say is true.

Mungo Jerry are just ordinary guys. They've all been in the business a long while, playing different music in assorted bands. And it's been a combination of these tastes—rock, folk, jazz, skiffle, C-n-W — which has produced and perpetrated their sudden appeal today.

"We've all been into different things and this is what has come out," says singer Ray Dorset, the dark, swarthy group spokesman, whose raw voice is vaguely reminiscent of Chris Farlowe. He jokingly tags Mungo music as "beer-drinking" or "happy" music — but concedes that it stems "like everything else" from rock.

Says Colin Earl, whose brother is Savoy Brown's drummer: "There's no secret to our success. Except perhaps that people feel part of our music—and can join in and have a good time."

This was certainly true at "Hollywood." When Mungo set the mood the masses joined in. They jumped up and down, stamped, clapped and improvised their own instruments with whatever they could lay hands on.

"We don't feel like stars"—Mungo Jerry (left to right) Ray Dorset, Paul King, Mike Cole, Colin Earl.

Mungo Jerry are happy with their 'beer drinking' music

formed some years ago by Ray and Colin. In those days they had a friend, Joe Rush, in the line-up; and at "Hollywood" he "jammed" with them on washboard!

Recalls Ray: "We first realised our possibilities the night we played a gig opposite Keef Hartley in December 1968. They put us on at the end of the evening—about 3 a.m.—as the 'group-to-go-home-to.' But instead everyone stayed till 5 a.m.!"

When Rush left to return to his love, trad, Paul replaced him before last Chris-

Unlike a lot of groups Mungo have made quite a bit of bread for themselves over the years. Two of them are married and own their own homes. And they once arrived at a £25 booking in a mini cavalcade of cars ranging from an Aston Martin to an Anglia.

"We've never been on the breadline like a lot of bands simply because we've been careful," volunteered Colin. "We work often as we can because we really enjoy playing. And if people enjoy us we get return bookings.

"Really all we want to do now festival euphoria is wearing consolidate our success as

Eddie Cochran never actually played the venue, though he may have passed through its doors. But there was no mystery to the way his one and only British tour ended. After the final date at the Bristol Hippodrome, the taxi ferrying him to London Airport crashed into a concrete post. The rising star of rock'n'roll was killed instantly.

On July 1, 1970, with the stars doubtless fortuitously aligned, Marc Bolan was ready to record 'Ride A White Swan'. The moment had been given added urgency by the recent success of Mungo Jerry's 'In The Summertime', already four weeks into its seven-week run at No. 1. Channelling Larry the Lamb, singer Ray Dorset had prompted an epidemic of vibrato mimicry.

Bolan was exasperated.

What had prompted him to adopt the voice, late in 1966, for his flop solo 45 'Hippy Gumbo' remains obscure. Had he really listened to old Bessie Smith records at 16rpm? He'd certainly heard Canadian protest singer Buffy Sainte-Marie at the correct speed and shared a bill with New York's finest flower-child warbler, Melanie.

By 1970, having endured endless taunts for possessing the most far-out voice in rock, Marc had become sensitive to imposters. He could tolerate The Kinks' Ray Davies ('King Kong') and John Lennon ('Cold Turkey'), though Family's Roger Chapman was a bit close for comfort. But good-natured skiffle act Mungo Jerry at No. 1, hailed as pop's new messiahs?

Marc Bolan was feeling revved up and ready for his close-up.

Many years ago, your author found the original tape of the 'Ride A White Swan' session gathering dust in a London archive. Contained within was The Moment.

From the control room, producer Tony Visconti announces, 'Let's call it "Swan".' Bolan, playing a late-fifties Gibson Les Paul stained orange in homage to Cochran's Gretsch, holds down an open E shape above the capo he'd strapped over the fourth fret.

With minuscule finger movements, he knocks out a clipped rock'n'roll sequence worthy of James Burton on an old Ricky Nelson B-side. Visconti moves fast, flicks a reverb switch and everything opens up.

A light goes on in Bolan's head. He calls back. 'I want that sound!'

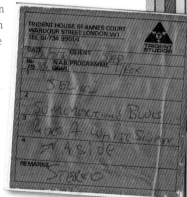

Chapter 2
Don't Believe the Hype

In September 1969, *Top Of The Pops*, the UK's premier pop TV show, had its broadcast time cut from its customary half-hour to twenty-five minutes. Weeks later, it was announced that sales of singles in Britain had plummeted by twenty percent since 1968. Album and singles sales had been roughly on par that year at forty-nine million. By the start of 1970, while the singles market continued to shrink, album sales were nudging sixty million.

Had pop's bubble burst? Or were the big acts simply turning their attention to the long-playing format?

There was money in albums, an obvious attraction to all those sixties acts who lost out due to a deadly combination of mercenary managers and minuscule royalty rates. Since The Beatles exploded the format in 1967 with *Sgt Pepper's Lonely Hearts Club Band*, the album was also the place where creativity had space to breathe.

A simple equation became the new orthodoxy: pop acts knocked out singles; rock musicians recorded LPs. That was why, for example, Steve Marriott walked out on Small Faces to form Humble Pie, and why talented hitmakers The Kinks and The Move were seen to lack credibility in the album market.

In December 1969, *Top Of The Pops* producer Mel Cornish made a surprise announcement. From January 22, 1970, the BBC's flagship television pop show would run from 7.15 until 8pm in its regular Thursday evening slot. The focus was widened from top twenty to top thirty, and there would be more scope to feature new, non-chart singles and album acts.

The show received a boost in February when John Lennon brought his ad hoc Plastic Ono Band into the *TOTP* studio. Lennon – *Time* magazine's 'Man Of The

John Lennon for P.M. say new voters pages 6-7

Fantastic

Today the Mirror chooses..

THE CLOWN OF THE YEAR

JOHN LENNON means well. Behind the preposterous facade of that sack, the saintly chemise or the un-won sergeant's stripes, there is evidence of honesty and good intent.

He and Yoko Ono—that high priestess of the human posterior — have made so many public declarations of love and peace

by

Decade' – was still a Beatle, despite rumours that the group was disintegrating fast.

The last (and only) time he had appeared before *TOTP*'s live studio audience was in June 1966, when The Beatles promoted 'Paperback Writer'. The Fab Four wore matching suits that day, their Beatle boots were shiny, their hair still mop-topped. In a sign of changing times, they dispensed with their ties and wore their shirt collars open.

When the Plastic Ono Band performed 'Instant Karma!' for the *TOTP* cameras, Lennon and his wife Yoko Ono drew a visual line under the Beatles era, wearing utilitarian denim and sporting brutalist crop haircuts. Lennon sat at the piano and sang with grim-faced commitment. Yoko, seated with a sanitary-towel blindfold around her face, held up a series of cards bearing messages such as 'Hope', 'Peace' and 'Smile'.

It was a remarkable provocation, one that likely increased the Great British Public's growing antipathy to the man they now knew as the 'Bed Beatle' or the 'Naked Beatle'.

The chorus rang out with post-hippie positivity. There would be life beyond The Beatles, beyond the already mythologised sixties. But there was anger in Lennon's voice, bitterness and sarcasm in his verses.

The song's biggest putdown came when Lennon – his voice bathed in an Elvis Sun Studio echo – taunted, 'Who on earth do you think you are? A superstar?' Given his estrangement from The Beatles' camp, the assumed target was Paul McCartney. But Lennon's disillusionment was with the wider rock culture.

'Nothing happened,' he told *Rolling Stone*'s Jann Wenner months later. 'We all dressed up. The same bastards are in control… The dream is over.'

The rock generation's lionisation of the superstar was both a nod to and a parody of vintage Hollywood. 'More stars than there are in heaven!' had been the boast of mogul Louis B. Mayer's MGM Studios, back in the thirties.

In 1962, pop artist Andy Warhol gave a twist to the idea of stardom. His *Marilyn Diptych* presented screen goddess Marilyn Monroe as an object of glamour and an easily reproduced commodity, both a star and an empty soul.

No one could agree whether Warhol was celebrating the world of media stardom or parodying its emptiness. The artist, ever inscrutable, liked it that way.

By 1965, Warhol had extended the idea by acquiring his own stable of stars. He found them among the misfits that hung around his Factory

LEFT: No one created more controversy in pop at the start of the new decade than John Lennon. Performing 'Instant Karma!' on *Top Of The Pops* in February, John and Yoko used the appearance to upend all the old showbiz rules. The song's lyric included a disparaging mention of the word 'superstar'.

ABOVE LEFT: Pop Art man of mystery Andy Warhol propagated the idea of 'The Superstar' during the mid-sixties. The term was applied to many of the misfits and creatives that hung around his New York studio The Factory, most notably Edie Sedgwick, star of several of his low-budget films.

ABOVE: In January 1970, pop was experiencing growing pains. 'The next big attraction group-wise will have to be good musicians as well as good looking,' predicted Love Affair's Steve Ellis.

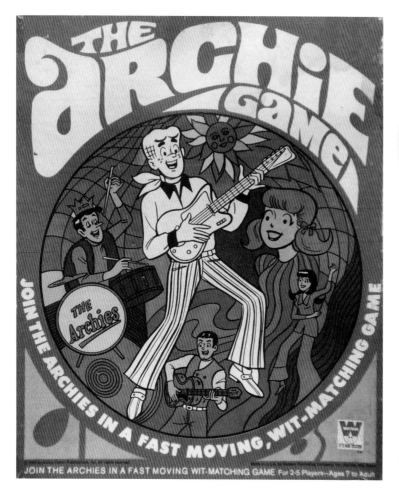

JOIN THE ARCHIES IN A FAST MOVING WIT-MATCHING GAME For 2-5 Players—Ages 7 to Adult

ABOVE: Don Kirshner, the man behind The Monkees, hastened the drive towards bubblegum pop with television series cartoon pop group The Archies. The enormous success of 'Sugar, Sugar' spurred noted British hitmakers Barry Mason and Tony Macauley to write 'Love Grows (Where My Rosemary Goes)' for Edison Lighthouse.

studio, viewing reflections of themselves in the silver foil that covered its walls. He declared them 'Superstars', destined for the grainy, low-budget films he co-directed with Paul Morrissey.

'Everyone will be famous for fifteen minutes,' Warhol said, a phrase that reverberated around the world. But some – like Edie Sedgwick, his most celebrated, ill-fated Superstar – would become more famous than others.

Superstardom soon migrated to pop music. 'Everyone in England is talking about this Warhol bloke,' said The Who's Pete Townshend in 1966, whilst in New York. 'How he's changed everyone's idea of what things look like, and what time is, and what feeling is, and style.'

In turn, *Dateline* reporter and future protopunk talent-spotter Danny Fields described London's best-known equipment wrecker as an 'angry superstar'.

By 1968, The Doors' Jim Morrison was no longer a mere rock frontman but a shamanic superstar;

Janis Joplin received the 'S' billing too. The following year, deciding that Jimi Hendrix had outgrown his superstar status, *Life* magazine elevated him to the status of 'Rock Demigod'.

Rock superstars shunned pop. Led Zeppelin refused to release singles and spent most of their time touring the US rock circuit. The January 31, 1970 edition of *Melody Maker* led with Zep superstar Jimmy Page in guitar-god pose and the news that the band expected to earn close to a million dollars on their spring tour of the States – their fifth since December 1968.

But not every hard or progressive rock act was so territorial. Jethro Tull worked the US circuit while keeping one foot in the UK singles market. Promoting 'The Witch's Promise' on the new-look *TOTP*, Tull's flute-playing frontman, Ian Anderson, gurned and hopped around in his rock-tramp persona, a folk hero both for kids and 'heads'. Three weeks later, in mid-February, the single went top-five.

Still, crossing the great divide remained a touchy business. 'Radio 1 and the majority of top ten records make me want to spew up,' confessed Tull guitarist Martin Barre. The band's *TOTP* appearance prompted a flurry of Tull-sell-out letters in the rock press, revealing the depth of feeling as rock and pop continued to go their separate ways.

★

Pop music itself was undergoing a transformation. *Record Mirror*'s January 10, 1970 edition plastered the faces of three contemporary chart stars on its cover to promote a dramatic 'Crisis In Pop' feature.

'The recognised teenybopper groups have had their day,' declared Love Affair's Steve Ellis. 'I couldn't work in the teenybopper scene anymore,' confessed Amen Corner's Andy Fairweather-Low. Dean Ford, singer with Marmalade, who'd had a 1969 hit with The Beatles' 'Ob-La-Di, Ob-La-Da', announced that the group planned to pull away from their teenybopper image.

Ellis and Fairweather-Low had their own eponymous projects to pursue, reflecting a desire for recognition as artists; Ford was staying put. Marmalade had recently signed a new deal giving them control over their work, with new single 'Reflections Of My Life' as its signature statement – a song of change, maturity and deep sorrow wrapped in life-affirming harmonies.

Steve Ellis made a prediction: 'The next big attraction group-wise will have to be good musicians as well as just good looking.'

Getting sophisticated – like Marmalade – or going solo – like Ellis, Fairweather-Low, the Bee Gees' Robin Gibb or Dave Dee – was a natural evolution. The process was given extra impetus by the enormous success of a cartoon pop group from a Saturday morning US kids' TV series.

The Archies' hit 'Sugar, Sugar' was still dominating singles charts worldwide long after hitting No. 1 in the US in September 1969. The project was overseen by Don Kirshner, the man behind The Monkees. Once again, Kirshner had used studio session musicians, but this time there were no real-life group members to complicate things.

After a misfiring Archies album in 1968, Kirshner and Brill Building writer-producer Jeff Barry had something to prove. They brought in co-writer Andy Kim and cooked up 'Sugar, Sugar' – honeyed, singalong pop with a killer hook and some Babycham sparkle.

'Sugar, Sugar' was 1969's biggest selling single in the States. It also hit No. 1 in Britain on October 19, staying there until mid-December. (After twenty weeks in the top thirty, it eventually dropped out in early March 1970.)

The song was a one-off – but it had a galvanising effect on other hitmakers and huge consequences for the pop charts. Another New York studio

Superman of the year

BY RAYMOND TELFORD

IF THERE was a Superman of the Year award for a pop singer, no one could touch Tony Burrows.

Chartbusters syndicate!

Disc looks at today's top chart names. Names that crop up again and again in various groups. Are they computerising music—or giving fans what they want? Two pertinent names give their views

Radio 1 and the majority of top ten records make me want to spew up.

creation, The Cuff Links, soon followed through with 'Tracy' featuring Ron Dante, anonymous lead voice of The Archies.

'Tracy' fell out of the UK top ten on January 25, 1970. That same week, studio group Edison Lighthouse hit No. 1 with 'Love Grows (Where My Rosemary Goes)', by esteemed songwriters Barry Mason and Tony Macaulay. Mason admitted the extraordinary success of 'Sugar, Sugar' had prompted the pair to come up with 'a Tamla Bubbletown smash'.

Once again, the act was a front for the writers/producers. Edison Lighthouse was in fact gigging

ABOVE TOP: Session singing ace Tony Burrows was declared 1970's 'Superman Of The Year' – and it was still only springtime. Burrows sang 'Love Grows' for Edison Lighthouse, before turning up on a streak of hits by White Plains, Brotherhood Of Man and 'Gimme Dat Ding' novelty act The Pipkins.

ABOVE: Songwriter and Blue Mink co-vocalist Roger Cook described the recent pop 'factory' explosion as a flash in the pan. 'Really, we're all doing a lot of uncreative things for a lot of money,' he confessed.

The Star Maker

Producer Tony Visconti Meets Bolan And Bowie

I'd come to England [in April 1967] to find the next Beatles. I didn't think it would take long to find a superstar in the rough; I considered British rock to be superior in every way to American rock.

I had my radar turned on full, but the only real tremors I felt were when I met Bowie and Bolan within weeks of each other.

It was my first night of talent scouting. I saw a poster for a group called Tyrannosaurus Rex, walked in and heard the music wafting out of the cellar. There were about three hundred people sitting around a small stage in silence, watching this strange little person on the floor singing in what I didn't take to be the English language. I thought it was French or something.

I felt awkward approaching Marc. He threw his head back to sing, and no one else did that then. And he gave off an air of being very precious, very special, very charismatic. I fell in love with him.

Steve [Peregrin Took] looked like a hippie. Marc was something else, like a gypsy with his curly hair, his little waistcoat, a tattered silk shirt and a scarf tied around his arm.

I said I was a record producer, 'I really like you and I'd like to work with you.' Marc replied – in perfect English of course – 'Oh, man, you're the eighth producer that's come to me this week. John Lennon came up to me last night…'

I thought his confidence was wonderful. He had the arrogance of a New Yorker and I loved it.

I walked in the office at ten next morning and the phone was ringing – it was Marc. He said, 'Can we come and see you?' I told Denny [Cordell, producer] he was great, the voice, the strange songs – that everything about it was extraordinary.

They showed up and unrolled the oriental carpet. The £12 guitar had a missing peg on the G string; Marc used a pair of pliers to tune it. Steve took out his bells, Pixiphone and one-string fiddle and they played the whole set from the night before. I'm just glowing with pride. Denny said, 'I don't understand them at all, but we'll sign them as our token underground group.'

Marc said, 'If you're gonna record me, you gotta read these,' and gave me all three [volumes] of *The Lord of the Rings* plus *The Hobbit*.

When I met Bowie [at the offices of Essex Music, Dumbarton House, 68 Oxford Street, London W1], I thought he was very vulnerable and it made me want to protect him. [Music publisher] David Platz didn't know what to do with him and [manager] Ken Pitt didn't see him as a rock star at all. He had no steady musicians to play with. He was trying to break into a successful situation by pursuing several things at once – going to film auditions, being part of Lindsay Kemp's mime troupe. Music took up about fifty percent of his efforts.

I'd just come from New York where I led quite an LSD-laced life – long hair, colourful clothing, embracing Eastern philosophies. I was called a 'fag' at least once a day. David had gone through a similar experience in the mid-sixties with his 'Long Hair Society' [a brief stunt in 1964] and for being a misfit generally.

I knew he was listening to The Fugs and The Velvet Underground at the time I met him, groups with a greater depth of musical freedom. We set the stage for being cool and obscure right from the beginning. I could see we'd have to keep each other honest when we started making records together. ★

On September 1, 1967, Visconti produced a projected new Bowie single, coupling 'Let Me Sleep Beside You' with 'Karma Man', at Advision Studios. Decca Records rejected it.

ABOVE: New Yorker Tony Visconti came to London in 1967 hoping to find the new Beatles. Instead, he stumbled upon two struggling individuals: Marc Bolan and David Bowie. '[Marc] had the arrogance of a New Yorker and I loved it,' he says. 'I thought [David] was very vulnerable and it made me want to protect him.'

Hype and David Bowie's future

group Greenfield Hammer, augmented by session singer Tony Burrows – the uncredited lead voice of 'Let's Go To San Francisco', by 1967 studio pop-psych pretenders The Flower Pot Men.

On February 22, both White Plains' 'My Baby Loves Lovin'' and Brotherhood Of Man's 'United We Stand' hit the top ten. Seven weeks later, The Pipkins' 'Gimme Dat Ding' peaked at No. 6. Tony Burrows, the voice of 'Love Grows', sang on all of them.

This revolving door of studio-hatched acts gave *Top Of The Pops* a headache. Between January 29 and February 26, four episodes featured two Burrows-fronted acts. With a politely disapproving shake of the head, *Melody Maker* hailed him as 'Superman Of The Year'.

Burrows had an explanation for the success of what he called 'manufactured' acts: 'People buy sounds and records, not artists.'

'Love Grows' spent five weeks at No. 1 and sold a million copies. By late March it had gone top-five in the States. Production-line studio hits were back in fashion.

Momentarily, Barry Mason had imagined a big career for Edison Lighthouse. But their work was done. '"Love Grows" is just fun music,' he told *Melody Maker*. 'It's not written to last.'

ABOVE: The Roundhouse, March 11, 1970. Performing as part of the Atomic Sunrise week of gigs celebrating 'living theatre', Bowie's new electric band Hype dressed for the occasion, with Bowie as Hypeman and Tony Visconti as Superman. 'David [once] showed me some contact prints,' Visconti says, 'and [there] was Marc Bolan in blue jeans and a floppy hat leaning on the stage. He wasn't in his glam thing yet. We were!'

The idea that a string of fictitious acts could dominate the singles charts, with loyalty to artistes a total irrelevance, was a grim scenario for two of pop's most enthusiastic devotees. Marc Bolan and David Bowie had spent much of their young lives cultivating themselves as artistes/artists. Both adored pop. But it had to show its creator's face.

The pair, friendly rivals since 1964, began the new decade with a rare collaboration. Bowie had already recorded the basics of 'The Prettiest Star' – the follow-up to his recent top-five hit 'Space Oddity' – on January 8, 1970, his twenty-third birthday.

Tony Visconti, who'd been working with both Bolan and Bowie since late '67, felt the song needed a lead guitar part. He gave a tape of the basic recording to Marc and invited him to an overdub session days later.

Initially, Bolan was hesitant. But he'd now been playing electric for months and had recently told the producer he'd been taking instruction from 'the Master', Eric Clapton.

(This has some credibility. Clapton's girlfriend, Alice Ormsby-Gore, would be a witness at Marc and June's wedding at the end of the month.)

> **Bowie was openly in awe. He made all the effort to be Marc's friend.**

'The Prettiest Star' was a love song for Bowie's girlfriend and wife-to-be, Angela 'Angie' Barnett. Its dramatic 'cold fire' opening was a quote from Shakespeare's *Romeo And Juliet*. Yet the song's key line, 'One day… You and I will rise up all the way,' could have just as easily applied to Marc and David, the fast-maturing star-seekers.

'Bowie was openly in awe [of Bolan],' says Visconti, 'always respectful, affectionately calling him a cosmic punk. He made all the effort to become Marc's friend – and it was Marc who was covertly in awe of Bowie. He secretly admired him.'

When Bolan and wife-to-be June arrived, 'it was daggers' says the producer. That cold fire enveloped the room. Working on the song, however, Bolan's mood changed. He found a warm, distinctive, almost conversational tone for his guitar; shadowing the melody without upstaging it, adding a light dust of melancholy.

As the song played out, Bolan bent his notes, as if making them 'rise up high' – and fall – like shooting stars. Then the take was done. The song's lilting melody and healing sound now had its perfect electric guideline.

ABOVE: 'The Prettiest Star', Bowie's March 1970 follow-up to 'Space Oddity', featured Bolan on guest guitar. After he taped his part, his partner June turned to Bowie and said, 'This song is crap!' The couple then walked out.

ABOVE RIGHT: The January 31, 1970 issue of *Mirabelle* described cover co-star Bowie as 'A Real Pop Oddity'. By the time the issue hit the streets, the 'Space Oddity' hitmaker had already moved on from pop.

As Bolan packed away his guitar, the mood of mutual generosity was rudely shattered. 'June viciously turns on David,' Visconti recalls, 'and says, "This song is crap! The best thing about it is Marc's guitar."' The couple walked out.

'The Prettiest Star' was released two months later to a deafening silence. Neither Bolan nor Bowie cared much. Both had moved on.

Bolan was in a broom cupboard perfecting his rock'n'roll twang. Bowie had reclaimed the stage after a tough time the previous autumn supporting Steve Marriott's rockin' new outfit, Humble Pie. Like Bolan, he was also taking counsel from his partner and main cheerleader.

Angie was a fast-talking American, free-thinking like Bowie but with none of his English reserve. Bowie believed in his talent but was reluctant to shout about it. Angie knew he was the great genius-in-waiting and was happy to tell the world. She also realised that a

fresh project would reel in a new record deal – and prompt a clean break with his recently acquired pop-folkie image.

The catalyst was Mick Ronson, a powerful yet versatile guitarist with classical training. On February 5, two days after meeting backstage at The Marquee, Ronson was part of Bowie's makeshift band for an hour-long broadcast on John Peel's *Sunday Show* on BBC Radio 1.

A new style of Bowie song was premiered that day. Long, meandering and under-rehearsed, 'The Width Of A Circle' nevertheless gave impetus to Bowie's next album project, one that would draw a line under his dispiriting months as a pop star the previous autumn.

Bowie named his new backing band Hype. It was a provocation. Only 'bubblegum' was a more offensive term to rock fans during those first, frenetic weeks of 1970.

ABOVE: The Move, October 1967. L-R: Carl Wayne, Bev Bevan, manager Tony Secunda, Trevor Burton, Roy Wood, Ace Kefford. Like Bolan and Bowie, The Move were part of Essex Music's late-sixties talent pool, albeit considerably more successful. With a foot in both singles and album markets, they were seen by some as having the potential to emulate The Beatles.

Angie and Visconti's girlfriend, Liz Hartley, knocked up the costumes. While the band played, mischievous hands backstage knocked off their daywear. Hype returned to Haddon Hall, their shared residence in the southeast London suburb of Beckenham, still dressed in character.

The venture was a throwback to Bowie's serious/not serious days, before he'd got himself a Dylan perm and a regular Arts Lab gig, fashioning himself into a deeply sensitive singer-songwriter.

Hype were loud and more impulsive. They even threw in the occasional chart hit, like Canned Heat's boogie-rock blast 'Let's Work Together' and, more aptly, Lennon's statement singalong 'Instant Karma!'.

In the audience for Hype's second Roundhouse gig was at least one keen observer. 'David [once] showed me some contact prints,' Visconti says, 'and [there] was Marc Bolan in blue jeans and a floppy hat leaning on the stage.'

Bolan didn't leave with any fashion tips. But he had witnessed the germ of a new aesthetic, one where mischief could mess with rock's lofty aspirations without going full Bonzo Dog Band. Two weeks later, he was playing his own pop game – in secret.

When Tony Visconti was offered free time at a west London studio, there was no 'What next for T. Rex?' conversation. Instead, fascinated by the recent proliferation of pop-by-numbers hit singles, Bolan suggested something different. On March 24, the pair played at pop bandwagon-jumpers for the day.

ABOVE: After the departure of singer Carl Wayne in January 1970, The Move's costume-conscious songwriter/guitarist Roy Wood – shown here performing riff-rocking new single 'Brontosaurus' for the BBC cameras – stepped up. Wood was 'obsessed with *Top Of The Pops*,' says Move drummer Bev Bevan. 'He wanted a new look each time.'

ABOVE RIGHT: The Beatles had been drifting apart since the death of manager Brian Epstein in August 1967. But there was no going back after April 10, 1970, when Paul McCartney's statement that he couldn't imagine writing with John Lennon again went around the world.

After debuting at the Roundhouse in north London's Chalk Farm, Hype played the White Bear pub in Hounslow on March 3. Ronson and drummer John Cambridge wore jeans and T-shirts. Bowie, his hair now longer and Bolan-shaggy, dressed in red trousers and a patterned tank top.

On March 11, Hype returned to the Roundhouse as part of the week-long Atomic Sunrise festival. This time, encouraged by Angie, they dressed in a manner worthy of the band's name, each member adopting a comic book-style alter ego.

Bowie's Rainbowman wore a blue cape draped over a shiny silver blouse. In a flash velvet jacket Bowie had worn at a recent *Disc and Music Echo* awards ceremony, Mick Ronson came on as Gangsterman. Tony 'Hypeman' Visconti wore a T-shirt under his cape emblazoned with the letter 'H', while drummer John Cambridge was Stetson-hatted Cowboyman. The audience was nonplussed.

> Roy is Britain's best commercial songwriter after Lennon and McCartney.

'Oh Baby' wasn't much more than a glib phrase on repeat with an occasional verse thrown in – but it blew a gust of fresh air through Rex-world. Visconti organised a funky bubblegum-beat rhythm section and upped the drama with a bold string arrangement. To spare Bolan's blushes – and avoid any contractual wrangles – the producer also sang the vocal lead.

'Loads of fun,' remembers Visconti. He placed the song with Bell Records, who released it in August to a resounding silence. In another indication of where all this had come from, the single was credited to Dib Cochran & The Earwigs.

By this time, pop's centre – or what remained of it – had collapsed.

On April 9, 1970, in an interview circulated to promote his first solo LP, Paul McCartney stated that he could never see himself writing with John Lennon again. The following morning, a *Daily Mirror* headline declared, 'Paul Is Quitting The Beatles'. It severed another tie with the previous decade, emotionally perhaps the most significant one.

One group with potential to step up to the vacant pedestal were The Move. Like The Beatles, they came from a large provincial city (Birmingham), made clever commercial hit singles, had strong visual appeal and – more relevant in 1970 than in 1962 – possessed the talent and creative ambition to excel in the album format.

Guitarist/vocalist Roy Wood was a natural talent. Some of The Move's biggest hits featured lyrics culled from a big book of fairy stories stories he'd written as a schoolboy. Almost as soon as the band broke big late in 1966, Roy talked about writing a pop opera.

Like Bolan, with whom The Move shared the same production company, Wood had a strong sense of his his own private world. Unlike Bolan, Wood, *Top Of The Pops*' flamboyant clown prince in the late sixties, was a reluctant star.

That began to change during 1970, when he struck up a lively working relationship with fellow Brummie Jeff Lynne. Lynne's previous band The Idle Race had been Peel show regulars, no doubt helped by featuring an electrified version of Tyrannosaurus Rex's 'Debora' in their live set.

Like Wood, Lynne regarded The Beatles as the band to beat. That was the real reason Lynne was in The Move – to assist in Wood's Big Idea, the Electric Light Orchestra, a classically driven project that took

The Beatles' 'I Am The Walrus' as its touchstone.

But first there was the main band's commercial reputation to consider.

The revamped Move returned in spring 1970 with 'Brontosaurus'. Wood stepped out as a frontman for the first time, dressed in a harlequin outfit with multicoloured stars painted around his eyes and on his forehead. His hair was long and wild, more finger-in-the-electric-toaster than ever. He looked every bit the rockin' wizard.

The song itself was no less dramatic. The riff was a Black Country crypt-kicker, the equal of anything by the city's brand-new heavies, Black Sabbath. Towards the end, the dirge breaks and 'Brontosaurus' – in Wood's imagination a new dance craze – erupts into jubilant, revivalist rock'n'roll.

'Brontosaurus' hit the top ten for three weeks in May. Back on the singles trail and with a simmering side project aimed at the album market, The Move were perfectly poised to fill any vacuum left by The Beatles.

Instead, Roy Wood spent much of the year playing pub-league football. 'We have our own Move team,' he told *Beat Instrumental*. 'I used to get lots of phone calls about the group. Now the only people that phone up are trying to find out about when the next match is!'

'Roy Wood is the best commercial songwriter in Britain after Lennon and McCartney,' insisted ex-Move lead vocalist Carl Wayne, who'd quit in January 1970. Many in the industry shared his view. 'The unfortunate thing,' continued the singer, 'was that Roy was the songwriter and yet the least leader-like member of the group.'

Chapter 3
I'm With the Band

In the spring of 1970, Hollywood impresario Marty Krofft arrived in London to audition teenagers for his latest project – 'a British Monkees'. He had a name, *The Bugaloos*, for a TV series lined up with NBC. Future Genesis drummer Phil Collins and the UK label manager for Tamla Motown, John Reid – whose fortunes would soon change dramatically – were among those turned down for parts in the show.

Krofft found his cast. *The Bugaloos* Saturday morning show would run from September 1970 until September 1972. But The Bugaloos, who dressed as insects and battled evil, were no Monkees. Spin-off records flopped; and, despite featuring British actors, the show never made it across the water. But 'boogaloo' did.

'Boogaloo' rivalled 'hype' and 'superstar' as the word of the moment. In the early sixties, it described a hybrid of Latin and R&B rhythms popular in US cities. By 1970, it had jumped cultures.

When a new British band gave *Melody Maker* a sneak preview of their debut album in February, Chris Welch praised its 'boogaloo beat'. They were The Faces and, like Zep and Tull, they too had an Atlantic crossing in mind.

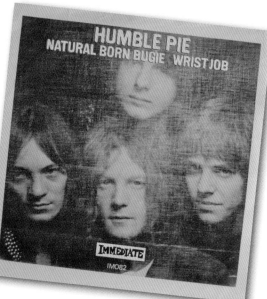

Present at the playback was frontman Rod Stewart, just home from the States where he'd been promoting his debut solo album. He'd made the trip with manager Billy Gaff, who was there to set up The Faces' first US tour.

It was a slightly awkward arrangement. Stewart had been offered a deal back during his time with The Jeff Beck Group, veterans of a trailblazing five US tours during 1968-69. Two Faces, Ronnie Wood and Ian McLagan, had also guested on Rod's record and their frontman was already making waves as a solo artist.

Released in the States in November '69 as *The Rod Stewart Album* and in Britain four months later as *An Old Raincoat Won't Ever Let You Down*, it positioned him close to Joe Cocker: a distinctive sandpaper voice; well-chosen material; and a remarkable ability to dig into the soul of a song.

But there the comparisons stopped. While Cocker sweated and idiot-danced his way through performances, Rod was meticulous and controlled in his appearance. He dressed in red satin jackets and strutted around the stage swinging his mike-stand. To all-girl Zappa protégés and cover stars of the emerging groupie scene the GTOs (Girls Together Outrageously), he was 'Rodney Rooster' because, wrote GTO Pamela Des Barres, 'of his choppy stick-up hairdo'.

There was little doubt that Rod Stewart was a superstar-in-waiting – but what he liked best of all was being part of a band.

A superstar was the last thing Ronnie 'Plonk' Lane, Ian 'Mac' McLagan and Kenny 'Kenney' Jones were looking for. Between 1965-68, the three had enjoyed huge pop success as Small Faces, London Mods turned Britain's favourite cheeky boys.

By 1968, they'd broken into the album market with the chart-topping *Ogdens' Nut Gone Flake*. But it wasn't enough for frontman Steve Marriott, who walked out on New Year's Eve to launch new band Humble Pie, which he'd co-front with 'Face Of '68' Peter Frampton from The Herd.

Neither Small Faces nor The Herd had made much impact in the States, so Humble Pie were created with US success in mind. Initially described as a 'pop supergroup', they debuted with 'Natural Born Bugie', a top-five hit in September 1969. Like The Beatles' 'Get Back', it owed a large debt to Chuck Berry. On their two 1969 albums Humble Pie covered Steppenwolf's 'Desperation' and embraced country rock. By the end of the year they were supporting the Grateful Dead in the States and playing twenty-minute versions of Dr John's 'I Walk On Gilded Splinters'.

the new LPs

ROD GOES SOLO—BUT NOT ALONE!

ROD STEWART'S "Gasolene Alley" is his second solo album. It seems rather incongruous that he should choose to make a solo album and then get most of his group, the Faces, to back him on it— Ron Wood on guitar, Ronnie Lane on bass, Kenny Jones on drums.

Anyway, it makes nice listening, and Rod does a variety of songs ranging from a couple of sad little folky things he wrote himself— "Lady Day" and "Jo's Lament"— to "It's All Over Now," which seems too high pitched to suit his voice. His version of Dylan's "Only A Hobo" is good; his voice sounds as if he's just gargled—great. The whole thing is well produced and thoughtfully presented. **(Vertigo)**
★★★

SAMMY DAVIS JR's first for Tamla Motown, **"Something For Everyone,"** doesn't quite live up

Caswell Galliard, are on two tracks—" "Change." Guitari Anderson except for Dave C tion"—w swing an playing instrumen beautiful Time Is' The s big-band the usual the big and Gar

Marriott's departure had crushed his three bandmates. 'I don't think any of us really forgave Steve,' remembers Kenney Jones. 'It hurt.'

The trio initially sounded out Peter Frampton as a replacement. 'They said, "Steve's left. Would you take his place?"' Frampton recalls. 'I said, "It'll take two people to replace Steve. I'm not worthy."' Besides, Frampton was already committed to Humble Pie.

After fulfilling their Small Faces obligations, Lane, McLagan and Jones looked for inspiration in a basement rehearsal studio at The Rolling Stones' storage warehouse in London's Docklands.

'If we could have pulled it off without a lead vocalist,

LEFT: Commonly used in Afro-American and Hispanic communities during the sixties, 'Boogaloo' hit the rock press by 1970, defining funky, US-friendly rock acts like Joe Cocker. Boogaloo piggybacked 'boogie', used by jazz and blues musicians for decades and picked up by Humble Pie in 1969 for 'Natural Born Bugie'. As rock recoiled from psychedelia, the turn of the decade saw a wider embrace of 'the boogie'.

like The Band,' said McLagan, 'that would have been great.' The last thing they wanted was a new singer full of what Ronnie Lane called 'superstar crap'.

Firstly, guitarist Ronnie Wood was invited by Lane to sit in. He was just back from one last Jeff Beck Group tour, where he'd played bass. Like Beck bandmate Rod, he was also cultivating the rooster look.

To Wood, the remaining Small Faces were Britain's

answer to Booker T. & The MG's. They tentatively worked on some new songs, with the guitarist sometimes inviting his fellow Beck Group renegade along. Rodney Rooster would sit upstairs and watch – then one day Kenney Jones gave Rod the nod.

'It was like seeing a girl from the corner of your eye,' said McLagan. 'It's a fucking singer!'

The five worked their way through the *Muddy*

the old one in half to accommodate Stewart and Wood's extra inches.

But it wasn't easy avoiding 'superstar crap' during the early months of 1970. Even Judas Jump, formed by Peter Frampton's Herd colleague Andy Bown with musicians from Amen Corner and The Mindbenders, were hyped up as a 'supergroup'.

But The Faces weren't Judas Jump. Despite lukewarm reviews for *First Step*, their modestly titled March '70 debut, they had recognisable faces and big reputations. Touring the States that spring, supporting acts like Canned Heat and Johnny Winter, promoters billed them variously as Rod Stewart & The Faces, The Small Faces or even occasionally The Faces. Decent-sized audiences silenced the band's grumbles. Their boogaloo groove went down particularly well in Detroit, where The Jeff Beck Group had often blown the roof off the city's famed Grande Ballroom.

It was a different story back home, particularly away from London. On June 5, The Faces played a one-day rock festival at Dudley Zoo. Backstage, someone from a rival band called them 'East End tarts'. Out front, an unruly contingent bunged beer cans at them. Only the intervention of local-lad-turned-Zep-superstar Robert Plant – who in pre-fame days used to invite himself backstage at Small Faces gigs – saved them from further ignominy.

> It was like seeing a girl from the corner of your eye. 'It's a fucking singer!'

The Faces couldn't wait to return to the States, where Small Faces' reputation was akin to that of a more cultish Kinks – London boy exotics, rather than a nattily dressed pop act that played to screamers. When they played their second major tour in October, Rod Stewart's second solo album, *Gasoline Alley*, had already gone top-thirty.

There were no hard feelings. The Faces had happily sat in on some of the sessions, notably on a reworked version of Small Faces' 'My Way Of Giving'. Stewart, who lost girlfriend Jenny Rylance to Steve Marriott back in 1967, exacted his revenge by dismissing the original as 'monstrous'.

The album also included 'Country Comfort', a slow, sepia-tinged slice of Americana and a neat fit for Stewart's lived-in delivery. Its writers were a musician-lyricist duo named Elton John and Bernie Taupin.

Waters At Newport songbook. 'Rod could sing them like you couldn't believe,' said McLagan. 'As soon as he started singing, we were a band – a blues band, a soul band, a rock'n'roll band. We were The Faces.'

Lane and McLagan set aside their doubts about flakey frontmen: Rod was in.

The Faces preferred fuss-free solutions. When it came to finding a band name, they simply chopped

ABOVE LEFT: Faces, November 1, 1969. L-R: Kenny 'Kenney' Jones, Ron Wood, Rod Stewart, Ronnie 'Plonk' Lane, Ian 'Mac' McLagan. Ex-Jeff Beck Group duo Wood and Stewart joined forces with three Small Faces with a view to breaking the US market. Back home, their pop past and passion for fashion sometimes saw them dismissed as 'East End tarts'.

ABOVE: Elton John came to prominence in spring 1970 with a sophisticated second album that had reviewers comparing him to Van Morrison and Neil Young. Tie-in single 'Border Song' was even described as a piece of 'God Rock' to rival The Beatles' 'Let It Be'.

The April 18, 1970 edition of *Melody Maker* included a half-page piece headlined, 'Is This The Year Of Elton John?'

Writer Richard Williams thought so, describing Elton's new single, 'Border Song', as 'an amazing God Rock ballad which quite put the insipid "Let It Be" into true perspective'. Soon afterwards, Aretha Franklin recorded a version for the US market.

Elton's own version flopped at home. But his new self-titled album was picking up rave reviews, some comparing him to Van Morrison, Neil Young or James Taylor. 'He is emerging as one of the most fascinating new talents around,' Anne Nightingale told her *Daily Sketch* readers.

Meanwhile, Elton was busy rehearsing a drummer and bassist to back him for a showcase gig at the second annual Pop Proms at the Roundhouse. With Traffic, Fleetwood Mac and visiting US bluesman Johnny Winter among the headliners, he'd be in good company.

There was just one hitch: Elton John wasn't sure he was ready to face the public. 'I really hate the showbiz thing,' he said from behind owlish spectacles.

The cover of his new album smacked of contempt for the whole star-making racket. Shot side-on and unsmiling, encased in darkness, it placed him firmly in the Harry Nilsson/Randy Newman category – more hip record company executive than raving Superstar.

Elton John had a right to feel camera shy. He'd spent the mid-sixties side-stage in club combos hunched over a Vox Continental. After meeting the young poet/lyricist Taupin in 1967, he'd concentrate on songwriting – which was just as well, because the man paying his wages, Beatles music publisher Dick James, told him he didn't look like a pop star.

The John-Taupin duo believed in their partnership. The British public wasn't so sure. The songwriters' 'I Can't Go On Living Without You' came last out of six in the national vote for Lulu's 1969 Eurovision Song Contest entry.

When James's DJM label eventually gave Elton a crack at his own material, he was knocked back again – this time by the rather more exclusive BBC Radio audition panel. 'Pretentious material – self-written – sung in an extremely dull fashion, without any feeling and precious little musical ability,' sniffed one panellist.

Eighteen months later, on April 21, 1970, Elton John was midway through his hour-long Pop Proms set backed by bassist Dee Murray and drummer Nigel Olsson. The mood was respectful, almost sombre.

Then, an accident: Elton knocked over his piano stool. The audience cheered. It was the cue he'd been waiting for – even if he hadn't realised it.

His instinct for showmanship, buried since his early teens, took over. This was Elton John the entertainer, standing on a piano stool and whipping up the crowd.

He knew how to do it too. As young Reg Dwight from Pinner, Middlesex, he was always banging out music-hall favourites on the family upright and entertaining locals in a nearby pub.

Critics agreed that Elton stole the show from headliners Tyrannosaurus Rex. He'd surprised the audience, one of the best things about his set being the opener, 'Your Song' – written over breakfast with Bernie one morning in fifteen minutes.

As the lyric intended, the song was a gift from the lyricist to his musical partner. On hearing it for the first time, arranger Paul Buckmaster said it was so beautiful he was reluctant to add anything to it. To Ray Williams, the Liberty Records A&R man who hooked the pair up in the first place, it was 'so grown up'.

Popular US rock act Three Dog Night – who'd already recorded Elton's early '69 'radio hit', 'Lady Samantha' – released their version of 'Your Song' simultaneously to Elton's on their *It Ain't Easy* album.

Its wider appeal was indicative of how, early on, Elton and Bernie had taken their writing cues from The Beatles, Cat Stevens, The Moody Blues and, on 'Lady Samantha', Procol Harum.

But it was hearing The Band's 1968 debut, *Music From Big Pink*, which changed everything. Rich in American myth and history, richer still in its embrace of various musical traditions, *Big Pink* brought lyricism, storytelling and narrators' voices that listeners could trust to rock's top table.

Eric Clapton was so affected by what he heard that he dissolved psychedelic power-trio Cream and sought out American musicians to play with. 'Border Song', and much else on *Elton John*, would have been unthinkable without The Band.

Once DJM's US outlet Uni Records in Los Angeles heard the *Elton John* album, they wanted him over there. The label saw parallels with the fashionable singer-songwriter aristos of Laurel Canyon – Crosby, Stills, Nash & Young, James Taylor – and had one eye on those artists' vast audiences.

Elton's instinct had been to concentrate on Britain, but Dick James convinced him to go. Before he did, in mid-August 1970, there was one last job to do – knock

out a few versions of current chart hits, including 'In The Summertime' and Free's 'All Right Now'.

Elton had been recording facsimile pop songs for budget titles such as Hallmark's *Top Of The Pops* LP series since late 1968. It supplemented his wages, satisfied his compulsion to play – and along the way, he'd learned how hits were made. Over two years, he played on some fifty soundalike songs, everything from Bee Gees ballads to Canned Heat's 'Let's Work Together'.

When Elton's small entourage stepped off the plane in Los Angeles, they were driven to a hotel in a red London bus plastered with a large 'Elton John Has Arrived' slogan.

The publicists had been busy – there were 'Elton Who?' stickers everywhere. Elton panicked and called Dick James to say he was coming home. James assured him that he wasn't.

Everything was geared up for August 25, 1970: opening night at the Troubadour. Neil Diamond brought Elton and his band out on stage to introduce them. Quincy Jones and Henry Mancini, David Crosby and Graham Nash, Mike Love and Van Dyke Parks headed up a long line of VIPs eager to see Britain's latest export. No one anticipated his outfit.

ABOVE LEFT: March 27, 1971: Lyricist Bernie Taupin wore white velvet to his wedding to Maxine Feibelman – the inspiration for 'Tiny Dancer', released later that year. Best man Elton opted for a Mr Freedom suit appliquéd with rhinestone flowers. Guests at the Lincolnshire ceremony included Marc Bolan and Blue Mink's Roger Cook.

ABOVE TOP: During the late sixties, Elton John made numerous appearances as an anonymous session musician performing hits of the day for budget LP releases. His last significant job was singing lead on Mungo Jerry's 'In The Summertime' and Christie's 'Yellow River' for *16 Hit Songs*, released in late 1970.

ABOVE: Elton John's career turned with a six-night residency at the Troubadour in Los Angeles during the last week of August 1970.

The man from Pinner was bringing showbiz back to Hollywood.

Before leaving London, Elton splurged at Mr Freedom, Tommy Roberts' King's Road fashion emporium. The fashion guru had once put Hendrix in frilly shirts and zodiac signs on T-shirts. Now Tommy had gone comic book – all vivid colours and star emblems.

Elton stepped onto the Troubadour stage as if bussed in from an old *Looney Tunes* cartoon. He wore yellow dungarees with a piano motif appliquéd on the back. His boots spouted green wings. The star motif was all over his shirt. The man from Pinner was bringing showbiz back to Hollywood.

He began with 'Your Song', which sounded like pop's best love song since George Harrison's 'Something'. Once the band joined Elton on stage, he treated his piano like a gymnast's prop, pounding the Stones' 'Honky Tonk Women' all the way back to the saloon bar. The grand finale, 'Burn Down The Mission', was a labyrinthine epic worthy of The Band or Grateful Dead.

The *LA Times*' influential rock critic, Robert Hilburn, was in no doubt. 'Rock music has a new star,' he announced two days later.

Word spread fast. America begged Elton to extend his stay. After the six-night Troubadour residency he hit San Francisco, then the East Coast. He started throwing rock'n'roll oldies into the set, Little Richard's 'The Girl Can't Help It' and 'At The Hop' – the latter a highlight of the recent *Woodstock* film as performed by Sha Na Na, a bunch of lamé-clad revivalists from New York.

Shortly after he left for home, three whirlwind weeks later, *Elton John* entered the US chart. The secret was out: here was a natural born entertainer with a huge talent.

RIGHT: On 21 April, 1970, Elton supported Tyrannosaurus Rex at the Roundhouse as part of the annual 'Pop Proms'. At one point, he knocked over his piano stool by accident. Elton expected humiliation. Instead, the audience cheered. From that moment on, he released his inner 'showman', and tore into the rest of the set like a man unleashed.

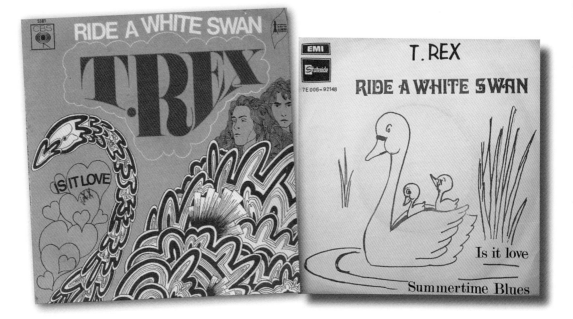

ABOVE: Released on October 9, 1970, 'Ride A White Swan' – here in French and Swedish editions – was a slow mover, eventually peaking at No. 2 in late January 1971. In concert, the shift was immediate. By mid-October, Rex publicist BP Fallon noted the queues of young women outside the stage door. 'One knew undeniably that this whole mad boogaloo was about to explode.'

ABOVE RIGHT: A 1971 unisex wedding. Both bride and groom wore blue dungarees, white polo-neck sweaters, large white hats and (not pictured) matching furry shoulder-bags. 'We are far from being alike,' said Liverpool University undergraduate Tom Stock. 'We've got different shoes and I have a beard.'

Stuffed into his luggage alongside the huge quantity of records he took home with him was a gift from an admirer – a gold lamé tail suit, a perfectly preserved relic from an old Busby Berkeley musical. It seemed apt.

Back home, new rock weekly *Sounds* gave Elton the full homecoming hero treatment. Writer Penny Valentine also noted the dichotomy at the heart of the man: the 'gentle, serious bumbling soul' who'd pour his heart out at the piano and the man-child, with Mickey Mouse badges pinned to his clothes.

There was even support from the fading underground scene. 'He will possibly become the finest, and almost certainly the most popular songwriter in England, and eventually the world,' predicted John Coleman in *Friends* magazine.

At an October press reception at the Revolution Club in Mayfair, Elton performed songs from his next album, *Tumbleweed Connection*. He said 'hello' to everyone and introduced them to a toy clown pinned to the lapel of his plastic coat. It lit up when he pulled a string.

After the reception, he had an appointment with Tommy Roberts. No longer did Elton John need to trek across to Mr Freedom's World's End premises. Now Mr Freedom came to Elton, still operating from Dick James' offices along New Oxford Street.

While *Friends* magazine was endorsing Elton John, thinking woman's monthly *Nova* – where hip exquisite Chelita Secunda was fashion editor – backed Ladbroke Grove mystics Quintessence. A two-page piece titled 'From Underground To Overground' in the May 1970

issue predicted that the raga-influenced festival band would soon follow Fleetwood Mac and Jethro Tull into the singles chart.

It was a wild hunch. *Nova* might just as well have nominated Tyrannosaurus Rex. But then, as Bolan had told *Zigzag* that spring: 'The ego pop things are a drag. As people, we're all important, but Marc Bolan as a plastic cut-out has got to be a drag.'

By the summer, Rex – still Tyrannosaurus – were back on the rock circuit. On June 27, in front of film cameras, dungarees-wearing Bolan soloed long and hard in the sunshine at the Kralingen Festival in Holland. A month later, *Melody Maker* caught him at the Lyceum 'cross-legged bawling like a child throwing a tantrum'.

No one outside Bolan's tight inner circle could see what was coming. Tony Visconti could:

'He had a clear understanding that he was going to be a big star – and he had everything to back it up: talent, imagination, great songs, extremely good looking. His melodies were superb. He just had the little matter of making a hit record…'

Bolan knew what he had with 'Ride A White Swan'. 'It sounded like a hit,' he told Michael Wale the following year. 'I felt it was going to be a hit. It was a two-minute thirty seconds funky, snappy, foot-tapper.'

There was plenty of goodwill towards the single. Long-term Rex watchers like Chris Welch virtually willed it into daylight. Decades later, Elton John said that hearing 'Ride A White Swan' was like meeting Bolan in person: whimsical, full of joy, a one-off.

There was good fortune too. The single – a maxi with 'Summertime Blues' and 'Is It Love?' on the flip –

would be the first on new label Fly, formed after Rex's production/publishing company's deal with Regal Zonophone had run out.

During a meeting between Fly boss David Platz and Bolan, it was agreed that the label's launch record would be credited to 'T. Rex'. Tony Visconti had been shortening the band name on paperwork for some time. Besides, it was slicker, more seventies and avoided any tongue-twisting at the tills.

'Ride A White Swan' hit the shops on October 9. Six days later, T. Rex played Sheffield City Hall. Bolan's PR man, BP Fallon, was there:

'After the gig, these girls were gathered outside the stage door, singing Marc's songs. Nothing unusual in that except these new chicks were less wispy and more feral, freaked out and heated up at their proximity to the hot new rock cock on the block… One knew undeniably that this whole mad boogaloo was about to explode.'

By late October 1970, Elton John was back in the States, this time for a six-week tour. Everyone had something to say about him, from Bob Dylan to The Beach Boys' Brian Wilson, who greeted him at the doorstep of his Bel Air mansion with the words, 'I hope you don't mind' – quoting Elton's 'Your Song'.

The Band flew to see him play in Philadelphia. His hero Leon Russell, who'd seen him headline at the Troubadour, sat in with him at New York's Fillmore East.

Elton was still mostly playing support slots – leaving audiences wanting more – but was now trousering ten grand a night. By the end of the year, the *Elton John* album was at No. 17 and still rising.

Tumbleweed Connection, already released in Britain, was due in January. There were big hopes for it, for within its sepia-tinted, Old West-style sleeve – albeit shot thirty miles outside of London – was an unabashed, extended love letter to the States. Truth was that the windswept, well-crafted material had been written months before Elton and Bernie had ever set foot in the country.

Back in London, Elton and his new manager/partner John Reid were living in The Water Gardens, an exclusive development just off Edgware Road. A purple Aston Martin DB6 sat in the private car park.

In February 1971, 'Your Song' – released back in autumn 1970, two weeks after 'Ride A White Swan' – finally hit the UK top ten. Elton also made the back cover of *Jackie*.

'In our search for someone to replace fallen heroes,' wrote Bill McAllister in *Record Mirror*, 'we pick on an extrovert pianist from Pinner, North London.'

The Faces also made a return six-week visit to the States in autumn 1970. They were still arriving at venues to discover that Rod Stewart & The Small Faces were playing.

With *Gasoline Alley* a top-thirty album, Stewart's star had risen considerably since the spring. The band were tighter now. They'd alchemised Paul McCartney's 'Maybe I'm Amazed' into a set highlight. Screamers started showing up, notably in Detroit and San Francisco.

Rod's conspicuous frontman flash, coupled with 'It's All Over Now' in the live set, brought the inevitable Rolling Stones comparisons. More often, though, The Faces came across like a rough-house version of The Band.

They returned for a triumphant tour of Britain in the weeks before Christmas. Rod Stewart – insouciant, white suited and shirtless – made the cover of *Rolling Stone*'s final issue of the year. And a new Faces album, *Long Player*, was virtually in the bag.

Asked by *Rolling Stone*'s John Morthland about the trend towards solo stars over groups, Stewart disagreed: 'I don't think it's a trend toward solo stars; I think it's a trend toward singers…'

Chapter 4
Nobody Likes Us

The story had been of the bold and cheeky 'Limey Kid Loves Yank Football' variety. The November 11, 1960 edition of *The Bromley & Kentish Times* had found further evidence of the continuing – and possibly dubious – US cultural invasion.

A local lad, 13-year-old David Jones, of Plaistow Grove, Bromley, had discovered the exotic pleasures of American football on his father's short-wave radio. An accompanying photograph showed him all dressed up in huge shoulder pads, holding a protective helmet and the sport's characteristic oval-shaped ball – gifts from the US Navy's London HQ, presented to him by a uniformed naval officer.

A decade later, on January 23, 1971, the boy – now 24-year-old David Bowie – left Heathrow Airport on a plane bound for Washington DC. His enthusiasm for the land of colossal quarterbacks and Bowie knives, of Little Richard and 'Over The Rainbow', might have become more selective. But it hadn't dimmed.

Bowie arrived as a stranger in a strange land – and with a mission. He had no intention of playing second or third on the bill to some standard-issue rock band. (Besides, he had no work permit.) Nor was he there to seek approval from America's cosy new rock aristocracy. He'd come to look, listen and promote the album he'd finished eight months earlier – *The Man Who Sold The World*.

Two and a half weeks into the trip, Bowie was introduced to *Rolling Stone* magazine's resident Anglophile, John Mendelsohn. The writer accompanied the English singer-songwriter on the West Coast leg of his visit, taking in San Francisco and Los Angeles. Bowie was on an inspirational high. Mendelsohn's resulting half-page feature, 'David Bowie? Pantomime Rock?', in

the magazine's April 1 issue, amounted to a manifesto, a blueprint for Bowie's future intentions.

His central idea was 'performance-as-spectacle'. It would be existential rather than empty showmanship, more about testing limits and personal liberation. 'I don't want to climb out of my fantasies in order to go on stage,' Bowie said. 'I want to take them onstage with me.'

In a remarkable interview, Bowie – 'ravishing, almost disconcertingly reminiscent of Lauren Bacall,' observed Mendelsohn – spoke not of Woodstock or the new sepia-tinted way of life but of Erté and Cleopatra, Japanese style and mime.

'I think [rock performance] should be tarted up, made into a prostitute, a parody of itself,' he continued. For rock had lost its subversive edge, relinquished its cultural power. It needed a new approach, new saviours.

'I refuse to be thought of as mediocre,' Bowie concluded. 'If I am mediocre, I'll get out of the business. There's enough fog around.'

The Man Who Sold The World had been one giant leap for the newly belligerent Bowie. It was loud, angry, phantasmagorical, a psychologically powered pie in the face of pop. During the sessions, Bowie had also broken from his long-time showbiz manager, Kenneth Pitt. Younger, sharper characters were running rock now. His partner, Angie, for one, could open doors, talk him up, dispense with old-school formalities.

At one of his low-key gigs during 1970, someone

PREVIOUS PAGE: David and Angie Bowie at Haddon Hall, spring 1971. 'When he started writing *Hunky Dory*, there was a definite change,' says future Spiders drummer Mick 'Woody' Woodmansey. 'He'd open the door and say, "I've just finished one." He'd play it and you'd go, "Fuck, that's a good song."'

ABOVE: After the failure of his 1963 solo single, 'The Feminine Look', Mickie Most turned to production, enjoying huge international success with The Animals, Herman's Hermits, Donovan, Lulu and The Jeff Beck Group. By 1970, Most was a wealthy man and running his own label, RAK.

had flicked lit cigarettes in Bowie's face. It served as a warning: the days of gentle conduct were over. Now there was too much fighting in the dancehalls. He needed someone to wade in on his behalf.

He brought in Tony Defries, a creative property-rights expert who'd worked with starmaker Mickie Most and businessman Allen Klein – now administering The Beatles' affairs – and understood the art of the deal. By 1970, Defries had turned his attentions to management. That autumn, he and GEM business associate Laurence Myers had landed Bowie a five-year publishing deal with Chrysalis.

A piano was installed in Haddon Hall, in a large room empty save for a chaise longue, an art-nouveau screen and a freestanding ashtray filled with dogends. Despite limited ability, Bowie worked hard at the instrument; soon the songs started coming. One of the first was 'Changes', which said everything about

PETER
OH YOU PRETTY THINGS
together forever

his career setbacks and the showdown with his old self. The song also addressed the young whose voices continued to go unheard.

In the early hours of January 19, 1971, Bowie was kept awake by a melody in his head. He called publisher Bob Grace; by the afternoon, he was laying the song – 'Oh! You Pretty Things' – down in a small demo studio. The following day, Grace took the demo with him to MIDEM, the music industry's annual pow-wow in Cannes. He made a beeline for Mickie Most.

Most was the most successful independent producer in Britain. Once a frontman himself, he'd switched to scouting and developing artists after the failure of his 1963 single, 'The Feminine Look'.

Nailing The Animals' 'The House Of The Rising Sun' in fifteen minutes and masterminding its worldwide success in 1964 put Most on the map. The era's most prolific one-man hit factory, he guided Donovan, Herman's Hermits, Lulu and The Jeff Beck Group to international stardom.

By 1970, Most was fabulously rich and fiercely independent, running his own record label. He still believed wholeheartedly in the pop single. It was quick, profitable – and besides, turning songs into hits was what he did best. To launch RAK Records, he had folksinger Julie Felix record 'El Cóndor Pasa', a Peruvian folk song recently covered by Simon & Garfunkel, renaming it 'If I Could'. It went top-twenty.

By January 1971, and yet to release a dud, RAK had two singles in the chart: CCS's cover of Led Zep's 'Whole

Lotta Love' and Herman's Hermits' 'Lady Barbara'. The Hermits had been the linchpin of Most's success. Noting singer Peter Noone's resemblance to the late US President John F. Kennedy alerted the producer to the group's potential in the States. He was right: Herman's Hermits were far more successful in the US, where they notched up eleven top-ten hits between 1965-67, than they were at home. But 'Lady Barbara' was a swansong. Most knew it was time for fresh-faced 'Herman', Peter Noone, to grow up and go it alone.

Down on the French Riviera, Bob Grace played Bowie's new song to Most. The producer stuck with it – he was usually done by the first chorus – and pronounced it a 'smash'. He rang Noone and said he'd just heard his first solo hit.

Three days later, Bowie flew to the States filled with confidence. 'Oh! You Pretty Things' and 'Changes' had redrawn his sonic landscape completely. He had a sophisticated new rock album to promote. And now Mickie Most was listening too. Suddenly anything was possible.

> **Someone flicked lit cigarettes in Bowie's face**

In New York City, Bowie saw The Velvet Underground at the Electric Circus. Backstage, he mistook Doug Yule for the recently departed Lou Reed – but at least he got to tell someone who mattered that he was one of the Velvets' first British fans. (Ken Pitt had returned from New York over the winter of 1966-67 with an acetate of the 'banana album' – *The Velvet Underground & Nico*.) Over on the West Coast, John Mendelsohn introduced him to the music of The Stooges.

Bowie was called a 'fag' in Houston, Texas, but was fêted in Hollywood, where he swanned around in his Mr Fish 'man's dress' and performed a few songs at a private Valentine's Day party. One new tune, 'Hang On To Yourself', was a guitar number that Bowie hoped leather-clad fifties rocker Gene Vincent would record.

Some insist he was already talking about a new fictional rock character named Ziggy Stardust. What's definite is that he returned home with a handful of singles by The Legendary Stardust Cowboy of *Rowan & Martin's Laugh-In* infamy.

On February 18, 1971, as David Bowie was on a plane back to London, Andy Warhol was creating scenes at the Tate Gallery. It was opening day for the first major exhibition of Warhol's work in Britain. Colour supplements ran lengthy profiles of the pasty-faced

ABOVE: In January 1971, Herman's Hermits were bowing out with 'Lady Barbara' and David Bowie was writing 'Oh! You Pretty Things' on piano. After hearing the demo, Mickie Most called Peter 'Herman' Noone and told him he'd found his first solo hit. The singer agreed. 'I only heard the first few bars, and I knew he was right.'

ABOVE: In June 1970, when the Alice Cooper band played a residency at Toronto's Electric Circus, their set was mostly pulverising rock with psychedelic overtones. Three months later, rookie producer Bob Ezrin saw them play Max's Kansas City in New York. No more those 'Worst Band In The World' accusations. 'I saw something that captivated me,' says Ezrin. 'The theatre had a lot to do with it.'

single – subtly retitled 'Oh You Pretty Thing' by Most. It charted in late May and stayed there for nine weeks, peaking at No. 12. By contrast, *The Man Who Sold The World*, when finally released at home in April, flopped – though it did earn Bowie some column inches for his man's dress on the cover shot.

'I think David is the best songwriter in England since Paul McCartney and Lennon,' Noone told *Record Mirror*'s Val Mabbs. Some noted that Noone's hit shared a stylistic similarity to Paul McCartney's piano songs, 'Martha My Dear' in particular.

While becoming a songwriter of note, Bowie increasingly took his cues from Andy Warhol. He broke out from cosy Beckenham and joined the social whirl, mostly at the predominantly gay Sombrero club in Kensington High Street. Inspired by Warhol's relationship with The Velvet Underground, he created and named a protégé band, Arnold Corns, with Sombrero regular Freddi Burretti, alias Rudi Valentino, earmarked as the front man.

At home, between plays of Neil Young's *After The Goldrush*, new songs poured out of him – 'Life On Mars?' on the piano, 'Andy Warhol' and 'Queen Bitch', his Velvet Underground homage, on guitar. Stepping outside his music room, the new husband and father (to son Zowie) was photographed by the *Daily Mirror* pushing a pram, dressed in the widest baggies imaginable.

To journalist George Tremlett, Bowie streamlined his 'pantomime rock' idea. He was going to become 'much more theatrical… more outrageous than Iggy Pop and the Stooges have ever been'.

artist who had assistants to do his work, sent stand-ins to fulfil his public duties, ruthlessly parodied Hollywood in underground films like *Hedy* and inspired endless 'It's clever but is it art?' dinner-party conversations.

The Warhol aesthetic flew in the face of rock musicians' desire for 'authenticity'. Rock was a young art desperate to be taken seriously. The Who and Deep Purple had worked with orchestras. New, keyboard-led 'progressive' rock acts aspired towards classical music.

Andy Warhol was the man most responsible for dethroning the seriousness from art – whilst reflecting the contemporary, commercially driven art world better than anyone. He was also becoming the wealthiest, most celebrated artist of his times.

March saw the release of Peter Noone's first solo

Over in the States, that was already happening. The real story there in spring 1971 was not Bowie's pantomime rock but the surprise success of Alice Cooper. *Love It To Death*, the band's third album, was well reviewed. A single, 'I'm Eighteen', was nudging the top twenty. Industry weekly *Billboard* led the applause: 'Alice and the group have become the first stars of future-rock.'

Back in 1968, the band Alice Cooper were among a menagerie of mavericks signed by Frank Zappa for his new Bizarre and Straight label imprints. Zappa had been impressed by their ability to clear a room in less than two songs. 'He said, "You guys are like a walking piece of Dada,"' recalls eponymous vocalist Alice (née Vince Furnier).

Word got around: Alice Cooper were 'The Worst Band In The World', a stain on rock's high-art aspirations.

Alice Cooper didn't play blues, rarely jammed their

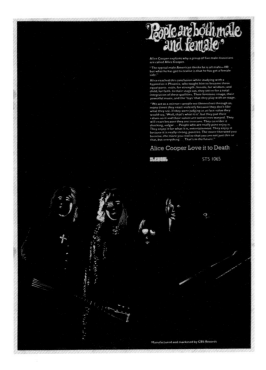

way to a sonic high and avoided anything po-faced and worthy. Outsiders in the Big Nowhere, the group of one-time track athletes from Phoenix, Arizona revelled in their runt-of-the-litter status. The big set-piece was 'Nobody Likes Me', sung by their big-nosed, Tiny Tim-lookalike singer peering through an empty doorframe. Often shows would end in a mass pillow fight.

'There were two divisions in the LA scene,' says bassist Dennis Dunaway, 'the hippies and the freaks. We associated with the freaks. They made fun of hippies. And they were more artistic in a lot of ways.'

There were enough freak-scene adventurers across the States in 1969 to nudge the Zappa-sanctioned *Pretties For You* album briefly into the *Billboard* 200. It sounded more like a series of theatrical skits than a rock record, though there were nods to the Syd Barrett-era Pink Floyd (who they'd seen at Santa Monica's Cheetah Club in November '67) and The Who's vocal arrangements.

'Frank would say, "'10 Minutes Before The Worm' is one minute and thirty-two seconds long and it's got thirty-five changes in it. What are you thinking?"' remembers Alice. 'I'd say, "That's the way we write." We could play that stuff live dead on every time.'

Straight stablemates The GTOs – alias Girls Together Outrageously – adored Alice Cooper, turning up at shows and shrieking approvingly. The Girls' philosophy was neatly summarised by panda-eyed Miss Mercy on the sleeve of their 1969 album, *Permanent Damage*: 'The

GTOs are to me a combination of the world's beauty and ugliness, we are supreme, yet the gutter…'

In a diary entry from October 1968, Miss Pamela (Des Barres) noted that fellow GTO Miss Christine was now seeing 'Alice', a 'new fave rave… a skinny, caved-in guy from Arizona whose real name was Vince'.

The pair looked like crypt-kickers, two super-skinny figures who stooped as they strolled in the streets around LA's Landmark Hotel. Frizzed-out Miss Christine, her face chalk-white like a vamp from the silent era, mixed hippie patchworks with glittering silver thrift-store outfits from the Roaring Twenties.

Alice later claimed he took his style from three sources: Anita Pallenberg as the Black Queen in *Barbarella*, *The Avengers*' Mrs Peel and Bette Davis in *What Ever Happened To Baby Jane?* But Miss Christine was the catalyst, colouring his hair, darkening his eyes, putting him in feminine blouses – the full Hollywood Babylon.

By January 1970, Miss Christine was over in London buying up unauthorised Mickey Mouse T-shirts from Granny Takes A Trip, with budding songwriter/producer Todd Rundgren in tow. Alice Cooper, now going out with a wink as 'The Most Beautiful Band In The World', had boutique owner Cindy Smith – sister of band drummer

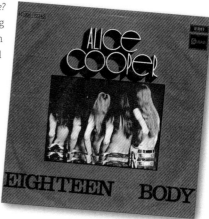

Neal – working on a new metallic/reflective look for their stage act: mirrors, an aluminium backdrop and plenty of silver.

The band began 1970 with two nights at the Eastown Theatre in Detroit. By the summer, they were back in Michigan on a more permanent basis. Post-Manson, LA had become a frightened town, hardly the place for five freaks loaded on booze and black humour. Detroit was a loud, dynamic, blue-collar city, home to The Stooges and MC5. The band took over a farm in Pontiac, thirty miles north of Detroit, installed pet monkey Otto Fellatio, whose party piece was sucking his own cock, and rehearsed like mad.

'It was a farm in the middle of nowhere next door to a prison farm,' says Dunaway. 'When we rehearsed, on a nice summer's day, we'd open the barn doors. If a song was working, we'd hear applause from prisoners.'

On September 9, 1970, Bob Ezrin, an aspiring young producer, was at Max's Kansas City in New York to see the band. 'My job was to go there and get rid of them,' says Ezrin, protégé of Guess Who producer Jack Richardson, who'd been approached by Alice Cooper manager Shep Gordon. 'My boss didn't want anything to do with them.'

The band arrived demoralised. For the first time in their career, they'd even considered not playing. 'We did the most pissed off set that we ever did,' says Dunaway.

'I was shocked, enthralled and entertained,' says Ezrin. 'I said, "You guys are the angriest band I've ever seen. I think I can get you a deal."' The clincher in Ezrin's mind was a song impressively titled 'I'm Edgy'.

Ezrin visited the farm, sat in on rehearsals and made an announcement, as recorded in Dunaway's memoir: 'We are going to invent Alice Cooper.'

The rookie producer had an instinct for what the Cooper band wanted – a tighter, more powerful rock sound for songs that would also work as onstage set-pieces.

'He said, "You have no handle,"' says Alice. '"When you hear The Doors or the Stones, you know who it is. When you hear you guys, it's fluff, it doesn't go anywhere. We need to give you a voice, a sound." And that's what he did. He reconstructed us.'

By the end of the year, Bob Ezrin and the Alice Cooper band emerged with *Love It To Death*. Each song was clearly defined and everything fitted together. 'We'd found our George Martin,' says Alice.

The producer's first instinct was right. 'I'm Edgy' – actually 'I'm Eighteen' – was the obvious single. 'We didn't wanna tell him that "I'm Edgy" was actually "I'm Eighteen",' says Dennis Dunaway. But the young producer got it; it was a powerful three-minute glorification of what Cooper describes as 'being eighteen and being confused'.

It clinched Alice Cooper's upgraded Warner Bros deal. But while the original song had meandered around for several minutes, Ezrin did his stuff, chopping pieces out and moving sections around.

Warners seized the moment. Both album and single were heavily promoted. There were Alice Cooper T-shirts, posters and stickers, even 'I'm Eighteen' and 'I Love You, Alice Cooper' fortune cookies. The single peaked at No. 21 in the *Billboard* chart on April 24, 1971.

Alice, hitherto an oddly reluctant, 'first among equals' frontman, was now obliged to step up. Pop needed an anti-hero and Alice Cooper – growling about teenage angst and madness, with mascara spider-legs around his eyes – was ready for the role.

Alice Cooper the band was giving way to Alice Cooper the man out front. The four accomplices behind him – all hollowed-out eyes, with the longest hair in rock – saw the sense in that.

'Of course, you cater to the vocalist,' says Dunaway. 'We were writing songs to develop and strengthen this character. We were all focused on pushing Alice out front.'

By the summer, the theatrical elements had been ramped up. The band still wore silver costumes designed by Cindy Smith (now Dunaway's partner). Other props included a boa constrictor named Kachina, fencing swords, a hammer and the usual cloudburst of feathers. The big centrepiece was 'Ballad Of Dwight Fry', where 'Nurse Cindy' leads Alice offstage only to return in a straitjacket, yell 'I gotta get out of here!' repeatedly and break his bonds. Then, to the queasy accompaniment of 'Black Juju', he was led to a homemade electric chair, where he'd fry each night in a blaze of flashing lights. The show ended with his resurrection for 'Return Of The Spiders'.

There hadn't been anything like this since the flame-headed Crazy World Of Arthur Brown performed 'Fire' three years earlier. But Brown quickly returned to the margins. Alice Cooper had no intention of doing that. Shock rock was here to stay.

The *Love It To Death* tour created headlines. Alice Cooper were selling records, appearing on magazine covers and prompting much debate – about the role of theatre in rock, about the dubious aesthetics of horror and about the emergence of 'gay rock'.

Jazz/counterculture critic Albert Goldman, writing for *Life* magazine in July 1971, had a hunch about Alice Cooper. In a piece titled 'Rock In The Androgynous Zone', he wrote: 'Far from being a freaky aberrant, Alice was a shrewd operator intent on translating to the fagged-out rock stage some perverse excitement of the Andy-Warhol, Sado-Masochist, Low-Camp Drama and Cinema.'

Calling the band 'Alice Cooper' had been a provocation – but it was all in the name of entertainment. 'The idea was that the audience would expect somebody like folksinger Mary Travers singing on a stool,' says drummer Neal Smith, who was there on the night the Ouija board spelled out the name 'Alice Cooper' – said to be a 16th-century witch. 'Then we'd come out all shiny and loud. It was an all-American name.'

And, insisted the band's designated spokesman, Alice Cooper were an all-American band. 'I love television, really crummy shows,' Alice would say between sips from his ever-present can of Budweiser. 'It's a constant source of useless information. If you look at what we do on stage, it's a kind of useless information too.'

'Everything was discordant and weird and strange,' says Bob Ezrin, 'but underneath it all was the American TV show – *Leave It To Beaver*, *The Andy Griffith Show*. That informed what they did as a band as much as late-night black-and-white horror movies. Alice never attended a black mass. He saw them on TV.'

On July 14, 1971, Alice Cooper were presented

You guys are the angriest band I've seen. I think I can get you a deal.

to the press and select dignitaries from the world of music (The Beach Boys) and television (Richard 'Dr Kildare' Chamberlain). The event was held in the Venetian Room at the Ambassador Hotel in Los Angeles.

Three years earlier, Senator Robert Kennedy had been assassinated in an adjoining room. Now, a rock band that prided itself as 'merely the end product of an affluent society' arrived at the venue in limousines, dressed in black tie and tuxedos.

Inside, a meaty lady called TV Mama, wearing a large pair of pink knickers and nothing else, sang some blues songs. The Plaster Casters were there, on the lookout for hot rock cocks. After canapés, Alice Cooper changed into their silver-lamé stage gear and played a short set.

Afterwards, Miss Mercy from the now defunct GTOs leapt out from a giant cake iced with the words, 'Happy Bastille Day, Alice Cooper.'

The second American revolution would, it seemed, be televised after all.

Chapter 5

Across the Great Divide

'I'm sure there are still a lot of people around who associate our name with the underground,' Marc Bolan told *Sounds'* Penny Valentine late in October 1970. 'But we're not.'

'I'm a pop star on any level and it doesn't frighten me.'

'Ride A White Swan' had just charted at No. 47. 'Doing amazingly well,' said Bolan, already warming to the idea of success. The single hit the top thirty by mid-November, hovered in and around the top ten for weeks before peaking at 'No. 2 on January 23, 1971.

Its success was welcomed as a happy fluke. After all, Tyrannosaurus Rex had a reputation as the quintessential John Peel act. Even the rock press usually treated them with condescension, an amusing reminder of those flower-power days. Bolan saw things differently. He'd spent his life waiting for this.

'Reaching a wider public is what we want,' he told *Beat Instrumental*'s Steve Turner as 'Swan' rose gently up the charts. 'If "underground" means being on a show screened at midnight and watched by fifteen people, we're out of it. If we're asked to do *Top Of The Pops*, we do it.'

'With "Ride A White Swan", two things happened,' says Tony Visconti. 'The image changed. They started to look more glossy, more teen magazine. And we put a string section on the song. I begged four

violins, which we used on a few songs from the [1970 album] sessions. Everything came together on "Ride A White Swan".'

Change came quickly. The October tour of select venues – with a maximum ticket price of ten shillings – had originally been billed 'For Rex Friends'. With dates being added all the time, subsequent ads read: 'T. Rex – Last Of The Great Underground Groups'.

'The trick is not to follow the vogue but to create the new vogue,' says BP Fallon, who as T. Rex's PR man coined the phrase. 'The word "Underground" conjured up images of Middle-earth and strobe lights and freaks dancing around completely off their trolleys. It had a certain gravitas.' It was effective. It was also a red herring.

T. Rex's break from the underground intensified once Marc and Mickey – as they were becoming known in the teen press – made their *Top Of The Pops* debut. Shirtless under blue dungarees, corkscrew locks cascading over his benignly angled head, Bolan held his Cochran-coloured Les Paul and mimed the riff with a smile on his face.

T. Rex —'last of the great underground groups'

THE Last of the Great Underground Groups is how their

Q. Then the ideals have fail
" I don't think so, because groups are pop groups. I think there's any pretence anyone who knows about mu assume that a lot of those are anything more than that. of those people, if there w money in being a progressive would, perhaps, immed become a bubblegum group." Q. Have musical standards proved at all then?

Mickey Finn, in crushed velvet trousers, switched from bongos to fake the bass part. That same evening, November 12, 1970, Tony Visconti sat in on bass at T. Rex's Oxford Town Hall gig. On November 27, at the Bournemouth Winter Gardens, the duo became a hippiefied Johnny Burnette Trio with the addition of new bassist Steve Currie.

Over in the States, where Tyrannosaurus Rex had aroused little interest, Bolan had been described as someone who dwelt 'in a hole in a tree'. In Britain, the big question was what Rex would do next.

'Fans who held on to T. Rex as the last stand of flower power have been startled by the recent introduction of electric guitars into the act,' wrote Rosalind Russell in the November 28 edition of *Disc and Music Echo*. 'Mickey [Finn] feels that fans will gradually come round to the idea.'

Bolan had no doubts about his next move. He'd written another hit – but it needed a drummer. Tony Visconti recommended Bill Fifield from Essex band Legend. Bolan might well have seen them on stage at the Rockin' The Roundhouse event, but what mattered now was Fifield's unfussy style. He had 'the feel'.

At the first meeting, sometime over the New Year period, Fifield was surprised to find that the diminutive man in ballet-style shoes and a black cloak needed something as basic as a rock'n'roll drummer. Fifield would take the moniker 'Bill Legend' at

The Turtles called Marc a cosmic punk. They just took the piss!

Bolan's prompting. His audition session also provided the basic track for 'Hot Love'. It came easily: Bolan was no procrastinator in the studio, preferring to work fast and channel the moment. But 'Hot Love' was too precious a gift to leave unadorned.

When Visconti reminded him of how strings had been used on 'Swan', Bolan's superstitiousness kicked in; while the songs were very different, strings would at least provide some continuity. The final touch came courtesy of Bolan's friendship with Turtles vocalists Mark Volman and Howard Kaylan, struck up during Tyrannosaurus Rex's 1969 US tour. Now going out with Frank Zappa as Flo & Eddie, the duo were in town.

'Marc said how much he loved The Turtles. They called him a cosmic punk. They just took the piss!' says Visconti, who kept a tape running to preserve all the robust ad-libbing. 'Marc was in there with them trying to match the quips.'

Two long orchestral swoops at the start of the song sounded like a nerve-steadying intake of breath before a major undertaking. By the end, Flo & Eddie's joyfully high-pitched voices had turned 'Hot Love' into a party.

On January 25, 1971, the night before the vocal overdub session, the still three-piece T. Rex played a packed Lyceum Ballroom in London. *Melody Maker*'s Chris Welch was knocked out by what he heard and

ABOVE LEFT: Coined by Rex PR man BP 'Beep' Fallon, 'The Last Of The Great Underground Groups' turned the idea of Rex as an anachronism on its head. What had once been a burden was now a cryptic calling-card. On a similar vibe, Bolan began describing his new music as 'Cosmic Rock'.

ABOVE: 'The minute he came in and played it, we all said it was a 'No. 1 hit,' says John Gaydon, then Rex's co-manager. 'Suddenly, we lost the hairy hippies and went into girls lining up outside wanting a kiss.'

ABOVE LEFT: During 1971, Marc Bolan and Mickey Finn became pop culture's most distinctive double act since *Batman* (and Robin) hit TV screens five years earlier. 'Mickey Finn was actually more beautiful than Marc was,' insisted co-manager David Enthoven. 'Lovely man, too. Bongo player, ladies' man and a drug-taker par excellence.'

It's such a hassle— sometimes I feel like giving up MARC

TRIDENT HOUSE, ST ANNES COURT
WARDOUR STREET, LONDON, W.I.
TEL 01-734 9901/4

TRIDENT STUDIOS

DATE 30-3-71   CLIENT S.A.P
15   NIAB   PROGRAMME
7½   CCIB   T.REX

1 MAMBO SUN

2 COSMIC DANCER

3

4

REMARKS   ROUGH MONO MIXES

saw. It was, he declared, the moment 'Marc Bolan became a star and T. Rex a supergroup'.

'Hot Love' met with similarly ecstatic praise on its February 12 release. 'CHART CERT,' announced *Record Mirror*'s Peter Jones. 'It's plain-centre, dead commercial.'

True to the accolades, 'Hot Love' hit No. 1 on March 20, staying there for six weeks. The record it replaced was 'Baby Jump' by Mungo Jerry. This time, singer Ray Dorset had no need to redeploy the Bolan-like warble of 'In The Summertime', for 'Baby Jump' sounded more like a punch-up outside a bikers' pub.

'Hot Love' offered a distinct change in the national mood. It was poetry in motion, with Bolan cooing seductively over a bright horse-trot rhythm. The long, euphoric 'la-la-la' singalong that played out the track could have gone on forever, like The Beatles' 'Hey Jude' three years earlier.

On March 24, Marc Bolan was at BBC Television Centre in the *Top Of The Pops* dressing room. It was the big one – 'Hot Love' had just hit No. 1.

Chelita Secunda, along to celebrate the moment, applied two daubs of glitter beneath his eyes. Under the glare of the studio lights, they shone like silver teardrops.

Fashion dynamo Chelita had all the attitude and elegance of silent-screen vamp Gloria Swanson. Now she was bringing some vintage Hollywood sparkle to British pop.

ABOVE: Early versions of 'Mambo Sun' and 'Cosmic Dancer' were taped days before T. Rex took off for the first US tour as a four-piece. Twenty years later, David Bowie and Rex superfan Morrissey paid tribute to Bolan with a duetted live version of 'Cosmic Dancer'.

RIGHT: As louche TV sleuth Jason King, actor Peter Wyngarde helped redraw the boundaries of masculinity during the early seventies. 'Jason King was always a failure,' he said, 'but in an amusing way. I camped it up, but a lot of people didn't get it, especially in America. They don't have that sense of the ridiculous.'

According to David Enthoven, one half of Bolan's management company EG, it was Bolan's wife, June, who had the widescreen perspective.

'June was fantastic,' he said. 'She understood what fans wanted – this beautiful, almost transgendered man. And she dressed him accordingly. He might not have made it without her.'

With his otherworldly looks, fondness for girls' shoes and Fenjal soap, Bolan was an ideal poster-boy alternative to the recent glut of cock-rock beefcake.

A quote from television funnyman Benny Hill on a recent issue of *TV Times* caught the mood: 'It's the twinkle that makes a star.'

Timing also played its part. A new, softer masculinity, nurtured in unisex boutiques and salons during the Summer Of Love, had worked its way into the adult mainstream.

The *Observer* magazine was now running features on facelifts for men. Fabergé was shaking up male grooming – albeit with a boxer's punch – via 'The Great Smell of Brut'. Then there was Jason King, TV's dandy author turned sleuth, played by distinguished actor Peter Wyngarde.

Having stolen every scene in the 1969-70 TV series *Department S*, King was now allotted his own series. But such was the aphrodisiacal effect of his gaily-coloured cravats, Zapata moustache and fondness for silks that large swathes of middle-aged men embraced the character's style in the vain hope of emulating his success rate.

Similarly flamboyant, Bolan was seized on by the teenage girls' magazine market. The rock press, still in shock at the unlikely transformation, mostly got behind an act that had been one of its own. 'Bolan Booms With Cosmic Rock!' declared *Melody Maker* approvingly.

Marc had thrown out the phrase during the long fade-out of 'Hot Love'. 'Cosmic rock' was hardly a new idea, though its pedigree was good: Hendrix, Bowie, Pink Floyd and Grateful Dead had all looked to the stars for inspiration.

Hawkwind, from Ladbroke Grove's glaze-eyed zone, had cornered the market for 'space rock'. Now Bolan, once cross-legged and rooted to the spot, was astral travelling.

'Marc Bolan is ready to take on the world,' announced Keith Altham in a *Record Mirror* cover story. 'It's been a long time since I've interviewed anyone with the kind of mental sparks that Bolan is spitting out in all directions.'

Bolan himself was remarkably unguarded in the piece, discussing his fears of exposure ('giving of my real self') and making no effort to conceal his contact high from success.

'I've suddenly tuned into that mental channel which makes a record a hit,' he explained. 'I feel at present as though I could go on writing No. 1's forever.'

Bolan had long prepared for this moment. His head had been changed by Elvis Presley and Bob Dylan. He didn't just consume pop; he believed in it as a life-force. He knew the job came with responsibilities.

'If there's going to be any kind of revolution in pop it must come from the young people,' he insisted.

'Marc believed that it was history,' said Mickey Finn in retrospect. 'He loved music so much that he believed he was making his mark.'

Despite the outward confidence, Bolan was in uncharted territory. 'I'm forcing myself to grow,' he admitted to *NME*'s Nick Logan. 'In the past I wouldn't have taken any risks, but everything I'm doing now is a risk.'

For years, Bolan had lived a frugal, abstemious existence. Tyrannosaurus Rex had been as much cottage industry as career. Now he was letting the sunshine in, opening himself up to everything.

'I'm very self-destructive,' he also acknowledged

at one point during the interview. It seemed out of context, out of character and nobody took much notice.

In the first week of April, 'Hot Love' was at No. 1 for the third week of its six-week run. The *T. Rex* album was nudging the top ten, and an opportunist – and misleading – *Best Of T. Rex* was also in the racks, plundering the Tyrannosaurus Rex archive.

But what mattered most to Bolan were two new songs he'd recently demoed, 'Mambo Sun' and 'Cosmic Dancer'. Everything stood or fell on the quality of his work – and this pair stood tall.

With drummer Bill Legend now on board, T. Rex left for the United States on April 6, 1971. Bolan was flying.

'America is really important to me,' he said before leaving. 'I want to have a sixteen-track in my home and make my own movies.'

In the States, Rex were barely remembered as a psychedelic folk duo who – with Steve Took perma-stoned and estranged from Bolan – created bad vibes on their visit two years earlier. Now the more distinguished sounding T. Rex stepped out on stage as a rock band, second or third on the bill to hard-bitten acts like Humble Pie (for four nights at New York's

NORTH-EAST LONDON POLYTECHNIC
ARTS FESTIVAL
(IN AID OF COMMUNITY ACTION)

SATURDAY, 13th FEB., at 8 p.m.

T. REX
COMUS
(LAST LONDON APPEARANCE BEFORE U.S. TOUR)
At BARKING PRECINCT
Tickets 70p (60p in advance)

MONDAY, 15th FEB., at 8 p.m.   IN CONCERT

CYRIL TAWNEY
CHINGFORD MORRIS MEN
DAVE & TONI ARTHUR
at BARKING PRECINCT   Tickets 35p (25p in advance)

TUESDAY, 16th FEB., at 8 p.m.
IN CONCERT FROM U.S.A

TOM PAXTON
at THE BARKING PRECINCT
Tickets 80p (70p in advance)
(By arrangement with M.A.M.)

WEDNESDAY, 17th FEB.
At WALTHAM FOREST PREC...
ALICE'S RESTAU
...SUBM...

FRIDAY, 19th FEB., at 8 p.m.

DAVY GRAHAM
TOM PALEY & THE NEW DEAL STRING BAND
STEVE RYE, SIMON PRAGER & BOB HALL
At BARKING PRECINCT   Tickets 45p (35p in advance)

SATURDAY, 20th FEB.   Members' Bar
WALTHAM FOREST PRECINCT

HUMPHREY LYTTELTON
with **KATHY STOBART**
and the **ED FAULTLESS TRIO**
Non-members 10p

Also **SATURDAY, 20th FEB. FESTIVAL ROCK**
At BARKING PRECINCT

WILD WALLY
...OUSESHAKE...

> Bolan urged the band on, stomping out the beat on the wooden floor.

famed Fillmore East) and Mountain.

They were under-rehearsed. Bolan had no experience of managing a four-piece. Too often, his guitar was turned up to the max, his voice and every sonic nuance lost in the din. Reviewers compared them unfavourably to Led Zeppelin and The Who.

In the States, T. Rex were still a work in progress. Away from the stage, the month-long visit reaped unexpected dividends. They returned home in early May with the core of the first full-band T. Rex album, taped on the hoof in New York and Los Angeles.

Bolan believed his new work represented a complete artistic renaissance. 'What I did,' he explained to Penny Valentine back in London, 'was not rehearse the band [but] go in, mike everything live and play.'

'He'd say, "I've got this number," he'd play it with us once then go and get a soundcheck,' recalls Bill Legend. 'We'd change the tempo around and he'd say, "That's the one!" It was spontaneous. Maybe that was good.'

In defiance of the self-conscious mindset of progressive rock, Marc Bolan wanted to recapture the impulsiveness of Elvis's early sides for Sun Records, of rock'n'roll raw and unrestrained, forged in the moment.

One song had it all: a vintage R&B riff inspired by Howlin' Wolf's 'You'll Be Mine', the natural echo of New York's Media Sound Studios (a converted Baptist church with stained-glass windows) and Bolan urging the band on, stomping out the beat on the wooden floor. He called it 'Jeepster', the latest in a long line of car-related songs.

Bolan rolled with it. There were parallels with John Lennon's recent confessional, clean-slate approach. But while Lennon was compelled to scream out his pain, Bolan wanted to tell some gentler truths – however elliptical – about his inner self.

'There's nothing in my life that I've felt is as important as this,' he said of the US sessions. 'I've never actually ever written about me. I've always disguised it.'

It had long been assumed that Bolan's greatest

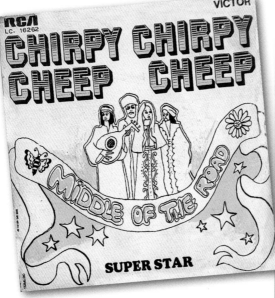

instrument was his wild imagination. In spring 1971, it was his feelings. Previously, he would 'give people pictures', he explained to *Record Mirror*'s Val Mabbs. 'But communication is more important to me at the moment.'

On May 9, T. Rex set off on a month-long sell-out tour of Britain. The set included extended versions of the two hits, featured new songs 'Girl' and 'Get It On', and revived 'Debora' and 'Elemental Child' from Tyrannosaurus times.

The most significant difference was out in the stalls, where the fans were younger, mostly girls in their early and mid-teens. Sometimes they listened. More often they gravitated towards the stage and shrieked: 'MARC!' 'MICKEY!' 'HOT LOVE!'

After the tour, T. Rex returned to the studio to record a five-minute, three-part suite for the flip of forthcoming 45 'Get It On' – once again, a value-for-money maxi-single. The prelude, 'There Was A Time', bade one final, sentimental farewell to those with 'flowers in their hair'. 'Raw Ramp' was all metal knees and crazy breasts, delivered with a vibrant chug-a-lug – the A-side that got away. 'Electric Boogie' saw out the B-side with a rousing call to 'boogie on'.

Between May and July 1971, two singles hogged the No. 1 spot for five weeks apiece. 'Knock Three Times' was credited to Dawn, a session trio fronted by US music-biz executive Tony Orlando. It was another success for Bell Records' UK division, more than compensating for their continued faith in Edison Lighthouse – whose 'It's Up To You Petula' spent one week at No. 49

in January 1971, before the band disappeared abroad.

The second, 'Chirpy Chirpy Cheep Cheep', featured *Opportunity Knocks* winners Middle Of The Road, a cabaret act from Glasgow with a name that made no secret of their generic aspirations.

In light of these successes, Bell label PR Chris Denning reiterated the view, widely expressed the previous spring, that the 'star system' was over. The public, he believed, was 'now more interested in sounds than images'.

The conclusion reached by Bob Dawbarn in his 1970 *Melody Maker* piece 'Singles: Who Buys Them?' was – despite inroads made by T. Rex – still valid: 'The singles market is now largely maintained by housewives and pre-teens. Whereas the teenagers, formerly the mainstay of the singles, generally go for LPs.'

The evidence kept piling up. Tony Burrows was back, fronting White Plains for the pitiful 'When You Are A King'. Even Britain's original homegrown star, Cliff Richard, was succumbing to the trend towards anonymity, by growing a beard and covering bubblegum handclapper 'Sunny Honey Girl' by studio act The Pipkins.

Wherever there was lightweight novelty-pop, master opportunist Jonathan King was rarely far away. He had successes with two alter-ego productions in the summer: a revamped 'Sugar, Sugar', credited to Sakkarin, and St Cecilia's 'Leap Up And Down (Wave

ABOVE: As *Opportunity Knocks* winners Middle Of The Road spent five midsummer weeks at the top with 'Chirpy Chirpy Cheep Cheep', industry spokesmen like Bell Records' PR man Chris Denning returned to the previous year's theme that 'the star system' was finished. T. Rex's 'Get It On', which spent four weeks at No. 1 that summer, suggested otherwise.

Your Knickers In The Air)'. Both peaked at No. 12.

But one act sought to strike a balance between what was often called a 'format' sound and genuine pop-star appeal. The Sweet's summer hit, 'Co-Co', had what monthly lyric mag *Disco 45* described as a 'happy making quality'. The use of steel drums, which had worked wonders for Bobby Bloom's 'Montego Bay' the previous summer, evoked the holiday season.

The Sweet also had a cheeky-faced and photogenic frontman with a fine mop of long blond hair, tonged in at the sides like the girl from the Harmony hairspray ad. The band's big visual asset, Brian Connolly was also the only band member present on the recording of 'Co-Co' and its predecessor, the 'Sugar, Sugar' take-off 'Funny, Funny'.

'When I first joined [in August 1970],' says guitarist Andy Scott, 'Brian was the go-to guy. He was a bit older than the rest of us and looked fantastic.'

'He was streetwise, the hustler,' confirmed Steve Priest, the band's bassist. 'More front than Selfridges.'

The Sweet had been together since 1968, slogging round the clubs and releasing flop singles. By 1970, they were covering The Archies ('Get On The Line', their third and last 45 for Parlophone) and doing session work for producer Phil Wainman.

Then the producer introduced the band to an ambitious new songwriting team, Nicky Chinn and Mike Chapman. The well-heeled Chinn had co-written a couple of songs with ex-Manfred Mann singer Mike d'Abo, for the 1970 film *There's A Girl In My Soup*.

ABOVE: The Sweet, 1971. L-R: Mick Tucker, Brian Connolly, Andy Scott, Steve Priest. 'Everyone thought we were gay before we were doing the gayness because we were a pretty bunch of boys,' said Priest. But only one of Middlesex's tight-shirted pretties performed on early hits 'Funny, Funny' and 'Co-Co' and that was singer Brian Connolly.

ABOVE: Mike Chapman and
Nicky Chinn, alias 'Chinnichap'.
After meeting early in 1970, the
fledgling songwriters set their
sights on singles chart success –
and soon found it with The Sweet.

ABOVE RIGHT: 'Funny, Funny',
the duo's first composition and
a hit for The Sweet in May 1971,
was another song inspired by
The Archies' 'Sugar, Sugar'. In
concert, The Sweet preferred to
play their own material.

Australian-born Chapman arrived in London in 1967, played psychedelic pop in a band called Tangerine Peel then met Chinn in Tramp – where Chapman was waiting tables. Unabashed pop lovers with a desire to break into songwriting, the pair formed a partnership in early summer 1970. An offer was put on the table.

'They'd written "Funny, Funny" and wanted a band to go out and sell it,' said Steve Priest. 'It was either carry on playing the *Wheeltappers And Shunters* circuit for £25 a night or move on.'

Yet Andy Scott's arrival soon afterwards brought a different dimension to The Sweet's ambitions. He'd been an *Opportunity Knocks* winner in 1966 with the Silverstone Set; then, with the Elastic Band, he'd played 'Georgie Fame meets Jethro Tull' music. By 1970, Scott

They'd written 'Funny, Funny' and wanted a band to go out and sell it.

was playing progressive rock with Mayfield's Mule.

'He came in with a long overcoat and hair down to his feet like Cousin It from *The Addams Family*,' Priest remembered. 'He was rather avant-garde.'

But Scott blitzed 'Summertime Blues' – loudly – and passed the audition.

With a new guitarist in place, and producers keen to break them as a singles act, The Sweet sidestepped the dichotomy and returned to the road. The success of 'Funny, Funny' – No. 13 in May 1971 – hiked up their booking fees. Further success with 'Co-Co' even earned Scott the full-colour treatment in *Fab 208*.

'A lot of bands like Edison Lighthouse had one hit and that was it,' Scott recalls. 'We could have been like that. But when you've grasped something, you don't want to let it go, especially when you think you can do better than the others.'

The Sweet made themselves heard on the B-sides. On the back of 'Co-Co' was the self-penned 'Done Me Wrong All Right', a tough rocker about a bad girl that namechecked Jerry Lee Lewis.

Meanwhile, Chinn and Chapman had turned to Mickie Most for advice. They also played him a batch of songs. Most took 'Tom Tom Turnaround' and worked it up for recent RAK signings New World, a cabaret-style folk trio from Australia. Come July, 'Co-Co' peaked at No. 2 while 'Tom Tom Turnaround' stalled at 6.

The Sweet owed their new-found reputation to their songwriters. They were happy to pose with 600lbs of cocoa (based on the band's combined weight) for charity photoshoots. But it was difficult to hide from *Gimme Dat Ding*, a popular budget-priced album split with novelty studio act The Pipkins.

It featured the A- and B-sides of three singles released before Scott's arrival – including the Archies cover. A biographical note on the back sleeve stated: '[They] have no pretensions about the kind of music they play but are quite happy to provide good commercial pop.'

The proliferation of manufactured, character-free pop posed no threat to T. Rex. Marc Bolan had stated he wanted to release singles as important as The Who's 'Pinball Wizard' and The Beatles' 'Day Tripper'. 'Get It On', issued on July 2, 1971, sounded like the fulfilment of that ambition: hypnotic Chuck Berry strut, breathy sensuality, artfully restrained – all that and polished to perfection.

Ringo Starr certainly thought so. 'T. Rex are fantastic,' he said during the four-week run at the top for 'Get It On' during July and August. 'I think they're doing the best stuff now they've ever done.'

But a 'Bolan-sells-out' contingent, which had manifested earlier in the year, was growing. There was resentment at how Marc was now redeploying the roots rock'n'roll of Chuck Berry, and a dislike of the low-status company he was keeping in the pop chart. John Peel, whose support for Bolan since August 1967 bordered on the fanatical, chose not

to play the new song. The pair's famous friendship collapsed.

Peel's protégé, DJ Bob Harris, picked up the slack. 'I think [Marc] peaked with "Get It On",' he says. 'Those early T. Rex singles were absolutely great – yet they were dismissed as fluffy pop singles.'

Twenty-five years later, Mickey Finn and Bill Legend relived the debate while seated around a table in central London:

Finn: 'It was a bit uncool to like T. Rex because we were bubblegum.'

Legend: 'In no way was it bubblegum!'

Finn: 'No, but that's what they termed it as. Musicians used to look at us and say it.'

Legend: 'We were all listening to Elvis and Rick Nelson. We were rock'n'rollers! We knew where it came from – the blues, Howlin' Wolf, Muddy Waters. Marc was the biggest rock'n'roller you could ever wish for. That's where our music was at.'

PR guru BP Fallon says the whole Bolan-sells-out press campaign was cooked up between him and Marc as a publicity wheeze. Only now it was threatening to backfire.

'I see no reason why freaks shouldn't be in the charts,' Bolan complained to *Zigzag*'s Pete Frame. 'But then they turn around and resent you for it.'

Marc flipped back into fantasy. His next venture would, he announced, be a big-budget Hollywood production. 'It's a very futuristic film,' he said, 'with a sort of Cosmic Messiah.'

Chapter 6

Boots on the Ground

New Year's Day 1971 and Slade were back on home turf, playing Wolverhampton Civic Hall. The band had spent the past year trying to play down their reputation as a skinhead act.

Slade were frustrated but never let their heads drop. 'Spencer Davis had made it, Moody Blues had made it, The Move had made it,' says bassist Jim Lea of their fellow Black Country rockers. 'But we were just so much better than anybody else. I was like, "Where's the group that's as good as us?" I wasn't being arrogant. That's the way it was.'

On February 2, Slade were back at the Civic, this time as spectators. Another West Midlands band, Mott The Hoople, were in town as part of a major British tour.

Mott were hairies who played ballsy rock and liked to fire up a crowd. It was 'honest', frontman Ian Hunter would say. It wasn't progressive rock.

Slade sensed common ground. 'We were a genuine group,' says lead guitarist Dave Hill. 'We were never indulgent. We didn't want to bore an audience. It was about the tunes.'

Mott's performance left Slade 'gobsmacked', Hill admits in his autobiography. They wanted that 'thick, strong sound' too. Manager Chas Chandler agreed. Days later, Slade were playing through powerful new amps.

Something else caught Hill's attention that evening. '[Mott] had this slightly hippy thing going where they had their trousers tucked into knee-length boots,' he writes. Slade's obsessive clobber-hound – as fond of the colour orange as his bandmates were of dark clothing – hadn't seen that before.

The four herberts from Wolverhampton had been doing the rounds of clubs and ballrooms since the mid-sixties. Three years younger than the rest, Jim Lea was the last to join. 'I was always a bit hunched over, wouldn't look at anybody,' he says. 'Dave said, "Son, you've gotta walk like you're in a band, hold your head up and look important. That's the way we do it."'

They were The 'N Betweens then, forever zigzagging up and down the country in an Austin J2 van they called Betsy. When Fontana Records showed interest early in 1969, an album deal came on condition that they change their name – 'N Betweens was deemed too sexually ambiguous. The band came up with Knicky Knacky Noo. Label boss Jack Baverstock much preferred Ambrose Slade.

Beginnings, the May 1969 debut, was a mish-mash – covers of Steppenwolf and The Amboy Dukes, Frank Zappa and Marvin Gaye were interspersed with the band's hastily knocked-up first attempts at songwriting.

'People would be baffled at the cross section of stuff we'd play,' says singer/guitarist Noddy Holder. 'Don was big on Harry Nilsson so we did some of his songs. I brought Motown, soul and old rock'n'roll stuff to the band. Jim was into The Moody Blues and Traffic.

Skinheads launched on record!

THERE IS ONLY ONE

SLADE

DON   JIMMY   DAVE   NODDY

Management: Chas. Chandler and John Gunnell in Association with
The Robert Stigwood Organisation, 67 Brook Street, W.1. Tel. MAYfair 9121

PR: Jigsaw PR Consultants. Tel. 01-836 0077

'It all went into this melting pot. But with a very rocky sound, and my singing, we'd make the songs ours. That melting pot stood us in good stead when we started writing our own stuff.'

Former Hendrix manager Chas Chandler dropped in on an Ambrose Slade session that spring. 'I remember looking through the control-room window and I could see him standing there,' says drummer Don Powell. 'I started to shake. This was the man from The Animals, the man who found Jimi Hendrix.'

Chandler had encouraged all the wild, guitar-burning showmanship that had turned Hendrix from a little-known American in London into an international superstar in less than a year. But by 1968, with Hendrix resenting all the crowd-pleasing showmanship, the partnership crumbled.

For his part, Chandler had little patience for the endless studio sessions that went into the making of Hendrix's *Electric Ladyland*. A docker on the Newcastle shipyards while The Animals were getting off the ground, he liked to see a band get its hands dirty. After catching Ambrose Slade at Rasputin's club in London, he immediately offered them a management deal.

Chandler streamlined the name a year before the T. Rex truncation, claiming that Ambrose Slade sounded more like a solo singer. He insisted the band start writing their own material in earnest, pairing Don Powell with Jim Lea and Noddy Holder with Dave Hill. He also came up with a publicity gimmick.

Skinheads had emerged during 1968-69. Some were ex-Mods that had gravitated towards a more brutalist, class-conscious style that turned the decade's appetite for flamboyance on its head. Others, often with football club badges pinned onto their Crombie lapels, were simply more into administering a good kicking to their hairy arch-enemies.

Slade weren't happy about taking on a skinhead image – they'd recently been burning incense at gigs – but Chandler was persuasive. 'He says if I do this, I'll be a millionaire,' Dave Hill told his girlfriend after Chandler had announced the plan over a few whiskies.

The makeover certainly thrust the band out of anonymity via a few fast headlines in October 1969. But it played badly with the rock press, some of whose readers were exactly those scruffy drug-takers that skinheads despised.

ABOVE: In spring 1969, Ambrose Slade were spotted by manager Chas Chandler, the man who'd launched Jimi Hendrix. Won over by the group's work ethic and onstage energy, Chandler took journalist Keith Altham's advice and convinced them to adopt the newly fashionable skinhead look. He also slimmed down the band name.

ABOVE: 'We went along with it because we understood the premise [was] to get us noticed,' says Don Powell. 'But we didn't play skinhead music.' The gimmick didn't play too well in the rock press, especially after January 1970 when The Who's Keith Moon accidentally ran over and killed his chauffeur while the pair were escaping from a gang of skinheads.

Noddy Holder and Don Powell looked the part, Dave Hill less so. It hardly mattered; the skins didn't show up much anyway. Their preferred habitat was the youth club, not dingy live music venues. Besides, reggae was their thing. So Slade carried on gigging, grew out their hair and kept up with changing musical tastes.

'We'd really got three lead guitarists in the band,' says Noddy Holder, 'and we'd play all the riffs together in different octaves. It was very much progressive and fiddly. We hadn't found the Slade style yet.'

The ensuing *Play It Loud* LP, released in late 1970, couldn't replicate the power of the band's live performances. 'It was dry and brittle with an awkwardness about the sound,' says Jim Lea.

The stage was Slade's kingdom. And by spring 1971, fired up by their powerful new gear, they were opening sets with a supercharged version of Ten Years After's 'Hear Me Calling'.

'We'd start with this subtle rhythm that carried on for ages,' says Holder. 'When a spotlight hit my face

by Little Richard – Holder's first and greatest idol. Sensing a breakthrough, Chas Chandler booked the band into the upmarket Olympic Studios in Barnes, west London, where he'd once worked world-beating miracles with Hendrix.

Holder, who'd made his stage debut aged seven, launched into the song as if he'd just leapt out in front of a festival crowd. His opening 'Well, all right!' rap had the gospel energy of Little Richard and the call-to-arms rabble-rousing of Plastic Ono-era Lennon.

Chandler, now keen to prioritise the voice at the expense of the drum kit, boosted Holder's declamation by running it through automatic double-tracking (ADT) – a process favoured by Lennon and, more recently, Bolan. For added atmosphere, the band overdubbed claps and foot-stomping.

'There was a real blokey thing about it,' wrote Dave Hill later, 'some sort of force, like rock'n'roll in its early days.'

'Get Down And Get With It' was released with great optimism in May 1971. Radio 1 breakfast show host Tony Blackburn, who could make or break a hit, claimed it gave him earache. But support came from an unexpected quarter.

> The skins' preferred habitat was the youth club, not dingy live music venues.

I'd start singing the verse. Then, out of the blue, all four of us would come in at full pelt – and all the lights too. It was shock tactics.'

Slade's predicament was how to translate those dynamics onto disc. One night, the penny dropped.

They'd recently been closing sets with 'Get Down And Get With It', a riotous rocker that sent everyone home with ringing ears, sore hands and a happy headache. Originally recorded by US R&B singer Bobby Marchan, Slade found the song on a 1967 single

ABOVE: 'We had to grow our hair again before we got successful,' says Dave Hill. '[But] what came from the skinhead thing was the hairstyles and... everything! I wanted to find my own look. The hair came first. I worked on it with a couple of people up in the Midlands.'

GET DOWN AND GET WITH IT
GOSPEL ACCORDING TO RASPUTIN

polydor
2058 123

SLADE

ABOVE: Once the boisterous 'Get Down And Get With It' charted, the headlines followed. 'Slade Fans "Get Down" To A Riot,' ran one, after 500 people were locked out of a gig at a youth centre in St Andrews, Fife, in late July 1971.

'John Peel hated us,' says Jim Lea. 'But he said, "I'm gonna play this record because I think I've made a mistake."' Radio 1's Johnnie Walker and Radio Luxembourg soon followed suit.

'Get Down And Get With It' – a three-track maxi – went top-thirty in mid-June. A month later, Slade received their *Top Of The Pops* invite.

'This was our moment,' says Jim Lea. 'There were eighteen million people watching.'

Noddy Holder, his beaming scoundrel's face a perfect match for his voice, put on his then-trademark cloth cap. Dave Hill wore a bright orange boilersuit from Mr Freedom with fake diamonds sewn down the legs, a long woman's coat in shocking pink and platform boots with red stripes on the side.

Even all this was eclipsed by his hair: long and straight at the sides, combed forward at the front bowl-style, it looked like it had been copied from a Ladybird book on the Crusades.

Hill had taken Bolan as his cue. 'Marc had an influence on everybody – his music and his look,' he acknowledges. But Hill himself was the complete exhibitionist – dancing, twirling, finger-pointing, stamping his feet, flashing his toothy smile. 'I certainly wasn't hiding!' he says.

'It was the Picasso thing,' adds Jim Lea. 'Square head with eyes on the side – get yourself noticed.

'The first time I saw The Beatles, nobody had their hair combed forward like that, or held the guitars up to their necks. And look at him with the bass that looks like a violin. Everything about them was funny.

'We soon got used to it and it became a trend. It was the seventies, everybody wanted to look idiotic.'

Slade's appearance might have proved a bit too shocking for the moment: 'Get Down And Get With It' peaked at No. 16 in late August.

Scoring a hit didn't erase the memory of Slade's crop-headed past – nor did they want it to. Ominously, *Melody Maker* predicted a flare-up of 'boot dancing' at gigs. And in a piece titled 'Bovver Boys Who Grew Their Hair And Got A Hit', Noddy Holder played up the band's streetwise credentials. 'Black Country yobbos,' he told *NME*'s Roy Carr. 'We like being like that.'

But success changed the nature of their concerts in an unexpected way, bringing in what Lea calls the 'screamage faction', hungry for blokes on stage who – costumes aside - looked little different to those they might meet on home ground.

Slade ramped up the excitement. 'After 'Get Down…',' says Jim Lea, 'we decided to make the whole show like that – cut out the clever stuff and rave it up. I don't think anybody else in the world was doing that, only in soul revues. It was like gospel. Everybody sing along.'

Despite good sales in the States, Mott The Hoople couldn't land a hit record at home. Their debut album had spent a week at No. 66 in May 1970 and follow-up *Mad Shadows* briefly went top fifty that October, but all the real action was taking place on stage.

On July 8, 1971, Mott celebrated two years in the business with an ambitious booking at the Royal Albert Hall. It sold out. The audience, according to a *Melody Maker* estimate, had an average age of 16 and they all came to enjoy themselves.

And so they did. There was so much stomping in two second-tier boxes that the ceilings below collapsed. Several fans were injured; the venue imposed a ban on rock acts.

But the rock press liked what it saw.

'When Mott The Hoople took the dear old Albert Hall by storm on Thursday evening, it was like a return to the halcyon days of rock,' wrote Roy Carr in the *NME*. 'The nearest scenes to Beatlemania I've seen this decade,' reckoned *Melody Maker*'s Chris Charlesworth. Mott also made the cover of *Disc and Music Echo*. At last, they seemed poised for greater things.

Like Slade, Hereford-based pre-Mott bands the Doc Thomas Group and Silence had also cut their teeth on soul and R&B covers before switching to psychedelic-era Beatles and Moby Grape songs. Everything changed when they caught the attention of Island Records A&R man Guy Stevens, recently out of prison after a stretch for a drugs conviction.

Stevens, one of Britain's leading R&B enthusiasts turned rock-culture schemer-dreamer, offered Silence a deal early in 1969. Part mentor, part spiritual advisor, he renamed them Mott The Hoople after an obscure US novel by Willard Manus ('hoople', claimed Manus, being regional slang for 'loser') and brought in a new singer, Ian Patterson.

Stevens also suggested they sharpen up their names: drummer Dale Griffin became Buffin; bassist Peter Watts and vocalist Patterson redeployed their middle names, Overend and Hunter respectively; Verden Allen (organ) and Mick Ralphs (guitar) passed the name game unscathed.

Ian Hunter was older than The Beatles, with a decade served at the twilight end of the music business by the time he joined the band. By day he turned a lathe in a factory in Archway, north London; by night he was knocking out songs for a publishing company.

But Stevens could see a diamond in the rust. He put the new man in a £100 white suit and Hunter did the rest – shed a few pounds, put on dark shades and let his curls sprout.

It was a good match. Stevens saw Mott as defenders of a tradition sidelined by psychedelia, pitched somewhere between mid-sixties Dylan, contemporary Rolling Stones and Jerry Lee Lewis. Mott had no desire to go progressive, like Island's other recent signings Renaissance and King Crimson. Neither did the band harbour any obvious superstar ambitions.

Shortly before the release of their November 1969 debut album, prominent underground magazine *International Times* welcomed Mott The Hoople with

BELOW: 'The nearest scenes to Beatlemania I've seen this decade,' raved *Melody Maker*'s Chris Charlesworth of Mott's July 1971 Albert Hall gig. The authorities were less enthusiastic – the venue slapped a ban on rock shows.

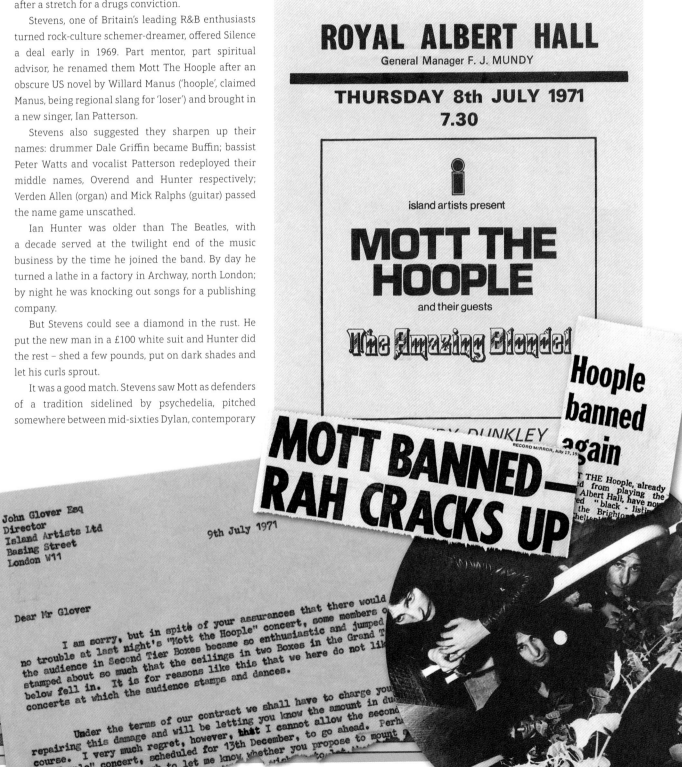

ROYAL ALBERT HALL
General Manager F. J. MUNDY

THURSDAY 8th JULY 1971
7.30

island artists present

MOTT THE HOOPLE
and their guests

The Amazing Blondel

MOTT BANNED —
RAH CRACKS UP

Hoople banned again

...T THE Hoople, already ...d from playing the ...Albert Hall, have now ...ed "black - listin... ...the Brighton...

John Glover Esq
Director
Island Artists Ltd
Basing Street
London W11

9th July 1971

Dear Mr Glover

I am sorry, but in spite of your assurances that there would ... no trouble at last night's "Mott the Hoople" concert, some members o... the audience in Second Tier Boxes became so enthusiastic and jumped ... stamped about so much that the ceilings in two Boxes in the Grand T... below fell in. It is for reasons like this that we here do not li... concerts at which the audience stamps and dances.

Under the terms of our contract we shall have to charge you... repairing this damage and will be letting you know the amount in du... course. I very much regret, however, that I cannot allow the second... the Hoople" concert, scheduled for 13th December, to go ahead. Perh...

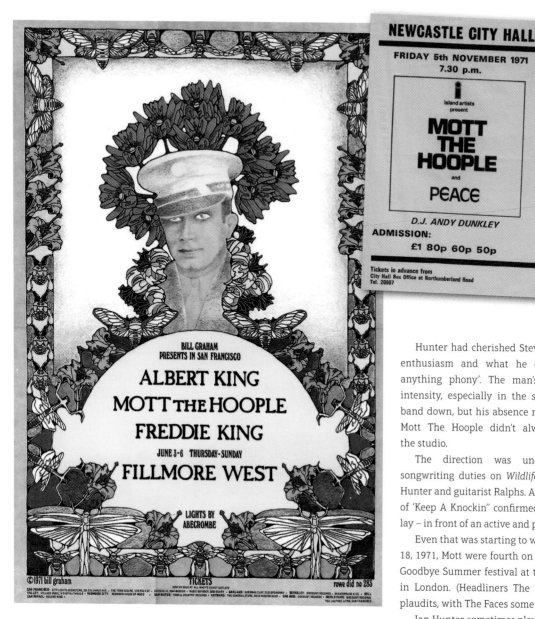

NEWCASTLE CITY HALL

FRIDAY 5th NOVEMBER 1971
7.30 p.m.

i
island artists
present

MOTT
THE
HOOPLE
and

PEACE

D.J. ANDY DUNKLEY

ADMISSION:
£1 80p 60p 50p

Tickets in advance from
City Hall Box Office at Northumberland Road
Tel. 20007

BILL GRAHAM
PRESENTS IN SAN FRANCISCO

ALBERT KING
MOTT THE HOOPLE
FREDDIE KING

JUNE 3-6 THURSDAY–SUNDAY

FILLMORE WEST

LIGHTS BY
ABECROMBE

©1971 bill graham

TICKETS

ABOVE: Mott The Hoople albums had some success in the States during 1970 and '71, but the band's reputation was mostly based on live performances. 'We give the customers what they want,' said Hunter, 'a good show and hard rock.'

RIGHT: Ian Hunter bought his Maltese Cross guitar from a pawnshop in San Francisco for $75. While it looked great on stage, Hunter later admitted it was 'useless'.

a prediction: 'The Only Rock'N'Roll Band Of The Seventies'.

It was a lot to live up to – and further evidence of the counterculture's exasperation with rock's fledgling Beethovens and the soft parade of singer-songwriters.

Mott gigged hard, especially in the States, where covers of Crosby, Stills, Nash & Young's 'Ohio', Little Richard's 'Keep A Knockin'' and The Kinks' 'You Really Got Me' endeared them to crowds that preferred familiar material over long freak-outs.

With that in mind, Mott targeted *Wildlife*, their summer 1971 album, at the US market. It was anything but wild – and Guy Stevens was nowhere to be seen.

Hunter had cherished Stevens' style, intelligence, enthusiasm and what he called his 'hatred for anything phony'. The man's amphetamine-driven intensity, especially in the studio, had ground the band down, but his absence revealed a shortcoming: Mott The Hoople didn't always move as one in the studio.

The direction was uncertain. Singing and songwriting duties on *Wildlife* were shared between Hunter and guitarist Ralphs. A ten-minute live version of 'Keep A Knockin'' confirmed where Mott's strength lay – in front of an active and participating audience.

Even that was starting to wear thin. On September 18, 1971, Mott were fourth on the bill at the day-long Goodbye Summer festival at the Oval cricket ground in London. (Headliners The Who took most of the plaudits, with The Faces some way behind.)

Ian Hunter sometimes played on Mott's reputation as underachievers. 'Led Zeppelin and Black Sabbath are on page one of the papers,' he'd tell audiences. 'We're on page nineteen – but that's where we belong.' Fans would cheer. But Mott knew they deserved better.

In mid-September 1971, they began work on a fourth album. Guy Stevens was back – dressed in a Lone Ranger outfit and riding shotgun more than ever. Sessions were interrupted by water-pistol fights and bouts of furniture smashing, but Stevens' provocations had the desired effect.

The resulting *Brain Capers* was a wild and belated adventure into ruined psychedelia, far closer to Ladbroke Grove's oblivion-seeking Pink Fairies than the aspiring prairie rockers who'd recorded *Wildlife*.

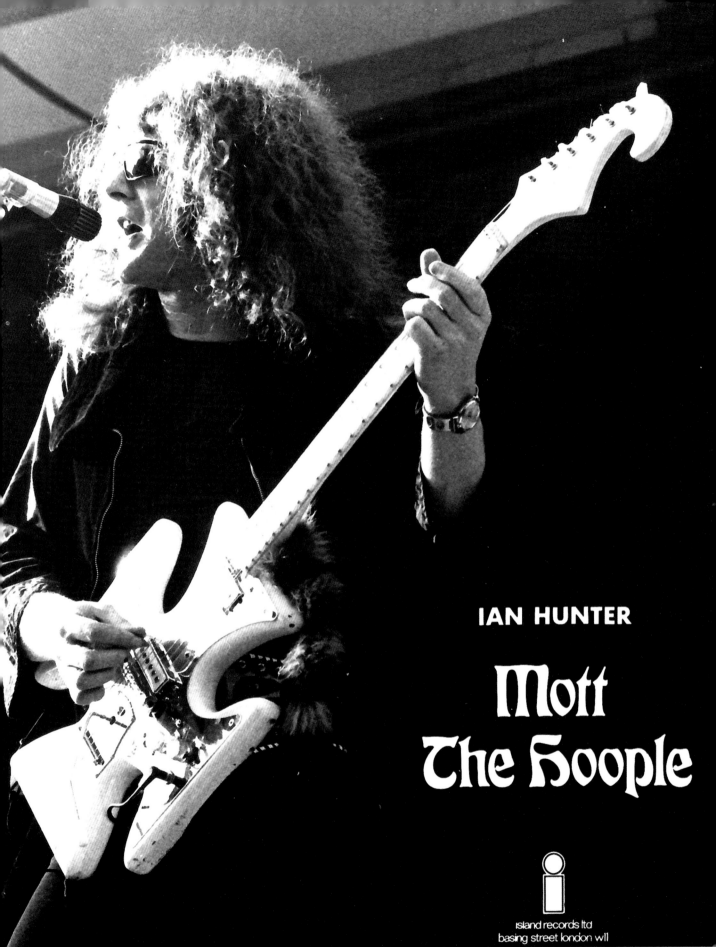

IAN HUNTER

Mott
The Hoople

island records ltd
basing street london w11

But it was out of time and when released, in November 1971, the album stiffed. Ian Hunter struggled to find an easy explanation. Inadvertently, his words hinted at a future course of action. 'Most of our following are working class people,' he told Keith Altham. 'Maybe they don't have the money for an album.'

A successful single would have eased Mott's predicament. Their late '71 cover of 'Downtown', a song Neil Young co-wrote for Crazy Horse, turned out not to be the answer. Hunter disliked the song so much that Mick Ralphs sang it.

Meanwhile, Mott The Hoople made plans to tour the States in February 1972.

With Chas Chandler's firm guidance, Slade remained focused in unity on their common cause. The manager's first instinct for a follow-up to 'Get Down And Get With It' was to record another cover. He had R&B standard 'Let The Good Times Roll' in mind, but

Jim Lea had other ideas:

'We were playing at this church hall in Wednesbury and the others had put their guitars down and buggered off. Don was playing this simple rhythm so I joined in going boom-boom-boom on bass. Don was laughing. Then he started doing it on the snare.

'Remember [The Move's] Trev Burton doing "Blackberry Way" on TV, holding the bass like he was shagging the audience? Well, I started doing this to the rhythm and it sounded gigantic.'

On the way home, Lea recalled how a John Dummer Blues Band song had been transformed by a Stéphane Grappelli-style fiddle part. He picked up his violin and acoustic guitar and turned up on Holder's doorstep.

'I sang a very basic lyric and in twenty minutes, we'd got it pretty much finished,' says Holder – who remembers the staccato shuffle being utilised as a dressing-room tune-up for the violin.

'We didn't think much of it. But we'd done what Chas had told us to do – come up with a simple three-minute pop song.'

ABOVE: Mott The Hoople, September 1970. L–R: Ian Hunter, Pete 'Overend' Watts, Dale 'Buffin' Griffin, mentor/manager Guy Stevens, Mick Ralphs, Verden Allen. After a spell away from the band, Stevens returned in August 1971 for the making of *Brain Capers*. To fire up the sessions, he'd don a Lone Ranger mask and start water-pistol fights. A Lone Ranger mask was used to promote the album in Germany.

Chandler heard it and announced that the pair had just written their first No. 1. He also rejigged the title, with 'Because I Love You' becoming the more eye-catching 'Coz I Luv You', coining the subliterate gimmick that became synonymous with golden-era Slade.

Hearing the recording back at Olympic, the band were disappointed. 'It was far too poppy,' says Holder. A decision was made to 'Sladify' it.

On the stairs outside the studio, the four added all the boot-stomping, handclapping and chanting they could muster. 'It went from a simple pop-rock song to a Slade song by adding elements from our stage show,' elaborates Noddy.

'Slade's Earbender,' raved *Record Mirror* on October 9, 1971. 'As they've been riot-raising round the B. Isles of late,' wrote editor Peter Jones, 'I've no doubt that this staccato building production will make it. And make it big. CHART CERT.'

On November 4, 1971, with 'Coz I Luv You' about to go top-ten, Slade returned to *Top Of The Pops*. The band were growing into their characters: Noddy Holder was assured in flat cap and mutton-chop sideburns; Don Powell chewed gum impassively; Dave Hill was resplendent in blue and silver satin; Jim Lea played a 'Danse Macabre' on violin.

Chandler called it right. 'Coz I Luv You' hit No. 1 on November 13 and stayed there for four weeks. During its run, he cannily negotiated a new, improved record deal for the band.

After the single's release, and sensing major success, Chandler booked three nights at the Command Theatre Studio in London. In front of an invited audience of fan-club members and industry insiders, Slade recorded what would be their next album – a live set under sonically advantageous conditions.

For a band now becoming popular in the teenage press, Slade still played it loud and lairy on stage. Even the ballad, John Sebastian's 'Darlin' Be Home Soon', was hooliganised by Noddy with a well-timed belch.

Days later, on October 25, Slade were at Portsmouth's Tricorn Centre. 'That was the first night we went crazy on stage,' says Jim Lea. 'There was a DJ down there who thought we were great, proggy rocky. This time, we came out with all our gear on, my tartan trousers done by my wife. He said, "You're ruining yourselves."'

That same night, Chas Chandler turned up at the gig. 'He said, "I've seen three and at every one you've gone down a storm. That means you're gonna be three times as big as Jimi Hendrix." I asked why. He said,

The band were disappointed. A decision was made to 'Sladify' it.

"Jimi died a death two out of every three gigs because he was stoned. But if you go out and win ten-nil every match, you're onto a winner."'

On December 29, 1971, Slade crowned the year with a gig at the Kew Boathouse. 'That was the first night I climbed on the gear,' says Lea.

He also recalls that Slade had visitors that evening. 'Sweet came down to see us. Chinnichap [Chinn and Chapman] with Andy [Scott] and Steve [Priest].'

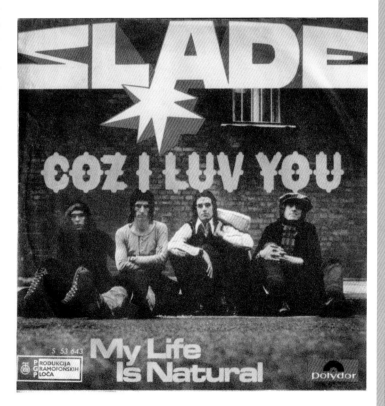

Chapter 7
Roll Away the Stones

In early March 1971, The Rolling Stones announced they were quitting Britain. With a new tax year approaching, the band – like the ex-Beatles – had woken up to the new decade with a financial headache. Exile on the French Riviera would ease the burden.

Before leaving they played a farewell tour, ending with two shows at the Roundhouse on March 14. They also filmed a video insert for *Top Of The Pops* of 'Brown Sugar', the launch release for Rolling Stones Records.

Jagger, hand on hip, wore a pink silk suit. It was shiny and gaudy, though hardly worthy of the 'Are you a boy or are you a girl?' backlash the group faced back in 1964. Yet still reporters were intrigued by his sexuality. 'If God wants me to become a woman, then a woman I'll become,' Jagger would say in response.

The Stones had been teasingly blurry about gender for years: cross-dressing for the 'Have You Seen Your Mother, Baby, Standing In The Shadow?' promo in 1966; then there was multi-instrumentalist Brian Jones, a phantom-like apparition with his floaty fabrics and angel hair. Jagger himself bade farewell to the deceased Jones, on stage at Hyde Park in July 1969, dressed in a white Mr Fish shirt-dress whilst quoting Shelley.

The Rolling Stones in cooperation with John and Tony Smith present

The Rolling Stones
UK Tour 1971

Thursday 4 March
Newcastle City Hall

Friday 5 March
Manchester Free Trade Hall

Saturday 6 March
Coventry Theatre

Monday 8 March
Glasgow, Green's Playhouse

Tuesday 9 March
Bristol, Colston Hall

Wednesday 10 March
Brighton, Big Apple

Friday 12 March
Liverpool Empire

Saturday 13 March
Leeds University

Sunday 14 March
London, The Roundhouse

ABOVE AND LEFT: The Rolling Stones played a short farewell tour in March 1971 before jet-setting off to France as tax exiles. 'The Stones are really showbiz now, thanks to Jagger,' sniffed Deep Purple drummer Ian Paice.

STONES QUIT U.K?

Vice. And Versa.

Mick Jagger.   And Mick Jagger.
This film is about madness. And sanity. Fantasy. And reality. Death. And life. Vice. And versa.

performance. x

James Fox/Mick Jagger/Anita Pallenberg/Michele Breton

Written by Donald Cammell/Directed by Donald Cammell & Nicolas Roeg/Produced by Sanford Lieberson in Technicolor*
A Goodtimes Enterprises Production from Warner Bros. Released by Warner Bros. Distributors Ltd.

This Stones shtick reached a zenith of sorts in *Performance*, a film so unlike anything else that it required more than a year of editing and accommodating censorship laws before being passed for release in 1970. A snapshot of worlds colliding, of gangland dust-ups and a rock star's disintegration, *Performance* starred Jagger as androgynous recluse Turner – a character based mostly on his by then fast-fading colleague, Brian.

Androgyny and blurred identities lay at the heart of the film. 'Did you never have a female feel?' asks Pherber – played by Jones' onetime girlfriend, Anita Pallenberg. 'No! Never! I feel like a man… all the time,' replies underworld interloper Chas, as portrayed by James Fox. 'That's awful,' says Pherber. 'That's what's wrong with you, isn't it?'

The Stones' departure from the UK domestic scene, a year on from The Beatles' split, looked like another blow to pop's middle ground. It also created an opportunity.

ABOVE AND RIGHT: The Rolling Stones in their foppish glory backstage at the London Palladium, January 1967. Floppy-hatted Brian Jones provided the inspiration for Jagger's portrayal of spun-out androgyne Turner in the 1970 film *Performance*.

RIGHT: Backstage at Weeley, August 1971, Rod Stewart – like Jagger had done earlier in the year – opted for the pink satin suit. Out front, The Faces lost out to T. Rex over top billing, but walked away with the plaudits in the following week's music press.

FACING PAGE: The Faces kicked a ball around on *Top Of The Pops*. Slade were attracting bovver boys from the terraces. But at Hurlingham Stadium, on February 28, 1971, models from two top agencies were taking part in 'The World's Most Beautiful Football Match'. Mr Freedom, alias Tommy Roberts, and Ossie Clark designed the strips.

> It would be 'a nice midnight-type album', nothing like the band's work.

A month later, on April 29, the Roundhouse hosted another evening of knockabout rock'n'roll. After a third tour of the States, The Faces were back.

'They're fantastic!' was the verdict on the cover of *Disc and Music Echo*. *Melody Maker* put them up there with The Who. But the Stones – from whose basement The Faces hatched – were the real inspiration.

Rod Stewart had launched his solo career with an unlikely if persuasive cover of the Stones' 'Street Fighting Man'. On stage, The Faces played 'Honky Tonk Women', 'It's All Over Now' (a Bobby Womack

original adopted by the Stones) and, more recently, Robert Johnson's 'Love In Vain', which the Stones had been playing since 1969.

Stewart and guitarist Ron Wood had a Jagger/Richards vibe going on. Rod, another pink satin enthusiast, was also showing plenty of Jagger's swagger and penchant for working a crowd.

On May 12, Ron Wood, Ronnie Lane and Kenney Jones were partying at Jagger's wedding reception in Saint-Tropez. Over in a New York studio, Rod Stewart was supervising the final touches on his third solo album, *Every Picture Tells A Story*.

As Rod told *Rolling Stone* months earlier, he was determined to keep his solo career separate from

The Faces. This latest release, he predicted, would be 'a nice midnight-type album', nothing like the band's work.

The Faces' second album, *Long Player*, released back in March, had once again suffered from a lack of band identity – the very thing they had in such abundance on stage. Band democracy was crucial to The Faces, but the record, while likeable enough, sounded as if no one was prepared to step up and take responsibility.

On *Every Picture Tells A Story*, released on May 29, each track stacked up as if to create a composite portrait of the singer. Yes, Rod Stewart was Mr Flash. But he was also a gifted vocal interpreter with an instinct for the right song and the voice to make it his own.

An album highlight was the cover of The Temptations' 1966 hit '(I Know) I'm Losing You', featuring David Ruffin. 'I nicked a few moves off him,' Stewart admitted later, including Ruffin's habit of holding the microphone behind his back. But the song featured all five Faces and had been a highlight of the band's early spring US tour. Its inclusion on a Rod Stewart solo record made the others uncomfortable.

By the time The Faces began their early summer tour of the States, on July 7, Stewart's album had gone top-twenty. By the time The Faces returned home a month later, it was in the top ten and rising.

It had been a messy tour. Onstage, support band Deep Purple stole some of The Faces' thunder with their virtuoso hard-rock. Offstage, it was rock'n'roll Babylon. Some of the tour's stag-like energy found its way into a new song, 'Stay With Me', likely written in a hotel room in Georgia.

Back home, The Faces played the Weeley Festival over the August bank holiday weekend. Rod Stewart arrived at the location – a large field outside Clacton-on-Sea, Essex – in his new white Rolls-Royce. His latest girlfriend, model Dee Harrington, was with him; his pink satin suit came too.

Backstage, a row had developed over which act merited the prime 9pm slot on Saturday night. Early publicity suggested The Faces were the headline act, but when T. Rex were added to the bill they were promised the slot. The Faces lost the battle but won the war, following Heads, Hands & Feet with a rapturously received early-evening set.

T. Rex walked out to a more subdued reaction. There were even a few boos. Hardy festivalgoers had little difficulty accepting Rod Stewart as a kind of Joe Cocker figure with added panache. But it took a wild stretch of the imagination to equate the four-piece, electric Rex with the woodland rock duo from dandelion-blowing days.

BELOW: A pre-Damned Captain Sensible (alias Ray Burns) saw T. Rex at Weeley. 'All the blokes in the audience wanted to kill him, and all the women wanted him.'

Marc Bolan, 1971: 'I thought it was a very good gig.'

RIGHT: Rod Stewart with new girlfriend Dee Harrington, pictured a few months after Weeley and with a different Roller.

ROD STEWART ON MERCURY RECORDS

MAGGIE MAY

Words and Music by ROD STEWART & MARTIN QUITTENTON

1 49034   CHAPPELL & CO. LTD., 68-70 Clarence St., Sydney
MELBOURNE — BRISBANE — WELLINGTON, N.Z.

chappell
Unichappell/New York

LEFT: Originally a B-side, 'Maggie May' was flipped and became a massive No. 1 hit on both sides of the Atlantic. 'We were happy for Rod,' remembered Ian McLagan. 'It never occurred to me that we wouldn't play it live.'

By Courtesy of The Trustees of the Surrey County Cricket Club

Goodbye Summer

A Rock Concert in aid of the Victims of Bangla Desh
at the **Oval Cricket Ground**, Kennington, London, S.E.11
September 18th, 11 a.m. to 9.30 p.m. (Gates open 9 a.m.)

THE WHO
ROD STEWART AND THE FACES

Mott the Hoople   Lindisfarne   Quintessence
+ Jeff Dexter   + Friends

Tickets now on sale. Price £1.25 at all branches of Harlequin Record Shops and all branches of One Stop Records or by post from The Oval Cricket Ground, Kennington, London, S.E.11

Some remember a set-opening provocation: 'I'm Marc Bolan. You may have seen me on *Top Of The Pops*.' But most agree that the three-hit finale of 'Ride A White Swan', 'Hot Love' and 'Get It On' had the crowd on its feet.

The rock weeklies weren't convinced. 'A one-group festival,' insisted *NME*. 'And they were The Faces.'

Days after Weeley, Rod Stewart was on course for his first British hit single. 'Maggie May' had been inspired by his teenage frolic with an older woman at the 1961 Beaulieu Jazz Festival. Yet, despite its folkish textures and rich sense of character, the song was initially dismissed as a yarn in search of a chorus.

'Maggie May' was duly dumped on the B-side of 'Reason To Believe', Rod's take on the beautifully downbeat Tim Hardin classic. But once a sharp-eared DJ from Cleveland, Ohio flipped sides, the song took off. By October, 'Maggie May' – with its arresting 'Wake up, Maggie' intro – had gone international.

For three weeks in October, 'Maggie May' and *Every Picture Tells A Story* topped both the singles and albums charts in Britain and the United States – a feat previously only achieved by Simon & Garfunkel in spring 1970. 'Maggie May' inevitably became the highlight of The Faces' set, though only Wood and McLagan had played on the recording.

The Faces frontman with a solo sideline – or 'Red Hot Rod', as he was sometimes described – was now the biggest-selling storyteller in the world. A Rod Stewart Day was declared in Amsterdam. He was Best British Singer in the annual *Melody Maker* poll; weeks later, he was *Rolling Stone*'s Rockstar of the Year.

Rod Stewart was more than ready for the superstar role. On September 18, with the single still climbing, he drove his Lamborghini to London's Kennington Oval for the Goodbye Summer festival.

'I had this overwhelming sensation of having arrived,' he'd recall in his autobiography. 'You're quite the rock star aren't you, son?'

The crowning moment didn't go quite as planned. With their set plagued – suspiciously, some felt – by sound problems, much of the acclaim went to headliners The Who.

But 'Maggie May', which brought the crowd to its feet, was the day's memorable moment. Resplendent in his leopard-skin suit from Granny Takes A Trip, Rod lapped it up.

'He looks like he always wanted to be a rock'n'roll star and now he is, he ain't ashamed to show it,' raved *Rolling Stone*.

On November 26, early into their third US tour of the year, The Faces played Madison Square Garden. Rod wore pink, wine was passed into the crowd and footballs booted around from stage to stalls. Everyone sang along.

'Of course, we still got the Rod Stewart and the Faces thing out there,' Ron Wood told *Disc*'s Penny Valentine on the band's return, 'but there's a reason for it there and you just can't fight it.'

'Red Hot Rod' was now the biggest-selling storyteller in the world.

YOUR SONG is Elton John's new single

D.J.M. (Distributors) Ltd.,
James House, 71/75 New Oxford St.,
London W.C.1 A1DP   Tel: 01.836.4864
Distributed by Pye Records (Sales) Ltd

Available now

DJS 233

Elton John had also spent much of 1971 crisscrossing the Atlantic, consolidating his US success while growing his audience at home.

He'd begun the year back at the Roundhouse, supporting The Who. Reviewing the show, *Record Mirror*'s Bill McAllister identified the contradiction that made Elton an awkward fit in Britain – a composer turned performer whose 'gaudy clothes and extravagant gestures go against the grain'.

The belated success of 'Your Song', peaking at No. 7 in mid-February, confirmed the general perception of Elton at home. He plugged the song on *Top Of The Pops*: a sensitive-looking man in a white jacket, seated at a piano, singing what already sounded like a heart-tugging standard.

But those who'd seen Elton do his Jerry Lee Lewis thing on stage, and read about his whirlwind success in the States, knew a different performer. The man in the tinted specs was no church mouse. 'Elton IS a superstar, joke or no joke,' McAllister insisted.

Elton John's success in the States – four albums in the chart that spring and two sell-out, career-capping performances at New York's Carnegie Hall – nevertheless prompted accusations of hype.

'It's kind of uncool to dig Elton John anymore,' said Carole King/James Taylor session guitarist Danny Kootch in July. 'Man, people make superstars, and eat them up the same day.'

Elton, who followed a busy schedule touring Britain and the States twice in 1971, began to play it down. Whenever asked if he was putting the showbiz back into pop, he'd shake his head and recoil from the idea. His role model, he insisted, was Paul Simon: 'To become someone like him, who is accepted by everyone, is my ultimate ambition.'

CRYSTAL PALACE BOWL GARDEN PARTY II
SAT. 31 JULY 1971
ELTON JOHN
DEE MURRAY NIGEL OLSSON
YES

1st ANNOUNCEMENT ONLY--MORE BIG NAMES STILL TO COME!
GATES OPEN AT 12.00 NOON

FREE CONTROLLED PARKING
TRAVEL
RAIL: Crystal Palace, Penge East/West from Victoria/London Bridge
UNDERGROUND: Northern Line to:

TICKETS AVAILABLE BY
MAIL ORDER
P.Os & Cheques made out to:

GARDEN PARTY at
42 Kings College Court
Primrose Hill Road
LONDON NW3

Please send me .... tickets
at £1.25 each plus S.A.E. to:
Name ....
Address ....

I enclose PO/Cheque for £ ....

ABOVE TOP: By the time 'Your Song' became a top-ten hit in Britain in February 1971, it had sold over 300,000 copies in the States, where it peaked at No. 8.

ABOVE: Elton stole the show with a two-hour set at the Crystal Palace Garden Party in July 1971.

But Elton took another view when asked for his verdict on pop at the end of the year. 'I wish the scene would change and people would get young idols,' he said. 'Rod Stewart's in his mid-20s. Dylan and Lennon are 30ish. Presley's an old man. And even I'm 24!'

Marc Bolan, who had passed Elton – as well as Bowie and The Move – on the stairs at Essex Music's Oxford Street offices in leaner times, had embraced stardom with both hands. But his reception at Weeley, and the reviews that followed, fed into the deep resentment he felt towards the rock mainstream – which had always struggled to take Tyrannosaurus Rex seriously.

T. Rex were already 1971's most successful singles act, and Bolan was pop's most visible, talked-about star. But he considered himself much more than that.

Back in July, *Record Mirror*'s Val Mabbs wrote of Marc's rejection of the idea that T. Rex had changed in any fundamental way. 'It's more a natural evolution for him,' she explained. 'He uses Jimi Hendrix as an example of the need to move constantly, musically.'

Neither The Beatles' split nor the Stones' self-exile meant much to Bolan. But the death of Hendrix moved him profoundly. When journalists visited him at his new flat in Little Venice, they noted the Hendrix posters on the wall and the copy of *The Cry Of Love* – a collection of Jimi's final recordings

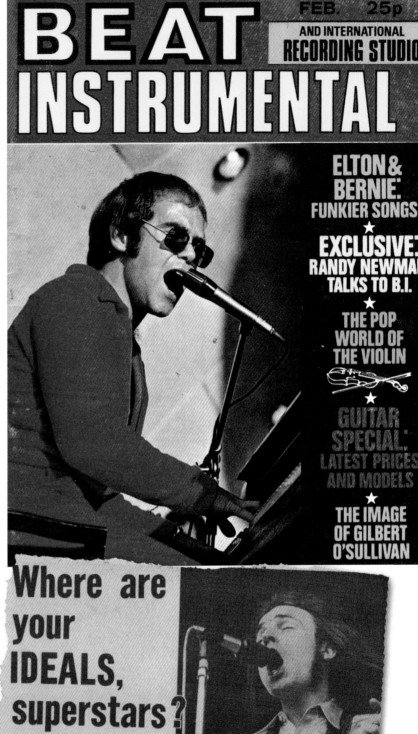

FEB.   25p

BEAT INSTRUMENTAL

AND INTERNATIONAL
RECORDING STUDIO

ELTON & BERNIE: FUNKIER SONGS?

★

EXCLUSIVE: RANDY NEWMAN TALKS TO B.I.

★

THE POP WORLD OF THE VIOLIN

★

GUITAR SPECIAL: LATEST PRICES AND MODELS

★

THE IMAGE OF GILBERT O'SULLIVAN

zigzag 25
FIFTEEN PENCE

Where are your IDEALS, superstars?

THE TIME has come to clarify what (if anything) it is that the hippie culture/rock sub-culture is striving for. I was under the impression that the ... and inequality ...

LEFT: Elton John's whirlwind twelve months prompted a retreat of sorts. His ambition, he announced, was to be more like Paul Simon.

ABOVE: The rock press was filled with misgivings about the new superstars. 'They are capitalists hiding behind a mask of freedom and anti-materialism,' accused one reader.

OK YOU WIN

We can't go on keeping a
good record down, so here
is the single*you asked for

JEEPSTER
T.REX

*from "Electric Warrior"

BUG 16

– on the turntable. He'd even bought a copy for Bill Legend.

A phrase on that album's first song, 'Freedom', leapt out at Bolan: 'electric warrior'. (It turned out to be 'electric water', but few non-American listeners heard it that way.) It provided him with the title for the new T. Rex album – and inspired the dramatic guitar-hero pose on the cover.

Electric Warrior was Bolan's own 'cry of love', his attempt to emulate what he called Hendrix's 'ability to give something so soulful and personal that it gives [his] music an extra dimension'.

One song in particular, 'Cosmic Dancer', seemed to achieve exactly that – with one key difference. While Hendrix's 'Angel', its spirit partner, had been inspired by Jimi's mother, 'Cosmic Dancer' was about Bolan himself. The backward guitar on the song's fade was his personal homage to the self-styled voodoo child.

'Cosmic Dancer' sounded more channelled than consciously written. But at the album's core was a deep understanding of popular music.

'It was a real rock'n'roll album,' says Tony Visconti. 'The "glam" was the dress code at that stage. Marc was into black R&B; we were both into Chuck Berry and The Beatles. We loved the strings on The Shirelles' "Will You Love Me Tomorrow". All those elements began to add up.'

Electric Warrior entered the chart at No. 2. By

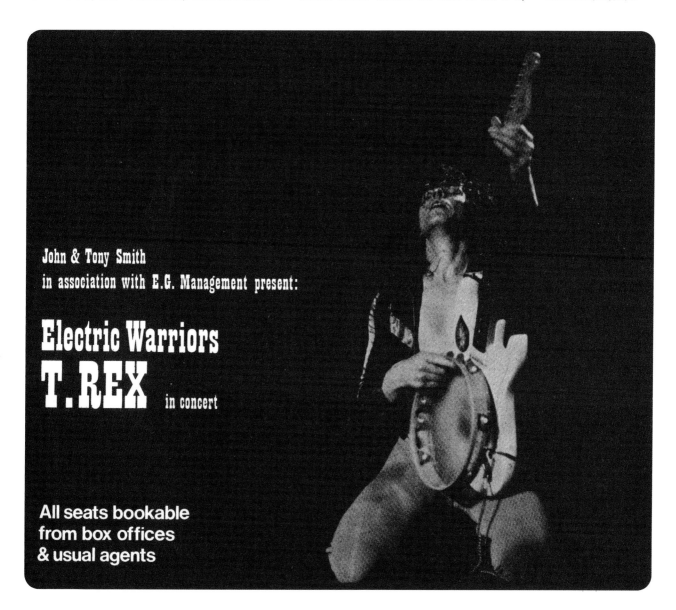

John & Tony Smith
in association with E.G. Management present:

Electric Warriors
T.REX in concert

**All seats bookable
from box offices
& usual agents**

ABOVE: George Underwood portrayed a more mythic Marc and Mickey for the *Warrior* inner sleeve illustrations. 'I don't think we will lose any of the freaks, but if they resent [me] then fuck 'em!' said Bolan.

December it was at the top spot, where, except for one week, it remained until mid-February. A single, 'Jeepster', was lifted from the set and spent almost two months in the top three. An obvious dancefloor number, it was also strangely intimate, courtesy of the glinting consonants and elongated, fluttering vowels that spilled from Bolan's voice.

Conscious of recent developments in the singles market, The Who's Pete Townshend lauded the pop 45 as 'concentrated energy into a compact form'. It was an art Bolan was fast perfecting.

CITY HALL
Northumberland Road, Newcastle upon Tyne 1

Sunday, 31st October, 1971 at 7.30 p.m.

JOHN & TONY SMITH PRESENT
ELECTRIC WARRIORS
T. REX
In Concert
Plus Supporting Band

AREA 60p

Booking Agents: City Hall Box Office
Northumberland Road, Newcastle upon Tyne (Tel 20007)

Phillips Printers Ltd., Newcastle upon Tyne

On October 19, 1971, T. Rex began their three-week Electric Warriors tour around Britain. Any cosmic connection made on the recent records was lost amid scenes of hysteria reminiscent of Beatlemania. BP Fallon conjured up a headline – 'T. Rextasy!' – and the national press seized on it.

Bob Harris, whose DJ set was the support act, remembers screaming teenage girls coming at Bolan's talismanic corkscrew hair with scissors. 'The scenes were beyond belief,' he says. 'We were getting police escorts in and out of town.'

With Bolan as its main draw, *Jackie* magazine for teenage girls was selling half a million copies a week. Hairdressers offered Bolan perms on a unisex basis. And cosmetic glitter, much in evidence in the stalls during the T. Rex tour, became the most desired accessory as Christmas approached. Many shops ran out of stock.

Meanwhile, Marc Bolan was being driven around – mostly by his wife, June – in a gleaming white 1956 Rolls-Royce Silver Cloud 1. 'It's not serious,' he assured Keith Altham in November. 'I'm serious about the music but I'm not serious about the fantasy.'

Sometime that autumn, journalist Tony Norman visited Bolan in Little Venice. He was about to interview him for Radio 1's magazine-style show, *Scene And Heard*.

'On the wall was a big poster, a classic pose of Marc on stage with his guitar,' recalls Norman. 'I said, "Why do you have a poster of yourself on the wall of your living room?"

'He said, "[Because] if I start to believe that I'm that guy, I'll know I'm in trouble. That guy is on the wall, and I'm sitting here, and we're OK." I thought that was great,' says Norman.

'He'd created a character. He was the guy on the wall.'

HE'S THE BIGGEST THING SINCE THE BEATLES

Chapter 8
On the Offensive

The featured pop musicians in the July 17, 1971 issue of *Jackie* magazine were Peter Noone, Rick Wakeman and Cat Stevens.

Stevens had been the first success for Decca's hip subsidiary, Deram, back in 1967 – pipping another young label hopeful, David Bowie. Keyboard virtuoso Wakeman – spilling the beans on 'The blackest day of his life… his wedding' – had played Mellotron on Bowie's 'Space Oddity' and was recently back working with him again. Peter Noone had just scored a top-twenty hit with Bowie's 'Oh! You Pretty Thing(s)'.

In September, *Jackie* finally caught up with Bowie himself. A half-page piece entitled 'Zowie: It's The Bowies' focused not on David's songwriting finesse, nor his eclecticism, but on the couple's unconventional relationship and their newborn son's zany name.

In the accompanying photo, Angie sported a layered shag hairstyle inspired by Jane Fonda in *Klute*. Bowie's appearance was all over the place, his 44-inch Oxford bags, loose blouse and wide-brimmed floppy hat a curious mix of forties Hollywood style and late-sixties androgyny.

His career was looking as flimsy as his outfits. April's *The Man Who Sold The World* – with its blistering psychodramas, twisted melodies and power-trio bluster – had attracted more commentary about its sleeve, with Bowie reclining on a chaise-longue in his Mr Fish 'man's dress', than its musical sophistication. It had barely shifted a thousand copies.

As he so often did, John Peel came to the rescue, inviting Bowie to perform on his Radio 1 *In Concert* programme, broadcast on June 20. Bowie used the occasion to play star-maker for the evening by opting for a 'David Bowie & Friends' format.

OPPOSITE: Bowie and Angie out walking with new-born Zowie, June 29, 1971. Bowie's high-waisted Oxford bags featured a pleasingly airy 44-inch flare.

Dressed up for the Bowie life

WHEN you're a fella and you wear a frock you get a deep feeling of freedom.

So says David Bowie, the pop scene's anti-hero, and he should know.

His wife Angela—she's expecting their first baby in two weeks—says: "I rather fancy him that way. He looks so lovely in a dress." And his mother sighs resignedly: "As long as he remains a boy, I can't see any harm in it."

Mind you, there are some people it upsets, as David found on his recent trip to America to plug his new album "The Man Who Sold The World."

He got to Texas to find himself staring down the barrel of a gun and a hunky rancher snarling at him: "If it wasn't against the law I'd blow your brains out, you fag. Quit town."

David Bowie a natural-born pacifist with long blond hair, got the message, decided The World could sell itself and took off for England pronto in his "Mr. Fish" dress, one of a collection of six he bought at £150 a throw.

Abuse

In his bizarre Becken-ham, Kent, pad, 24-year-old David told me: "I get all sorts of abuse showered on me. It doesn't worry me any more what people say. I get called a queer and all

Mick Ronson, Woody Woodmansey and bassist Trevor Bolder, until recently playing in their native Hull as Ronno, were his backing trio. Out front were old friends George Underwood, Dana Gillespie and Geoffrey Alexander; Mark Carr-Pritchard came from Bowie's local protégé band Arnold Corns.

It was a revue-like performance, with Underwood, Gillespie and Alexander all taking lead vocals at some point and plenty of relaxed conviviality. Bowie performed a range of new material, from swaggering opener 'Queen Bitch' to US country rock-style singalong 'Looking For A Friend'. The only barely familiar song was an acoustic version of 'The Supermen' from the recent album.

The session was another indication of the new father's relaxed, treading-water attitude to life and work. It was also an exorcism of sorts, one last Arts Lab-style blowout before the serious business began.

Bowie, like Bolan, was haunted by a suspicion that others might steal a march on him. He'd read about how Alice Cooper's rock theatre was creating headlines in the States; he'd watched Bolan turn his career around back home.

After one last session on June 4, Bowie called time on Arnold Corns. 'Bowie was gonna do all the writing and producing,' says drummer Woody Woodmansey, 'and Freddi Burretti, who looked like a Michelangelo statue come to life, was gonna be the rock star he created – like a Ziggy thing. But there was one flaw – he couldn't sing a fucking note.'

Instead, sticking with the three Ronno musicians, Bowie began work on a new album. He already had the title: *Hunky Dory*. 'When he started writing *Hunky Dory* songs there was a definite change,' says Woodmansey,

who had returned to Haddon Hall in late spring with Ronson. 'He plonked. He wasn't a pianist. But he was incredible at putting chords together.'

Bowie had big ambitions for new song 'Life On Mars?'. 'He invited me round to his house, which I used to call Beckenham Palace,' says Rick Wakeman, 'and played me all these songs on an old twelve-string. They were just unbelievable, one after the other. He said, "I want to come at this album from a different angle. I want them all to be based around the piano." He said, "Play them as you would a piano piece and we'll adapt everything else around that."'

After mixing 'Life On Mars?', co-producer Ken Scott called the band in for a playback. 'On these massive, high-quality speakers,' says Woodmansey. 'Is that us? Is that what we sound like? That's when I thought there's more to this guy than we'd imagined.'

Scott, who'd engineered Bowie's 1969 album and *The Man Who Sold The World*, noted another change. 'He'd come to terms with the music industry,' he says. 'He wanted success.'

There was another factor: timing. Bowie's contract with Mercury Records had expired. Manager Tony Defries – now sporting a fashionable afro – had waited a year to negotiate a new record deal for him. The artist needed a strong hand.

Hunky Dory was a songwriter's album, textured, sophisticated, expansive, but with a clear identity. Including tributes to Bob Dylan and Andy Warhol, a cover of Biff Rose's modern standard 'Fill Your Heart' and a musical homage to The Velvet Underground, it was made with the United States in mind.

Armed with acetates, a confident Tony Defries took off to New York. He came back ten days later, a two-year, three-album contract with RCA in the bag. On September 8, Defries was back out there – this time with the Bowies and Mick Ronson in tow to sign the deal.

Bowie and Angie were well primed for NYC, having recently seen the Ridiculous Theatre production of Andy Warhol's play *Pork* at the Roundhouse, based on tape-recorded conversations between Warhol and Factory habitué Brigid 'Polk' Berlin.

During the trip, Bowie finally got to meet Lou Reed over a dinner arranged by RCA (the ex-Velvet

Freddi looked like a Michelangelo statue. But he couldn't sing a fucking note!

Underground leader had recently signed to the label) and ex-Stooges frontman Iggy Pop in a back room at Max's Kansas City.

Tony Zanetta, who'd played Warhol in *Pork*, fixed up a meeting with the artist himself at The Factory. Bowie – in his favoured floppy hat and super-wide bags – got into the spirit of the place where anything goes by spilling his entrails in an improvised mime piece, captured on a handheld film camera.

ABOVE: Bowie had admired Warhol ever since his manager Ken Pitt returned from New York in December 1966 with an advance copy of The Velvet Underground's debut LP. When *Pork* came to the Roundhouse for a month-long season in August 1971, Bowie and Angie attended more than once. Various cast members would soon play significant roles in Bowie's career.

ABOVE: Andy Warhol with 'Superstar' Geri Miller, London, 1971. Some of the *Pork* cast knew Bowie as 'David Bowery' after the infamous 'skid row' district in New York.

RIGHT: Alice Cooper's London debut had a queasy effect on the domestic rock circuit. *Melody Maker* questioned whether the spectacle was 'enjoyment'. Bowie, who took his band along, left before the end.

One song on the upcoming album tapped directly into the camp, theatrical New York tradition that – aesthetically at least – Bowie was beginning to hitch himself to. 'Queen Bitch' sounded like The Velvet Underground riding an Eddie Cochran riff. Bowie cackled and threw his voice about; Ronson's upper-register guitar lines made everything hiss and sparkle.

Back in the UK, the early Velvet Underground albums were once again in circulation. They'd been barely noticed first time around, but *Melody Maker*'s Richard Williams now made a strong case for reappraisal: 'Please, please buy these albums. They're too beautiful, too damn important, to remain the property of a handful of converts.'

His plea went largely unheard. The Velvets' reputation was still too enmeshed in white noise and Warhol-associated transgression. A better indication of where rock's sexuality was at in 1971 could be found on the inner gatefold of Steppenwolf's album, *For Ladies Only*: a 'Dickmobile', a specially built penis-on-wheels.

Tiresome bloke-rock was in Bowie's sights that autumn. 'Changes', a manifesto song of sorts, carried a warning to its exponents: 'Oh, look out you rock'n'rollers.'

On November 7, 1971, with much fanfare, Alice Cooper made their British debut at London's new rock venue, the Rainbow Theatre. Bowie took the band along.

'It was very rock'n'roll,' says Woody Woodmansey, 'that American trashy [thing].' But David left before the end.

Bowie had followed the Cooper band's theatrical coming-out in the States with interest. In a June '71 cover story in British underground mag *Frendz*, spider-eyed singer Alice spoke of 'Third Generation Rock', of The Stooges, of sex, makeup and gender blur.

He also told writer Steve Mann about the Alice character. 'It's a complete Jekyll-and-Hyde thing,' he said. 'She's really a mean old broad.'

'Rock music is based on sex!', Alice explained to *Record Mirror*'s Rory O'Toole that same month. 'There's

Then Warhol was granted a preview of Bowie's homage from the forthcoming *Hunky Dory*. Angie remembered the artist leaving the room as soon as it finished without saying a word. All was not lost: the shoe fanatic approved of Bowie's canary-yellow Mary Janes, apparently a gift of peace from Bolan.

Bowie took it all in. 'It was fascinating,' he recalled years later. '[Warhol] had absolutely nothing to say at all.'

How do you figure out a drumbeat for a song about the end of the world?

Alice Cooper & Arthur Brown's Kingdom Come Sun. Nov. 7 8pm at the Rainbow
(formerly the Finsbury Park Astoria)

Tickets: £1.50, £1.25, £1.00, 75p, 50p telephone: 272 2224
Box office: 232 Seven Sisters Rd. N4 from 12 to 10pm

a big sexual liberation thing behind it. I think these [hung-up] people are all closet queens really.'

The day after Alice Cooper's Rainbow show, Bowie and the band were back in the studio. The *Hunky Dory* release was still several weeks away, but Bowie was fired up and ready – and convinced there was a young audience for his new project.

Before the sessions began, Bowie took Ken Scott aside. 'You're not going to like this album,' he told his co-producer. 'It's much more rock'n'roll.'

Scott was mystified. 'I've no idea why he thought I wouldn't like rock'n'roll,' he says.

Bowie was swept along by the freshness and immediacy of his song ideas. Half of the album was recorded in an initial week-long flourish. Two songs, 'Moonage Daydream' and 'Hang On To Yourself', had been reclaimed from the Arnold Corns project.

By the end of the week, the project also had its three cornerstone songs – 'Ziggy Stardust', 'Lady Stardust' and 'Five Years'. In place, respectively, were lyrics pertaining to an imaginary rock star, gender ambiguity and the filmic, fatalistic scenario that would set up the album.

'David said ["Five Years"] was going to be the first track and wanted it to start with a drumbeat,' says Woody Woodmansey. 'I thought, "How do you figure out a drumbeat for a song about the end of the world?"'

Woodmansey asked Ken Scott not to make the drum sound 'like Yorkshire puddings' and kept it frill-free: no cymbal smashes, no drum rolls. (Sometimes, as Warhol liked to say, the simplest idea is the most beautiful.)

Stepping loosely into the rock-band concept and then the Ziggy Stardust character, Bowie began to shake himself free from the burden of sincerity, the accepted hallmark of a rock artiste. Instead, he could unselfconsciously give himself to the role; inhabit the reality of the artifice.

That same month, Tony Defries employed a new publicist, Dai Davies. One of his first assignments was to visit Bowie at Haddon Hall and discuss the project. Bowie told him he was going to 'be Ziggy'.

Ziggy Stardust had been strummed into existence during one week in November 1971, by a man on a mission with long, flyaway hair. The man who sold him to the world would not resemble that same person.

Melody Maker's first issue of 1972 ran with a 'Giants Of The Year' cover story on the big stars of 1971, the year when 'glamour was back'. John Lennon, Rod Stewart, Marc Bolan and keyboard virtuoso Keith Emerson were chosen to illustrate the point.

'The one quality they all shared was their remoteness,' ran the accompanying text, 'a mental and physical inaccessibility which manifested itself in the purchasing of white Rolls-Royces and lightweight Lamborghinis.

'They gave the audience something to look up at again.'

But now all that was over, if the paper's New Year predictions were to be believed: Linda Lewis, Joe Egan, Dave Lambert, ELO, the Natural Acoustic Band and Annette Peacock were all supposedly destined to make waves in 1972.

On the left-hand side of the cover of *Melody Maker*'s January 22, 1972 edition, it was business as usual: 'Crimson Break Up' was the week's main story; 'Big Tull Tour' was right behind it.

Down the right-hand side was an image that required no bold type. The photo did all the talking – a man with a cigarette and a clownish smile, dressed in a geometric-patterned two-piece, unzipped to the navel, his hair trimmed, layered and elevated almost bouffant style.

This was the new Bowie, the 'Space Oddity' man, revived, refreshed and gunning for 1972. Gone was the curly Dylan perm from his Major Tom days, but the space theme was still there: he looked like the first Mod on the moon.

"shocking"
"thrilling"
"gets you thinking... carefully calculated and precisely performed"
'fascinating'
"overwhelming"
"downright inspiring"
"incredibly imaginative"
"pure entertainment"

Alice Cooper
Killer

New from the group which knows how to harness the power of shock. Theater in the round, engraved in vinyl, on Warner Bros. Records (and Ampex distributed tapes).

Alice Cooper
Killer
Includes the hit Single UNDER MY WHEELS

BS 2567

Bowie found Alice Cooper – 'Miss C' – 'quite fitting with our era'.

Turn to page nineteen. Bowie has plenty to say to journalist Michael Watts: he'd just written a new album about a fictitious rock group; he used different voices for different songs; he found Alice Cooper – 'Miss C' – 'very demeaning… premeditated, but quite fitting with our era'; as for Bowie himself, he was 'gay, and always have been, even when I was David Jones.'

Melody Maker knew it had a scoop and sold the story on the cover. 'David Bowie, rock's swishiest outrage: a self-confessed lover of effeminate clothes, Bowie, who has hardly performed in public since his "Space Oddity" hit of three years ago, is coming back in super-style.'

The forthcoming album was named in full: *The Rise And Fall Of Ziggy Stardust And The Spiders From Mars*. There was no suggestion of any Bowie/Ziggy conflation. Ziggy Stardust could have been as far removed a character as Sgt Pepper or The Archies.

Later that month, during a break from tour rehearsals, Bowie was more pointed in his interview with George Tremlett.

'Entertainment,' he said. 'That's what's missing in pop music now.

'There's not much outrageousness left in pop music anymore. There's only me and Marc Bolan.'

Chapter 9
I Am the Greatest

With scenes on T. Rex's late autumn '71 tour drawing comparisons with Beatlemania, Bolan's mind was made up. This is what he wanted.

ABOVE: T. Rex: singles artist of 1971. 'It had been what he was waiting for all of his life,' said John Peel. 'He'd been wanting to be a rock'n'roll star since he was 14... and it happened. It's bound to transform you.'

All those resentful festivalgoers and 'ex-Rex fan' letter writers could moan as much as they liked. A vibrant new generation was hailing him as a pop messiah. It was a calling.

But first there was business to attend to. 'He was broke,' said Tony Secunda. 'All the agreements had run out. It was a mess.'

Having masterminded the mid-sixties success of The Moody Blues, manager Secunda had switched to The Move. He came up with the name, put them in mob-style suits and had them destroying television sets when everyone else was going to love-ins.

'He saw himself as Napoleon,' says photographer Robert Davidson, who worked with Secunda in the mid-sixties. 'He was an extraordinary presence, always smartly turned out and approachable. But if you crossed him…'

'He was frightening,' says Move drummer Bev Bevan.

Secunda loved upsetting the establishment. But when a salacious postcard – designed to promote The Move's summer 1967 single 'Flowers In The Rain' – depicted Prime Minster Harold Wilson in a compromising position with an alleged mistress, the group ended up in court. The judgement meant the loss of all royalties on the song – leaving songwriter Roy Wood cruelly out of pocket. Secunda and The Move parted ways soon afterwards.

Bolan knew of Secunda through the Essex Music scene. As the colourful manager's ex-wife, Bolan's friend and sometime stylist Chelita Secunda had a

I told Bolan the full story of how everybody had screwed him.

much better handle on him. Understanding Bolan's predicament, she engineered a meeting.

'She's quite Machiavellian,' said Tony Secunda. 'There was Marc, June and some crazy French guy with this pure amphetamine sulphate. We sat and talked for fourteen hours and I told him the full story of how everybody had screwed him.'

While not privy to all the details, Bolan instinctively knew it. He'd recently vented all his frustration on 'Rip Off', the scorching blowout built around the repeated purgative title phrase. The song would close *Electric Warrior* and, hoped Bolan, end this long, impecunious chapter in his life.

'I didn't trust anyone in the business,' he told *NME* a few months later. 'I trusted the kids. But I regarded myself as having been screwed so many times.'

'He had a class complex,' said Secunda, 'an ingrained working-class attitude. He resented those [industry] guys, really.'

Secunda got busy. Late that autumn, he secured a 'favoured nations' deal with EMI, meaning Bolan would always enjoy the best royalty rate at the company; established the T. Rex Wax Co. record label; and cut separate deals with overseas territories. On at least one occasion, this involved a pyramid of cocaine and a briefcase stuffed with banknotes.

For the first time in his life, Marc Bolan was about to see serious money. And, of roughly equal importance, from January 1972, his distinctive head would appear on the label of every T. Rex record.

The rewards came fast. January 1972's 'Telegram Sam', the first release under the new arrangement, was the third T. Rex No. 1 in less than a year. Once again, it hinged on a blunt-edged Chuck Berry riff, this time gift-wrapped in a high-drama, Phil Spector-style production.

The song was stuffed with characters, including Bolan himself: 'I ain't no square with my corkscrew hair.' Bob Dylan was the 'natural born poet'. According to radio presenter Danny Baker, 'Jungle-faced Jake' was named after a boxer dog owned by the manager of One Stop Records in Soho, where Bolan was a regular

ABOVE LEFT: 'Telegram Sam', released in January 1972, was the launch record for Bolan's own, distinctively packaged label, T. Rex Wax Co. Bolan immortalised himself in the song with key line, 'I ain't no square with my corkscrew hair.'

I Am the Greatest 93

and the young Baker worked. As for Sam himself, insiders couldn't make up their mind whether he was Bolan's coke dealer or, more likely, Tony (T.S.) Secunda.

Bolan was trademarking rock'n'roll poetry like no one – except perhaps Keith Reid, lyricist of Procol Harum's 'A Whiter Shade Of Pale' – since late-fifties Chuck Berry. The chin-scratchers didn't dare approve, hearing only repetition and nonsense rhyme. Even the usually supportive Penny Valentine felt Marc was sending himself up.

'Telegram Sam' would be the great galvaniser, and Bolan the man to beat. But for *Top Of The Pops*, he wore stripes and vivid colours rather than shiny silver. The first man of 'glitter rock', as some were now describing pop's new showmen, was keen to distance himself from the pack. (Slade's Jim Lea remembers Bolan being sniffy backstage at *TOTP*.)

The record that replaced 'Telegram Sam' at the top was 'Son Of My Father' by Chicory Tip. From the band name – inspired by a bottle of chicory-enhanced Camp Coffee – to the song's prominent Moog synthesizer part, everything on the Giorgio Moroder-penned hit smacked of novelty.

But 'Son Of My Father' was huge, No. 1 for three weeks. A light stomper with an irresistible six-note synth hook, the song was soon adopted on football terraces, as fans refashioned its chorus to fit the name of their favourite striker. (Manchester City fans serenaded star striker Rodney Marsh with 'Oh Rodney, Rodney…')

Back in the world of pop, Chicory Tip soon adopted some of the era's most preposterous costumes: capes, belted underpants, spiderweb faces. But as they would discover, it took more than a dramatic image change to guarantee continued success.

Meanwhile, on February 15, Rolling Stone Mick Jagger was seen dancing in the wings to T. Rex at the Hollywood Palladium in Los Angeles. It was the opening night of a whirlwind two-week US tour.

The omens were good. 'Get It On', retitled 'Bang A Gong' to protect US innocence from sexual innuendo, was rising towards its eventual top-ten placing. *Electric Warrior* was in its fifteenth week on the *Billboard* 200. Bolan seemed justified in holding out for that headline tour.

Weeks earlier, he'd told Lisa Mehlman for *Disc and Music Echo* that Rex had been offered the support slot on Alice Cooper's much-anticipated *Killer* tour before Christmas but turned it down. When Cooper came to the Detroit show, he understood why: teenage fans chanted Bolan's name and a finale of 'Summertime Blues' brought the house down.

Tip's name was inspired by a bottle of chicory-enhanced Camp Coffee.

Detroit, as so often for visiting British bands, was a special case. In Chicago, support act Uriah Heep pulled the plugs on Bolan mid-set, earning them some hard-rock brownie points back home. Nevertheless, T. Rex moved on to a prestigious, tour-capping gig at New York's Carnegie Hall, scene of Elton John's triumph the previous year.

Eager to impress, Bolan had played at Grand Funk Railroad volumes throughout the tour. Now he was in a venue famed for its acoustics.

'Marc locked himself in the toilet and drunk two bottles of champagne,' said Tony Secunda. Eventually, the manager coaxed Bolan out. 'He got on stage wearing a T-shirt of himself and on the first number, fell flat on his face.' Bolan wasn't much better when he was back on his feet. 'It was so loud you couldn't hear a thing,' said Secunda.

Frustrated, the manager sought refuge on the steps outside. 'Paul Simon came running out and said, "This is fucking bullshit, man." I thought, "This is where it comes to a close." That was the end of it.'

Ten days later, T. Rex were staying at the Château D'Herouville outside Paris having made a trial visit early in February. The eighteenth-century country residence-turned-recording studio was once the love nest of Chopin and pseudonymous author George Sand. More recent visitors included Elton John and Pink Floyd.

Between March 8-12, the band put down the basis of a new album. Once again, Bolan dug deep for raw material. One song, 'The Slider', had a mercurial, almost hypnotic quality. It was mostly made up of his trademark random juxtapositions ('cosmic sea'/'bumblebee'), with one neat line of Bolanesque wisdom concerning the strangeness of schools and a repeat refrain – 'And when I'm sad/I slide' – that seemed to hide in plain sight.

ABOVE: On March 18, 1972, T. Rex played two sell-out shows at the Empire Pool, Wembley. 'Bolan's Triumph: The Day That Pop Came Back' roared *New Musical Express*. Bolanmania hit overdrive with poster magazines on newsstands and hairdressers offering 'Bolan perms' on a unisex basis. Over in the States, 'Get It On' – retitled 'Bang A Gong' – was about to go top ten.

'Metal Guru' was a dizzying Wurlitzer ride of can-this-be-true? euphoria.

It had never really gone away. But Bolan was clearly reigniting the idea of pop as a kind of heroic force, one capable of capturing the hearts and minds of a generation. You didn't get that from Chicory Tip.

'Fanmania reminiscent of The Beatles' touring days in 1964 and 1965 returned to London on Saturday,' raved *Melody Maker*'s front-page report. The paper also picked up on another aspect of Bolan's star power:

'Many fans wore Bolan-style clothing – satin trousers, glitter dust around the eyes and "corkscrew" curled hair over their shoulders.'

The shows were filmed by Ringo Starr for the Beatles-funded Apple Films. The pair had met the previous autumn and found common ground in first-generation rock'n'roll, cinema and, of course, enormous success.

Both outsiders in their own ways, Marc and Ringo seemed to understand each other. The pair soon dreamed up a film project, *Born To Boogie*: Bolanmania as witnessed by a Beatlemania survivor.

The film would be built around wild scenes from the second Wembley show, but the pair also wanted a more surrealistic element. A series of set-pieces and incidentals were filmed during late March and April, including a Mad Hatter's Tea Party shot in the grounds of John Lennon's Tittenhurst Park mansion, which Starr was housesitting at the time.

On April 20, 1972 the band – with Ringo and Elton John sitting in – debuted a new, big-sounding Bolan song in front of the cameras at Apple Studios. It was a theme for these times. Bolan called it 'Children Of The Revolution'.

Another song that defined the moment, albeit on a more personal level, was recorded in France and released in May. 'Metal Guru' was Bolanmania on 45. Opening with an exultant howl of happiness, the song was a dizzying Wurlitzer ride of can-this-be-true? euphoria.

It was a curious choice for a song title; Bolan later insisted it was a sexual metaphor. But a semi-whispered, 'Oh watch me now, I'm gonna slide,' as the song played out sounded far more ambiguous.

Any nuanced interpretation of his reaction to fame was impossible as Bolanmania swept through the country during the first months of 1972. 'Bolan's Triumph – The Day That Pop Came Back,' raved *NME* after two sell-out shows at the Empire Pool, Wembley on March 18.

ABOVE: Ringo Starr filmed the evening Wembley show for a feature-length documentary. Bolan had previously provided the spark for the ex-Beatle's March 1972 single, 'Back Off Boogaloo'. 'They both had to fight to get where they were,' says Apple Records sleeve designer Kosh. 'That probably explains why they got on so well.'

LEFT: On the sleeve, Bolan credited *The Slider* cover photo to Ringo Starr. Producer Tony Visconti remembers it differently. But the producer has no qualms with the record. 'Only a true artist would create something like that,' he says.

BELOW: Spending four weeks at No. 1 during May and June 1972, 'Metal Guru' marked the high point of Bolan's success. The illustration on the acetate is likely to be a Bolan original.

T. REX

TRIDENT STUDIOS
A side
Trident House, St Annes Court, Wardour St, London W1.
Telephone : 01-734 9901

time 2.24

"METAL GURU"
PUBLISHED BY WIZARD ARTISTS LTD
T. REX M. BOLAN
ALL WORK
COPYRIGHT

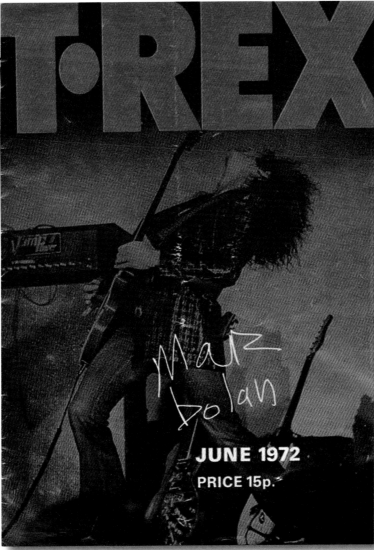

JUNE 1972
PRICE 15p.

Across the three different performances for *Top Of The Pops*, Bolan celebrated the moment in gleaming Superstar style – best of all in his favoured blue rose-patterned Alkasura jacket and holding his 'metal front' Zemaitis guitar. He even revived those daubs of shiny glitter under his eyes. And he beamed.

T. Rex were no longer simply making hits. On 'Telegram Sam' and 'Metal Guru', Visconti and Bolan had created a signature sound to emulate: vast, dense, dramatic. 'Marc supplied the raw materials, and I supplied the sophistication,' says the producer.

'Metal Guru' hit No. 1 on May 20 and stayed there for four weeks. By now, an entire industry had grown up around Bolan – super-size posters,

magazine specials, scarves, badges, curly perms. Even his obscure 45s from the mid-sixties were fetching extortionate prices.

Proud mum Phyllis Feld was giving interviews. Anello & Davide were now marketing their famous strap footwear as 'Bolan shoes'.

Bolan's old record company, Fly, began saturating the charts with Tyrannosaurus Rex records. 'Debora', the duo's freewheeling debut single from 1968, hit No. 7 in April 1972. The first two albums were repackaged as a budget-price 'doubleback', spending one unlikely week at No. 1. *Bolan Boogie*, a mix of A- and B-sides from 1970 and '71 spiced with album tracks, went in at No. 1 and stayed there for three weeks.

ABOVE: T. Rex kicked off a short four-city tour at the Birmingham Odeon on June 9. Noting Bolan's 'unconvincing smile [and] a hint of boredom in his hip-shaking', *Sounds*' Howard Fielding made a bold prediction that both star and audience would soon tire of each other.

MARC BOLAN TALKS ON RADIO LUXEMBOURG,
SUNDAY, 24th MAY AT 9.30 pm

Today I'm not making £40 a week but £40 every second.

By July, 'Metal Guru' was gone from the singles chart. The hit, both joyful and triumphant, had confirmed Bolan's place at pop's centre. But it was also the song that caused his remaining loyalists from the macrobiotic days to lose faith.

'Marc gave me a copy three weeks upfront, so I was the only person at Radio 1 to have it,' says Bob Harris. 'I played it because T. Rex were so hot at that time. But I played it more to support Marc rather than actually liking the record.

'I never liked it. I felt that the quality of Marc's music began to decline in equal measure to his growing sense of self-importance.'

In that regard, there was plenty for Bolan to feed off. The May '72 issue of *Cream* ran with: 'Hello. I'm Marc Bolan. I'm a superstar. You'd better believe it,' as the story headline.

Days later, the front page of family paper *The Weekly News* simply declared, 'Marc Bolan Superstar'. Inside, he thanked his parents. 'It just shows you how wise they were to let me go my own way. Because today

MAIN PHOTO: T. Rex's first British gig of 1972, at the Gliderdrome, Boston, on January 15, set the tone for the year. Rexmaniacs travelled from all parts of the country to pay their 60p entrance fee and be part of the 'T. Rextasy' phenomenon. Amid wild scenes, more than thirty fans fainted and had to be pulled to safety over the crash barriers.

I'm not making £40 a week but £40 every second.'

In May, Bolan and wife June were on a yacht off Cannes with Ringo Starr and George Harrison, Cilla Black and her husband Bobby Willis. Back home, the T. Rex office was about to lose BP Fallon, with Chelita Secunda following sometime later.

On June 9, T. Rex played Birmingham Odeon Theatre, the first of four dates on a short tour of Britain's major cities. Fans held scarves above their

heads, screamed Bolan's name and sang along. But *Sounds* reviewer Howard Fielding suspected the performance now had little to do with the music, even expressing concern for Bolan.

'There's a lack of conviction to the smile, a hint of boredom in the hip shaking,' Fielding wrote. He predicted the bubble would soon burst.

It was prescient. After eighteen rollercoaster months, Bolan was already considering his future.

Even before the gig, *NME* had run with a 'Bolan To Quit Tours?' headline after he told editor Nick Logan that security concerns were making touring 'almost impossible'.

A bigger truth was buried deep into the story. Bolan and June had recently moved to a high-rise flat in Bilton Towers, a prestigious block behind Marble Arch tube station in central London. He was, he admitted, becoming 'a recluse'.

Chapter 10

Opportunity Knocks

Rock's brief role as the spearhead for social revolution had passed. In Britain, the remnants of the free festival scene, principally Ladbroke Grove's Hawkwind and Pink Fairies, still sometimes pitched up and jammed to assorted speedfreaks and acidheads. But The Faces and Mott The Hoople were giving new meaning to the idea of a 'people's band', one that had no qualms about ticketed entertainment.

Meanwhile, Slade were offering Right To Work marchers – who'd descended on London from Liverpool, Glasgow and Swansea – half-price entry to their biggest appearance yet, at a multi-artist fundraiser held at London's Empire Pool, Wembley on March 12, 1972.

Slade had all the credentials to be a pop 'people's band'. But 'Look Wot You Dun', their first single of 1972, lacked the spark of its predecessor. Chas Chandler

suggested the heavy panting and whip-cracking overdubs, but that couldn't mask what was, in essence, a downbeat, piano-driven song.

Still, it was carried by Noddy Holder's hobnailed voice. Visually, too, the frontman was emerging as a fine foil to Dave Hill. Holder was part Dickensian rogue – all big features and bushy sideburns – and part terrace hooligan, legs akimbo in tartan trousers held up with red braces.

He had a mouth on him too, his between-song banter perfected over years on the club circuit. Dave Hill, by now the band's ace joker, was often the butt of Holder's colourful repartee.

But to *Top Of The Pops* audiences, Slade's Mr Sparkle was the band's chief asset. Promoting 'Look Wot You Dun', he roused the studio audience with compulsive arm-waving and finger-pointing, as he twirled away in a new silver cloak with matching platform boots.

'Silver was very good on black-and-white television,' Hill says. Black-and-white TV wasn't truly eclipsed by colour in Britain until the mid-seventies.

Drawing a line from Holder's bawdy masculinity and Hill's bowl haircut and deranged rabble-rousing to Slade's skinhead past wasn't difficult. And Jim Lea's short-on-top/long-at-the-sides look was virtually the skinhead girl's hairstyle and a forerunner of the glam 'mullet'.

Only drummer Don Powell sported a more traditional rock-star look: nonchalant behind the kit, poker-faced Powell chewed more gum than the Wolverhampton Wanderers bench on Saturdays.

There were no aspiring poets or mime artists to be found in Slade. The assorted roughs and ne'er-do-wells among their audiences appreciated that.

So did Chas Chandler. He had no problem with Slade slotting into the role of an anti-Rex act; The Rolling Stones had risen to fame on an anti-Beatles ticket, after all. The illiterate song titles – the antithesis of Bolan's precious poetry – helped too, giving the press another angle to pick up on.

Still, Chandler aimed higher. He'd always believed that Slade were his Beatles. That's why he'd encouraged them to write their own songs and perfect their stagecraft, even granting the B-side due respect with some top-notch material. And now each band member had his own distinctive character and style: with your eyes closed, Noddy Holder made a great Black Country John Lennon.

Ringo's Bolan documentary—picture page 4

SLADE TOUR NATIONWIDE

SLADE do an extensive British tour
also included in their schedule is a re
in France.
Slade, who rec
i Wet Sou

SLADE ALIVE!

BELOW: Slade taking a break from recording at Olympic Studios, August 10, 1972. 'We were into making ourselves look preposterous,' says Jim Lea.

Slade prove they're alive and well

SLADE ALIVE! (Polydor Super 2383 101: £2.15). Slade have learned a lot from past mistakes, and learned to fine effect. They invited a studio audience to fill out the clapping, stomping sounds and have managed to retain most of the atmosphere created on live gigs. Another good idea was to include more written by other people, although this invariably makes

'Look Wot You Dun' peaked at No. 4 in February. The bigger story was that *Slade Alive!* had gone top-ten in April. The album, which included canny endorsements from Paul McCartney and Deep Purple's Ritchie Blackmore on the inner gatefold, played up to Slade's strengths as a powerful working band. Roaring through Steppenwolf's 'Born To Be Wild', as well as their own blistering 'Know Who You Are', the live Slade were closer to The Who than T. Rex.

The band went out and proved it all over again by touring clubs and colleges during April and May. Many venues were besieged by large crowds, some of whom had to be turned away.

It was a different story over the May bank holiday, when Slade joined Humble Pie, The Faces and little-known newcomers Roxy Music at the Great Western Festival in Lincoln. They walked out to the traditional welcome reserved for singles chart acts – a grumble of boos.

Slade plugged in and soon turned it around. Ever the showman, Noddy had another card up his sleeve. He brought the festival's sponsor, actor Stanley Baker, out onto the stage. The crowd roared its approval, prompting Holder to start up the war chant from *Zulu*, one of Baker's biggest screen triumphs. Everyone joined in.

'That was a really important show for us,' says Dave Hill. 'We were having hits, but [Lincoln] helped us establish ourselves as a live band.'

Catching Slade at the Kew Boathouse at the end of 1971 didn't have an immediate effect on The Sweet – or at least not on disc. 'Poppa Joe', released in February 1972, was already in the bag, a safety-first confection after the disappointing showing of 'Alexander Graham Bell' the previous autumn.

Steel drums and references to coconuts revived the tropical vibe of the previous summer's 'Co-Co'. Even the title sounded recycled from The Equals' 1969 hit 'Viva Bobby Joe'.

At that point, songwriters Chinn and Chapman still had an interest in New World, having written 'Kara, Kara', a November top-twenty hit. But when the soft-rock trio took off for a thirteen-week run in a Christmas panto version of *Robinson Crusoe*, the pair focused their attentions on The Sweet.

While the cheery 'Poppa Joe' peaked at No. 11 on March 4, The Sweet were gigging around the country and letting the mask slip. After a show at Portsmouth's Mecca Ballroom, the venue manager complained: 'Their actions, words and everything were obscene.' Nicky Chinn insisted The Sweet had simply arrived

LEFT: 'You couldn't wear female boots because they'd break,' says Dave Hill. 'I went to Kensington Market, saw a singular platform, and discussed with the bloke who'd made them the idea of having a double platform. I'd go in with a design, especially for the silver ones. Silver was very good on black-and-white television.'

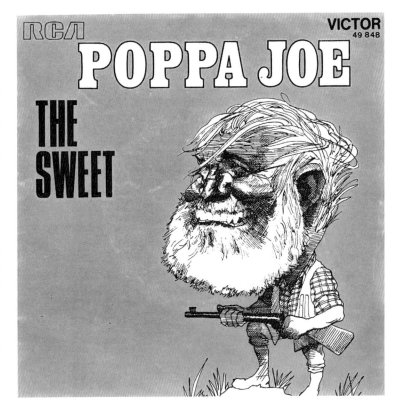

THE SWEET

ABOVE: Fans expecting a bubblegum-style performance at Sweet concerts sometimes got a rude surprise. In May 1972, after a gig in Belgium, Brian Connolly and Steve Priest were arrested for alleged obscenity and spent six days in custody.

twenty minutes late on stage but Mecca disagreed, banning the band from its nationwide circuit.

Weeks later, in May 1972, Brian Connolly and Steve Priest spent six days in custody in Belgium after being arrested for alleged obscenity on stage. They were freed after a brief court appearance.

Back in the pages of *Jackie* and *Diana*, smiling super-blond Brian Connolly continued to advertise the swoonsome side of The Sweet.

'Brian was the guy [they] went to,' says Andy Scott. 'He was a bit older than us and looked fantastic, no doubt about it. We were all sucked along with that in the early-ish period.

'But once you'd been given an opportunity, you've got to get it right. As Steve once put it, we weren't Ruby & The Romantics. It's The Sweet – not a singer with a backing band.'

Almost all the new stars – or superstars, as the press now preferred to describe them – were embedded in bands. One singer, however, a veteran of the pop scene for more than a decade, continued to plug away as a soloist. He'd gone out as Paul Raven, Paul Monday, Paul Russell, even as Rubber Bucket, but his real name was Paul Gadd.

Sometime in 1971, the veteran vocalist, who might as well have been called Paul Nobody at that point, sat around with a group of friends to watch a fifteenth anniversary screening of rock'n'roll cinema classic *Rock Around The Clock*. 'I said, "Wouldn't it be nice if there was some glamour about?"' he told *Disc*'s Caroline Boucher the following year.

The friends started throwing imaginary star names at each other. Someone suggested Terence Tinsel; Mike Leander, Raven's long-time producer, became Tommy Throb for the night.

'It was all a bit camp,' the singer continued. 'And I said I'd like to be called Gary Glitter.'

(It's also been claimed that original *Ready, Steady,*

Go! presenter Michael Aldred coined the name.)

From that day on, whenever he rang one of his friends, Paul Raven introduced himself as 'Gary Glitter'.

He and Mike Leander went back almost a decade. Leander had been a musical director at Decca, arranging strings for Marianne Faithfull, creating melodramatic backdrops for Billy Fury and even arranging Marc Bolan's 1965 debut, 'The Wizard'.

That same year Leander met Paul Raven, then working as a warm-up man on the set of *Ready, Steady, Go!* Once described by Parlophone as 'Our most exciting artist since Helen Shapiro,' Raven's ambitions had been thwarted by the emergence of The Beatles.

Leander gave him work as a singer for The Mike Leander Orchestra. Independently, Raven acted as producer on a couple of flop 45s: The Poets' 'Baby Don't You Do It' and Thane Russal's 'Security' – both became cult freakbeat singles years later. But mostly he worked the clubs in Germany, seven nights a week.

Meanwhile, the much-in-demand Leander arranged The Beatles' 'She's Leaving Home' and, in 1968, became a producer working out of US label MCA's new London office. He had Raven record a few

> **We were The Sweet – not a singer with a backing band.**

sides as Paul Monday, mostly fashionable covers like Sly & The Family Stone's 'Stand!' and The Beatles' 'Here Comes The Sun'. He also secured him a cameo on the *Jesus Christ Superstar* soundtrack album – and had him front Rubber Bucket.

As recounted to Glitter's first biographer, George Tremlett, one morning in summer 1969 Leander set up some speakers and recording equipment on the MCA balcony, beside two squatted buildings in Piccadilly. Raven, dressed in a white kaftan, sang a mantra, 'We're All Living In One Place', to the melody of 'Amazing Grace'. A large choir of squatters down below sang along. But the Rubber Bucket single went the same way as everything else Raven had touched up to that point.

By 1970, Leander was a paid writer for GEM, Laurence Myers' music management, production and publishing company, then successfully crafting hits for Bell Records. Raven, who'd recently supported Little Richard in Germany, was back in London where the rock'n'roll scene was stirring once more.

Sometimes, the pair took off for Hampshire and a day's fishing; other times, Paul Raven would drop into the GEM office, where he'd usually make the tea.

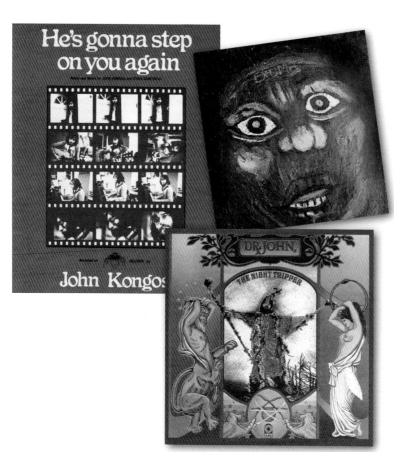

'We realised that what we'd produced was not black music at all,' Leander told Tremlett. 'We were making a great rock'n'roll record.'

The fifteen-minute recording was strangely reminiscent of the music Leander and Raven had loved in their youth – even though it hadn't been planned that way. But there was nothing revivalist about the sound. '[It] was a revelation,' Leander continued. 'It was unlike anything that either of us had heard before.'

Leander edited the fifteen-minute jam down to two 45rpm-sized segments and presented it to Bell label boss Dick Leahy. A deal was done. With a bank overdraft hanging over him, Raven grabbed at the opportunity.

'Until the single I'd always been serious about Paul Raven,' the singer told *Disc* in 1972. 'Then I thought, "Why the hell not change my name?" Since then, I haven't taken myself so seriously.'

The single, 'Rock And Roll (Parts 1 & 2)', was released on March 3, 1972. The spectacle out front was Gary Glitter. The man who did most of the writing, arranging, producing and playing was Mike Leander.

'Putting on a spectacle,' said Leander, 'that was what Glitter was about. And the records were geared to that. They were constructed to be seen, whereas in the sixties they were constructed to be heard, probably with a joint dangling from your lip.'

Leander's production tapped into that – and to the old Rubber Bucket/tribal idea of music as involving and communal. Reverb sent Glitter's voice into a starry swirl for 'Part 1'. The flip was a mostly instrumental stomp augmented by killer handclaps and the singer's exhorting cries of 'Hey-ey!' over syncopated, loose-skinned drums and fuzzed-up guitar and sax lines, coughing and wheezing sonic silver over everything.

Leander had caught 'Hey' fever before. 'Choc Ice', a 1964 flop he'd written and arranged for The Long And The Short – as covered by Lulu in Brit movie *Gonks Go Beat* – had a hook that went, 'Hey, hey, hey, hey.'

The first Gary Glitter single was snubbed initially by producers at the BBC. But within a month, Bell Records' London office began to receive calls from DJs up and down the country demanding copies. Then came the record dealers.

By mid-May, sales were reaching a thousand a day and rising. More unexpected still, it was the mostly instrumental flip side, popular in discotheques, that everyone was after.

After DJ Alan Freeman span it on his new Radio 1 mid-afternoon show, the single went nationwide,

Occasionally, he'd bump into a lank-haired hippie type there, checking that he still had a career. It was David Bowie.

GEM's hot shots for 1971 were Johnny Johnson & The Bandwagon and The New Seekers. Raven was by then considering taking a backroom job in the industry.

Meanwhile, Leander pursued his interest in chants and trance, picking up on mystical New Orleans 'night tripper' Dr John and a mesmerising 1970 LP by Bahamian musician Exuma. But the catalyst for change was hearing 'He's Gonna Step On You Again', a hard-groove top-five hit for John Kongos in July 1971.

Sometime before Christmas 1971, Leander booked an evening session at Mayfair Studios in central London. With a few session musicians and Paul Raven at the microphone, the producer induced a spontaneous jam session based around his approximation of a West African-style rhythm. The recent top-forty success of French producer Michel Bernholc's 'Burundi Black' single, based on a recording of the Royal Drummers of Burundi, had already confirmed its commercial validity.

entering the chart at No. 37 on June 10, 1972. Glitter – dressed in a sparkling silver suit – made his first *Top Of The Pops* appearance on June 21.

'Our heroes were Elvis and others who were very showbiz,' said Glitter, 'and rock'n'roll which was fun. I was more glitter than glam, but that was glamorous too.

'After the great message era, bands wearing beards and jeans, we wanted to kick it back into theatre again.'

The single was the slowest grower since Bowie's 'Space Oddity'; it was also that rare thing, a genuine grassroots success. It spent most of July at No. 2, tucked in behind Donny Osmond's 'Puppy Love', and stuck around the top thirty until September.

Pop's recent turn towards theatricality now had a figurehead who embodied all the pomp and pageantry of the British monarchy. Gary Glitter was an anachronism, but with a key difference – he was in on the joke. Audiences and critics laughed; he laughed louder still.

Portly, proudly hairy-chested, a Liberace figure turned medallion man, Glitter was also the spark for all manner of hopefuls – both in the recording studio and on the streets – to reach for the sparkle jar.

'Rock And Roll Part 2' was one of three mostly instrumental top-ten hits that summer. But neither Glitter nor Mike Leander had any intention of following Hot Butter ('Popcorn') or Terry Dactyl & The Dinosaurs ('Seaside Shuffle') into the book of one-hit wonders. They'd both worked too hard for that.

On July 1, three competing beneficiaries of the Bolan-inspired pop revival had stormed the top five: Slade's 'Take Me Bak 'Ome' was No. 1; Sweet's 'Little Willy' and Glitter's 'Rock And Roll (Parts 1 & 2)' had shot up to Nos. 4 and 5, respectively.

'Take Me Bak 'Ome' was Slade's 'Telegram Sam', a bells-and-whistles consolidation of their best assets. Whereas Bolan had gone for seduction, Slade upped the stomping and hectoring – with nuanced nods to

RCA
the sweet
little Willy
VICTOR STEREO
N 1663

On July 6, 1972, they appeared on *Top Of The Pops* to promote 'Little Willy'. David Bowie – in Ziggy mode – had just draped an arm around Mick Ronson. But at least as much of the talk the following morning was of The Sweet's performance.

The 'Little Willy' title and chorus was suggestive enough. The sight of bassist Steve Priest camping it up in gleaming silver boots, a chest-baring blouse (without a hair to be seen) and hot pants (actually a hastily butchered pair of trousers) was something else again.

Porcelain-faced Bowie played the alien stick-insect; Steve Priest roared headlong into slapstick. 'Bowie was looked upon as upper class,' said Priest. 'We were workingmen's crapola.

'I was in the studio piling my makeup on like a tart. He was sat next to me and says [adopts fancy voice], "Oh no, you're putting much too much on!"

'I went, "Nah, I'm not."'

'When I joined The Sweet,' says Andy Scott, 'I realised they all used a bit of pancake which I'd never used before. But under certain lighting, you want to make the best of what you've got. We all used to slap a bit on.'

Once the archetypal bubblegum puppets, The Sweet were now firmly aboard the sparkling fun train. They were also putting in a strong challenge for the most effeminate-looking male band in pop history. The pop world giggled. Chinn and Chapman toasted another hit and resolved to make it to No. 1 by the end of the year.

The songwriters were clearly capable of moving with the times. Ads for 'Little Willy' described the single as a 'rocking new disc from The Sweet'. It was a step in the right direction – for everyone.

'We'd sung on "Little Willy,"' said Steve Priest, 'but we were just brought in like choirboys. The thinking, as always, was that it was cheaper and quicker to use session musicians.

'Our lucky break was the Musicians' Union demand that anyone miming on *Top Of The Pops* had to re-record the song with an MU member watching. So we re-recorded "Little Willy".

'When Chapman heard our version, he went, "Wow! You just turned it into a rock'n'roll song.

'"You can play on the next record."'

Slade shared a joint and sang an impromptu 'When You Wish Upon A Star'.

The Beatles via Hill's lead fills and that significant pause after Nod's 'alright' (shades of The Beatles' 'Birthday').

Jim Lea's arranging skills were all over the song. 'We'd all chip in,' says Don Powell, 'but Jim's classical training helped a lot.'

Coming off the back of a successful nationwide tour supported by head-shaking, double-denimed crowd-pleasers Status Quo, Slade promoted the single with characteristic gusto. The contrast with Bolan's remote star power was stark. Slade were tilting the balance: they were rockier, sillier and more keen on good-time singalongs than in soliciting fan worship.

Late in July, as Don Powell recalls in his memoir, Slade played a short residency in Benidorm. As the foursome gazed across the harbour in Calpe, the small town where they were staying, they shared a joint and sang an impromptu 'When You Wish Upon A Star' from Walt Disney's *Pinocchio*.

Enjoying a moment of kinship and fulfilled childhood dreams on the Costa Brava, the boys from Wolverhampton knew they'd come far. The Sweet, the four-piece from the suburbs of west London, still had it all to do.

ABOVE: The Sweet re-recorded the 'Little Willy' backing track for the *Top Of The Pops* broadcast. Mike Chapman was so impressed that he let the band record their next single themselves.

RIGHT: July 6, 1972: while The Sweet played slapstick, David Bowie and Spider-in-chief Mick Ronson played androgynous aliens for the unsuspecting *Top Of The Pops* audience. Stagehands joked that that they'd just walked in from the *Doctor Who* set.

Chapter 11
Ziggy Goes Pop

Despite the hype, there was no corresponding bounce for 'Starman', the first new David Bowie single since his 'I'm Gay' controversy back in January. Released on April 28, 1972, 'Starman' didn't go top-twenty until July. Its success was down to the power of television – and long-term strategy.

'I'm going to be huge, and it's quite frightening in a way,' he'd told Michael Watts back in January.

Bowie had no intention of remaining a one-hit wonder. Having developed the *Ziggy Stardust* album/tour/alter-ego concept in late 1971, assisted by Tony Defries, Angie and a small but motivated team of stylists and industry grubbers, he'd firmly set success as the goal.

As so often with youth culture, the primary weapon was hair. Bowie bade fond *adieu* to his Veronica Lake locks early in January 1972, with the assistance of Beckenham stylist Suzi Fussey.

The cut harked back to the neat Mod style of mid-sixties Small Faces, albeit raised and layered over the crown like Rod Stewart. Hairspray was required to keep it upright. The colour, 'Schwarzkopf Red,' said Bowie, was added the following month.

The inspiration came from a pile of fashion magazines, from *Honey* to continental editions of *Vogue*. One photoshoot, in the August 1971 edition of French *Vogue*, had featured model Christine Walton sporting a fiery red 'bog-brush' crop.

Bowie himself liked to cite Japanese designer Kansai Yamamoto as an inspiration. The key point was that it was a unisex cut – and turned heads.

His Ziggy, an androgynous, comic book-style antihero, was almost complete. But pop's Dr Frankenstein was growing bigger ambitions for his creation. He wanted Ziggy to walk on his own.

'*Hunky Dory* had been about finding his legs as a songwriter,' says drummer Woody Woodmansey. '*Ziggy* was something that would communicate as a rock show.'

The *Ziggy Stardust And The Spiders From Mars* tour was launched on February 10, 1972. It began with sixty people gathered in a function room at The Toby Jug, a suburban pub in Tolworth on the edge of southwest London.

Eyewitness reports suggest minimal, theatrical lighting, with possibly a blast of Beethoven from the soundtrack of Stanley Kubrick's controversial new film *A Clockwork Orange*, which had just opened.

Bowie had instructed photographer Brian Ward

'Ziggy-zaggy' youths defied seaside police

By MIRROR REPORTER

CHANTS of "Ziggy-zaggy, Ziggy-zaggy . . . rah, rah, rah" sounded along a seaside promenade.

They came from a crowd of youths and girls who on Sunday night created a disturbance and defied the police, a court heard at Great Yarmouth, Norfolk, yesterday.

Bottles were thrown and a policeman was punched, Inspector Walter Painter told the court.

Another police witness said that one group of youngsters kept running up and down shouting "All coppers are bastards" and "Let's get them."

Seven youths, aged eighteen to twenty-four, were before the court variously charged with assaulting the police, obstruction, threatening behaviour, being drunk and disorderly, and stealing a petrol cap from a police van.

'Hot'

One of them told the court there was a "hot atmosphere." Another blamed "the heat of the

Being the adventures of a young man
whose principal interests are rape,
ultra-violence and Beethoven.

STANLEY KUBRICK'S

A Stanley Kubrick Production "A CLOCKWORK ORANGE" Starring Malcolm McDowell · Patrick Magee · Adrienne Corri
and Miriam Karlin · Screenplay by Stanley Kubrick · Based on the novel by Anthony Burgess · Produced and
Directed by Stanley Kubrick · Executive Producers Max L. Raab and Si Litvinoff · From Warner Bros., A Kinney Company

Exciting original soundtrack available on Warner Bros. Records

72/30

LEFT AND FAR LEFT: Random
acts of youth violence,
including crowd trouble
at football matches and
a growing concern about
'mugging', made headlines
during 1972. Stanley Kubrick's
new film, *A Clockwork Orange*,
starring Malcolm McDowell
as protagonist Alex, became
a convenient scapegoat
for contemporary ills. The
director was sufficiently
spooked and pulled the film
from cinemas the following
year.

David Bowie "Changes"
74-C625

REGIONAL BREAKOUT! LAST WEEK BOSTON, NOW WASHINGTON D.C. AND SEATTLE!
Everything's "Hunky Dory" with Bowie spreading!

FROM HIS SMASH HIT ALBUM

DAVID BOWIE
HUNKY DORY

LSP-4623, P8S-1350, PK-1850

RC/I Records and Tapes

to go for a *Clockwork Orange* effect at the *Ziggy* album photoshoot three weeks earlier. He'd drawn from Kubrick before. It was seeing the visionary director's *2001: A Space Odyssey* in 1968 that had inspired 'Space Oddity'. But *A Clockwork Orange* was closer to home, a near-future dystopian fantasy that chimed with Bowie's long-held views on alienation and social breakdown.

Based on Anthony Burgess's 1962 novel, the film followed a group of teenage 'droogs' prowling the concrete wasteland, dishing out ultraviolence for kicks to the sounds of electronically rearranged classical music. The poster depicted bowler-wearing ringleader Alex, played by Malcolm McDowell, all spider eyelashes and amoral grin, brandishing a knife that glinted like a jewel.

'*Clockwork Orange*: that was our world, not the bloody hippie thing,' Bowie would tell *MOJO*'s Paul Du Noyer in 2002. 'It all made sense to me. The idea of taking a present situation and doing a futuristic forecast and dressing it to suit.' He added his own twist, 'subvert[ing] it by using pretty materials'. It was, he said, the '*Clockwork Orange* look but with the violence taken out of it'.

Kubrick's black-comedy masterpiece prompted a moral panic in the press during February, with random incidents of street violence allegedly echoing scenes from the film. The following year, Kubrick would become sufficiently spooked to demand that the film be pulled from cinemas. All

the controversy did Ziggy's own faux-Droog Squad no harm at all.

As the band continued to tour, RCA blitzed the rock press in February with a promotional campaign for *Hunky Dory*, which had been lost amid the Christmas rush. Full-page ads were filled with glowing endorsements:

'David Bowie is the most singularly gifted artist creating music today,' declared *Rock* magazine. 'He has the genius to be to the seventies what Lennon, McCartney, Jagger and Dylan were to the sixties.'

'The most intellectually brilliant man yet to choose the long-playing album as his medium of expression,' raved the *New York Times*. An 'avant-garde superstar', announced *Billboard*.

The ads signed off in more prosaic fashion: '"Changes" is [Tony] Blackburn's record of the week.' Alas, neither 'Changes' nor *Hunky Dory* caught so much as a sniff of the charts – though the album eventually crept into the top fifty for two weeks during the autumn.

But the failure mattered little. The Bowie camp was fixated on the fast-evolving *Ziggy*; *Hunky Dory* was last year's thing.

As the tour continued, *A Clockwork Orange* soundtrack music and flashing strobe lights were

ABOVE: Bowie and the Spiders performing 'Starman' for the first time on TV for *Lift-Off With Ayshea*, June 15, 1972. 'It was all done with smoke and mirrors,' remembered Mick Rock, Bowie's newly appointed personal photographer. 'They rarely spent much money on it, not in the early days. The illusion was of this massive star, looking and acting like a star.'

DAVID BOWIE
His latest album
"Hunky Dory" is now
high in the US Charts!
His new single "Starman"
is released on April 28th.

David will be appearing at the Manchester Free Trade Hall
on April 21st

"STARMAN"
c/w "Suffragette City"
RCA 2199

RCA

Townshend said one day groups would be unafraid to mock the whole process.

ABOVE: April 1972's 'Starman', the launch record for the *Ziggy* project, was also used to boost sales of the poorly performing *Hunky Dory*. Another advert managed to namecheck all three releases: 'Can a young guy who went through truly incredible "Changes" and made it all "Hunky Dory" ever find true happiness as a "Starman"....?'

augmented by costume changes and a developing rapport between Bowie and his guitarist, Mick Ronson. The line between rock band and theatrical production began to blur.

'Rock'n'Roll Suicide', one of the last songs recorded for the *Ziggy* album, was the *coup de grâce*. Bowie appended the grand farewell with restorative howls of 'You're not alone!' and 'You're wonderful!', and the crowd responded with arms outstretched and happy/sad expressions on their faces. It was a Judy Garland-style *adieu* remade for rock.

Bowie's ambition to dress rock up and turn it into a plaything was threatening to become a reality. On May 6, at Kingston Polytechnic, whilst introducing himself as David Bowie, he suggested his band 'could be The Spiders From Mars'. He'd also added Cream's

'I Feel Free' to the set, perhaps more pertinent to his own psyche than to the character's.

Just as Warhol had destabilised the idea of 'the Artist', Bowie was putting quote marks around his role as 'singer fronting a rock band'. He'd already credited himself on the *Hunky Dory* sleeve as 'the Actor'.

'On the early tours, you'd seen him getting ready to be Ziggy,' says Woodmansey, 'putting the makeup on, two or three outfits. We'd do the encore and we'd be laughing, and he was still Ziggy. Then we'd get in the limo and it'd be a gang again.'

It was creatively provocative and a lot of fun. It was also all in the service of success. On one of those early Ziggy nights, the drummer recalls Bowie making an announcement: 'You're all going to be millionaires, so you'd better get used to that.'

★

'Starman' received its television premier on June 21, 1972 on *Lift Off With Ayshea* in ITV's back-from-school slot. But it was *Top Of The Pops*, with its fifteen million weekly viewers, that counted. On the July 6 edition, over two months after the record's release, Bowie got his chance.

Backstage, BBC staff joked that the band had walked in from the *Doctor Who* set. In front of the cameras, Bowie and his satin-clad musicians seemed to offer significantly more than The Sweet, with Steve Priest shifting around in his makeshift hot pants.

DAVID BOWIE AND HIS FOUR MINUTE GEM

Now this i

'Starman' peaked at No. 10 on July 29, 1972. Bowie's rising status in the weeklies was now matched by coverage in the pin-up magazines. Even *Daily Express* muckraker Jean Rook had a pop at 'the pop star with the poison green eyelids and the hair like an orange lavatory brush'.

The Rise And Fall Of Ziggy Stardust And The Spiders From Mars had hit the shops on June 16. Though credited to David Bowie, the concept of the album could have passed off as the creation of a fictional frontman and band. It was, perhaps, the first realisation of a prediction made by Pete Townshend in late 1967, that one day groups would be unafraid to 'mock the whole process'.

'This latest chunk of fantasy can only enhance [Bowie's] reputation further,' wrote *NME*'s James Johnson.

The storyline was threadbare. But Bowie himself was clear that role-play and identity lay at the heart of the project. Bassist Trevor Bolder, on the other hand, always maintained that *Ziggy Stardust* was nothing more than the title of a record.

DAVID BOWIE IS ZIGGY STARDUST

More and more, the truly bisexual nature of man will be acknowledged.

ABOVE: 'When I was asked to create a Ziggy character for the poster,' says George Underwood, 'David specifically said he didn't want it to look exactly like him. He wanted a cartoon version of Ziggy, that's all.' A set of five cartoon-style images, designed by the artist and based on characters from the *Ziggy* album, featured in the programme for the Rainbow concerts in August.

'We didn't want any of the cheesiness that started to come out around that time,' says Woodmansey. 'We were glamorous, but we never saw ourselves as glam rock.'

Bowie's carrot-top was set off against a quilted, multi-coloured two-piece bomber suit made from Asian-style furnishing fabric and designed by last year's protégé, Freddi Burretti. His guitar, an acoustic in Neptune blue, looked too big on him as he swayed slimline and grinning, a cosmic ragamuffin.

As the song hit the first chorus, Bowie flung an arm around the shoulders of Ronson, his bottle-blond, feather-cut foil. Even the Stones' two princely androgynes, Mick Jagger and Brian Jones, hadn't expressed their sartorial decadence in such a close, comradely manner.

It was an electric moment, at a time when the launch issue of *Gay News* had just hit discerning newsstands. Bowie and Ronson were nothing like the female impersonators and pantomime dames beloved of television audiences. If anything, they symbolised a daringly fluid, subterranean idea of sex and gender identity – though the decidedly hetero Mick Ronson later admitted to feeling 'funny' about it.

In *The Important Thing Is Love*, a 1971 television documentary on lesbianism, psychotherapist and sexologist Dr Charlotte Wolff had made a prediction: 'I believe that how the world is developing, that more and more the truly bisexual nature of man will be acknowledged.'

On a more prosaic level, the gesture may just have been Bowie playing a game of one-upmanship with Bolan. For months, his on-off rival had been teasing fans that he and Mickey Finn were married.

Bowie's debt to Bolan on 'Starman' was obvious: he sang of 'hazy cosmic jive', while cosmic Marc often referred to 'jive'; the Starman urged us to 'let all the children boogie'; even the 'la-la-la-la-la' outro sounded like the 'Hot Love' fade in miniature.

There was a small, Rex-like string section and a Bolan boogie breakout midway through. Performing the song live on *Top Of The Pops,* Bowie even slipped a reference to 'Get It On' into the opening lines.

Embedded in the song was another secret helper from Bowie's little box of acquired mythology. The 'Starman' chorus followed a similar melodic arc to the keyline of Judy Garland's 'Over The Rainbow'.

'David is taking longer than most to become a superstar,' observed Chris Welch reviewing the single in *Melody Maker*, 'but he should catch up with Rod and Marc soon.'

SUPERSTARMAN!

25/6/72 Greyhound.

At Tony Defries' prompting, RCA initially produced an in-store poster declaring, 'David Bowie Is Ziggy Stardust.' It depicted Ziggy as a gnome-like figure, more Tyrannosaurus Rex cosmic pixie than the 'Leper Messiah' hybrid of Hendrix, Iggy Pop and vintage-rocker-turned-space-cadet Vince Taylor.

As the album climbed the chart, peaking at No. 7 during an initial seven weeks in the top ten, RCA placed another full-page ad in the press. This time, the campaign went further: the image, shot by new personal photographer Mick Rock at Oxford Town Hall on June 17, depicted Bowie in full Ziggy mode, going down on Ronson's Les Paul guitar.

An accompanying message made it all about the fans: 'Thanx to all "OUR" people for making ZIGGY. I love you. Bowie x.'

After a Save the Whales benefit at London's Festival Hall, on July 8, *Melody Maker* editor Ray Coleman was the latest to invoke Judy Garland with a dramatic 'A Star Is Born' headline. 'He left the stage a true 1972-style pop giant,' Coleman wrote, 'slaying

us all with a deadly intensity, the undisputed King of Camp Rock.'

'David Bowie is probably the best rock musician in Britain now,' acclaimed Peter Holmes in that month's *Gay News*. 'One day, he'll become as popular as he deserves to be. And that'll give gay rock a potent spokesman.' Holmes was by no means alone in taking Bowie's 'I'm gay' stance literally at the time.

Coleman also noticed something else: 'Bowie is a flashback in many ways to the pop star theatrics of about ten years ago, carrying on a detached love affair with his audience, wooing them, yet never surrendering that vital aloofness that makes him untouchable.'

Days later, Defries had RCA fly in twenty-four influential music and arts journalists from the States – including the famed Lillian Roxon, the coltish Lenny Kaye and Glenn O'Brien from Warhol's *Interview* magazine. They would witness the Bowie/Ziggy phenomenon in person, then go home and spread the word.

ABOVE: As Ziggymania took off, fans gathered round stage doors for autographs and the daily press proclaimed yet another superstar. 'David had great music and great visual appeal,' said Mick Rock. 'He was ridiculously glamorous.'

Woody Woodmansey: 'If Ziggy
was going out with red hair,
costume changes, high kicks and
mime, it would never have looked
right if the band didn't look [to
be] on his team. It had to be four
people all on the same page to
pull it off.'

RIGHT: Bowie stepping into the
crowd at the climax of a very
early Ziggy show at London's
Imperial College, February 12,
1972. By the time of the Rainbow
shows six months later, his fame
was assured.

The July 15 show at Aylesbury Friars, a blessed
venue for Bowie, was a triumph. The next day,
journalists from both sides of the Atlantic attended
a press audience at The Dorchester Hotel in London.
Cameras were confiscated. Bowie was not to be
approached or, God forbid, touched. Then came the
announcement: he would be playing two nights at
north London's Rainbow Theatre on August 19/20;
after a few select British dates, Bowie would then tour
the States.

The billing for the London shows was 'David Bowie
Is Ziggy Stardust Live At The Rainbow.' According to
NME's Charles Shaar Murray, '[It] was perhaps the most
consciously theatrical rock show ever staged. It made
Alice Cooper look like a third-form dramatic society.'

The performance was built around a snakes and

ladders-style set fashioned from movable scaffolding.
His old mime mentor Lindsay Kemp choreographed
the show and his mime troupe danced. Images –
including Bolan's face during 'Lady Stardust' – were
projected onto a vast backdrop. The silver-clad Spiders
and the costume-changing man in the middle were
often bathed in a fog of dry ice.

For the first time, fans turned up in various shades
of Ziggy/cosmic yob apparel. Mick Jagger danced in
the aisles; Elton John said he couldn't see how Bowie
could fail in the States; Rod Stewart kept his thoughts
to himself. Lou Reed had such a good time he needed
to be helped from the theatre.

Three weeks later, David and Angie Bowie set sail
from Southampton to New York on the QE2. And Ziggy
came too.

Lou Reed had such a good time he had to be helped from the theatre.

Rainbow

MEL BUSH PRESENTS

DAVID BOWIE
ROXY MUSIC
LLOYD WATSON
SATURDAY, AUGUST 19th—SOLD OUT
EXTRA SHOW
SUNDAY, AUGUST 20th, 7.30

Tickets: 75p, £1.00, £1.25, £1.50
Rainbow Box Office open 11 a.m. to 8 p.m.
232 Seven Sisters Road, London, N.4
TEL. 01-272 2224

Chapter 12
Misfits, Dudes, Messiahs

Many years later, David Bowie would claim 'All The Young Dudes' had been written for an intended part of the *Ziggy Stardust* storyline where the electricity supply breaks down and songs become the main source of communication.

Back in September 1972, when Mott The Hoople accepted his gift and turned 'Dudes' into a top-three hit, its meaning owed nothing whatsoever to *Ziggy* and everything to the surge of optimism that had made pop come alive once more.

'It was all about young people being at a loose end,' says Mott guitarist Mick Ralphs. 'It unified them all.'

But when Mott The Hoople first heard the song late in March 1972, unity was in short supply.

'We'd split,' says Ian Hunter.

Hunter was inclined to shoulder the blame for Mott's inability to transition from a live act pulling in a solid £600 a night to a successful recording band. 'Sometimes I think the fault is mine,' he told *Record Mirror*'s Keith Altham in December 1971. 'Mott really don't have a very good vocalist.'

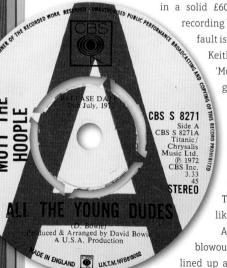

The band's reputation always boiled down to what Hunter called 'Good old Mott'. They had no desire to stun audiences with jaw-dropping feats of virtuosity. They were entertainers who liked to whip up a crowd.

And so, after the cathartic blowout that was *Brain Capers*, Mott lined up a Rock'n'Roll Circus tour for April 1972 – its name inspired by the failed Rolling Stones TV special filmed back in 1968. It was planned as a vaudevillian-style roadshow with jugglers, a knife-thrower and music-hall legend Max Wall – a huge inspiration to Steve Marriott and Ray Davies, crowd-pleasers both.

Wall's tragic clown persona and the hard-working band with little to show for their efforts seemed well suited. But days before the tour was due to start, Mott The Hoople brawled on stage during a performance in a converted gas container in Zurich. They agreed to split up and go home.

Back in London, Island Records stressed the financial implications of cancelling the tour. Platform-booted bassist Pete Overend Watts got on the phone to David Bowie.

Early in February, Bowie had sent Mott a reel-to-reel tape of the yet-to-be-released 'Suffragette City'. An accompanying note asked speculatively whether the band might wish to do something with the song. Bowie also left his phone number.

Watts picked up the phone, told Bowie Mott had split and asked if he needed a bass player. Bowie replied, 'You can't do that, you're in Mott The Hoople. It's a great band!'

Days later, towards the end of March, Bowie was seated in his manager's Regent Street office in front of various Mott members. He was strumming 'All The Young Dudes' on an acoustic guitar.

ALL THE YOUNG DUDES

Words and Music by DAVID BOWIE

Recorded by MOTT THE HOOPLE on Columbia Records

MOTH MUSIC INC.

Exclusive Selling Agent for
the United States and Canada
WARNER BROS. PUBLICATIONS INC.
1230 Avenue of the Americas, New York, N.Y. 10020

Design • Asterisk Assoc. Inc.

$1.00
In U.S.A.

'My first thought was, "I know I can sing this,"' says Ian Hunter. 'I'm a weird singer. I can't sing anything, you know. I just thought, "I can sing this. And it could be a monster."'

The *Ziggy Stardust* album was in the bag. The tour had built up a head of steam. Bowie now found time to throw himself into the second role he'd long felt destined for – The Mentor.

On Bowie's instructions Tony Defries moved to extricate Mott from their Island deal, fixing them up with a lucrative CBS contract in June. But the new creative partnership couldn't wait that long. On May 14, Bowie joined Mott The Hoople at Olympic Studios to oversee the 'All The Young Dudes' recording session.

Bowie sketched out a guide vocal for Hunter to follow, which in essence he did. Yet Hunter brought so much more to the song; his weary Mott's-last-stand delivery chimed with the undercurrent of melancholy that was hardwired into the new decade via a 'party's over' mindset exacerbated by political pessimism.

It was an inspired decision – either by Bowie or engineer Keith Harwood – to add repeat echo to Hunter's voice. It turned a fine performance into one of pop's epic monologues.

While Bowie and Mott were creating the song that would become the defining anthem of these times, T. Rex's 'Metal Guru' was already providing the era with its first crescendo. The song was Bolan's ode to joy, floating helium-like over everything.

'All The Young Dudes' just wasn't that kind of song. It had a more traditional establishing guitar hook, a conversational mid-Atlantic vocal, measured walking-pace verses, a classic-era Dylan organ sound and a contagious call-and-response chorus that spoke to a mixed-up new generation mindset.

Hunter's ad-lib on the song's fade introduced an extra layer of intrigue: 'I've wanted to do this for years!', he quipped, inspired by the memory of a particularly lairy Mott fan.

'We had what we called "a heckler's ten seconds",' says Hunter, 'when we all had to be quiet and let the idiots shout "Fuck off" or whatever they wanted to shout. Then when someone did that, we had his mates bring him down to the front and I'd empty a bottle of beer over him.'

But the context here was less primitive, more one of wish-fulfilment – for Bowie, for the band and for all those 'boogaloo dudes' out there, set free from all that 'revolution stuff'.

TOP: '"All The Young Dudes" was all about young people being at a loose end,' says Mott guitarist Mick Ralphs. 'It unified them all.' The anthem of the era, 'Dudes' peaked at No. 3 in September.

ABOVE AND LEFT: Mott's pop success didn't interrupt their hectic gigging schedule, but it did change their fanbase. Ian Hunter didn't mind. 'We wanted to be flash,' he says, 'Stones flash.'

Overend Watts
MOTT THE HOOPLE

ABOVE: 'Pete Watts was probably the first bloke I knew to have these
stacked-heeled boots made for himself,' says Mick Ralphs. 'It became
a trend, but Pete took it to extremes. He was so tall he could hardly
stand up.'

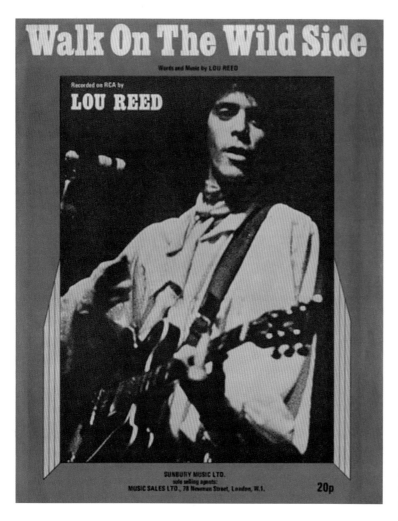

Walk On The Wild Side

Words and Music by LOU REED

Recorded on RCA by
LOU REED

SUNBURY MUSIC LTD.
sole selling agents:
MUSIC SALES LTD., 78 Newman Street, London, W.1.

20p

ABOVE: Back in 1962, *Walk On The Wild Side* was a gritty melodrama starring Barbara Stanwyck as a New Orleans brothel-keeper with an Elmer Bernstein soundtrack. A decade on, Lou Reed's similarly titled song celebrated the taboo-busting characters that inhabited Warhol's Factory. David Bowie and Mick Ronson co-produced. 'I love the guy,' said Reed of his new benefactor. 'The kid's got everything.'

During June and July, between promoting 'Starman', *Ziggy Stardust* and the never-ending tour, Bowie supervised sessions for a new Mott album. Mick Ronson assisted with the arrangements.

'David was a bit scared at first,' says Hunter. 'He thought Mott were a biker gang. We were normal guys – but if he wants to think of us as bikers, that was great by us.'

For all Bowie's talents, his production skills were still a work in progress.

'David heard things a little more fey than we did,' says Hunter. 'We were blood and thunder. David liked it more poppy. But people used to record like that, mixing [songs] specifically to be heard on a small transistor radio.'

Bowie's most effective input on the sessions was to introduce Mott to The Velvet Underground's 'Sweet Jane'. A passionate Velvets enthusiast, he'd been playing 'I'm Waiting For The Man' live as early as 1967 and namechecked the band on the *Hunky Dory* cover ('Some V.U. White Light returned with thanks') as inspiration for 'Queen Bitch'. The Velvets' speed-freak anthem, 'White Light/White Heat', was also part of Bowie's 1972 live set.

Lou Reed, The Velvet Underground's ex-frontman and songwriter, was now in town. Before leaving New York, he'd described Bowie as 'the only interesting person around. Everything has been tedious, rock'n'roll has been tedious, except for what David has been doing.'

Reed, who'd recorded his solo debut in London in late 1971, was back on the promise that Bowie would produce his next album. He sat in on the 'Sweet Jane' session at Olympic, to assist with the song's complex phraseology. But mostly, he was busy writing songs in a modest hideaway in leafy Wimbledon.

Bowie's endorsement of Reed went against the popular grain. The Velvet Underground were always an acquired taste – too close to Warhol's sensationalist aesthetic, too intense, abrasive and pop-art impulsive for the classical sensibilities of the prog-rock community. As a songwriter Reed was very much on the dark side of the street, with no laurels or canyons in view.

Yet the association of two highly visual cult figures, both cultural outsiders, was of mutual benefit. Reed was eager for the recognition he felt was long overdue; Bowie was keen to associate himself with a genuine subversive and leading light in what some regarded as an anti-rock tradition. 'White light makes me sound like Lou Reed!' he sang approvingly during a session for John Peel's *Sounds Of The 70s* in May.

The Reed charm offensive began at Bowie's July 8, 1972 Festival Hall show, when the man in black joined the main attraction to perform three of his own songs. The following week, Reed played a late-night set at the King's Cross Cinema in north London. Photographer Mick Rock was there to capture him, white-faced and panda-eyed.

'I was fooling around with this makeup from Japan that they used in Noh plays,' Reed later told me. 'It takes all the colour out of your face like *Nosferatu*. I loved that look.'

Reed also credited Angie Bowie for helping him restore his old 'Phantom of Rock' panache. 'She said I was not dressed appropriately and took me out shopping,' he admitted.

During sessions at Trident Studios in August for what would become Reed's *Transformer* album, the 'mutual empathy' he had expressed earlier that summer with Bowie was under some strain. Wearing his arranger's hat, Mick Ronson took a much more active role.

When the album was released in November, Bowie and Ronson shared production credits. A shot of Reed from Mick Rock's King's Cross portfolio, which had inadvertently – and fortuitously – blurred during the printing process, stared out from the cover.

Transformer was Reed's renaissance. It gave him his first chart album while its single, 'Walk On The Wild Side', immortalised the Warhol Superstars, bringing trans women, drugs and fellatio onto daytime radio whilst becoming a top-twenty hit on both sides of the Atlantic.

But *NME* Velvets purist Nick Kent was disappointed, calling *Transformer* 'a pitiful display of gross terminal self-parody'. Nick Tosches, for *Rolling Stone*, hailed Reed's genius yet lamented the album's sexual energy as 'timid and flaccid'.

Defiantly proud of the record, Reed nevertheless gave some succour to the critics. 'I mimic me probably better than anybody else,' he confessed. 'I can play him well.'

Bowie wasn't done with extending his rock'n'roll menagerie. It was on his advice that Tony Defries had signed Iggy Pop to a management deal the previous September. A new contract with CBS duly followed and, by March 1972, Iggy and his ferocious new guitarist, James 'The Skull' Williamson, had relocated to London.

It was a massive gamble. Hard drugs had been behind The Stooges' collapse the previous summer. But the idea was to team up Iggy and Williamson with a rhythm section from one of Britain's few

surviving community rock groups, perhaps the Edgar Broughton Band or Pink Fairies.

Instead, the pair reached out to ex-Stooges guitarist Ron Asheton (now obliged to switch to bass) and his brother, drummer Scott. Iggy had known the pair since high school; they were, he said, 'the laziest juvenile delinquent sort of pig snobs ever born'.

The new-look Stooges played just one UK gig, a thirty-minute set at the King's Cross Cinema on July 15, the night after Reed's show. Wearing silver lamé trousers and white face makeup, Iggy flung off his T. Rex T-shirt and hurled himself into the equipment and the crowd – among them Bowie, Mick Rock and the visiting New York press corps *en route* home from Bowie's Aylesbury gig.

'The total effect was more frightening than all the Alice Coopers and *Clockwork Orange* put together,' wrote Nick Kent in *NME*. 'These guys weren't joking.'

The following day, both Reed and Iggy joined Bowie for his momentous Dorchester Hotel press conference. In the same week, *NME* featured Bowie – 'Britain's high-priest of Camp Rock' – on the cover. *Ziggy Stardust* was the No. 7 album, while 'Starman' was a new entry in the singles chart.

Meanwhile, as the two misfits of American rock were finding favour in London, something stirred on Manhattan's Lower East Side.

Playing a lengthy residency at the Oscar Wilde Room in the Mercer Arts Center, the New York Dolls came on like a bunch of Rooster Rod caricatures with a Mick Jagger impersonator out front. Their song titles read like a list of unmade Andy Warhol films: 'Pills', 'Personality Crisis', 'Looking For A Kiss'. The description 'subterranean sleazoid trash' attached easily to them.

LEFT: On Bowie's advice, Tony Defries struck a management deal with Iggy Pop in September 1971. The following March, Iggy and his new-look Stooges arrived in London in various states of disrepair, played a show at the Scala Cinema in July and finally started recording in September. The tapes were hastily mixed by Bowie in Los Angeles, during a break in his US tour, and released the following year as the mighty *Raw Power*.

Fashion, Gigs and Playing Biba in Early 1970s London

By New York Dolls Guitarist Sylvain Sylvain

Biba was the high point of the New York Dolls. Two great sold-out shows [November 25/26, 1973 – one year after the Dolls' London debut] in this plush, decadent, art deco Rainbow Room up on the top floor. We'd just put our album out. We'd been on the BBC where Bob Harris called us 'mock rock'. And right outside Biba's, Mercury Records had put this bicycle completely covered in little round stickers of each New York Doll. Total kitsch.

Before one of the gigs, me and [bassist] Arthur Kane went to the women's department on one of the floors downstairs. Arthur fell in love with this long, black, woolly jacket with a fake leopard collar and cuff sleeves. But we didn't have much money. Arthur switched tags and got busted! The police were called. This was two hours before the show.

I was in the clothing business myself before the Dolls; I had this sweater company called Truth & Soul which I started with Billy Murcia, the first Dolls drummer. I'd fly to England every summer with all the money I'd made. I'd go to Biba before it moved to the department store, to Mr Freedom, Granny [Takes A Trip] and Malcolm [McLaren] and Vivienne [Westwood]'s shop Let It Rock, and to Kensington Market to pick up Levi's for a pound.

I'd always be at the Roundhouse. I saw *Pork*, the Andy Warhol play, there. I got totally hooked on the Pink Fairies, who were weird the way I liked to be weird. And I saw Rod Stewart with The Faces and Tyrannosaurus Rex several times. Bolan was an influence. T. Rex would shit out of me and [Dolls co-guitarist] Johnny [Thunders] – not just the music but the look and everything else.

People called it cross-dressing but I don't think it was, not compared to [singer] David Johansen who went for his mother's look!

I'd grown up with the early Who, Rolling Stones, Beatles, but that had all changed. They were making stadium rock, opera rock. Our whole thing was to rebel against that – but not just because it was groovy to do that. We were rebelling for a purpose – that shit sucked! The songs were

BELOW LEFT AND BELOW: The New York Dolls backstage and on stage at Biba, November 25, 1973. Below L-R: Arthur Kane, Sylvain Sylvain, David Johansen, Jerry Nolan, Johnny Thunders.

RIGHT: 'Arthur [Kane] went to the women's department and fell in love with this long, black, woolly jacket with a fake leopard collar and cuff sleeves. We didn't have much money, [so] he switched tags and got busted! The police were called.'

twenty minutes long and half of that was a drum solo. What about a fast, cool, three-minute song that speaks to you like 'Trash' – 'Don't throw your life away' – like 'Frankenstein', y'know, something has to happen over Manhattan.

The New York Dolls were ground zero for that sound and attitude. We didn't come home, take it off and hang it in the closet. Arthur and I would take three or four hours getting dressed up and made up just to go to a supermarket to buy chicken.

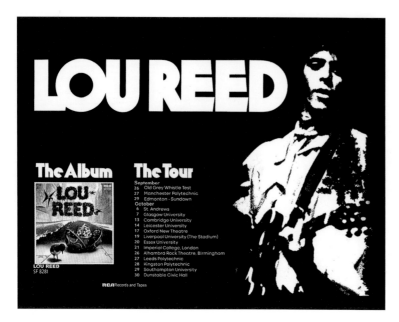

On October 29, 1972, the Dolls were in London to support The Faces at the Empire Pool, Wembley. In the flesh, they didn't look like The Faces at all, more a bunch of tarts from New York's blurred side. They were greeted with wolf whistles and a hail of projectiles.

The previous week, Lou Reed had turned down their offer to support him at Liverpool Stadium. The following week, drummer Billy Murcia would overdose at a party on 'quaaludes and red wine', as Bowie commemorated it, and die shortly after his twenty-first birthday.

Despite The Stooges' own predilections for nasty habits, the new album – credited to Iggy & The Stooges – came together in a series of sessions at CBS Studios beginning September 10. James Williamson had sketched out the riffs on acoustic guitar in a Kensington Gardens hotel room. But it was only when the Bowie roadshow took off for the States that the recordings, propelled by Williamson's razor-sharp playing, took shape.

'James is a very aggressive, controlled, brutal player,' says Iggy. 'The only problem with that is where do you find a hole for anybody else!'

In mid-October, Iggy brought the tapes over to Los Angeles for Bowie to perform the final mix. Midway through his first US tour, the Englishman only had a couple of days with the masters. Matters weren't helped by their primitive state. As Bowie remembered it, the recordings were split down three channels: one for the rhythm section, one for Iggy's vocals and one for lead guitar.

On its US release in February 1973, with another distinctive, defining Mick Rock shot dominating the sleeve, *Raw Power* would prove uncompromisingly raw – but somewhat shorn of its power. A 1997 Iggy Pop remix from the original masters would eventually restore the album to full power.

Lou Reed's career had turned on Bowie's intervention; Iggy Pop's less so. But the biggest beneficiaries were Mott The Hoople.

When 'All The Young Dudes' first charted, at No. 22 on August 12, 1972, the big summer hit was Alice Cooper's 'School's Out'. Despite Bowie's best efforts, Alice dominated the new trend for theatre-rock. Images of the vocalist chopping up a doll with an axe and fake blood on the *Killer* tour marked a shocking new departure.

'All The Young Dudes' appealed to a more modest aspect of new pop: the audience's sense of belonging. On August 13, three days after Mott premiered 'Dudes' on *Top Of The Pops*, Bowie turned up at Guildford's Civic Hall. He filled the backstage area with flowers and joined the band on stage for the song.

Afterwards, Ian Hunter sat with Bowie and Angie in their limo. 'It took him four hours to get ready!' whispered Mrs Bowie. The phrase stuck with Hunter, because Mott The Hoople just weren't that type of band.

'The lyric,' Hunter reflects, likely with the 'dresses

ABOVE: With *Transformer* in the bag, Lou Reed toured Britain during the autumn with young New York pick-up band The Tots. Sets mostly comprised songs from The Velvet Underground's *Loaded* and Reed's first solo album, issued back in the spring.

ABOVE RIGHT: October 29, 1972. Days after being snubbed by Lou Reed, the New York Dolls supported The Faces at Wembley as part of a two-day 'Festival Of Music'. 'Possibly the worst set I've seen,' wrote *Melody Maker*'s Mark Plummer.

RIGHT: 'We have a big debt to David because without ['Dudes'], I think we'd have been finished,' says Ian Hunter.

All the Young Dudes

recorded by

**MOTT
THE HOOPLE**

on C.B.S.

words and music by
DAVID BOWIE

Bowie photo/design by Mick Rock

TITANIC MUSIC / CHRYSALIS MUSIC LTD.
sole selling agents:
Music Sales Ltd., 78 Newman Street, London W1E 4JZ.

20p

like a queen' phrase in mind. 'Well, of course we were gay overnight!' Mott found that especially amusing, not least because, says Hunter, 'we all looked a bit bricklayer-ish. We wanted to be flash. We liked the idea of that. We didn't really wanna be gay flash. Stones flash – that was Mott's thing.'

'All The Young Dudes' peaked at No. 3 on September 9. Swept along by the single's success, the namesake album hit No. 21 later that month. 'Overnight, we became a pop group,' says Mick Ralphs.

Ian Hunter didn't see such a distinction. 'There was no such thing as pop or prog rock then,' he insists. 'You just went out and did it.

'[Mott] was a band that encompassed everything. We were like The Who. We embodied the spirit of rock'n'roll.'

Chapter 13
Tinseltown Rebellion

Wembley Stadium, Saturday August 5, 1972. The London Rock'N'Roll Show. A teenage girl sporting a Ziggy cut with a zesty marmalade finish sells 'Rock'n Roll Lives' T-shirts at the Let It Rock stall. The stallholder beside her, doing all the talking, wears a fifties-style Teddy Boy drape jacket and a leopard-skin-patterned flat cap. He is Malcolm McLaren. Three years later, he will scheme the Sex Pistols into existence.

McLaren was no bona fide Ted. He was a rabblerouser who admired the Teddy Boys' belligerent refusal to admit the world had moved on since Elvis joined the US Army. These walking anachronisms were his clientele, the ones that wide-stepped into his Let It Rock shop at the shabbier end of King's Road to buy drape jackets, brothel creepers, dayglo socks and bootlace ties – the glorious ruins of pop culture, remade and remodelled for a retrograde era.

to launch his new rock'n'roll big band, Wizzard.

If rock'n'roll music belonged to everyone now, a formidable Teddy Boy presence at the event made a famous last stand in defence of their hallowed territory. Teds policed the stage boundaries, denouncing imposters and charlatans with boos and bottles.

The MC5 – hairy, explosively loud and fronted by Afro'd Rob Tyner – were the Teds' worst nightmare. Guitarist Fred 'Sonic' Smith wore a superhero outfit with a cape around his shoulders and an 'SS' logo on his chest; hardly Brando in *The Wild One*.

Though fronted by two of rock'n'roll's biggest enthusiasts, the new British acts fared little better. Gary Glitter, whose 'Rock And Roll Part 2' was still in the top ten, stepped out in platforms and sequins to jeers and projectiles. Roy Wood's Wizzard were deemed too hairy, too musically eclectic, to be trusted. 'The rot'n'roll concert,' groaned Wood afterwards.

Just one freakshow passed the authenticity test. Screaming Lord Sutch, wearing a huge glittering gold cape, his face painted white with black markings, was Britain's original shock rocker. The regular Let It Rock patron arrived on stage by coffin to a rockin' death march amidst a clutch of scantily clad young women (including a stripper named Alice Cooper), pigeons and billowing orange smoke.

He'd created the template for glam back in the late fifties. But some booed.

At Wembley, dressed-to-kill retronauts weren't the only ones hovering around McLaren's stall. Since idealism had withered away, fifties nostalgia was fast taking its place in the collective consciousness of youth culture. And Marc Bolan had been emblematic of that change.

The cross-legged singer who once described his work as 'a happy, poetic, loving experience' was these days up on his feet, wearing a Chuck Berry T-shirt and announcing that his next book of poetry would be called *Teenage Animal*. He'd learned that Berry's fundamentalist rock'n'roll and the teenage sensibility were the keys to his survival.

Rock'n'roll was back – but events at Wembley proved it was hotly contested terrain. Chuck Berry, Jerry Lee Lewis, Bill Haley & The Comets and Little Richard were the marquee attractions. Billy Fury, Heinz and Screaming Lord Sutch & The Savages represented the home front. The MC5, who'd ditched White Panther revolutionary politics in favour of a fuzzier rebel-rock stance, had flown in from Detroit.

Then there was Gary Glitter, tottering along from the *Top Of The Pops* studio – as did The Move's Roy Wood. Wood had recently appeared on the show dressed in a drape jacket, his long hair quiffed, honking a baritone sax King Curtis-style on the band's rowdy revivalist hit 'California Man'. With The Move in a state of collapse and Jeff Lynne taking sole charge of the Electric Light Orchestra, Wood chose the occasion

RIGHT: The Rock'N'Roll Show, Wembley, London, August 5, 1972. Gloriously OTT, Little Richard had been an early inspiration to so many of the new superstars. Yet at this one-day celebration of rock'n'roll, both vintage and contemporary, some among his core audience were clearly discomfited by his act and booed.

Why do the 'oldies' continue to be 'goldies'? or the "boom from the tomb"!

But even for the younger, hairier crowd – including a hefty contingent of bikers – that swelled the event, the day was all about the legends. Jerry Lee Lewis, Bill Haley & The Comets, Bo Diddley and headliner Chuck Berry all received rapturous welcomes.

But something strange happened when Little Richard took the stage. He hollered, he leapt on top of his piano, he did everything the most outrageous rock'n'roller of them all was expected to do.

After all, this was the man who'd created the template for glam back in the late fifties – gaudy makeup, high-drama showmanship, braggadocio, onomatopoeia. But some of the old guard booed. It was almost as if Little Richard's perceived effeminacy had become a little too culturally relevant for their liking.

Rock'n'roll of various shades was by now making huge inroads into the top thirty. Days after Wembley, Little Eva's 1962 dancehall classic 'The Loco-Motion' was back for a nine-week run. Gifted weeny-bopper Michael Jackson charted with a version of Bobby Day's 1958 US smash 'Rockin' Robin'.

Arcade and K-Tel, aggressively marketed budget-label newcomers, both enjoyed huge success with densely packed fifties hits collections that summer. Elvis Presley notched up four top-ten hits between April and December 1972. Only south London rockers The Wild Angels, hotly tipped back in 1970 and now with a Decca Records deal, seemed unable to cash in.

But there was a dramatic new twist on retro culture that summer – one more aligned, at least in terms of spirit, to recently revived 1962 classical rock parody 'Nut Rocker' by B. Bumble & The Stingers.

On September 2, 1972, with 'School's Out' and 'All The Young Dudes' making their slow descent, 'Virginia Plain' by Roxy Music hit the top twenty. The band name evoked the popular Roxy cinemas of the thirties, forties and fifties, many since converted into bingo halls. The song title conjured up a similar vintage, a preoccupation of Roxy frontman and songwriter Bryan Ferry.

The original *Virginia Plain* was a 1964 art-school painting by Ferry, featuring a pack of Virginia Slims cigarettes adorned by 1964 'Girl Of The Year' Baby Jane Holzer. The perspective was Dali-like, the muse Warhol's.

ABOVE: Dressed in retro-futurist flash, Roxy Music gave a new twist to the vogue for vintage. August 1972 debut single 'Virginia Plain', inspired by an old brand of cigarettes and mid-sixties Warhol muse Baby Jane Holzer, sounded like the band looked. Some territories released the single in a modified version of Roxy's first album artwork.

Roxy wore retro-futurist flash: gold and silver lamé, mock animal skins, crepe-soled brothel creepers, Brylcreem-sculpted quiffs. Synthesizer player Eno claimed to be from Planet Xenon – and looked the part. The visuals were overdone to the point of parody but, despite the overtures, Roxy Music didn't exactly play rock'n'roll.

The band was as much designed as it was rehearsed. In that respect, Roxy shared plenty with Bowie's *Ziggy Stardust*. But while Bowie wanted to create something archetypal, a ready-made icon built for success, Roxy opted for a counter-intuitive approach.

'We knew we didn't sound like everybody else,' Eno would tell Robin Denselow that autumn, 'but we thought we sounded like everybody else plus something.'

Roxy Music were signed by Island Records in May '72 primarily as an album act. They were regarded as an acquired taste, though there was little in common with, say, Pink Floyd or King Crimson – for whom Ferry once failed an audition.

Neither did Roxy do the boogaloo, play blues-rock or harbour any ambition to become Britain's answer to The Band. They were an awkward fit, with only one real musical precedent.

'If I played any wacky free-form guitar,' says guitarist Phil Manzanera, the band's youngest member and the last to join, 'they'd say, "Oh, that's a bit like The Velvet Underground, we like that." Though we all had very different tastes, that was something we all had in common.'

The closest Roxy came to defining themselves was when they placed an ad in *Melody Maker*'s Musicians Wanted column in 1971: 'The Perfect Guitarist [wanted] for Avant-Rock group.'

While many of the era's new showmen and superstars had spent a decade changing hairstyles and managers, and slogging round the clubs, the nucleus of Roxy – Ferry, Eno and sax/oboe player Andy Mackay – came to pop on the rebound from fine arts and the teaching profession. Even if, like Ferry and Eno, there was no traditional musical training, they had the confidence to pick up an instrument and run with it. They weren't short on ambition either.

'We're not interested in scuffling,' Ferry told *Melody Maker*'s Richard Williams in August 1971, in a breakthrough piece on the band. 'If someone will invest some time and money in us, we'll be very good indeed.'

Ferry had studied art at Newcastle under Richard Hamilton, the father of British pop-art. Mackay had been an oboe player in the London Schools Symphony Orchestra before studying music at Reading University. Eno, a fine arts graduate from Winchester School of Art, brought with him a bag of ideas inspired by Marcel Duchamp, John Cage and Allan Kaprow – the ready made as art, abstract sound (and indeed silence) as music and human activity as performance, respectively.

They'd say, 'Oh, that's a bit like The Velvet Underground,' we like that.

"The Perfect Guitarist"
for AVANT-ROCK GROUP

Original, creative, adaptable, melodic, fast, slow, elegant, witty, scary, stable, tricky

QUALITY MUSICIANS ONLY
"ROXY" 223 0296.

HORIZON

New names that could break the sound barrier

A CURIOUS feature of modern rock music is the way it's taken potential artists away from other spheres. Men who might have become poets, painters, or even classical musicians have, instead, found an outlet for their creativity in the new medium, which also offers the chance of wide exposure — not to mention bags of loot.

Five years ago, for instance, it would have been unthinkable for Bryan Ferry to have entered rock and roll. Fine Arts graduates from Newcastle University just didn't do that sort of thing.

But now, in 1971, Bryan is leading a band called Roxy which has produced one of the most exciting demo tapes ever to come my way. Although it was recorded on a small home tape machine in what sounds like a Dutch barn, it carries enough innovatory excitement to suggest that Roxy may well be near the head of the field in the avant-rock stakes.

As some of you may already have realised, Roxy will have to change their name when they find a manager and a record company. Elektra already have a

BRYAN FERRY: interested in flash rock

LEFT: In a striking first piece on the band by *Melody Maker*'s Richard Williams, frontman Bryan Ferry displayed a rare eclecticism, citing influences that ranged from Ethel Merman and The Velvet Underground to jazz. 'The [band] were all a bit older than me,' says guitarist Phil Manzanera, who joined in January 1972. 'And they'd all been to art college. It was very grown up.'

LEFT: Roxy Music, 1972. L-R:
Andy Mackay, Paul Thompson,
Bryan Ferry, Eno, Phil Manzanera,
Rik Kenton. 'We knew we didn't
sound like everybody else,'
Eno said in autumn 1972. 'But
we thought we sounded like
everybody else plus something.'

ABOVE: Unique among the Class of '72, Roxy Music emerged without a backstory of soul-sapping gigs and flop 45s. 'We're not interested in scuffling,' said Ferry at the outset. Neither were they easily typecast. 'Some saw in us shades of the fifties,' says Phil Manzanera, 'others shades of a futuristic nineties.'

Yet Roxy's smart set was at least as transfixed by pop music. In 1967, while he was singing R&B with the Gas Board in Newcastle, Ferry had hitchhiked down to London to see Otis Redding head up the Stax/Volt tour. Gas Board bandmate and original Roxy bassist Graham Simpson taught himself to play by copying Brian Wilson's basslines on Beach Boys records. And Eno ditched the idea of a fine arts career after realising that pop 'seemed much more revolutionary'.

'Imagine if you'd been one of those fifties Colourfield painters like Barnett Newman,' Eno explains. 'And somebody walks into your studio with a briefcase and says, "In here I've got four thousand colours you've never seen before. They don't even have names." That was what pop music was like with the development of the recording studio and the sudden expansion of sounds in every dimension. I thought, "Why would you not want to play with that?"'

The perfect vehicle for Eno's perspective on pop was the synthesizer, developed commercially by Robert Moog in the mid-sixties. It was, he says, 'an instrument waiting for a new way of playing it. A complete beginner like me had as much right to say

"I'm a synthesizer player" as anybody else did. More so in a way.'

Invention and play were integral to Roxy's creative approach. Another factor, at once complementary and contradictory, can be traced back to the Ferry household in County Durham where, recounts Roxy biographer Michael Bracewell, Ferry's father kept an impeccably maintained vegetable garden and his mother baked cakes that emerged perfectly formed from the oven.

A sense of perfectionism, 'The Ideal', came easily to Ferry, who was fastidious in his pursuits: whether acquiring the car of his teenage dreams – a Studebaker in metallic green – or erasing his Geordie accent. By the time he'd settled in London in 1968, his voice and deportment were more in keeping with Evelyn Waugh's 'Bright Young Things'.

Ferry found a residence on fashionable Kensington High Street. With a harmonium at his disposal, he began writing during winter 1970/71. Despite his rudimentary keyboard skills, the songs – mostly in a ballad style – soon came.

The arrival of classically trained Mackay and

mischief man Eno – who quickly commandeered Mackay's EMS VCS3 synthesizer – helped turn Ferry's song sketches into full-blown tonal adventures.

'The Bob (Medley)' became a labyrinthine epic with long tape, synthesizer and oboe passages. '2HB', a tribute to Hollywood legend Humphrey Bogart (by way of a pencil), was prefaced with a passage that conjured up a street market in Casablanca. 'Chance Meeting' sounded like solo Ferry backed by Quintessence.

Bryan Ferry hand-delivered the recordings to the home of Richard Williams. 'One of the most exciting demo tapes ever to come my way,' Williams informed *Melody Maker* readers in August '71. He was spot-on: nothing had ever sounded like this.

The arrival of drummer Paul Thompson, who previously backed Billy Fury, and ex-Nice guitarist Davy O'List brought a new muscularity to the band. O'List's style, forged in London's 1967 psychedelic scene, was far more innovative and attack-minded than that of his contemporaries.

As the band emerged from rehearsals to perform, mostly at private functions such as the Friends of the Tate Gallery's 1971 Christmas party, a camaraderie had developed. Ferry and Mackay shared a fondness for old music-hall songs, and the singer's stagecraft, performed with the conviction of an old matinee idol, came from a similar place – superbly crafted but hammed-up to perfection.

In February 1972, after a disagreement at an audition for management company EG, Davy O'List was replaced by another guitarist with a psychedelic pedigree. 'When I'd dream about being in The Beatles, Roxy fulfilled all that side of it,' says Phil Manzanera. 'I could see that it was fulfilling Bryan's fantasy. But I was happy to contribute to it in every way I could.'

That same month, EG Management's David Enthoven agreed to finance a Roxy Music album. The band recorded their debut during two weeks in March. They also started playing more conventional rock-circuit gigs, beginning with a 'coming out' appearance at the Lincoln Festival on May 27 (with new bassist Rik Kenton) and a prestigious booking supporting Alice Cooper at the Empire Pool, Wembley, on June 30.

The Roxy live experience didn't always go smoothly, particularly when they ventured beyond their metropolitan bubble. On June 14, they played Liverpool Stadium, warming up for blues-rock guitarist Rory Gallagher. Gallagher was a checked-shirt and denim man; Roxy's outrageous sparkle was now in its pomp, completed by drummer Paul Thompson's sleeveless, Tarzan-style shirt and new

bassist Rik Kenton's overgrown schoolboy look.

Chants of 'Poofs!' broke out at regular intervals. The band left the stage prematurely to a chorus of boos.

Two days later, their self-titled debut album hit the racks. The first track, 'Re-Make/Re-Model', amounted to a virtual manifesto. Against the background chatter of a mock cocktail soiree, Ferry's Jerry Lee Lewis-style

FIRST ALBUM BY ROXY MUSIC (ILPS 9200) OUT NOW

Roxy Music

ABOVE: Bryan Ferry, who spotted model Kari-Ann Muller on a catwalk, knew exactly what he wanted for the album cover – a forties-style pin-up in marshmallow pinks and blues. Anthony – later Antony – Price did the styling; Kari-Ann received £20 for posing as a forces-style sweetheart.

RIGHT: After one last rock'n'roll blowout, the Jerry Lee Lewis-inspired 'California Man', Roy Wood walked away from both The Move and sister act Electric Light Orchestra to form big band Wizzard.

piano figure cued in what sounded like a rampantly glossy upgrade of The Velvet Underground's relentless 'White Light/White Heat' (the shared slash/stroke was a clue).

But as this was 1972, each instrument took a break midway through. It was a delicious subversion of the virtuoso routine: Mackay blew a fast phrase from Wagner's 'The Valkyrie'; Simpson played The Beatles' 'Day Tripper' riff; Manzanera did that Duane Eddy twang thang; Thompson thumped out a Sly Stone 'sock-it-to-me' groove; Ferry cruised atonally up the keyboard; Eno's VCS3 had hysterics. It was the Roxy Music style book in miniature.

For all the album's daring, at its heart was Bryan Ferry's crooner-on-the-moon stylings. He channelled 'Cry' guy Johnnie Ray on 'If There Is Something', Bogart on '2HB' and Noel Coward on the doo-wop-inspired closer 'Bitters End', where Eno led the backing singers in chorusing the word 'bizarre'. For the finale, Ferry moved in for his close-up with a (presumably) tongue-in-cheek statement of intent to 'make the cognoscenti think'.

The mischief and provocation were matched by the artwork. Ferry knew what he wanted: pouting cover model Kari-Ann Muller – who the singer had

spotted on a catwalk – was all dressed up like a US Forces 1940s sweetheart, a pin-up in pastel pink and blue. The striking image opened out like a vintage centrefold.

The inner gatefold featured stylised personality portraits of the band, a 'Clothes, makeup & hair' credit – to Anthony Price – straight out of *Vogue* and some words from band 'philosopher' Simon Puxley that further concealed the enigma at the core of Roxy's music: 'what's the date again? (it's so dark in here) 1962? or twenty years on?'

'Presentation is integral to how we think the audience hear the music,' Eno explained that September. 'Hearing is conditioned by what one sees.'

Certainly, when Island boss Chris Blackwell saw the proposed sleeve artwork, it proved the deal-clincher. Being presented to Bowie's audience at his two Rainbow shows in August 1972 also helped. Support act Roxy Music earned standing ovations on both nights.

Four days later, on August 24, Roxy debuted 'Virginia Plain' on *Top Of The Pops*. The band, mostly in their mid-to-late twenties, were clearly a breed apart. Bryan Ferry, a vampiric lounge lizard in black sequins and blue eyeshadow, screwed up his eyes and sang through a very deliberate rictus grin. Andy Mackay sparkled in green, and Eno's silver gloves danced across the synth's small keyboard.

There was a whiff of revivalism – that Duane Eddy twang, some ton-up boys-style motorbike revving and a reference to that 1950s icon the 'teenage rebel'.

But 'Virginia Plain' was mostly about Ferry's voice, as remarkable an abstraction as the 20th century art he favoured. It was the way he stretched the syllables (*Make me a deeeal!*) like a mobster Bob Dylan that made the song stick. At the end of the *TOTP* performance, he flashed a knowing wink.

'Virginia Plain' peaked at No. 4 in mid-September, staying in the top thirty for nine weeks before dropping out in late October. On the back of it, the album hit No. 10 at the end of September.

Meanwhile, the rock'n'roll nostalgia boom continued. Elton John's 'Crocodile Rock', an unabashed love letter to 1950s pop music, hit No. 5 in November. Wizzard charted in December with high-kickin' debut 45 'Ball Park Incident'. Another K-Tel compilation, *25 Rockin' & Rollin' Greats*, topped the album chart, while Chuck Berry – the man who brought the riff, the duckwalk and street poetry to rock'n'roll – was selling cock'n'bull humour back to the British with 'My-Ding-A-Ling'. It stayed at No. 1 for four weeks in the run-up to Christmas.

Roxy Music ended the year with a dispiriting tour of the States. They headlined LA's Whisky A Go Go but all too often found themselves supporting Humble Pie or Jethro Tull. The first flush of fame took its toll, especially on Ferry – already rivalling Bolan as pop's most distinctive voice. In October he was laid up in hospital, having his tonsils removed.

'There was no power struggle to become leader of the band at that point,' says Phil Manzanera.

'Bowie had his "Ziggy" persona at the time. We were more democratic. But all the agents and promoters told us that no band had ever succeeded without having a focal point. So Bryan became the frontman.'

Chuck Berry was selling cock'n' bull humour back to the British.

Chapter 14
Jesus Christ...
Superstars!

July 23, 1972: the Ace Face of British pop swivels nervously in the guest chair on Russell Harty's late-night chat show...

During the ten-minute interview, Marc Bolan admits he's a 'teenage crush thing' but insists that pop's an art and he a craftsman. He's rich, he says, but all he spends money on are books, records and cars.

He namedrops Victorian poet Lord Tennyson, Hollywood recluse Katharine Hepburn, and 1950s British singer Terry Dene. Once dubbed 'the British Elvis', Dene struggled with bad publicity and later turned his back on fame.

Bolan fiddles constantly with his long, cavalier-style locks. He talks straight but seems oddly defensive. Sometimes, his sincerity gets the better of him. 'If they don't want to listen, crap 'em' he says, laying into his critics. 'I do it because I believe in it. And I'm giving everything I can.'

As Harty draws the interview to a close, he asks his guest to imagine himself at 50 or 60. Bolan's face drops and he shakes his head. 'Never think about it,' he dead-pans. 'I don't think I'll live that long.'

Fame was a lonely place, and Dead Man's Curve was always looming on the horizon. Bolan had learned that from James Dean (killed in a car crash on Mark Feld's eighth birthday), Eddie Cochran (another car accident) and Jimi Hendrix (carelessness with pills and red wine, at a low ebb).

The Harty show appearance coincided with the release of T. Rex's *The Slider*. It was the most eagerly awaited album of 1972, with a title that sounded (to those who understood such things) daringly sexual.

RIGHT: Shot informally during a break in filming for *Born To Boogie* in spring 1972, this image captured Bolan at his most spectral. 'He was a sort of innocent abroad,' says Keith Altham. 'It gave him a very engaging innocence, a childlike perception. He had that in abundance.'

Cover star Marc was the cool cat in the top hat. Each side kicked off with a No. 1 hit: 'Metal Guru' and 'Telegram Sam' respectively. Other songs – 'Rock On', 'Baby Strange' and 'Chariot Choogle' – offered variations on Rex's trademark electric boogie. Triumphalism was in the air and there was much to celebrate.

In a neat visual gag, a reverse shot of the star featured on the rear sleeve. It hinted at the possibility of a quite different take on *The Slider*.

In May, after the album had been completed, *Melody Maker*'s Chris Welch and Michael Watts asked Bolan whether success had changed him. 'Well, I'm still the same little boy I was,' he said. Then his inner adult kicked in. 'You just get sadder. You see more pain and suffering… You end up disliking yourself.'

There was space for that on *The Slider* too. 'It's a pity that I'm like me,' Bolan sang on the wistfully downbeat 'Spaceball Ricochet'. The title track spelled it out more robustly. Album closer 'Main Man' sounded like a requiem to a fallen star, still kicking ('Bolan likes to rock now / Yes he does') but deeply aware that his time as main man was limited. 'It's a song about me,' he said. 'I've never cried so much in my whole life as this last year.'

Even *Jackie* readers weren't spared Bolan's jarring honesty. In a cut-out-and-keep special that itemised his favourite drink (Dom Pérignon), preferred perfumes (Chanel N° 5 and Onyx) and worthiest dish (brown rice), he admitted: 'Of course I have doubts about my own ability. I have doubts about everything.'

Bolan had an open face, looked great in unisex fashions and sang with his heart. Fans believed him. But he was gripped by a mistrust of everything and prone to gaucheries.

While Bowie had been schooled in showbiz etiquette by his PR man father and 'theatrical manager' Ken Pitt, there was no urbane male mentor in Bolan's life. His first lesson in doing business was watching his mother Phyllis work her stall in Soho's Berwick Street market – all fast hands, big voices, territorial disputes and fierce rivalry.

After the departure of Tony Secunda – whose next venture, plotting a comeback by Steve Took, failed miserably – Bolan appointed his wife June's long-time friend Tony Howard as business manager. Howard's first duty was to take orders.

Meanwhile, old friends and associates continued to drift away – from photographer Kieron 'Spud' Murphy to Marc's oldest mate in the business, Jeff Dexter. Even Tony Visconti, master builder of T. Rex's pocket symphonies, had been obliged to take a fifty per cent pay cut before starting work on *The Slider* and was quietly seething about it.

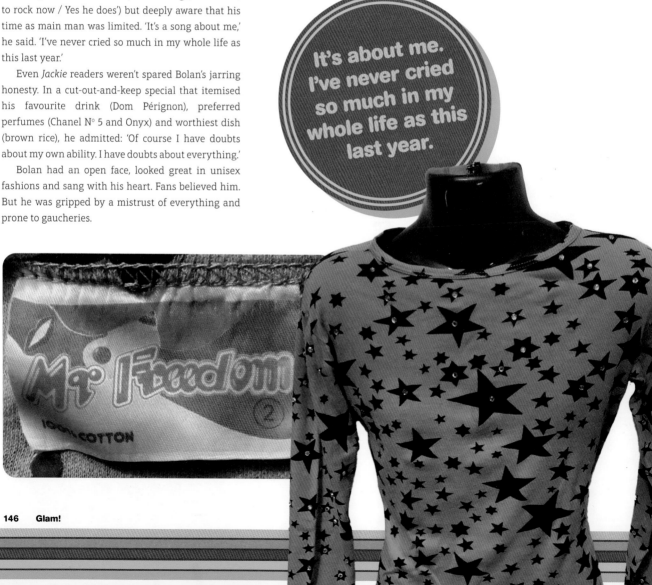

It's about me. I've never cried so much in my whole life as this last year.

Mr Freedom 100% COTTON

CHILDREN OF THE REVOLUTION

Words and Music by MARC BOLAN

Recorded by

T. REX

WIZARD ARTISTS LTD.
sole selling agents
KPM MUSIC GROUP, 21 Denmark Street, Lond

'In 1971, it was like a family,' remembers an insider. 'Before every show, we would form a circle, hold hands and chant.' After a collective whoop, T. Rex would hit the stage running. By summer 1972, the goodwill was ebbing away.

T. Rex were no longer the sole traders in glitter rock and Bolan no longer the lone superstar in the singles chart. Slade and Bowie were on a roll. Rod was a massive personality. And now the younger end of the market had ignited. David Cassidy, The Jackson 5/Michael Jackson and The Osmonds/Donny Osmond, all clean-cut US acts that had long threatened to break big in Britain, were poaching audiences.

In scenes reminiscent of 1967's Monkeemania, each act's arrival at Heathrow was welcomed by crowds of screaming, fainting young girls. To the dailies, they were 'weenyboppers'. To Bolan, whose audience was mostly young and female, they were competition – even if he still pitched himself closer to Dylan and Lennon than Donny and David.

And, indeed, to Shakespeare: 'To Be Or Not To Be, That is *The Slider*,' ran the ad campaign for the new album, released on July 21.

Since 'Metal Guru', however, the antipathy of the rock press had gathered pace. 'Dangerously close to a complete artistic collapse,' was Charles Shaar Murray's damning verdict in *NME*. 'Marc is just not trying.'

The Bolan backlash that gained traction over the spring and summer seemed unduly harsh.

Tyrannosaurus Rex had always existed as outsiders on the rock scene. And while BP Fallon had fed the press headlines during T. Rex's rise, there was never the necessary muscle (sometimes literally) that kept journalists onside for, say, Led Zeppelin.

Part of that was down to Bolan's just-look-at-the-sales-figures arrogance. But there was also something endearingly Heath Robinson-like about his approach to the business of pop.

There was another factor too. The rock press had a new saviour: David Bowie.

Asked in July if he considered Bowie a rival, Bolan was having none of it. 'They said Dave Clark [was] gonna topple The Beatles,' he demurred, 'it's as bullshit as you can possibly get.'

Sales were on his side. *The Slider* hit No. 4 early in August, higher than *Ziggy Stardust* would ever go. But Bolan was spooked. 'All The Young Dudes', released that same week, sounded more like stealing a march than homage to his ears. On a bad day, even the line 'I need TV when I got T. Rex' might have sounded like a threat to poach producer Tony Visconti from him. Besides, Bolan didn't need any pat on the back. He'd already written the year's anthem.

So highly did Bolan value 'Children Of The Revolution' that he wanted the song – featuring Ringo Starr and Elton John – to be a centrepiece of the *Born To Boogie* film. It would be his 'Blue Suede Shoes' or 'My Generation', a song for the times, an inspiration to those sparky high-heeled teenagers who once again were taking their cues from pop.

A studio version of 'Children Of The Revolution', recorded at the Château d'Hérouville in early August, was released on September 8. The riff was heavy, the beat warlike and Bolan's vocal filled with defiance.

BELOW: 'I wasn't allowed to photo Marc Bolan 'cos he and David weren't talking at the time,' said Mick Rock. 'Marc liked my work and wanted to stick his finger up to David. But David wasn't having it. He would have been very upset if I did. That was cute, their dispute! They were young and close for a long time, then something went wrong.'

ZIGGY STARDUST OUTSHINES BOLAN?

DAVID BOWIE AND The Spiders From Mars spun a golden web at the Carnegie Hall. New York's dudes and dudesses had been waiting for this knight in shining armour, and they were not

Linda Solomon, NEW YORK

admitted until well after the appointed hour. So they stood in front of Carnegie and observed

knees. Velvet was all over the place. Sequins galore. Leather and suede. Plus silver lame, golden gauze, floppy feathers, and ridiculously dangerous high platform shoes and boots for both genders, in metallic leather and snakeskins.

A TREND at right should

Even Visconti's signature T. Rex string arrangement sounded more strident than seductive. Reviewers speculated as to the precise nature of Bolan's 'revolution'; no one was entirely sure.

Surprisingly, though hardly catastrophically, it stalled at No. 2. Excepting 'Jeepster', which was released against Bolan's wishes, it was the first time a T. Rex 45 had failed to top the singles chart since 'Ride A White Swan'.

The Slider's chart run didn't portend so well either. By mid-September, with the still rising *Ziggy* hitting No. 6, a perfectly fine T. Rex album dropped out of the top ten.

But Bowie was building more than a lean, mean chart machine. And he had no intention of taking on the world alone. In Manchester on September 2-3 for two shows at the new Hardrock, his manager Tony Defries sat the entourage down for a pep talk before the US tour later that month.

'So far as RCA in America is concerned,' Defries said, 'the man with the red hair at the end of the table is the biggest thing to have come out of England since The Beatles. You've all got to learn how to look and act like a million dollars.'

On September 10, David and Angie Bowie left Southampton on the QE2 bound for New York. The week-long trip was artfully reminiscent of Greta Garbo – the inspiration for Bowie's *Hunky Dory* cover pose – leaving Sweden in 1925 *en route* to Hollywood, where her white-faced mystique introduced a new kind of screen goddess to cinema.

With the Bowies installed in the Plaza Hotel on Fifth Avenue, Defries pulled strings: albums were piled high in record shops; the vast network of local radio was primed; RCA forked out for an entourage of fifty, including a week at the Beverly Hills Hotel.

Defries also set up an office for his new company, MainMan, in New York. Figures from the theatrical cast and crew of Warhol's *Pork*, including Cherry Vanilla and Leee Black Childers, joined the staff and further boosted Bowie's allure.

The tour opened on September 22 at Cleveland's Music Hall. Days later, on September 28, all the heavyweight critics descended on Carnegie Hall. *Melody Maker*'s Ray Hollingworth was there to take the temperature. Standing outside the venue, he overheard the words, 'The sixties are over, well and truly over.'

Lillian Roxon reprised the now familiar *A Star Is Born* theme. Robert Christgau, for *Newsday*, was mostly impressed but wondered if the USA's 'jaded

DOUG CLARK & KDKB PRESENT
DAVID BOWIE

Saturday, Nov. 4 8:30pm
CELEBRITY THEATRE
FORMERLY TRAVELODGE THEATRE IN-THE-ROUND

RESERVED SEAT TICKETS: $3.50, $4.50, $5.50. AVAILABLE AT THE CELEBRITY THEATRE TICKET OFFICE, THOMAS MALL BOX OFFICE, GORDONS CASUALS in Christown, BILL'S RECORDS in Tempe, and ALL COMMUNITY BOX OFFICES. FOR MAIL ORDERS, MAKE CHECK PAYABLE TO CELEBRITY THEATRE, INC. & SEND TO CELEBRITY THEATRE, BOX 5178, PHOENIX 85010.   CELEBRITY PRESENTATIONS, INC.

rock' audiences would appreciate songs about Andy Warhol written by a man they might regard as 'some English fairy'.

The New Yorker's Ellen Willis expressed similar reservations, noting, 'British rock musicians have always been less uptight than Americans about displaying, and even flaunting, their "feminine" side.'

ABOVE: When Bowie returned home in February 1971, after his first visit to the States, wife Angie remembered him complaining about the crime and commercialism he'd witnessed there. In December 1972, having spent three months in the States touring the Ziggy show, Bowie turned up at a press conference – without eyebrows – and had a new twist on the territory: 'America is the loneliest place in the world.' Despite his misgivings, Bowie was winning over the critics, the coasts and Philadelphia.

Despite some critical reservations, Bowie's first US tour was successful enough to warrant being extended from one month to almost three, criss-crossing the States until mid-December.

During November, he hit the coveted cover of *Rolling Stone*. In a piece subtitled 'The Iceman, Having Calculated, Cometh', writer Timothy Ferris characterised Defries as Machiavellian and Bowie as cosseted, talented and – for a rock musician – unusually ambivalent about the direction of his work. 'I'm pretty unstable about my stability as an artist,' he said.

Bowie's lengthy stay in the States was eagerly reported back home. But it had come at great expense – some estimates put the cost at $300,000 – and Bowie's success was by no means assured. Just 250 turned up for a show in Kansas City. Two shows in San Francisco, gay capital of the US, were barely half full.

By the time the tour ended, in mid-December, *Ziggy Stardust* had stalled at No. 88 in the *Billboard* chart. That same week, Elton John's *Honky Château* was at No. 47, down from its chart-topping peak. T. Rex's *The Slider* was still at No. 36, having peaked at 17.

If Bolan was winning the war in terms of record sales, T. Rex's US tour during September and October struggled. For all the razzmatazz surrounding Bowie's visit, the *Ziggy* show was a slick machine, well-rehearsed and tightly structured. As audiences left to the strains of Wendy Carlos' electronic arrangement of Beethoven's 'Ode To Joy', many wondered whether they'd just seen a rock band or an actor in a musical.

But if the theatricality of Bowie's show prompted some happy head-scratching, T. Rex presented critics with a different problem: performances were often regarded as one-dimensional. 'I love the albums,' wrote *Melody Maker*'s US correspondent, Richard Cromelin. '[But] the live T. Rex is a terrible disappointment.'

'Warner Brothers didn't work hard enough,' deflected Mickey Finn, and there was some truth in that. T. Rex's US label was busy riding the Alice Cooper gravy train, while support act The Doobie Brothers – Warners' bright new hope – were far more suited to mainstream US AOR tastes.

Bolan overcompensated with volume and long, muddled versions of his hits. His frustration sometimes boiled over. Drummer Bill Legend vividly recalls a night when 'Marc fell on his knees and banged his fists against a radiator.'

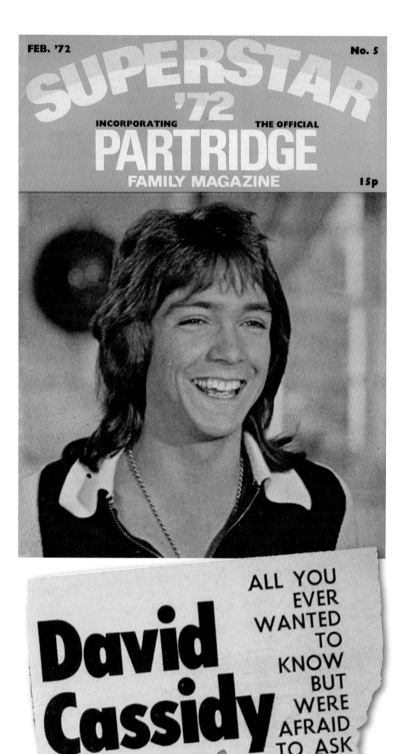

FEB. '72   **No. 5**

SUPERSTAR '72

INCORPORATING THE OFFICIAL

PARTRIDGE FAMILY MAGAZINE

15p

David Cassidy

ALL YOU EVER WANTED TO KNOW BUT WERE AFRAID TO ASK

ABOVE: David Cassidy, another Don Kirshner protégé, shot to fame in 1970 as the singing lead in US TV series *The Partridge Family*.

With Bolan and Bowie away, the British pop charts became even more hotly contested. Slade's 'Mama Weer All Crazee Now', a roaring, daft, brilliant boot up pop's backside, spent three weeks at No. 1 in September. The song that unseated it was an enchanting, soft-focus remake of The Young Rascals' 1967 blue-eyed soul ballad, 'How Can I Be Sure', by David Cassidy.

Cassidy was the archetypal all-American kid in blue jeans, albeit with genuine Hollywood genes and poster-boy looks. His big break had come in 1970, when he won the part of singer Keith Partridge in TV musical sitcom *The Partridge Family* – another Screen Gems production, like *The Monkees*, buttressed by top-notch LA session musicians.

By the end of the year, the Partridges had hit No. 1 in the States with 'I Think I Love You', a breathtaking blend of bubblegum and '67-era Beach Boys vocal arrangement.

Cassidy was key to the series' success and had fronted the hit. No one was surprised when he launched a solo career late in 1971.

His first single, a cover of The Association's 1966 No. 1 'Cherish', hit the US top ten. Meanwhile, *The Partridge Family* began airing in Britain – where an official monthly tie-in magazine was launched. By early 1972, the publication had been incorporated into another glossy A5 magazine titled *Superstar*. Early cover crushes included Cassidy, Ben 'Kid' Murphy from TV Western series *Alias Smith And Jones* – and Marc Bolan.

Cassidy's music was impeccably crafted LA balladry. But in May 1972, he busted out of his Mr Clean image by posing naked on the cover of *Rolling Stone* and spilling the beans on his private life – including suggestions of dope-smoking.

Bell Records chose the moment to launch Cassidy in Britain. The double A-side 'Could It Be

ABOVE: September 10, 1972: Cassidy is seen off at Heathrow Airport by thousands of hysterical fans. Having broken in the States as a solo artist during 1971, he was launched in Britain the following year, quickly becoming a threat to Bolan's dominance in the pin-up magazines.

Forever'/'Cherish' hit No. 2 and – with the *Rolling Stone* story gaining little mileage in Britain – 1972 had its first Mr Clean teen heartthrob.

Cassidy's main competitors were The Jackson 5 and The Osmonds. But as pop's premier pin-up for the past year, Bolan had more to lose than most from the blossoming 'weenybopper' market – certainly more than Bowie.

At the other end of this fast-growing market for pin-ups, glittering stars and feather-cut crowd-pleasers was the act that would knock 'How Can I Be Sure' off its No. 1 perch in October and raise pop's tickled tone a hundredfold.

Forget Gary Glitter. Forget Bowie's six-string fellatio. Forget Steve Priest's butch pouts. Lieutenant Pigeon evoked fancy-dress nights down the local pub. Their 'Mouldy Old Dough' was the novelty hit the times deserved, the 7-inch equivalent of Mr Humphries, the camp character on TV sitcom *Are You Being Served?*, passing himself off as Ziggy Stardust.

Pigeon's unlikely star was 58 year-old Hilda Woodward, a bespectacled Mrs Mills-a-like in a witch's hat rolling out a music-hall melody on upright piano. The instrumental sounded steam-powered, majestic in its minimalism. Occasionally, drummer Nigel Fletcher growled out 'Mouldy old dough!', a gimmick that had listeners keenly awaiting its next arrival.

This was a 'people's band' with a difference, one that sat lightly in the gaping chasm between English music-hall and Fellini-style commedia dell'arte. 'Mouldy Old Dough' spent four weeks at No. 1 and became the second biggest-selling single of the year.

The bona fide satin'n'tat acts also raised the stakes that autumn. On October 8, while Pigeon sat at the apex, Gary Glitter went top-five with 'I Didn't Know I Loved You (Till I Saw You Rock And Roll)'. The man acclaimed by *Disc* for 'sparkling bravely' wasn't going away anytime soon. Neither was the act he'd surpassed on his way up.

'Wig-Wam Bam' was the first Sweet A-side to feature the band as instrumentalists. It was the perfect compromise – a bubblegum single that rocked.

BELOW: Autumn 1972 was a bumper season for big-hitting singles, with Glitter, Slade and The Sweet all consolidating earlier successes. 'Mouldy Old Dough' outdid them all.

Fresh out of hot pants and by now rivalling comedy-sketch eminence Dick Emery as the prince of disguises, Steve Priest didn't disappoint – wearing a full-length American Indian headdress for *Top Of The Pops*. He'd also stepped up in the recording studio, cooing a camp, 'Try a little touch…' before each chorus.

'That was Chapman's idea,' Priest said. 'He knew I'd sung some of our early songs like [Willie Parker's] "You Got Your Finger In My Eye", the more soulful songs which Brian wasn't into. But it was my idea to play it up. It had to be witchypoo.'

Bolan, too, was feeling the magic. During an otherwise restful August, T. Rex spent several days back at the Château, stockpiling songs for a new album. The band also nailed a new single.

'Marc had gone to the control room, and we started doing [this] rhythm,' remembers Bill Legend.

'He came back and said, "Keep going, guys." Within ten minutes, he was back with some words and we recorded it.'

'Solid Gold Easy Action' was a much-needed personal victory for Bolan, proof he could still conjure up a hit from nothing. He even weaved the spirit of the moment into the song: 'Easy as picking foxes from a tree.'

There wasn't much to it: a rockabilly shuffle, a pugilistic 'Hey, hey, hey!' refrain, a threadbare lyric, all over in little more than two minutes. It was – perish the thought – as if Bolan was mocking his critics and all those now upgrading their wardrobe to join what some were now calling pop's 'glamwagon'. Effortlessly dynamic, 'Solid Gold Easy Action' hit No. 2. T. Rex still had the power.

The chorus was built around a lyrical nod to The Rolling Stones' career-changing 1965 hit, '(I Can't Get No) Satisfaction'. Bolan was playing games. Back in May, he'd claimed that the Stones' latest, 'Tumbling

ABOVE: The Sweet performing 'Wig-Wam Bam', *Top Of The Pops*, September 1972. 'We all had a go with that headdress,' says guitarist Andy Scott.

Dice', was ripped off from 'Get It On'. 'They're just not that important anymore,' he'd told *Melody Maker*.

Jagger, still in exile, was having none of it. 'I'm not interested in going back to small English towns and turning on all the ten-year-olds,' he sniffed the following week.

It was a sideshow. Bolan's real beef was far closer to home. Sipping iced white wine in T. Rex's Holborn office, he gave *NME*'s James Johnson a lesson in pop's pecking-order in a piece published on November 11, 1972.

'With no disrespect to David [Bowie], it's much too soon to put him in the same class as me,' he explained, conceding that Slade were more worthy of comparison. 'He's still very much a one-hit wonder, I'm afraid… I've always thought Mott The Hoople were bigger than David.'

Bolan also suggested that Bowie had been 'sucked into something that's unhealthy for him' – the Ziggy Stardust trip into alter ego. 'You can't create an image,' he said. 'It's only what you are.'

Bolan's attitude boiled down to this: 'I believe the ultimate star is the star who makes it just by being themselves.' It was both his strength and his weakness.

James Johnson noted how Bolan seemed 'almost too sensitive to criticism… desperate to defend himself'. There were reasons for that: Bowie was still touring the States; *The Slider* had dropped out of the album chart in October, after eleven weeks; *The Rise And Fall Of Ziggy Stardust…* was well into its year-long run in the top twenty. Most damning of all, Bolan's latest interview barely merited a mention on the cover.

Even Slade's resident ray of sunshine, Dave Hill, was sticking the boot in, telling *Sounds*: 'I like [Bolan's] songs, but there doesn't seem to be much going on as far as the group is concerned.'

The rivalry was real, insists Slade's co-songwriter Jim Lea. 'I'd read this Q&A piece where [Bolan] was asked about the competition. "What competition?" Slade, for instance. "No competition!"'

BELOW: December 1972 saw 'Solid Gold Easy Action' at No. 2 and Bolan's film, *Born To Boogie*, in cinemas. The single, written in a matter of minutes, was a personal victory for Bolan. The film, a 67-minute Bolan love-in, was cherished by fans, though critics were less convinced.

40 pages – still 6p

DISC

NOVEMBER 11, 1972   6p   USA 30c

Marc Bolan

The slaggers strike, but he's not dead yet!

David Cassidy

to quit Partridge TV?

Jackson Five

another British date this month

'That got my back up and I was gunning for him. But it was a bit like Richard the Lionheart and Saladin. You respected the man on the other side. You knew they were good.'

Over December 22-23, T. Rex played three Christmas shows in London. The lights flashed 'Rexmas', fake snow filled the venues – and thousands of hysterical fans were still capable of drowning out the band.

On the 'Solid Gold Easy Action' B-side, Bolan wished fans a 'super-funk Christmas and a golden new year' before new song 'Born To Boogie' trailered the long-awaited film of that same title. It hit selected screens in London on December 18.

The reviews were poor. Within weeks of the premiere, director Ringo Starr was pleading for forgiveness. 'It's not like *A Hard Day's Night*,' he told *Record Mirror*. 'This took three days to make. *A Hard Day's Night* took ten weeks!'

Born To Boogie was a sixty-seven-minute Bolan love-in. Had it been released six months earlier, with its 'comic' interludes reined in, it may well have sustained Bolanmania a little longer.

But much had happened since the summer – as confirmed in the end-of-year music press polls. One artiste had made a virtual clean sweep – and that was Bowie. He too, though, was experiencing rivalry issues, from an unexpected quarter.

The latest Bowie single, 'The Jean Genie', looked a dead cert to give him his first No. 1. Instead, on January 27, 1973, he was pipped by a song featuring the very same staccato guitar riff – 'Blockbuster!' by The Sweet.

Bowie could hardly have claimed it as his own. The riff, standard fare for 1960s R&B acts, had been utilised by The Yardbirds for their 1965 hit 'I'm A Man' – an intense take on the mid-fifties Bo Diddley original. But how two high-profile singles bearing the same riff came to be released by the same record label (RCA) within a week of each other was a mystery.

Bowie had written 'The Jean Genie' during the first days of the US tour. With his howling, Stones-like harmonica and Mick Ronson's dirty chording, the new single was tense, trashy and strangely mythic – as befitting its main inspiration, Iggy Pop.

Sundown

SILVER STREET, EDMONTON, N. 18.

EVENING 8-0 p.m.
FRIDAY, 22nd DECEMBER, 1972
T. REX

ARENA
£1·25   2124

Cameras & Tape Recorders are not allowed in the Auditorium.

For conditions of sale see over

Gay rock, whitewashed soul and bubblegum

...AND THAT WAS THE SOUND OF 1972

HE dearth
ingles this
eviewer
Holloway
ack over
of hot and
hot licks.
the verdict:

'l be marked
od of transi-
e history of

e glam rock,
lack music
attempt to
h itself in
of sophisti-
) soul. Bub-
tayed. And
5's did bet-
ness than
as a mixed-

> I was gunning for him. It was a bit like Richard The Lionheart and Saladin.

The Sweet recorded 'Blockbuster!' on November 1, time enough for them to have heard 'The Jean Genie', mixed in the States in mid-October. Then again, Steve Priest insisted that Mike Chapman had sprung the song on the band backstage at *Top Of The Pops* as early as September.

On January 20, 1973, with both songs in the top three, it was Bowie's turn to warm the guest's chair on Russell Harty's show. He'd changed again – just as he'd done at the start of the previous year. This makeover was at least as shocking.

Now stick-thin, his eyebrows shaved off, his face pastier than Warhol's (albeit with rouged cheeks), Bowie wore a dangly glass earring from one ear and a pair of what he called '3-D shoes' on his feet. He giggled nervously, as if Ziggy had stepped out of the song and 'came on so loaded, man'.

The audience giggled nervously too. No one, probably not even Bowie himself, could now be sure whether Bolan's warning about his persona sucking him 'into something unhealthy' was catty invective or simply good advice.

'It's not at all real,' said Bowie/Ziggy. 'It's all a total fantasy.

FACING PAGE: While the rock weeklies continued to write Bolan off, T. Rex's London Christmas shows were joyous affairs packed with screamers and fainters. Behind the scenes, Bolan had new plans for 1973. 'I want it to be the year I diversify.'

LEFT: Quite how The Sweet and David Bowie emerged with new singles at the turn of the year, both bearing the same staccato guitar riff and issued on the same label, has never been fully explained. On January 27, 1973, 'Blockbuster!' pipped 'The Jean Genie' to the top spot.

Chapter 15
The Powder-Puff Bandwagon

January 6, 1973: *Record Mirror* was sharing its 'New Year Pop Predictions'. 'Is Marc on the way out?' 'Is this the end for Alice Cooper?' posited the music paper.

'It looks like it's getting back to the days of conveyor belt pop,' said The Moody Blues' Justin Hayward. 'I hope that only real talent, like David Bowie, will become prominent.'

'Bowie's got it all sussed,' reckoned Status Quo's Francis Rossi. 'He's such a weird human being but he looks so good.'

MANUFACTURER AND THE OWNER OF THE RECORDED WORK RESERVED. UNAUTHORISED PUBLIC PERFORMANCE, BROADCASTING AND COPYING OF THIS RECORD

THIS IS A SNEEKY EARFUL OF A TRACK FROM THE NEXT SLADE ALBUM 'SLAYED' (POLYDOR 2383 163) GIVEN TO YOU BY MUSIC SCENE NOVEMBER ISSUE 1972

SLADE

33⅓ rpm

THE WHOLE WORLD'S GOING CRAZY

COMPOSED BY HOLDER
PUBLISHED BY BARN MUSIC
PRODUCED BY CHAS CHANDLER
FOR BARN PRODUCTIONS—

David Bowie
25p

The full exciting story of pop's newest superstar.

Pages of exclusive pictures.

Free Poster Inside

a Record Mirror special

POPSWOP
January 6 1973 No14   5p

MICHAEL JACKSON ROD & THE FACES BEN MURPHY NEW SEEKERS they're all here in gorgeous colour

ARE YOU DATING A DOUBLE? meet the girls who are! Inside!

RECOGNISE THOSE EYES? KNOW THAT NOSE? try our GUESS WHO quiz 'n' see

PLUS! loads of Songwords... Pop Gossip... and Fun!

The Sweet's Brian Connolly anticipated more success for Bowie, Slade and Gary Glitter – though his big pick was Junior Campbell, the onetime Marmalade keyboard man who'd had a recent hit with 'Hallelujah Freedom'.

Judge Dread, whose very rude-boy white reggae 45s were banned from the airwaves, predicted that Slade and T. Rex would be gone in six months. 'They just turn out the same rhythm,' he belched.

And *Record Mirror*'s first cover star of 1973?

Marc Bolan. He was still big enough to sell the issue, even if the year's predictions on the back page queried whether his career was ending.

The magazine was also busily promoting a spin-off publication, *The David Bowie Story* – a 28-page colour special 'on the life and times of pop's newest superstar'.

Another plug introduced readers to *Easy Listening*, the latest addition to the magazine racks, aimed at lovers of 'middle of the road music'.

Pop in all its various shades was booming. Even Gilbert O'Sullivan, who'd ditched Depression-era thrift-wear for bigger hair and chunky jumpers, was now deemed starry enough for the covers of recent newsstand additions *Popswop* and *Music Scene*.

But the real tempo for the year had already been set by the chart battle between The Sweet's 'Blockbuster!' and Bowie's 'The Jean Genie'. It was billed as a clear-cut case of 'gum hit-machine versus The Artist.

Bowie resented being dragged into the face-off, though he reputedly called Nicky Chinn a 'cunt' for stealing a march on his song of subversion – accentuated by the title's allusion to a voice from the margins, author Jean Genet.

On *The Russell Harty Show*, Bowie blithely ignored the contest and instead premiered a new song, 'Drive-In Saturday'. It was the same week that 'Blockbuster!' leapfrogged 'The Jean Genie', going on to spend five weeks at No. 1 through to the end of February.

The song was a watershed moment for The Sweet – their first No. 1 and a milestone in the battle for Chinn and Chapman to recognise the band's rock-star ambitions. 'The group is

more convinced now that they're breaking out of the narrow rut they were trapped in,' reported *Record Mirror*'s Val Mabbs.

Mike Chapman's starting point for a song was usually the title, and 'Blockbuster!' marked a clear break with the past. The music was pitched perfectly too, a full-on pop melodrama that allowed the band to display their tougher selves – and their own well-worked backing vocals. But there were still niggles.

When Mick Tucker suggested adding a thumping kettledrum interlude, there was some disapproval in the studio. Steve Priest remembered Mike Chapman stepping in: 'He said, "They're the band. Let them put their own personality into it." He was on our side.'

The song was a production triumph. The scene-setting siren, the suspenseful rhythm

It was billed as a clear-cut case of 'gum hit-machine versus The Artist.

RIGHT: The Sweet's Brian Connolly turned on the melodrama for 'Blockbuster!', especially for its long, maniacal fade. He also toughened up his look for *Top Of The Pops* with a pair of black gloves offsetting his monogrammed satin jacket. 'Blockbuster!' was The Sweet's first No. 1 hit.

ABOVE: 'It had a different edge
to it,' says Andy Scott of The
Sweet's new sound. 'The guitars
were right up front, and the
drums had that bang-on-the-floor
tom sound. We'd found our feet.'

and tipsy guitar chording, the neo-psychedelic cries
of 'Blockbuster!' climaxing in a spinetingling 'Buster,
Buster… Blockbuster!' fade.

Pop's fastest-growing hit factory, now commonly
known as 'Chinnichap', had flipped the recipe. With
'Blockbuster!', The Sweet took one giant leap into a
feverish, seductive, slightly dangerous kind of pop music
– just as the term 'glam rock' was gaining currency.

The band had sorted out their wardrobe, too. On
the January 25, 1973 edition of *Top Of The Pops*, they
celebrated 'Blockbuster!' hitting No. 1 in style. Brian
Connolly toughened up his look with black gloves and
a silver monogrammed jacket. Mick Tucker sparkled
at the huge kettledrums. Andy Scott poked his tongue

out whenever he found the camera. Steve Priest
sported bright red lipstick and wildly exaggerated,
Clockwork Orange-style eyelashes.

Best of all, for the second hit running, Priest
had made one of his brief but unforgettable vocal
cameos. 'We just haven't got a clue what to do!' he
squealed, while fanning his hand over his face. It was
in deliciously bad taste, far more a case of lads at a
fancy-dress party than the dissolute, Factory-style
look Bowie adapted for his Ziggy Stardust persona.

Now The Sweet waltzed through the teen-
pop media with confidence. Brian Sweet was the
romantic, easy-going one; Andy Sweet was the
enigmatic one who let his guitar do the talking; Mick

Sweet was the all-smiling Mr Nice Guy; and, despite his outrageousness on TV, Steve Sweet was quiet and reserved. Now they could speak about their music in earnest.

The makeover didn't convince everyone. As 'Blockbuster!' climbed the chart, The Sweet played an industry showcase at – of all places – Ronnie Scott's in Soho, home of the British jazz scene.

'The worst group performance to be allowed on stage since the discovery of electricity,' reckoned NME's Nick Kent. Chris Welch in Melody Maker was more forgiving, commending the band's guts and energy.

At one point during the set, singer Connolly appealed to the invited audience of media assassins. 'You'll have to help us out,' he said, requesting a singalong. 'We're not used to this. We're used to screamers…'

★

On the windy Sunday afternoon of January 14, 1973, Gary Glitter stood on the deck of chartered riverboat the Sloop John B. With the assistance of six young women in fishnet stockings and DJ Alan 'Fluff' Freeman, he lowered a sequin-studded coffin into the Thames. Inside, so reporters were told, were his old Paul Raven records and publicity photos. Glitter was burying his past.

BACKSIDE
(Strawbs)

Side 2
STEREO
12 396 AT
12 396-B
STEMRA
Made in Holland

CIGGY BARLUST &
THE WHALES FROM VENUS
Produced by Strawbs
Engineered by Tom Allom

ABOVE LEFT: Gary Glitter began 1973 by lowering a coffin filled with all his pre-fame records into the River Thames. The publicity stunt was hardly necessary. Glitter's first single of the year, 'Do You Wanna Touch Me? (Oh Yeah!)', was another top-three triumph of massed, terrace-style chants over a thick vibrato sound.

ABOVE RIGHT: Over the winter, folk rockers The Strawbs were one of several unlikely acts to sparkle up on *Top Of The Pops*. But only they braved having a pop at the whole glittering scene, releasing a song titled 'Backside' credited to Ciggy Barlust & The Whales From Venus. Bowie had once performed a mime to one of their songs on BBC2's *Colour Me Pop*.

'That's Paul Raven all over,' he joked. 'Always sank to the bottom.'

Glitter had emerged from 1972 in good standing. With just two hits behind him, he scored highly in the polls. 'Rock And Roll Part 2' had outflanked every T. Rex and Slade single in the official end-of-year chart poll – though Chicory Tip's 'Son Of My Father' and 'Mouldy Old Dough' by Lieutenant Pigeon fared better still.

Just as belly-laugh comedy had prevailed in the 1972 TV schedules – from the enormously popular *On The Buses* to self-deprecating king of camp innuendo Larry Grayson – so too had the fun side of pop.

By January 1973, Glitter was hitting the stage via a long moveable staircase, dressed in a huge cloak with a collar made from ostrich feathers. This wasn't exhibitionism with a wry smile; it was a full-blown panto night with large helpings of self-parody. Apart from a few rock press snipers, no one even minded that Glitter was approaching 30. If anything, it added to the preposterous, stiff-limbed incongruity of his act.

By early February, his 'Do You Wanna Touch Me (Oh Yeah!)' was installed at No. 2, right behind 'Blockbuster!'. The musical blueprint he'd established with Mike Leander was now proving addictive.

'Gary Glitter has virtually revolutionised pop music,' wrote *Record Mirror*'s Charles Webster. 'He's put stomp into pop and chanting into singing and has turned a lot of people on to the *heyeyey* sound.'

This was Webster's way of introducing a piece on The Strawbs, prog-inclined folkies, whose latest 45, 'Part Of The Union', was said to incorporate 'a Glitterish approach'. That single – 'a gentle knock at the trade unions,' said co-writer John Ford – marked a 'decision to go in for a bit of rock and rouge, glam and glitter, a little bit of sparkle,' noted Webster. The move had already prompted sell-out catcalls.

The Strawbs, who'd shared bills with Bowie in 1969 during his Arts Lab days, had already dipped a toe in 'glam and glitter' on the B-side of their previous hit, 'Lay Down'. The song, 'Backside', was credited to Ciggy Barlust & The Whales From Venus.

It was hardly The Strawbs' finest moment, given the innuendo-laden lyric plus the fact that one or two of them slapped on blue eyeshadow – with unflattering results – when promoting the A-side.

But if going glam was a strategy to improve the prospects of a band not known for its visual flair, it was clear that a shift was taking place right across the pop spectrum. *Music Scene* had a phrase for it: 'The Powder-Puff Bandwagon'.

Inevitably, Mick Jagger led the way, stepping out in a silver tiara, a silk sash and a glittering blue jump suit at a fundraiser gig at the LA Forum in January. Back in the UK, The Sensational Alex Harvey Band were in the process of going full-on vaudeville, with guitarist Zal Cleminson slapping sinister clown makeup over his face. Even The Osmonds went in for Vegas jump suits.

But there was no one more perfectly poised to join the powdery frolics than Roy Wood. Wood, who donned a wig for Dusty Springfield impressions during his Birmingham club days, had been bringing costume drama to the small screen virtually every season since January 1967.

When he went full harlequin in March 1970 to promote The Move's 'Brontosaurus', even his bandmates were shocked. 'We had no idea that Roy was gonna turn up wearing all this makeup,' says drummer Bev Bevan. 'It was as if this madman had suddenly appeared on stage with us.'

Roy Wood was significantly more than pop's gentle jester. With more than a dozen hit singles to his name, he was also the era's finest one-man hit factory and,

It was as if this madman had suddenly appeared on stage with us.

LEFT: 'There's no way he could go on stage as Roy Wood,' says Wizzard's Mr Bassman Rick Price. 'He was absolutely petrified without his makeup on.'

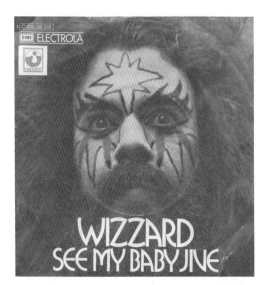

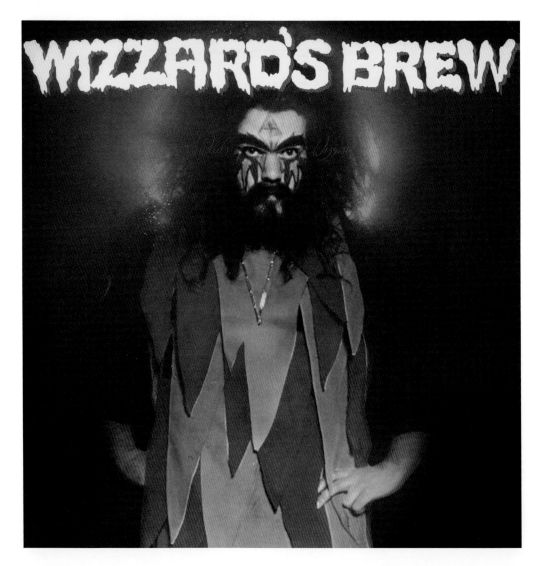

ABOVE: 'We had two double drum kits, two sax players, two cellists,' remembers Roy Wood. 'I thought, "What can we do with that? Phil Spector might be pretty good..."' Wood's vast production job on 'See My Baby Jive', which also included vocal backing from The Suedettes – alias Rick Price and *Lift Off* host Ayshea – gave Wizzard their first No. 1. 'It's just a good-time rock'n'roll number,' he said.

RIGHT: Wood's characteristic eclecticism was all over Wizzard's debut album, a heady mix of jazz, classic, hard rock and rock'n'roll. Titled *Wizzard Brew* in Britain, where it went top-thirty, in the States it featured a different cover and modified title.

FACING PAGE: Encouraged by the success of 'Blockbuster!' Chinnichap and The Sweet went all out for 'Hell Raiser', a sort of glam rock answer to Steppenwolf's 'Born To Be Wild'.

according to Tony Visconti, 'one of the cleverest people in British rock'. He changed styles so often and came up with so many new ideas that it wasn't easy to keep up with him.

That same year, he'd also formed Electric Light Orchestra with Bevan and Move latecomer Jeff Lynne as a vent for his classical rock fusion ambitions. It was a long time coming. Once talks of a tie-in film foundered, a debut album appeared in December 1971, followed by '10538 Overture', a summer 1972 hit single. But soon afterwards, Wood's partnership with Lynne, which had seemed such a golden prospect, soured.

'We didn't mix very well to be quite honest,' said Wood. Musically, Lynne favoured piano and Wood wind instruments. Personally, Wood was inclined to walk rather than face up to any conflict over musical differences.

By early 1973, Wood's Wizzard and the Lynne-led ELO were both onboard for the rock'n'roll nostalgia trip. ELO went route one with a Beethoven's Fifth-enriched update of Chuck Berry's 'Roll Over Beethoven'.

Wizzard's 'Ball Park Incident' was a brassy production reminiscent of Lloyd Price's 1959 hit 'Stagger Lee', with a *West Side Story*-like narrative about a girl gunned down in a baseball ground. It was quintessential Roy Wood – big band rock'n'roll couched in a Phil Spector Wall of Sound, with an added dollop of chaos. Both Wizzard and ELO hit No. 6 in the singles chart.

ELO had their sights firmly set on the States. Wood rolled with the Christmas-all-year-round spirit that was now gripping pop. His ambition for Wizzard was, he said, to be a seventies version of Lord Rockingham's XI, the resident big band on late fifties pop show *Oh Boy!* The band's debut album, *Wizzard Brew*, released in the spring, took that idea and ran with it, mixing jazz, classical and hard rock with rock'n'roll. While baffling reviewers, the album briefly hit the top thirty in May.

Despite his bigger ambitions, Roy Wood's gift was writing hit singles. On May 19, 1973, 'See My Baby Jive' – even more Spector, even more rock'n'roll, even more clowning around on *TOTP* – gave Wizzard a No. 1 for four weeks, seeing off competition from both Gary Glitter ('Hello! Hello! I'm Back Again') and The Sweet ('Hell Raiser').

'Hell Raiser' – more metallic intensity with a hard-rocking mid-section – hit No. 2, but The Sweet were already looking beyond singles. 'Mick Tucker and me were certainly getting a bit more mouthy by early 1973,' says Andy Scott.

The band had also found new management, with a view to trying their luck in the States. Meanwhile, Brian Connolly was telling the press about The Sweet's first proper LP project.

'The album's going to start at 1956 with a song that'll be like a Presley,' he told *Record Mirror*'s Rick Sanders. 'Then it'll change to a Little Richard sort of song, and so on, through the years.' The projected concept album, covering the history of rock and pop music, would end, he said, with 'a futuristic number for 1976'.

The Sweet were on a roll. But Connolly had just one reservation. 'I could do without "Hell Raiser" coming out just at the moment,' he said. 'A little breathing space would have been nice.'

Chapter 16
Trouble at the Fantasy Factory

During the three-week run of 'School's Out' at No. 1 in August 1972, Alice Cooper whipped up the *Top Of The Pops* crowd with an exhibition of roaring, sword-wielding malevolence. Not since devil-faced Arthur Brown screamed 'Fire!' with a burning crown on his head, back in 1968, had pop witnessed anything quite like this.

'School's Out' was every teenager's perfect summer holiday singalong. Cleanup campaigner Mary Whitehouse, founder of the National Viewers' and Listeners' Association, dutifully denounced the song as 'violent' and 'anarchic', and demanded the BBC stop giving 'gratuitous publicity to a record which can only be described as anti-law and order.'

'Millions of young people are now imbibing a philosophy of violence and anarchy,' she said. 'This is surely utterly irresponsible in a social climate which grows ever more violent.'

'We sent her flowers!' band namesake vocalist Cooper remembers. 'The more they banned us, the more the records just went crazy. We sold out Wembley in a second. And we delivered, that was the thing.'

Alice Cooper categorically won over the British rock press with a sensational June 30 appearance at the Empire Pool, Wembley, which brought the curtain – and the blade – down on the controversy-packed *Killer* tour. 'Cool Ghoul' was just one of many approving headlines.

In a two-page *Melody Maker* spread entitled 'Beauty And The Beast', Alice seized the moment. 'There's got to be more theatre,' he argued. 'Groups have to go out and form an image. The Beatles had an image, the Stones had an image…'

During autumn and winter 1972, the Alice Cooper band were back in the States and planning an even more elaborate theatre-rock extravaganza. Cooper had often claimed the band's performances were a blend of *West Side Story* and *A Clockwork Orange*. 'Cheap, vulgar and mean as hell,' he'd say. And everyone in the band had a role to play. But now came the twist.

FACING PAGE: 'We were sending Mary Whitehouse flowers for banning us!' says Alice. 'We were sending [Labour MP] Leo Abse cigars. The more they hated us, and the more they banned us, the more the records went crazy.'

LEFT: Early copies of the 1972 *School's Out* album came with a free pair of knickers. Alice claimed he hated underwear and refused to wear any.

Dennis Dunaway, bassist and Vince 'Alice' Furnier's friend since schooldays, could sense change. 'It seemed as if [manager Shep Gordon] decided it was time to throw all that out and go for making Alice a household name,' he states in his memoir.

It was a process that had been going on since early 1971, when Alice was sent out to do the lion's share of the *Love It To Death* album publicity alone. It worked, so no one questioned it. Besides, the band members welcomed time off from the endless gigging.

'It was the hardest work we ever did,' says Alice, 'but it was paying off. We were indestructible. I was with my best friends. We were getting rich. Everything was perfect. Even the hard times were perfect.'

The band decided to draw on everything that had happened to them since for the latest album project: *Billion Dollar Babies*. 'We wrote the songs around the concept of wealthy brats who could do anything they wanted,' wrote Dunaway.

LEFT: When Alice Cooper arrived at the *Top Of The Pops* studio to film 'School's Out' – one of the era's key performances – the singer was told he couldn't use the snake. The boa constrictor had to be kept locked in the band's dressing-room.

RIGHT: *The Sunday Telegraph* predictably denounced Alice Cooper as 'like a cross between Rasputin and Bela Lugosi'. *Melody Maker* was sniffy about the Wembley show too: 'He looks like a middle-aged Soho tart with ladders in her tights.' The overwhelming view was that it was a gloriously gory triumph.

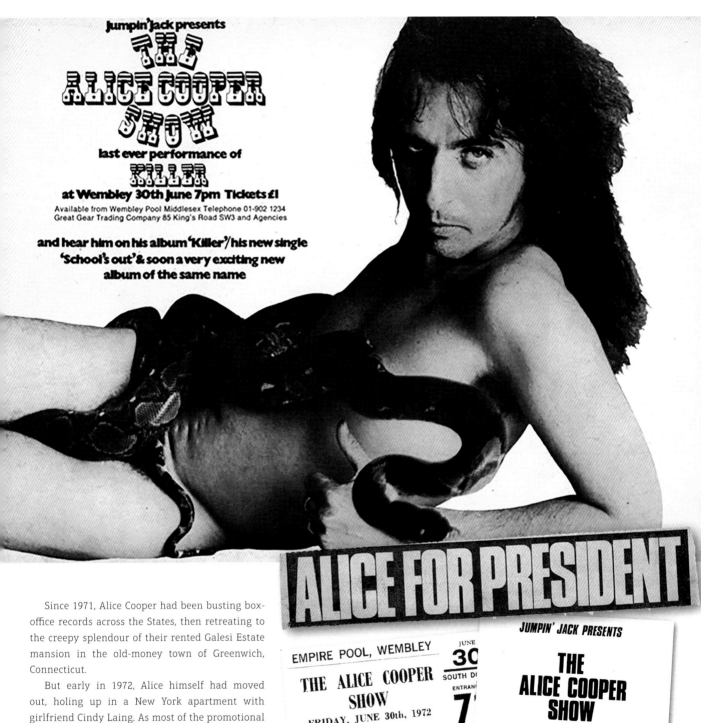

jumpin' jack presents

THE ALICE COOPER SHOW

last ever performance of

KILLER

at Wembley 30th June 7pm Tickets £1

Available from Wembley Pool Middlesex Telephone 01-902 1234
Great Gear Trading Company 85 King's Road SW3 and Agencies

and hear him on his album 'Killer'/his new single
'School's out' & soon a very exciting new
album of the same name

ALICE FOR PRESIDENT

Since 1971, Alice Cooper had been busting box-office records across the States, then retreating to the creepy splendour of their rented Galesi Estate mansion in the old-money town of Greenwich, Connecticut.

But early in 1972, Alice himself had moved out, holing up in a New York apartment with girlfriend Cindy Laing. As most of the promotional work was being done in New York, once again it made good sense.

By August, a mobile studio was set up in the mansion's driveway and the house wired up for early sessions for the new album. There was just one problem: booze was laying waste to lead guitarist Glen Buxton's talents.

EMPIRE POOL, WEMBLEY

THE ALICE COOPER SHOW

FRIDAY, JUNE 30th, 1972
at 7 p.m.
Doors open at 6.30 p.m.

SOUTH GRAND TIER

£1.00

TO BE RETAINED   See conditions on back

JUMPIN' JACK PRESENTS

THE
ALICE COOPER
SHOW

Glen put cigarette ash under his eyes to make himself look dark and diabolical.

'All the group were heterosexual, beer swilling, all American guys,' fellow guitarist Michael Bruce later wrote in his memoir. But Glen was playing it too hard.

'Glen was the Charles Bukowski of the group,' says producer Bob Ezrin, 'hard drinking, hard living, curmudgeonly, anti-social, anti-government, anti-everything. But underneath it all, he was the sweetest, kindest, gentlest person who was just hoping that people would like him.'

Glen was the band member who'd led the others in terms of musical proficiency; he was also the one, says Cindy Smith, 'who'd put cigarette ash under his eyes to make himself look dark and diabolical'.

'He smashed the guitar on "Sick Things",' says Dennis Dunaway, 'but it was the only thing he played on [*Billion Dollar Babies*].'

As work progressed, later moving to The Record Plant in New York, session musicians were called in – guitarists Steve Hunter, Dick Wagner and Mick Mashbir, plus keyboard player Bob Dolin. Hunter handled most of the guitar solos.

Had Buxton been able to contribute more, *Billion Dollar Babies* might have been Alice Cooper's answer to the Stones' *Exile On Main St.* – a free-wheeling affair from battle-scarred musicians let off the leash, successful enough to take their audience in whichever direction they wanted.

Bob Ezrin had other ideas. This time, he took an even more controlled approach than usual, applied more polish – and delivered the band's masterpiece.

After 'All The Young Dudes', Mott The Hoople were obliged to confront the gnarly matter of stardom and leadership.

When Mott the Hoople takes the stage, there's bound to be a commotion. The headline excitement and energy of their month-long tour of 14 major cities have been blowing audiences out of their seats and making them scream for more. And here's more. "Mott."

It's the audacious new Hoople, who brought you "All The Young Dudes." Featuring "All The Young Dudes", "Honaloochie Boogie," "Hymn for the Dudes," Mott the Hoople," Mott is glittering outrageous, driving Hoople-philes wild.

Diary of a rock'n'roll star
ian hunter
Lead Singer for
mott the hoople

On December 10, 1972, while both Mott and David Bowie were touring the States, Ian Hunter paid Bowie an early-hours visit to his suite in New York's Warwick Hotel. Bowie played him 'Drive-In Saturday'. There had been a suggestion it should be Mott's next single, but Hunter thought it sounded too complicated.

In *Diary Of A Rock'n'Roll Star*, his memoir of the tour, Hunter recalls that Bowie dressed in loose-fitting Japanese trousers with clogs. He radiated positivity, seemed entirely comfortable with stardom and was getting back into the saxophone. *Lenny Bruce Live At Carnegie Hall* was on the turntable.

Hunter's own feelings on the fame game were all over the place. 'Fuck stardom,' he wrote in his

LEFT: 'The snake was easy,' says Alice, 'it was very gentle. It wasn't in any way as dangerous as the guillotine.'

ABOVE: Ian Hunter's *Diary Of A Rock'n'Roll Star* was a sobering account of five weeks on the road in the States over the winter of 1972.

MOTT SHOCK ALLEN QUITS

Hoople to continue as four piece

HOOPLE QUITS

ORGANIST VERDEN Allen has quit Mott The Hoople. He is not being replaced. Mott are to carry on as a four-piece. They played their first gig with the depleted line-up at Cheltenham last week. Allen left the group because Hunter and Mick Ralphs are writing the majority of Mott's material and Allen felt there wouldn't be scope in the band for his songs. Founder-member Allen, the MM understands, wants to develop as a singer and work in a band that is more organ-based.

ABOVE: Given their origins at the tail end of the underground scene, Mott's pop success during 1972 prompted some soul-searching. Keyboard player Verden Allen decided to quit in the new year, leaving Mott to work on their next album as a four-piece.

diary afterwards. Days later, on a plane to Texas, he spotted Tony Defries up in First Class. 'Perhaps he's thinking of how he's going to make us stars,' he wrote hopefully. 'I want to be a star,' he continued, 'but I keep thinking we're just ordinary blokes and we don't have the killer instinct.'

Then, right on cue, in another case of Mott's characteristic bad luck, the Texas gigs were cancelled.

Back in Britain, Hunter reflected on something Bowie had told him; that for Mott to succeed in any meaningful way, he needed to take control of the band. But first, the band needed to assert its own independence.

'David insisted that Defries manage us but he had his hands full,' Hunter says. 'If David wanted an elephant outside Harrods at nine in the morning, it was there.'

'We were getting bigger, but David was meteoric. There was a parting on the business side of things.'

The success of 'All The Young Dudes' had brought an illusion of unity to Mott. But by January 1973 cracks were showing. After an onstage row,

keyboardist Verden Allen played his last gig on January 19 at Sheffield University. Allen wasn't keen on the new association with glitzy pop – though his songs weren't getting much of a look-in either.

Hunter's call to capitalise on what the band had achieved was heeded. Sessions for a new album in April revealed a focused, confident-sounding Mott, though the lyrics often told a different story.

'Ballad Of Mott The Hoople' revealed a continuing ambivalence to fame. 'Hymn For The Dudes' included what seemed to be a coded message to the band's mentor ('You ain't the Nazz / You're just a buzz'). Album opener 'All The Way From Memphis' was the keynote song, steaming into the vicissitudes of fame while sounding like a love-letter to early rock'n'roll.

Mott was packaged for success – its die-cut gatefold sleeve boldly featuring the head of Roman emperor Augustus on the inner laminate. Released in July, it was the band's best-performing album to date, peaking at No. 7. Its first single, 'Honaloochie Boogie' featuring Roxy Music's Andy Mackay on sax, may have been a little tame by the band's standards but only narrowly missed the top ten.

Still, Mott remained uneasy. 'The only thing that pisses us off a bit about [Status] Quo,' said bassist Overend Watts, 'is that people say, "Isn't it great to see a band up on stage rock'n'rolling like that?" But that's what we got off on in the early days… We were the working class heroes.'

HONALOOCHIE BOOGIE

Words and Music by IAN HUNTER

Recorded on CBS Records by

MOTT THE HOOPLE

LAND MUSIC LIMITED, 155/157 Oxford Street, London, W.1.
le selling agents:
USIC SALES LIMITED, 78 Newman Street, London, W.1.

20p

Seadivers

Kris Needs on Running the Mott The Hoople Fan Club

ABOVE: Seadivers fan club secretaries Kris Needs and girlfriend Caroline Bain in AIR Studios, London, 1973, listening to a playback of the *Mott* album. 'It pissed all over the *Dudes* album,' Needs remembers.

FACING PAGE: 'I designed the membership card,' says Needs. 'Angie Bowie had this idea that we'd blow up balloons with the fan club address on and fling them over the balcony at the Rainbow. But blowing them up fell to me and I was already manning the stall.'

When I was 10, in 1964, I joined The Rolling Stones fan club. A few years later, I joined the Jimi Hendrix fan club. It was great getting all those newsletters and photos through the post.

I first saw Mott at [Aylesbury's] Friars Club in December 1969, then again a week later at my school's sixth form dance. I was too young to be allowed in so the band smuggled me in and I watched from under a table. I followed them around after that. That's how I met [future Clash guitarist] Mick Jones.

By May '72, Mott had hooked up with Bowie and MainMan. Bowie's fan club had started in Aylesbury when a local girl, Hilda Williams, got MainMan's backing. She enlisted me to design the membership card. Then we had an idea: instead of me helping with Bowie's fan club, why didn't I start one for Mott?

Hilda asked Tony Defries, and I was summoned to the MainMan office where I was grilled by Stan Tippins, the former Mott singer turned road manager.

By the time I got the call, 'Dudes' had taken off, so I went back to MainMan, got loaded up with an itinerary, interviewed the band and had them fill in questionnaires.

I was a nervous 17-year-old, naturally shy, and here I was talking to David Bowie and Mott The Hoople. They were all so nice. I think they realised this frightened rabbit sitting in front of them was totally into the band and wasn't gonna screw up.

Angie Bowie decided she was going to help me. She suggested I had a stall when Bowie played the Rainbow. I had a membership form – it was 50p to join – and membership cards printed up. I never got paid for any of this!

MOTT THE HOOPLE

SEA-DIVERS

Secretaries – Kris Needs and Caroline Bain, 53, Richmond Road, Aylesbury, Bucks.

Then I took an ad out in the rock press classifieds. It didn't get much response, so someone came up with the idea of writing a letter to the NME. I would complain about the lack of Mott coverage and put the fan club address at the bottom. It worked.

When I'd go to MainMan, Defries would always be on the phone, sometimes three at a time. I barely got a grunt. Stuey George, Bowie's bodyguard, would give me the photos and stuff for the Mott club [called Seadivers after 'Sea Diver' on the Dudes album].

Once Bowie got really big, Mott started writing and recording on their own. I was there with my girlfriend Caroline at a playback for Mott in AIR Studios. That was such a landmark album during that whole glam period. They put my address on the back and the membership went up.

It went up even more after the December '73 show at Hammersmith Odeon. That was probably Mott's peak. It was never huge – we never topped a thousand. But they were devoted fans who liked to write letters. One was Steven Morrissey from Stretford. He'd write about once a week. He'd talk about the lyrics, about that track 'Whizz Kid', and say he'd sit and play Mott for hours. I'd always write back.

Another member was Benazir Bhutto. She was studying at Lady Margaret Hall, Oxford. One day she turned up at the front door with a mate. I think they were hoping to find a funky MainMan-style office. Instead, they got me and my mum! Next time I saw her name she was Prime Minister of Pakistan.

The perks were great. I could turn up to a gig, get in free and hang out with the band. Overend and Buffin were two of the nicest blokes I've ever met. I was there at the Isle Of Man, which turned out to be their last UK gig. [Ariel] Bender was out of control! Mott had become a different band.

When 'Saturday Gigs' died, so did Mott. I was at journalist college in Harlow by then and I had to

send out letters telling fans that Mott had split – a sad moment.

A couple of years later, punk came along. I was 22 and had outgrown fan clubs. That's when Pete Frame, who lived in a nearby village, kindly gave me *Zigzag* magazine.

Kris Needs edited *Zigzag* between 1977 and 1981. He went on to become – and remains – one of a small handful of 'rock star' journalists.

There was one early surprise at Alice Cooper's *Billion Dollar Babies* sessions. Ezrin had found an obscure song, 'Hello Hooray', on a 1968 Judy Collins album. The band felt it far too mellow for Alice. Producer Ezrin, again thinking visually, saw it as a vehicle to present Alice in a different light, amidst a vast theatrical set-piece with heart-stopping pauses and fist-pumping exaltations.

'Hello Hooray' was a deliberate change of pace, elegant yet jumpy, with a unison slide-guitar break that sounded like Pink Floyd's David Gilmour in one of his more celestial moments. When Cooper yelled a climactic, 'God, I feel so strong!' against the sound of percussion bells, it was easy to imagine Samson breaking his chains and bringing the house down all over again. Alice had the power.

By mid-March 1973, 'Hello Hooray' hit No. 6 in Britain on the singles chart; *Billion Dollar Babies* was the best-selling album on both sides of the Atlantic; Alice Cooper, as a band, were on a three-month tour across the States. The session players came too.

Each show began with Alice, dressed all in white, singing, 'Hello, Hooray, let the show begin,' his nasal whine removing all traces of Judy Collins' famed purity. The vintage Hollywood buff – who now counted Groucho Marx and Burgess 'The Penguin' Meredith from *Batman* among his friends – was putting on the style.

Alice drank all the time, 24 hours a day. It frightened the hell outta me.

When he got to the line about having waited so long for this moment to come, however, alarm bells went off in the minds of those in the shadows behind him.

'His Hollywood vision was a little different to Dennis's or mine,' says Michael Bruce. 'The top hat and cane thing, the Fred Astaire thing. I was thinking, "I dunno…"'

The tour, which ran almost nightly until May, brought Broadway slickness and Busby Berkeley extravagance to the Alice Cooper horror show. Baby dolls were still being put to the sword and Alice still ended up on the guillotine, but now everything was more professionally executed.

The split-level set featured statues and mannequins. A stage magician, The Amazing Randi, operated the guillotine giving the death scene a more circus-like quality. The big new set-piece was a battle between a giant tooth and an even bigger toothbrush.

Film cameras rolled to capture one of the highest grossing, most headline-grabbing rock tours yet. Backstage, with the entourage walking around in 'No Head, No Backstage Pass' T-shirts, it was business as usual.

Controversy continued to follow the band. In February 1973, an 'Alice Cooper Is Dead' story spread fast. It seemed there had been a terrible accident with the guillotine. The press was flooded with calls from distraught fans and Warner Brothers was

HELLO HURRAY · GENERATION LANDSLIDE

ALICE COOPER

STEREO
WB 16248

New depths of vulgarity and depravity, achieved by Alice

forced to quash the story as a hoax. It created a ton of publicity for 'Hello Hooray', *Billion Dollar Babies* and the tour.

Over in Britain, Labour MP Leo Abse picked up on Mary Whitehouse's campaign to get the band barred from entering Britain. 'Cooper is peddling the culture of the concentration camp,' Abse accused. 'Pop is one thing. Anthems of necrophilia are another' – a reference to 'I Love The Dead' on the latest album.

'Oh, he hated us!' says Alice. 'We sent him cigars.' In fact, the band had no immediate plans to visit the UK. There was yet another album scheduled first.

Late in the *Billion Dollar Babies* tour, which ended in early June '73, ads started to appear for a new line in unisex cosmetics, Whiplash Mascara: 'Whip the one you love – get a tube for your best friend too!' Alice's name was all over both publicity and packaging.

Truer to the band was a spoof written by journalist Ben Edmonds, 'Alice Cooper's Alcohol Cookbook', published in the June issue of Detroit-based rock mag *Creem*. 'Buxton's Bomber', a potent mix of cognac, Cointreau, anisette and vodka, came with a recommendation to 'Repeat indefinitely.' Some even speculated – incorrectly as it turned out – whether a sponsorship tie-up was behind Alice's very public drinking too.

It looked good for the cameras, reinforcing Cooper's insistence that, at heart, he was a gore-loving, beer-swilling, all-American boy. But he too was hitting it hard, getting through a crate of beer a day between slugs of Seagram's VO whisky.

Drinking wasn't unduly affecting his performances – Alice was a high-functioning boozer. But it was another reason why the band were finding their frontman more difficult to reach.

'He drank all the time, twenty-four hours a day,' says Ezrin, who remembers Alice spending an increasing amount of time recording his vocals alone in the studio. 'It frightened the hell outta me.'

In May, Alice Cooper were back in the British top ten. 'No More Mr Nice Guy' perpetrated one of pop's great misnomers: sonically at least, this was Mr Filth as Mr Clean, all flyaway falsettos and cruisin'-down-the-freeway choruses.

Alice insisted the bad-boy lyric had been inspired by a long-in-the-past episode from teenage times. Others in the Cooper camp wondered whether Mr Nice Guy really was no more; whether there might yet be another twist in this killer thriller.

Chapter 17
In a Broken Dream

In March 1973, Rod Stewart described The Faces' new release, *Ooh La La*, as 'a stinking, rotten album'. The following month, *Melody Maker* splashed with 'Rod: Our New Album Is A Disgrace'. A week later, on April 28, *Ooh La La* became The Faces' first No. 1 LP.

But no one was in the mood for celebration. Certainly not bassist Ronnie Lane, who was unconvinced that all the long, disjointed hours which went into making the record – clocking in at an underwhelming thirty minutes – had been worth it. 'I wanted it to be good,' he said, 'but I don't think it's the best thing we're going to achieve.'

Twelve months earlier, The Faces had been flying. 'Stay With Me', a top-twenty hit in the States, peaked at No. 6 at home. Their third album, *A Nod's As Good As A Wink…*, was an even bigger transatlantic success.

Rod was now living in Cranbourne Court, a thirty-two-roomed mansion set in 18 acres close to Windsor, with girlfriend Dee Harrington. Ron Wood had purchased The Wick, a prestigious property at the top of Richmond Hill, from distinguished British actor John Mills. Ronnie Lane, who'd stayed put in his flat at the bottom of the hill through all the band's early success, had his arm twisted by Wood to purchase Wick Cottage, the modest property at the bottom of the garden.

Rod Stewart was a different breed of flash to the late-sixties rock superstars. He loved cars, women and football, and enjoyed a beer down the local boozer. He could reach out and touch with his voice but he was no voodoo child, no chronicler of strange days, no end-times nihilist. Rod was the classic geezer-done-good and the embodiment of rock's new *modus operandi*: pleasure first, a better world later.

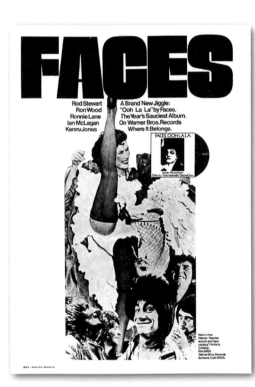

ABOVE: Ads hailed *Ooh La La* as The Faces' 'sauciest album'. Rod Stewart disagreed. 'A stinking, rotten album,' said the man who didn't show up for some of the sessions.

RIGHT: Rod Stewart collects yet another trophy, this time at the *Disc* awards ceremony in February 1973. It joined the others in the lavatory at his Windsor mansion.

During The Faces' three-night stand at the Rainbow in February 1972, British rock's brothers in arms had arrived on stage in a vintage yellow Rolls-Royce made from cardboard. The crowd gave a football-style of chant of 'Rod-er-nee' between songs (though he's 'Roderick' by birth). At the end, the band were hauled off stage by buxom, middle-aged comedy actress Janet Webb.

But as 1972 wore on, The Faces' famed conviviality grew strained. Rod's album *Never A Dull Moment*, released that July, continued where *Every Picture Tells A Story* left off both creatively and commercially. While the band laboured over *Ooh La La* in the autumn, Stewart notched up two more hit 45s: the No. 1 'You Wear It Well' and the double A-side of classic covers, 'What Made Milwaukee Famous (Has Made A Loser Out Of Me)'/'Angel', which peaked at No. 4 in early December.

Unexpectedly, the singer also featured on a third hit that autumn. 'In A Broken Dream', credited to Python Lee Jackson, had been recorded back in April 1969, when he was still with The Jeff Beck Group. The band were Australians who John Peel was trying out for his new Dandelion label. Stewart was roped in to sing on the promise of a set of carpets to doll up his silver Marcos sports car.

The recording was sold on and released as a single late in 1970. It went nowhere. In 1972, however, rereleased on the back of 'You Wear It Well', 'In A Broken Dream' hit No. 3 in late October.

The only major media coverage the song received was when dance troupe Pan's People interpreted it on *Top Of The Pops*. Its belated success by now had everything to do with Rod's reputation – and his impassioned, instinctive performance, equal to the band's stinging blues-rock backing. But its lament paralleled an encroaching sense of unease in The Faces' camp that autumn.

When Stewart appeared on *TOTP* in August that year, to promote 'You Wear It Well', he'd been joined by Ronnie Lane during the violin break for a highland fling. The pair looked inseparable.

But when the band spent two weeks kicking around ideas for *Ooh La La* that same month, Rod hadn't bothered to show up. Nor did he even hide his lack of enthusiasm, telling *Disc*'s Mike Ledgerwood, 'I wish I could give The Faces a lot more attention than I do.'

By November, Rod Stewart – once again with The Faces – was back at the *TOTP* studio performing his solo cover of Hendrix's 'Angel'. This time, it was the tartan scarfed Rod and Ronnie Wood show.

"We never foresaw the Rod thing being quite so big. It's a wonder we survived, but I suppose we are an extraordinarily close group"

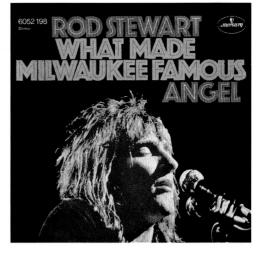

ABOVE: Rod Stewart performing
'Cindy Incidentally' with The
Faces at the *Top Of The Pops*
studio, February 1973. Meanwhile,
his solo career continued apace
with 1972's *Never A Dull Moment*
and singles 'You Wear It Well' and
a double A-side of 'What Made
Milwaukee Famous' and a cover
of Hendrix's 'Angel'. 'The hit
records weren't a problem,' said
Ian McLagan. 'We were happy
for Rod, for fuck's sake. I was on
most of them!'

FACING PAGE: Ronnie Lane
announced he was quitting The
Faces during the band's spring
'73 US tour. 'It was the right
thing for him,' said McLagan, 'but
it was a shame for The Faces.'
Lane, whose first solo single
'How Come' hit No. 11 in February
1974, turned his back on stardom
for a new life fronting a travelling
roadshow.

Switching between xylophone and congas, Ian
McLagan looked grim-faced. Ronnie Lane stood stiff
and expressionless – indeed, he'd sent in a life-size
cardboard cutout of himself.

The real Ronnie was in Ibiza, writing songs. He'd
made huge changes to his life that autumn and The
Faces were no longer at the centre of it. In October,
dispirited after another US tour, he'd left his wife
Sue and taken off to Ireland with Kate McInnerney,
the wife of longtime Faces and Who associate Mike.
Lane, a keen student of the teachings of Meher Baba,
wanted to make substantial changes to his life.

The bassist returned from Ibiza with one gypsy-
style earring and several songs for the next round
of *Ooh La La* sessions, including a sketch for the title
track. When Rod Stewart complained that it wasn't in
his key, co-writer Ronnie Wood stepped up and sang it.

Another Ronnie Lane original, the bittersweet
'Glad And Sorry', asked: 'Can you show me a dream?'
Lane shared the vocals with Wood and McLagan. Rod
was conspicuously absent, as he was on three other
tracks on the album.

Ooh La La's huge success was matched by the
advance single, the low-slung 'Cindy Incidentally',
which hit No. 2 in early March 1973. The following

month, The Faces were back in the States – where
Ooh La La peaked at twenty-one but the single had
been a relative flop – for their eighth US tour in three
years.

Before leaving for the States, Lane spoke to the
press. He'd recently finished work on a low-budget
film score with bandmate and namesake Wood:
Mahoney's Last Stand, a tale of a man who quits the
city for the countryside. 'The times the thought of
moving out has gone through my head!' he said with
a smile to *Record Mirror*'s Val Mabbs.

Ronnie Lane signed off with a hot flush concerning
pop's current state. 'We must have been one of the first

bands that didn't go out on stage in jeans,' he said. 'But then you always get people [who] tear the arse out of things and take the showbiz bit too far.'

During the US tour, the band bickered on stage, backstage and behind each other's backs. They travelled by Lear jet, but Lane preferred to rent a Land Rover and take the scenic route with partner Kate in tow.

He was craving a more spiritually satisfying, down-to-earth existence. Seeing Rod drift from the band into a superstar world filled with fawning courtiers was difficult to take. Ronnie had no doubt that Small Faces' experience with Steve Marriott was happening all over again.

On May 12, 1973, before a gig in Roanoke, Virginia, Ronnie Lane announced he was leaving the band. It was big news. 'Plonk Quits Faces' made the front page in the British music press. US rock writer Lester Bangs commemorated the moment with an imaginary resignation letter from Lane to Rod Stewart, citing the singer's 'busy schedule of ascending stardom' and his race to get to the top before Elton John.

Lane was unburdened – but he wasn't allowed to leave quietly. The farewell gig at the Edmonton Sundown, northeast London, on June 4 was an emotional affair. There were can-can dancers and plastic palm trees on stage; 'Farewell Ronnie' signs in the crowd.

Rod twirled his now-familiar tartan scarf and, as happened at all Faces gigs, everyone sang along. The set ended with an emotional 'We'll Meet Again' – the popular song that helped Britain through the Second World War.

'He asked me to leave with him,' said Ian McLagan, 'but I told him, "This is the band we made. I don't wanna leave our band." It was the right thing for Ronnie but a shame for The Faces.' Rod Stewart later compared Lane's departure to a car losing its engine. Plonk was, he said, The Faces' Keith Richards.

Ron Wood might have begged to differ. Weeks later, on July 24, 1973 at a night-time session in the basement studio he'd built at The Wick, he was playing 'Keef' to man-at-the-mike Mick Jagger. David Bowie sang backing vocals; Kenney Jones answered a late-night call for a drummer to drive over.

The demo they worked on, with T. Rex's 'Get It On' as loose inspiration, was 'It's Only Rock'n'Roll (But I Like It)'. Jagger liked the song so much he later worked it up as the next Stones single. In a swift bit of negotiation, he left Wood with the Jagger-enhanced (if distinctly inferior) 'I Can Feel The Fire' for the guitarist's solo album.

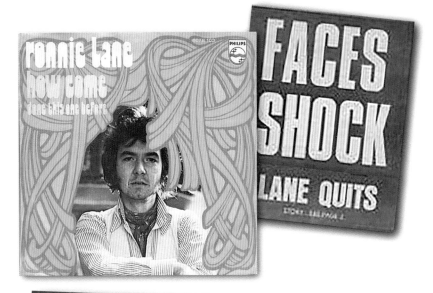

Elton's Year of Triumph
and who could begrudge it

A personal view of contemporary British pop at this time was given by one of its key instigators. 'I like to send it all up,' Elton John told *Record Mirror* in January 1973. 'I like to wear outrageous things.

'I started that about three years ago. I got knocked for it then, but a lot of people have come along and done the same things since.'

Elton's main market was still the States. 'Crocodile Rock' topped the *Billboard* singles chart in February, while his new album, *Don't Shoot Me I'm Only The Piano Player*, would soon hit No. 2. When Elton turned up at the launch for Bolan's *Born To Boogie* film, he proudly displayed a gold dollar-sign accessory on his jacket lapel.

(Elton also paid homage to Marc on the new album with the affectionate and astute 'I'm Gonna Be A Teenage Idol'. 'He likes it,' confirmed the piano player.)

Now Britain was following suit. 'Daniel', a gentle ballad about a soldier returning from Vietnam said lyricist Bernie Taupin, peaked at No. 5. The new album entered the chart at No. 1 on February 10, where it stayed for six weeks.

Elton toured Britain extensively during February and March. His audience had changed – younger, more girlish, more inclined to scream, rush the stage and sing along.

Elton lapped it up, dropping to his knees as he rocked the piano, tossing handkerchiefs into the crowd and – unlike most rival acts – delivering two-hour sets that stimulated both mind and body.

'Elton is bringing something back to show business that show business very badly needs and this is genuine showmanship,' said a proud Dick James, the man who invested in him.

Off stage, Elton posed in 8-inch heels with 5-inch platforms and paraded a fleet of Rolls-Royce and Mercedes cars outside Hercules, his

LEFT: Elton John frolics on a chopper bike in front of his fleet of cars at his new Hercules home in Virginia Water, Surrey, 1972. Near neighbours included Donovan, Keith Moon, Ringo Starr and mum, Sheila.

bungalow-style residence in affluent Virginia Water, Surrey. Donovan, Keith Moon and Rod Stewart were neighbours; so too were Bernie Taupin and Elton's mother, Sheila.

Elton's new friend, film director Bryan Forbes, introduced him to Hollywood legends and British royalty. He also acquired a taste for art deco and ever more extravagant eyewear – his most recent commission was a pair of glasses in the shape of a poodle.

By May 1973, Elton John and his band were back at the 'Honky Château' in France, recording his next album. While at work, the atmosphere was both monastic and factory-like. Bernie Taupin would write lyrics at a typewriter and pass them to Elton over breakfast.

In half an hour, or often less, he'd whip up a new song. One such, 'Candle In The Wind', was inspired by the short, difficult life of Marilyn Monroe. It hit Elton more than most.

'When I think of Marilyn Monroe, I think of pain, of complete torment,' he explained in *Elton John and Bernie Taupin Say Goodbye Norma Jean and Other Things*, a 1973 TV documentary directed by Forbes. 'I could write sad songs all day long. That's the sort of person I am.'

A similar strain of melancholy ran through the documentary. 'He's had darker moods since he's made it into the pop world than he ever did before,' explained his mother, Sheila.

'The artist lives with failure magnificently,' piped in Dick James, who'd worked closely with The Beatles during the sixties. 'I've never yet met one that can live with success,' he cautioned.

With the documentary still in production, the first fruit from the spring sessions revealed a remarkably upbeat Elton John. 'Saturday Night's Alright For Fighting', released in June, benefited from the energy and bite of a full rock band. Years later, Elton would claim he felt 6 ft 2 in at the height of glam. On this record, he sounded like it.

Guitarist Davey Johnstone had once played in prog-folk band Magna Carta, but on the new single he tore into the chords, Ronnie Wood-style. Channelling Jerry Lee Lewis on piano, Elton snarled, 'I'm a juvenile product of the working class' with conviction. The 'get a little action in' line spoke to everyone from football hooligans to women newly liberated by driving lessons and the 1970 Equal Pay Act.

Though the wildly upbeat single seemed to spook the States, where it failed to reach the top ten, 'Saturday Night's Alright For Fighting' was the song that changed perceptions of Elton John back home. The gifted all-rounder could play it tough, too.

I've never met an artist that can live with success, cautioned Dick James.

Chapter 18
The Gang's All Here

Finding himself competing with David Cassidy as much as David Bowie by winter 1972, Marc Bolan was determined to make a pitch for the rock market and those mostly male fans who had deserted him. It was, wrote Penny Valentine in *Sounds*, 'a pretty crucial time for Bolan'.

He came out fighting. On March 10, 1973, the first T. Rex single of the year hit No. 3 in its week of release. '20th Century Boy' kicked off like Led Zeppelin and pushed on like classic Sly & The Family Stone. Two throat-clearing staccato chords and a life-or-death howl announced a reinvigorated, gutsy Bolan; the song's driving riff refined that old Johnny Burnette style for the Marshall stack era.

But this was more rock'n'soul than rock'n'roll, the inspiration more Muhammad Ali ('sting like a bee') than Elvis or Jerry Lee. Bolan's fighting spirit was all over it. '"20th Century Boy" is erection rock,' he told Radio 1's magazine-style show, *Scene And Heard*. 'This is an energy record… Every young man in the 20th century is a super stud.'

The rock press mostly applauded the single, with *NME*'s Charles Shaar Murray back on side and hailing Bolan's 'thunder guitar'.

'Super Marc' was back – wrapped in feather boas on TV, guesting with ELO on 'Ma-Ma-Ma Belle' and still the subject of unfounded playground rumours of his imminent demise from some incurable illness.

Bolan extended the macho theme to new album *Tanx*. While the original release didn't include '20th Century Boy', Marc posed provocatively astride a large toy tank on the cover and served up a couple more erection rockers in 'Mad Donna' and 'Shock Rock'. But the main point of *Tanx* was to break with the trademark Bolan boogie and ballad methodology.

To that end, Bolan and Visconti added Mellotron, brass and soul-style vocal backings to the mix. Sessions were guided by a desire for greater sophistication and spontaneity. They were successful up to a point. In contrast to the latest hit single, the first three songs on *Tanx* sounded as much self-sabotage as dramatic regeneration: muddled ('Tenement Lady'), pedestrian ('Rapids'), lightweight ('Mister Mister').

From that point on, everything perked up. The final quartet of songs – some more emotionally engaged ('Life Is Strange', 'Highway Knees') others breaking fresh ground ('The Street And Babe Shadow', 'Left Hand Luke And The Beggar Boys') – were high points in what otherwise sounded like a transitional album.

FACING PAGE: Ever since the press began talking about 'Glam Rock' as a collective thing, Bolan had distanced himself from it. By 1973, he was dismissing glam as 'Sham Rock'.

LEFT: First T. Rex hit of 1973 '20th Century Boy' found Bolan crunching big rock chords and quoting Muhammad Ali. *Tanx*, also released in the spring, was a more hit-and-miss affair, suggesting there was something half-hearted about Bolan's desire to leave glam rock behind.

It kicked off like Led Zeppelin and pushed on like classic Sly & The Family Stone.

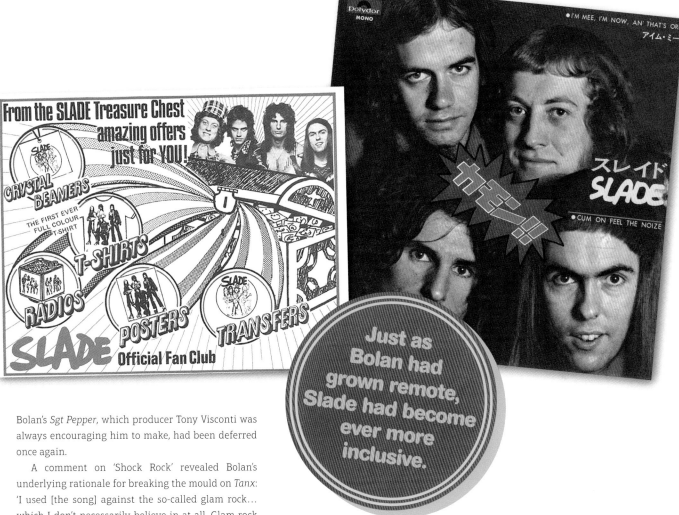

Bolan's *Sgt Pepper*, which producer Tony Visconti was always encouraging him to make, had been deferred once again.

A comment on 'Shock Rock' revealed Bolan's underlying rationale for breaking the mould on *Tanx*: 'I used [the song] against the so-called glam rock… which I don't necessarily believe in at all. Glam rock is sham rock.'

The phrase 'glam rock', thrown around during autumn 1972, was beginning to take hold.

Tanx hit No. 4 for a couple of weeks; it would exit the top thirty after two months. In the week it dropped out, Bowie's latest album, *Aladdin Sane*, was spending its fifth week at No. 1. Bolan's desire to leave glam rock behind was a risky strategy. Like The Move back in 1970, his pop success left him a little compromised in the album market.

Slade's Jim Lea had previously considered T. Rex the act to beat. That moment came, he says, when 'Mama Weer All Crazee Now' held off 'Children Of The Revolution' to retain the No. 1 spot for the third week running back in September 1972. Now, in March 1973, Slade – Top British Band in the recent *NME* readers' poll – took it up another notch.

'Cum On Feel The Noize' began with another of Noddy Holder's throat-ripping yells: 'Baby, baby, BABY!' The verses rolled as effortlessly as well-oiled Bolan boogie, while the 'girls grab the boys!' choruses took Slade's you-can-all-join-in philosophy to new levels of euphoria. Just as Bolan had grown remote, Slade had become ever more inclusive.

Promoting the single on *Top Of The Pops* in late February, Holder switched his now familiar mirrored top-hat for a tartan one. No doubt mindful of Steve Priest's recent headline-grabbing appearances, Dave Hill came out in a cape and headscarf covered in circular mirrors; his so-called 'Metal Nun' outfit.

If Bolan had reprised Beatlemania in concert halls, Slade were beginning to compete with the Fab Four in chart terms. For the first time since The Beatles' 'Get Back' in 1969, 'Cum On Feel The Noize' went straight to No. 1 in its first week of release, staying there for four weeks; *Slayed?* had recently topped the album

LEFT: Slade in the *Top Of The Pops* studio running through latest hit 'Cum On Feel The Noize', for broadcast on the February 22, 1973 edition. Dave Hill unveils his custom-made 'Super Yob' guitar and matching outfit. After rehearsals, Hill changed into his latest outfit, his so-called 'Metal Nun' costume complete with mirrored headscarf, for the broadcast performance.

Suzi writes own songs

ABOVE: Suzi Quatro backstage at Newcastle City Hall, November 4, 1972, during a short tour supporting Slade and Thin Lizzy. Pianist Alastair McKenzie and drummer Keith Hodge are recent recruits to her new backing band. Out of shot is burly bassist and Quatro's future husband Len Tuckey.

RIGHT: Suzi's debut single, May 1972's 'Rolling Stone', featured Peter Frampton on guitar. The record flopped but it earned Quatro some press coverage.

RAK

RADIO STATION COPY

Suggested
Side
45 RPM
ZS7 4512
JZS7 4512-1
2:41
Publisher:
Rak Publ. Ltd.
(ASCAP)

ROLLING STONE
D. Brown
SUSIE QUATRO
Produced by Mickie Most
A Mickie Most Production
℗ 1972 RAK Records Ltd.

chart; *Slade Alive!*, which had spent the past year in the chart, was still going strong.

Slade were inspiring others, too. At the London Palladium in January, they'd been supported by Geordie, who were soon engulfed by a rash of 'We Don't Copy Slade' headlines.

But fellow Midlands act Blackfoot Sue, whose stompy, Slade-inspired 'Standing In The Road' hit the top ten in September 1972, had already turned. Their debut album, *Nothing To Hide*, included 'Glittery Obituary', which put the boot into all those 'overrated, celebrated… chromium-plated' acts in Max Factor 'blue eyeshade'.

Back in November '72, Slade had toured Britain with Thin Lizzy. Third on the bill at several gigs was a Mickie Most protégé whose brief set was best remembered for its obligatory Chuck Berry cover, 'Sweet Little Rock And Roller'. Dressed in jeans, T-shirt and knee-length platform boots with a Mickey Mouse motif, Suzi Quatro was fronting her own band for the first time.

Quatro derived her energy less from contemporary glitter acts than from her native

Detroit. 'It's black, it's white, it's rich and poor, it's Motown and it's rock,' she affectionately recalls. Detroit's rock tradition was always louder, tougher, more cathartic than anywhere else in the States. 'There's a desperation in Detroit, and the only thing that relieves it is the music,' Quatro observes.

Home to The Stooges, MC5 and Grand Funk Railroad, the incubator for Alice Cooper (whose frontman was born there), Detroit had warmly welcomed The Jeff Beck Group, The Faces and Mott

The Hoople. But Suzi Quatro, who'd played garage rock with her sisters in The Pleasure Seekers, had to cross the Atlantic to find success.

Sometime in autumn 1970, Mickie Most was in Detroit to record Jeff Beck and Cozy Powell in the Motown studio. One evening, apparently persuaded by Quatro's brother Mike, the producer saw Suzi – now playing harder rock with her sisters in the band Cradle – at Detroit's Eastown Theater. The idea was that Most might sign the band. Instead, the producer

ABOVE LEFT: Early publicity shots featured Quatro in denim with fluffed-up two-tone hair and a pop smile. That all changed by the time of 'Can The Can', No. 1 in June 1973, when all talk was of the girl in leather and 'Suzi Power'.

SUZI QUATRO

il sexy rock d' oltremare

Can the Can

ain't ya somethin' honey

EMI Italiana SpA

SUZI QUATRO

48 crash
Little Bitch Blue

saw the singing bass player as Cradle's big asset and invited her to the studio. Once there, she picked up a bass and jammed along with Beck and Powell as they played The Meters' 'Cissy Strut'.

Reluctant to break up the Quatro sisters' latest band, Most bided his time. Meanwhile, others had spotted Quatro's potential. 'Elektra offered me a solo contract,' Suzi says. 'Jac Holzman wanted to take me to New York and make me the new Janis Joplin.'

Mickie Most had a much better proposition. 'He wanted me to come to England and be the first Suzi Quatro. Guess which offer I took? I didn't wanna be the second anybody.'

Quatro arrived in October 1971 with two pairs of jeans, her Les Paul bass and one song, the autobiographical 'Suitcase Lizzie' with its key line, 'She can do anything.'

The producer installed Quatro in a west London hotel, where she wrote and occasionally demoed songs. One, 'Rolling Stone', with Peter Frampton guesting on guitar, made it onto 45. Released on RAK in May '72, the single flopped, but it gave the then big-haired Quatro – in double denim – her first flurry of publicity.

Most persevered with his protégé. 'Mickie saw me as I was,' she says, 'androgynous – a female that could rock with the best of them. He let me be who I was and watched me develop.'

After the Slade dates, Mickie Most knew Quatro was ready and got to work. A promotional piece co-sponsored by Radio Luxembourg tipped 'Little Suzi Quatro' for success in 1973. Shortly before 'Blockbuster!' broke, Most decided to call up Nicky Chinn and Mike Chapman.

'Mickie asked if I'd mind if they tried to craft a single based on what I did,' she says. 'They came to a gig, saw my music was very boogie and Mike went away and wrote "Can The Can".'

Quatro was knocked out by the song. 'Absolutely great,' she says. It was boogie, it had the all-important glitter beat and it allowed Suzi to add her own trademarks: driving bass, a tough-talking vocal and those high-powered yells she'd been doing ever since belting out Otis Redding songs back in sixties Detroit.

Once 'Can The Can' was recorded, Chapman played it down the phone to Most, who was in the States. The producer had one suggestion – twist everything up a semitone. It was a masterstroke. Now 'Can The Can' had the intensity of 'Blockbuster!' – all topped with a cat-scratchin' lyric and vocal from the trailblazing Quatro.

Reviewers raved about 'Suzi Power!' RAK turned up the heat with a series of publicity shots featuring Quatro in a black leather suit unzipped to the navel.

'Mickie asked me what I wanted to wear and I said "leather". We had a big argument. He said it was old hat. I said, "It might have been done but it ain't been done by a woman!" I got my way.

'Then he said, "What about a jump suit?" I said, "Great." I always used to say, "Don't treat me as a sex symbol." And there I am in a leather jump suit! I swear to God I had no idea it was going to be sexy.'

Now clad in leather, during interviews conducted at RAK's offices, Suzi played up to the image. 'I like men,' she'd say. 'I like to be surrounded by masculine boys.

'The bass is the horniest instrument. It gets right in there, between the hips,' she elaborated provocatively. She described her backing band as 'hooligans'.

Suzi Quatro made her *Top Of The Pops* debut on May 11, 1973. Five weeks later, 'Can The Can' was at No. 1.

Mickie Most commissioned Chinn and Chapman to write a follow-up along similar lines. By mid-August, the equally intense '48 Crash', featuring another ear-splitting vocal, had gone top-three. Quatro and Len Tuckey, the band's guitarist – and Suzi's future husband – blitzed an album's worth of songs. Commanding a fee of a grand a night (an instant hike from £125), glam rock's newest star hit the road.

The spotlight also turned back on Chinn and Chapman. They'd notched up eight hits by June 1973, most of them million-sellers. The Sweet's 'Little Willy' had just entered the US top three; 'Hell Raiser', their latest, had spent three weeks at No. 2 in Britain. The pair were now writing for Suzi Quatro and another RAK act, Mud.

NME decided it was time to investigate the 'Chinnichap' phenomenon. The piece was headlined 'The Dynamic Duo Of Plastic Pop', but The Sweet dominated the conversation. 'They want to become more outrageous,' said Chinn. 'And the loonier they get, the bigger they'll become.'

'In two or three years' time,' added Chapman, 'they'll be competing with bands like Emerson, Lake & Palmer.'

The pair made a stout defence of their work. 'It's not easy to write plastic songs,' said Chinn. 'Every Tom, Dick and Harry would like to be a plastic songwriter and earn twenty grand out of every song that hits the charts.'

Over at *Record Mirror*, Mike Beatty raised the popular rock press accusation that their work was banal garbage. 'I'll tell you what's garbage,' Chapman hit back, 'a record that never sells!'

Chinn and Chapman were at the top of their game. So too was Mike Leander.

Back in the spring, Gary Glitter had peaked at No. 2 for three weeks with 'Hello! Hello! I'm Back Again'. By June, Leander finally had the song that would put his protégé out front.

'We all tried to outdo each other,' Glitter would reminisce. 'It was a healthy competition. We – Marc Bolan, David Bowie, myself, Slade and Sweet – were pre-video times but we'd think like video. When we did *Top Of The Pops*, our major outlet, we'd try and create a video in one slot. I'd stand on moons, come up with motorbikes…'

And there I am in a leather jump suit! I had no idea it was going to be sexy.

JUNE 30th. 1973

Music Star

7p
EVERY SATURDAY

How does BOWIE live – you'll never believe it!

Did you write a poem for DONNY?

Who's wild about Ricky?

HAVE BREAKFAST WITH THE STARS!

Why the New Seekers split?

Rod, Michael, Slade, Mickey Finn. And David and more, more, more

Mike Leander's strongest card were those bronchial saxes and guitars.

With the term 'glam rock' now in everyday usage, Glitter seized the crown. His second album, *Touch Me*, had just hit No. 2 and the huge, six-week *Glitter Over England* tour was running into three months across Europe.

It was another peak of sorts, the heyday of big-sounding sparkle as a familiar and faintly ludicrous pop phenomenon. But for some, Glitter's triumph was a moment of reckoning.

★

Marc Bolan had a distinctly nasty smell under his nose. 'I think glam rock/sham rock is as dead as a doornail,' he reiterated to *Sounds*' Penny Valentine in June. 'I want to wait until people are ready for the next phase.'

It was a good moment for him to step back. 'The Groover' – 'Why make the T. Rex single again?' grumbled one reviewer – had peaked at No. 4 in June and dropped from the twenty in just five weeks. Bolan had also taken to hiding behind huge, space-age specs and looked puffy.

His latest big idea was to create what he called 'a cosmic ensemble'. He was now working with two soul singers from Los Angeles, Gloria Jones and Pat Hall, and had brought in a second guitarist, Jack Green – ostensibly for an upcoming US tour supporting Three Dog Night.

'Marc walked in with his short bolero jacket with wide sleeves and feathers coming out from the collars,' says Green of his hasty audition. 'He looked remarkably flash [and] was incredibly full of himself.

'The Bolan I knew was nearly always nice. Then again, he was Marc Bolan – having hit singles, enjoying cocaine, brandy, all the fame! Walking around in that cocooned way – it's gonna affect you.'

RIGHT: Competition winner Deborah Loads from Darwen, Lancashire, wearing Marc Bolan's two-tone checked shirt, summer 1973. Her illustration of Bolan wearing a feather boa was judged by *Tanx* sleeve designer John Kosh to be the best from a healthy postbag of submissions by T. Rex Fan Club members.

'I'm The Leader Of The Gang (I Am!)' had it all: roadkill motorbike intro, an instant terrace chant of 'Come on, come on!', a crazy-paced rhythm wrapped in what sounded like galvanised tinsel and – always Leander's strongest card – those bronchial saxes and guitars, all bolstering Glitter's bold and brassy leadership bid.

'It's not a formula,' Glitter told *Record Mirror*'s Peter Harvey that May. '[It's] a sound, just like T. Rex or The Beatles. I don't intend people to sit down and listen. It's totally mindless music and there's a place for it.'

In July 1973, 'Leader Of The Gang' put Glitter at No. 1 for the first time – after three No. 2s and a No. 4 – where it stayed for a month. Bowie's 'Life On Mars?', Elton's 'Saturday Night's Alright For Fighting', Quatro's '48 Crash', Mud's 'Hypnosis' and The Osmonds' Slade-like 'Goin' Home' ('I gotta fight, fight, fight!'), strong suits all, were seen off by the man some were now calling 'the Big G'.

T·REX
T.Rex Fan Club London W1A 4XQ

18th July, 1973.

Dear Debbie,

Congratulations Debbie. As you see you have won the drawing competition for one of Marc's shirts.

We had so many entries that John Kosh, the judge, had a very hard time deciding. However, he thought your picture was the most original especially with the feather boa.

The July/August Newsletter will be out soon and you will see the complete results then.

Things are very hectic at the office at the moment. Vicky has left to get married and I have only just taken her place. You'll read all about it in the Newsletter.

Till then, Debbie, congratulations once again, and I hope you like the shirt.

Bye for now,

Linda

Linda

T-REX
SUMMER '78

Chapter 19

Death Trip

On January 17, 1973, David Bowie filmed his Russell Harty interview and forthcoming single, 'Drive-In Saturday', for broadcast three days later. A second song was taped that day: 'My Death (La Mort)', written by Belgian *chansonnier* Jacques Brel in 1959.

Bowie first heard 'My Death' in 1967 via a girlfriend with a passion for Scott Walker and a copy of Scott's debut solo album. The singer, who preferred monastic retreats to pop package tours, had sensationally quit The Walker Brothers to plough his own furrow, inspired more by Brel and the films of Ingmar Bergman than The Beatles. Bowie, still then a Buddhist 'child of Tibet', as in his early song 'Silly Boy Blue', admired Walker's decision to fly in the face of fame.

By the time Bowie introduced 'My Death' into his set, at the Rainbow in August 1972, Walker was – after a string of illustrious solo albums – fading into obscurity. More pertinently, with Bowie now settling into the role of Ziggy Stardust and closing each night with 'Rock'N'Roll Suicide', 'My Death' was a far more appropriate moment of dark cabaret than 'Amsterdam', the Brel song it replaced in the set.

Bowie had always resented Alice Cooper's pack-up-the-props-and-go-home approach to rock theatre. *Ziggy Stardust* was as much private psychodrama as it was provocative pantomime. It provided camouflage for a sometimes insecure and desperately aspiring singer to express his inner ambition and showmanship without reserve.

Designing Ziggy as a ready-made star also brought with it a sense of wish-fulfilment. Whilst killing him off for the album's finale made melodramatic sense, it also reflected Bowie's keen interest in finitude. Whether through the existentialist literature he'd read as a teenager, his fascination with Buddhism, madness or tragi-heroic stars, fame, struggle and ruination provided natural territory for him.

As the *Ziggy* project passed into 1973, the lines between Bowie the rising star, Bowie the superstar and Ziggy Stardust the archetypal rise-and-fall guy blurred. On February 24, 1973, *Melody Maker* ran an explosive 'Bowie's Last Tour?' cover story. Its main purpose was to announce a major British tour starting in May. However, manager Tony Defries gave it an extra twist. '[David] may not make another British tour after this one for a long,

LEFT: Jacques Brel's 'La Mort' ('My Death') was first released in 1959 on the chansonnier's acclaimed *N° 4* album. Bowie, who came across the song on Scott Walker's debut album eight years later, introduced 'My Death' into the Ziggy live set at the Rainbow in August 1972.

RIGHT: Bowie's second US tour began with two nights at the Radio City Hall in New York on February 14/15, 1973. 'By that time, he'd be in his own limousine, in a different hotel,' remembers Woody Woodmansey. 'Maybe he was just letting us know that he was the star.'

BOWIE U.S. TOUR II

NEW YORK CITY	FEB. 14	RADIO CITY MUSIC HALL
PHILADELPHIA	FEB. 16, 17, 18	THE TOWER THEATRE
NASHVILLE	FEB. 23	WAR MEMORIAL AUDITORIUM
MEMPHIS	FEB. 25, 26	ELLIS AUDITORIUM
DETROIT	MARCH 1	MASONIC AUDITORIUM
CHICAGO	MARCH 5	ARAGON BALLROOM
LOS ANGELES	MARCH 10	THE LONG BEACH ARENA

AND MORE DATES TO BE ANNOUNCED.

long time, maybe even years,' he said, 'especially if he gets into films.'

It sounded like classic Colonel Tom Parker salesmanship. Bowie was already touring the States, with Japan to follow. *Aladdin Sane*, his follow up to *Ziggy Stardust*, was in the bag. The touring band had been expanded and its leader was on a mission.

'That's what pop's for,' he reminded *Music Scene* in January, 'to shock people out of their complacency. Remember when pop was kids versus their parents? Well, that's what I'm trying to stir up again.'

Bowie was determined to do things differently. He'd sailed to the States on the QE2 and again by boat to Japan via Hawaii – better suited both to his aerophobia and his romantic view of classic travel. Whilst in New York and later in Japan, he spent more time with fashion designer Kansai Yamamoto than the band, watching kabuki performances and commissioning a range of new outfits inspired by Japan's Noh theatre tradition.

Bowie made the final leg of his journey back to Britain via the Trans-Siberian Express, stopping off in Moscow to see the May Day Parade, before alighting at Paris and spending an evening with Jacques Brel.

Mobbed at Charing Cross Station on May 4, Bowie returned to a welcome-home party at Haddon Hall. Guests included Chelita Secunda and – taking a night off from producing T. Rex's 'The Groover' at AIR Studios – Tony Visconti and his wife, Mary Hopkin.

'He wasn't really the same David,' Visconti recalled. 'He was Ziggy…'

Behind the scenes, Bowie's success brought its own problems. On discovering that pianist Mike Garson was earning $800 a week, around ten times their weekly wage, bassist Trevor Bolder and drummer Woody Woodmansey confronted Tony Defries. The matter was smoothed over rather than healed.

Around the same time, Woodmansey also noted a distinct cooling off between star and band. 'A few tours in, "Ziggy" walked off stage and got in the limo. When you started talking to [David], it was what you expected Ziggy Stardust to say. It wasn't David Bowie; it was… an oddness.

I suppose
I'm some
kind of
cosmic yob
—DAVID BOWIE

HAS THE STAR GONE TOO FAR?

'If he wanted to communicate, he would. If he didn't, he'd snub you or give you a dirty look. It was weird. Was it the fame or something I said? Maybe it was the meeting [with Defries].

'On that American tour, he'd be in his own limousine, in a different hotel. Maybe he was just letting us know that he was the star. But we knew that anyway.'

There was another problem. RCA Records were mystified that all the publicity and prestigious write-ups had not translated into record sales. In the week that the US tour ended, in mid-March, *Ziggy Stardust* had climbed no higher than No. 78 on the *Billboard* Hot 100. There was some compensation in 'Space Oddity' becoming a belated top-twenty singles hit, with the 1969 folkie album (now retitled *Space Oddity*) in the US top thirty and rising. But that wasn't the man-of-the-moment Bowie they wanted to market – or the one that Bowie himself was projecting.

The US tour was notable for the emergence of Ziggy lookalikes, particularly at New York's Radio City Music Hall on Valentine's Day. There was real, unexpected drama that night, too. At the end of the set, returning in massive heels for 'Rock'N'Roll Suicide', Bowie fell over and was hastily carried offstage. Some – perhaps including Bowie himself – initially imagined hearing gun-shots and watching Bowie/Ziggy die on stage. But he'd simply collapsed after a fan leapt up and kissed him on the cheek. It seemed like a portent.

Bowie later described *Aladdin Sane*, released in April while he was touring overseas, as his 'Ziggy Goes To America' album. Consumerism, violence, hi-tech and Hollywood all found their way into songs such

LEFT: With carrot-topped Ziggy lookalikes turning up at gigs in greater numbers, Bowie continued to evolve the image. By 1973, he was wearing Kansai Yamamoto's Kabuki-influenced costumes and a La Roche-designed astral motif on his forehead.

ABOVE: Bowie's sell-out 1973 British tour prompted plenty of coverage in the national press. 'Bowie behaves more like a Soho stripper than a top pop star,' noted one scandalised report.

ALADDIN SANE

BOWIE'S LATEST ALBUM

BOWIE ALBUMS AND TOUR

RS. 1001 (L.P.) PK 2134 (C) P8S 2134 (S8)

SIDE 1 : 1. WATCH THAT MAN (New York) ;
2. ALADDIN SANE (1913-1938-197?) (R.H.M.S.
''Ellinis'') ; 3. DRIVE-IN SATURDAY (Seattle –
Phoenix) ; 4. PANIC IN DETROIT (Detroit) ;
5. CRACKED ACTOR (Los Angeles).

SIDE 2 : 1. TIME (New Orleans) ; 2. THE
PRETTIEST STAR (Gloucester Road) ; 3. LET'S
SPEND THE NIGHT TOGETHER (Jagger/
Richard) ; 4. THE JEAN GENIE (Detroit and New
York) ; 5. LADY GRINNING SOUL (London).

RCA
Records and Tapes

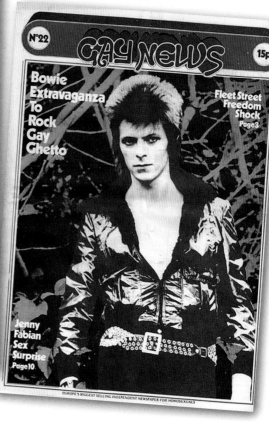

RIGHT: The experimental cabaret
ambience of *Aladdin Sane* finale
'Lady Grinning Soul' mirrored
the cut-glass despair of 1972 film
Cabaret, set during the last days
of Germany's Weimar Republic.

as 'Watch That Man', 'Panic In Detroit' and the single 'Drive-In Saturday'.

There was faded grandeur, too, particularly when Mike Garson's scintillating, cut-glass piano was allowed free rein. The blood-pumping yet oddly languid title track, and especially the Brecht/Weill-influenced 'Time', owed as much to the spirit of *Cabaret* – the 1972 film about the last days of the Weimar Republic and the rise of Nazism – as the Ziggy experience did to *A Clockwork Orange*. The 'Aladdin Sane' subtitle '(1913-1938-197?)' suggested that Bowie's apocalyptic premonitions had been intensified by his star experience.

There were also hints of self-destruction. 'Cracked Actor' was a graphic take on the excesses of (fading) fame. The cover sent an even less subtle warning. On a personal level, the lightning flash across Bowie's face was a visible representation of the 'crack in the sky' madness he'd alluded to on 'Oh! You Pretty Things'.

Politically, though he never acknowledged any connection, its shape and cosmetic tones evoked the flag of Mosley's British Union of Fascists. The graveness of this seemingly subliminal warning was echoed in the lyric of the album's title track, with its allusions to the inter-war period, and in Bowie's growing fascination with decadence (and, indeed, fascism).

Blank-faced and with eyes closed, *Aladdin Sane* was Bowie's – and perhaps everyone's – death mask. As he had claimed months earlier, 'Any society that allows people like Lou [Reed] and me to become rampant is pretty well lost.'

The album topped the UK chart on the week of release and stayed there for five weeks. It remained in the top ten until mid-November. Despite its lunar doo-wop light-headedness, 'Drive-In Saturday' still hit No. 3. By the time Bowie was back in London in early May, *Ziggy Stardust*, the retitled *Space Oddity* album and *Hunky Dory* were all in the top fifty.

The '100-day worldwide tour', as it was promoted, was swiftly followed by a home-coming tour of fifty-six gigs, beginning on May 12 with the first-ever rock show at the vast Earls Court Arena in west London. Tickets sold out in three hours. *Gay News* made it a cover story, announcing that '17,000 of us will be there'. Inside the venue, the audience – whether straight or gay – waved souvenir programmes and were now literally screaming for 'Ziggy!'

But the sound was poor and the vision, due to a low stage, even worse. A stampede early in the show prompted Bowie to walk off as roadies begged the crowd to move back. The gig resulted in the first bad press – 'Bowie Blows It' claimed *Melody Maker* – since his 1972 breakthrough. A second show at the venue was promptly cancelled and replaced by a two-night end-of-tour finale at the more intimate Hammersmith Odeon.

Elsewhere, ticket prices on the tour were at a premium; local journalists were told 'Mr Bowie doesn't give interviews,' but wrote up their 'New Hero Of Camp Rock' pieces anyway; Bowie's bodyguard, Stuart 'Stuey' George from Hull, shadowed him everywhere.

By now, performances involved up to six costume changes. Minus eyebrows, but with silver lips and a golden astral sphere on his forehead, resplendent in a Yamamoto gown, Bowie stripped down to a G-string for his 'invisible wall' mime routine during 'The Width Of A Circle'. Each night ended with audiences screaming 'Bowie!' and 'Ziggy!' with arms outstretched, and the performer responding with the grand mock-showbiz pay-off of 'Rock'N'Roll Suicide'.

On June 5, in a report on the Bowie phenomenon for BBC1's current-affairs programme *Nationwide*, presenter Bernard Falk told his family audience: 'It's said that Bowie will soon be the world's number one beat singer. If he achieves such eminence, he will be the first superstar of pop to wear shorty [sic] dresses on stage.'

That same month a mystified Cliff Richard expressed his bemusement to the *Daily Mirror*, under the headline 'What Is David Bowie Trying To Prove?': 'When you get a married man with a child who drags up and does an effeminate act, there's got to be a reason for it. He says he's playing a part. But what part? And why? And who gave him the part?'

Bowie was now infiltrating the mainstream in the way that Bolan had back in late 1971-72 – albeit with as much shock as awe. Meanwhile, 'Life On Mars?', which had grown into a high-point of the live set, was released as the new single; Lou Reed's 'Walk On The Wild Side' hit No. 10 in the singles chart; and Iggy & The Stooges' *Raw Power* finally received a UK release in June 1973. It fell straight down a commercial black hole.

Once again, Bowie shunned *Top Of The Pops*. Both 'Drive-In Saturday' and 'Life On Mars?' were determinedly far removed from the conga-line of glam hits now cramming the chart. Ever since the press prediction of a final tour back in February, rumours of a career change had rumbled on. In May, *Music Scene* stated that Bowie was considering playing Valentine Michael Smith – described, somewhat misleadingly, as 'a peace and love messenger from another planet' – in a screen version

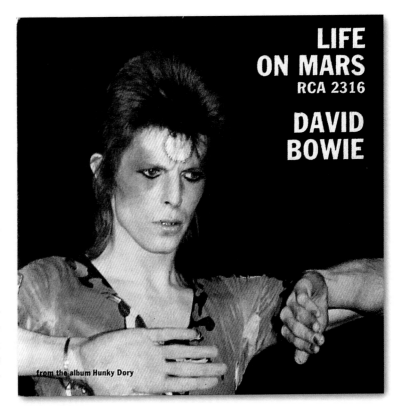

from the album Hunky Dory

LIFE ON MARS RCA 2316

DAVID BOWIE

BELOW: Fan Michael Warley about to hit Hammersmith Odeon, July 3, 1973. 'I'd borrowed my sister's lime green satin Biba smock and teamed it with raspberry velvet flares and orange platforms. My uncle added the lightning flash. Hammersmith was like a Lurex Lourdes. When David made his announcement, we gasped. People were crying. Surely, he wouldn't do that to us. We all wanted to give him our hands forever.'

OPPOSITE: On July 9, six days after Hammersmith, Bowie stepped onto the boat train at London's Victoria Station bound for the famed Château d'Hérouville recording studio near Paris. He spent three weeks there recording *Pin Ups*. 'I get that David had to end Ziggy,' says Woody Woodmansey. 'I didn't get it that night. It knocked the shitout of me.'

of Robert A. Heinlein's 1961 sci-fi novel, *Stranger In A Strange Land*.

For the time being Bowie remained earthbound, arriving at the Hammersmith Odeon on July 3, 1973 for the last night of the *Aladdin Sane* tour via limo, dressed in dungarees.

The evening began with a piano medley as Mike Garson tapped into his inner Liberace, for a grandiose mixed grill of 'Space Oddity', 'Ziggy Stardust', 'John, I'm Only Dancing' and 'Life On Mars?'.

The first half of the show was brought to a climax when Bowie announced he was resurrecting a song from 'long, long ago'. 'This is called a quiet song,' he said, a subtle plea for calm. 'My Death', dropped from the tour, had now been resurrected, he added, 'as it's the last show'.

The symmetry of its inclusion was made apparent towards the end of the second act. 'Not only is it the last show of the tour, but it's the last show that we'll ever do. Thank you,' announced Bowie, before launching into 'Rock'N'Roll' Suicide'. There were gasps and screams but mostly open-mouthed disbelief.

As the crowd joined Bowie/Ziggy for gushing *en masse* exclamations, it was as if every Dusty/Fury/ Shangri-Las/Orbison heartbreaker ballad had been rolled into one. Vintage pop always did melodrama well, but never like this – and in real time, too.

The audience filed out – their faces watery with mascara, sweat and tears – to the familiar stiff-upper-lip sound of 'Land Of Hope And Glory'. It was the *coup de grâce*, a pompous blast of chauvinism that served to underline the high camp of the occasion.

Nothing sheds light on Bowie's glam-pantomime era better than Susan Sontag's *Notes On 'Camp'*, written back in 1964. 'The whole point of Camp is to dethrone the serious,' she wrote in Note 41.

'Camp involves a new, more complex relation to "the serious". One can be serious about the frivolous, frivolous about the serious.'

Bowie understood that sincerity – the guiding spirit behind much of the rock era – was never enough. In Sontag's words, it was another form of 'simple philistinism, intellectual narrowness'.

As with every good melodrama – whether camp or straight-faced – the final Ziggy show had a cliff-hanger. 'It was the last gig of the tour,' says Woody Woodmansey. 'You pull out all the stops. Obviously, David knew it was the last show, so he was really on form that night. I'm thankful I didn't know because it's there on film forever and it was a great show.'

Outside the venue, the 'We're All Working Together With David Bowie' sign on the hoarding was still up – as if band, backstage crew and audience alike were moving as one. But, like most of the Bowie entourage and everyone out in the stalls, Woodmansey was in the dark as to the significance of Bowie's valedictory speech.

'Has David decided to quit the business?' the drummer retrospectively reflects. 'Is that what he was saying? Everything was up in the air.'

A huge farewell party was thrown afterwards at the Café Royal. Dr John played on the small stage while an all-star cast feasted on champagne, smoked salmon and strawberries 'n' cream. Bowie was pictured deep in conversation with Lou Reed and Mick Jagger, or eyeing up his next protégé, Lulu. Neither Woodmansey nor bassist Trevor Bolder were any the wiser when the night was over.

BOWIE FINISHED WITH LIVE GIGS

Four days later, on July 7, Woody Woodmansey married his childhood sweetheart in East Grinstead. Though both were invited, the Bowies didn't attend. 'I got the call a few minutes after getting married,' Woodmansey says. 'I'd assumed it was just to say, "Congratulations, your present's in the post."' Instead, the drummer was told that his services were no longer required.

A statement issued by MainMan the day after the show declared that Bowie 'was leaving the concert stage forever'. But at the party, MainMan PR Cherry Vanilla had told select reporters, 'David could be performing sooner than you think, but in a different way.'

When Bowie eventually raised his head, he cited exhaustion and suggested he was likely to take up a film offer. But of one thing he was certain: 'It's been a great run, but this scene is finished for me now.'

Due to deadlines, the news was mostly reported on the inside pages of the rock papers rather than the cover. Only *NME*, whose Charles Shaar Murray had the scoop, ran with a massive 'Bowie Quits… That's It' cover headline.

According to MainMan's latest newsletter, Bowie's vast arena tour of the USA and Canada had been cancelled. Instead, he was going to 'spend the summer in France and Italy recording, relaxing and writing the script of his future'.

'I knew it was the end of the Spiders,' Bowie admitted on a Radio 1 documentary years later. 'I'd done as much as I could in the context of that band. And I was so weary of touring that I wondered whether I wanted to tour again.'

Within days of his July 3, 1973 proclamation, Bowie seemed to be reconsidering his actions: 'What have I said? I'm feeling better already!'. But the script prevailed. 'That's what Ziggy did so I had to do it too. Ziggy broke up the band. It was a self-fulfilling prophecy.'

Ultimately, Bowie was taking back control. The masquerade had enabled him to do things that the pre-Ziggy Bowie would have found uncomfortable: a naked lunge for stardom; compromising with the music business. Now that he was a real star – more Dean or Brando than Elton, Marc or Rod, as Defries liked to tell everyone – Bowie had given himself the freedom to play any part he fancied.

'He'll be back,' Mick Ronson told Ray Hollingworth under an 'Is Bowie Really Quitting?' headline in the July 14 issue of *Melody Maker*. 'We haven't even started yet. David has to keep changing.'

BOWIE QUITS

That same month, in a late, lukewarm review of *Aladdin Sane*, *Let It Rock* contributor Simon Frith predicted: 'In the long run, I suppose Bowie will become a Judy Garland-type performer, putting on a show. Rock will be one of his tools but only one. He'll be our answer to Bette Midler.'

A week later, with Ronson, a reinstated Bolder and producer Ken Scott, David Bowie decamped to the Château d'Hérouville for a project that screamed, 'There's no business like show business': an album covering favourite sixties beat-band 45s and B-sides.

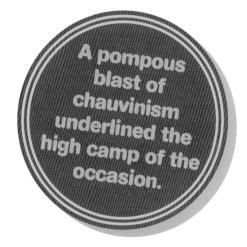

A pompous blast of chauvinism underlined the high camp of the occasion.

Chapter 20
Cover Girls, Cover Boys

By January 1973, Eno was favouring a dual-tone brown hairstyle with a patch of blond over one ear. He was similarly meticulous about his outfits, flamboyant and 'terribly feminine', as he put it.

Yet in conversation with NME writer Nick Kent late that month, Roxy Music's self-styled 'non-musician' and the man widely tipped to become Face of '73 was clearly narked by the conspicuous consumption of fashion. 'I'm really fed up with all this thing about glamour,' he said. 'We had to get a girl in to pose for the cover of the new album, which I thought was a drag because it's all becoming too stereotyped.'

He'd have preferred, he said, an 'unpretentious, unglamorous picture of the band, wearing false beards and denims and standing around a tree with "Support Ecology" on the back of the sleeve'. But Eno had no say in the matter – and that, perhaps, lay at the root of his disgust.

The sleeve artwork for Roxy's as yet unrecorded second album was in the vein of the first – with a high-class model in a high-gloss glamour setting. Once again, it was Bryan Ferry's domain. He conceptualised the cover, assisted by regular collaborators Anthony Price (wardrobe, makeup), Nick De Ville (art director) and Karl Stoecker (photographer).

This time, the model was Amanda Lear, muse to Salvador Dalí, one-time lover of her lookalike, Rolling Stone Brian Jones, and an enigma of apparently indeterminate gender and ancestry. Ferry spotted her on an Ossie Clark catwalk. Lear's glamour-with-a-twist matched Roxy's arch take on pop culture perfectly.

Shot in January in a London studio, the cover image visualised a futuristic Tinseltown – high in the Hollywood Hills with an ultra-modern cityscape below, the archetypal femme fatale taking centre-stage with a black panther as companion.

To the left of the picture, flipped to the back cover for the eventual album, Ferry posed as the limo driver. This was sex and the city noir style, all lipstick traces and dirty plot twists.

The scenario was far removed from the America experienced by the band during their coast-to-coast

This was sex and the city noir style, all lipstick traces and dirty plot twists.

December '72 tour. 'Very, very down,' was Ferry's impression of the place from the vantage point of his Earl's Court flat weeks later. The only Roxy song to connect was 'Re-Make/Re-Model' because, he said, 'it's crude'.

Bryan didn't think New York's 'drab' residents deserved the city that they lived in. Only Los Angeles, where the band enjoyed an appreciative audience at the Whisky A Go Go, met his exacting standards.

Playing warm-up to acts such as Edgar Winter, Humble Pie and Jethro Tull (supporting the latter at New York's Madison Square Garden), Roxy Music made little impression. '[Audiences] seem to be three to five years out of date,' Ferry told *Sounds*' Steve Peacock.

Even the rare favourable stateside review seemed to disapprove of the Roxy aesthetic. Writing about the first album for *Creem* in January 1973, Robert Christgau spoke of the music's 'polished deformity', the celebration of 'the kind of artifice that could come to seem as unhealthy as the sheen on a piece of rotten meat'. But at least Eno got noticed: 'a balding, long-haired eunuch lookalike'.

On the plus side, Bowie sent the band some poinsettias for good luck and ex-Velvet Underground viola/keyboard/bass player John Cale offered to produce the new album in LA. Eno was all for doing it cheaply in half a day, with a view to achieving a sound like the Velvets' thrillingly overdriven *White Light/White Heat*. But Ferry was just happy to go home.

Roxy Music had cleaned up in every UK 'Best New Act' poll at the end of 1972. They had an eye-boggling look that kept them in the rock and pop press, and a fearsome reputation for musical innovation. Still, much was riding on their first release of the year: 'Pyjamarama', issued in late February 1973, managed to sound simultaneously cautious, baffling and inspired.

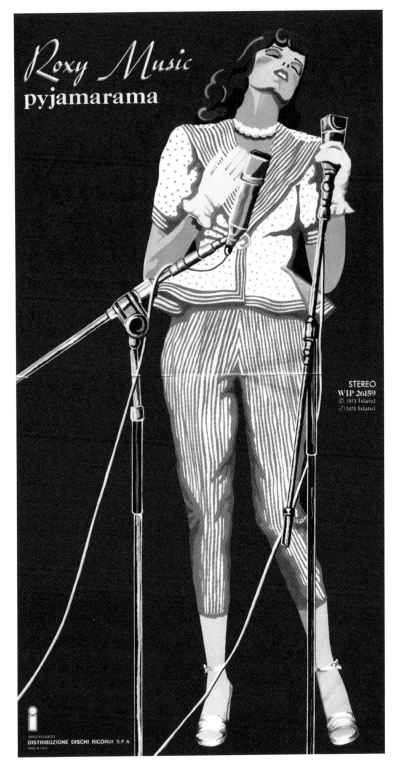

LEFT: Tipped by some as the 'Face of 1973', Eno charmed journalists with his pop theorising and lively Maida Vale abode.

ABOVE: Second Roxy single 'Pyjamarama' – shown here in its Italian form – was a masterclass in understated pop sophistication.

Sock It To Me!
The Now Generation
Sock Me Your Love · Baby Don't You Weep · Sockerina
Old Time Sock · Frankie And Johnny · & Others

MARBLE
ARCH

SHOW SOUVENIR

THIS BOOK IS DESIGNED FOR YOUR FURTHER ENJOYMENT OF THE SHOW
IT IS NOT A PROGRAMME

ROXY MUSIC

ABOVE: Continental model, singer and *Sock It To Me!* cover girl Amanda Lear was and remains an enigma of Warhol Superstar proportions. After seeing her on an Ossie Clark catwalk, Bryan Ferry put Lear on the cover of second Roxy album, *For Your Pleasure*, with himself masquerading as her chauffeur.

ABOVE RIGHT: Putting Phil Manzanera – in his customary 'fly' glasses – on the front of Roxy's 1973 tour programme hid the fact that relations between Bryan Ferry and Eno were deteriorating.

RIGHT: While Eno fantasised about feeding Roxy's instruments through the VCS3 synthesizer, Ferry's vision was to ditch the messy retro futurism and go for a cleaner, less accident-prone sound. A switch to writing songs on guitar, starting with 'Pyjamarama', was indicative of his new, more controlled approach.

Unusually, Ferry had written 'Pyjamarama' on guitar, sending out a strong statement of how he wanted the band to keep evolving. The song, with a more refined allure than the beaty wallop of 'Virginia Plain', was quietly seductive, with a bubbling rhythm that evoked the hapless chickens Colonel Tom made to dance on hotplates, pre-Elvis. In an era of bold introductions, the ringing guitar chords that set the song up provided a masterclass in counterintuitive pop fanfare.

'Pyjamarama' hit No. 10 on April 14 and stayed there for three weeks. John Peel, reviewing it in

Disc, lauded the single as 'a handsome row'. It was the band's first collaboration with producer Chris Thomas, who cut his teeth working on The Beatles' 'White Album' and with Procol Harum.

'He showed us how to construct things, how instruments locked together without being overplayed,' says guitarist Phil Manzanera. 'Pyjamarama' was an almost exact expression of that modus operandi, so Thomas was kept on board for the February second album sessions at AIR Studios.

With all but a couple of vocals and mixes left to do, Eno broke off at the end of the sessions to talk to *Sounds*' Steve Peacock. In a wide-ranging piece titled 'Unease Of The Bogus Man', he discussed a new costume that would require feathers from the tail of a lyrebird as well as Roxy's blossoming confidence.

Songs were now 'anchored to a strong base' he said approvingly, rather than the 'dilettantism' that characterised the first album. He was particularly excited about one piece, the nine-minute-plus 'The Bogus Man': 'It's probably the most successful track because it's the one on which the band is most obviously working together,' he said of the extended, Can-like improvisation topped off by Ferry playing the ghoul.

That same week *NME* featured Eno in its 'Under The Influence' column, where he discussed his admiration for Buddy Holly, systems music, The Velvet Underground's 'overpowering' third album and Mike Oldfield's percussive use of 'snake guitar' on Kevin Ayers' 'Song From The Bottom Of A Well'.

Eno was a genial and generous host. Journalists came away from his Maida Vale bachelor pad with plenty to report. Ducks on the wall; mischievous women lurking about the place; conversations on the joys of muzak and working with his new musical playmate, 'Rodney Frock', alias King Crimson's Robert Fripp – a collaboration that would yield the experimental, proto-ambient, tape-loop extravaganza (*No Pussyfooting*) in November.

Ferry, by his own admission, was a reluctant interviewee. When, in January 1973, Nick Kent, Ian MacDonald and Charles Shaar Murray all turned up at the singer's Earl's Court abode on behalf of *NME*, Ferry greeted them in an exquisitely tailored dove-grey jacket, offered them champagne and spoke from behind green-tinted shades.

There was a fine line between poise and pose, and Ferry – sometimes lampooned as 'Byron Ferrari', or even 'Biryani Ferret', in gossip columns – seemed to have a well-heeled foot in both camps. But diffidence,

and a belief that the work should speak for itself, was part of Ferry's makeup too.

For Your Pleasure was released on March 23 to huge acclaim. 'This isn't rock. It's Roxy,' claimed the ad campaign ambitiously. Where once the band's fashion fixation and sonic eclecticism had intrigued, or more often baffled, now Roxy seemed synonymous with an elevated sense of glamour that most glam acts would barely recognise. They rocked with as much passion as any 'people's band' and, in terms of innovation, left the progressive acts covered in dust.

Side one was filled with Ferry's most recent songs. None was more impressive than opener 'Do The Strand', jump-started by Ferry's conspiratorial 'There's a new sensation!', delivered as if performing some clunky magic-show trick. There was more high drama at the end of the first side, where 'In Every Dream Home A Heartache' explored the limits of comfort and desire via a darkly comic tale involving a blow-up doll.

The second side was dominated by the krautrock-like persistence of 'The Bogus Man' and the title track, a slow-burn awash in loops and echo with the longest fade since Soft Machine's 'Moon In June' – and with a brief walk-on for actress Judi Dench, whispering 'You don't ask why,' as sampled by the band's extraterrestrial boffin.

When Roxy Music returned to BBC2's *The Old Grey Whistle Test* in April, the show's presenter, DJ Bob Harris, was uncharacteristically downbeat, suggesting his views hadn't changed since their previous appearance when he'd claimed the band were 'style over substance' and their music 'somewhat computerised'.

In the TV presenter's favour, on that occasion Roxy had mostly mimed to pre-recorded backing tracks. By spring 1973, however, he was in the minority: *For Your Pleasure* spent six weeks in the top ten, peaking at No. 4.

During the spring promotional tour, Roxy played two nights at the Rainbow. A section of the crowd – 'Roxettes', as they were sometimes known – turned up in various shades of vintage glamour: young women with net face veils, pencil skirts and strap shoes; young men with high-rise fifties D.A.s, streaked and

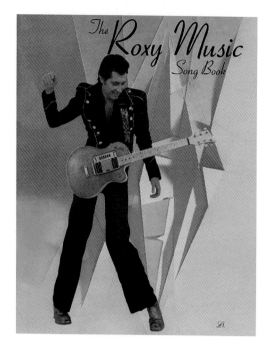

When, on May 26, Nick Kent caught up with Roxy in Amsterdam for the last night of the tour, he noted how Ferry hung out with publicist Simon Puxley and management; Andy Mackay and Phil Manzanera stuck together, while Eno seemed to be alone.

Within two weeks, Ferry was back in London to record his first solo album. 'It will be all old classics,' he told *Sounds*' Martin Hayman. 'I don't want to compromise the next Roxy Music album.'

Ferry had been dropping hints about his desire to record what he called 'my favourite things' since January. He eventually settled on a set of mostly familiar material, ranging from The Rolling Stones' revolution rocker 'Sympathy For The Devil' to the 1930s standard that would give the album its title.

Because several of the songs required strong keyboard or faux-orchestral elements, Ferry looked outside the band for a talented multi-instrumentalist. A loose family connection led him to Eddie Jobson, Curved Air's violin-playing teenage whizz-kid, who joined Roxy's Paul Thompson and current bassist John Porter for the sessions. Manzanera played the guitar break on Beatles cover 'You Won't See Me'; neither Mackay nor Eno were invited.

On July 2, Roxy Music regrouped for an open-air festival gig at the Museum Gardens in York. Ferry invited Jobson along to watch. Mackay and Manzanera both felt uncomfortable about it.

Matters were made worse when a handful of enthusiastic Eno fans kept yelling out his name while Ferry was at the microphone. Eno even slunk off stage – to contemplate his laundry, he quipped later – in a bid to ease the situation.

Shortly afterwards, Ferry swore that he'd never perform on stage with Eno again. Rather than wait to be pushed, pop's most celebrated non-musician walked.

The July 21 issue of *Melody Maker* carried 'Eno Quits Roxy' on its front page. 'The group's electronic wizard wants to become a vocalist and plans to form a group called Loana And The Little Girls,' stated the report – though Eno's never-to-be-fulfilled, all-femme line-up was actually christened Luana And The Lizard Girls.

It was also announced that Eddie Jobson was leaving Curved Air and would be joining Roxy Music in the studio to record their third album, imminently.

'I was cramping Eno's style,' Ferry rationalised a week later. 'Two non-musicians in a band is one too many. I think he'll do very well by himself.'

Eno was bugged enough to consider calling a press conference to air his grievances, before telling Nick Kent, 'My thirst for revenge has died down.

tinted. Faces sparkled with neatly applied cosmetics. 'A combination of the great and the grotesque,' noted *Record Mirror*'s Val Mabbs.

Now that Ferry spent more time out front than stage-side at his keyboard, his skills as a performer were commanding attention. 'The group has the new Mick Jagger,' wrote Tony Palmer in *The Observer*. 'He has the same magnetic brilliance, the same supreme self-confidence… He looks mean and cold and struts with the precision of a matador.'

Back in the music press, Eno was still the personality everyone wanted more of. 'My make-up is the same both on and off stage to a greater or lesser degree,' he answered a reader's enquiry in *Melody Maker*. 'It consists of a large selection of things including Quant, Revlon, Schwarzkopf and Yardley. On my eyes I use six different colours by three or four different makers. I'm using Quant crayons quite a lot at present.'

In March *Disc*'s Caroline Boucher hinted at friction, stating that Roxy 'contains more strong-willed individuals than a lot of bands'. The live dates seemed to exacerbate differences between Bryan Ferry and Brian Eno.

Elsewhere on the tour, in a post-gig interview with *Sounds*' Barry Dillon, Eno dominated the conversation while Ferry and saxophonist Mackay stayed silent. Breaking ranks, he insisted the band would have preferred 'Do The Strand' as the recent single.

RIGHT: After Eno's departure in July 1973, Ferry's *These Foolish Things*, a solo collection of covers that spanned the decades, portrayed the singer as a classically minded sophisticate. 'The standard of songwriting is abominable,' he said of the contemporary scene.

Ziggy for the stage?

'There was a tension between me and Bryan,' he said. 'Bryan felt the focus was divided by me being on stage and that wasn't what he wanted.'

Ferry's power grab destabilised the band. 'When Eno left, we were in great danger of imploding completely,' admits Manzanera, though he lays the blame elsewhere. 'It's always the people behind the scenes, the managers and agents, who stir things up. Me and Andy kept [the band] together.'

★

In March 1973, the *NME* letters page had carried a blunt headline: 'Bowie: Pseud Or Sage?' Six months later, Bowie's actions cut such debate dead. He was opting out to become a covers artist.

To the rock press, releasing an album of cover versions was barely a step up from Elton John's jobbing days singing White Plains' 'My Baby Loves Lovin'' and Christie's 'Yellow River' for budget labels such as Hallmark and Marble Arch. Except that, Bowie being Bowie, he was in effect curating a micro-era.

Two days after the Ziggy retirement show, Bowie sat down in a London hotel with a pile of his most cherished singles from the mid-sixties. Picking out songs such as The Pretty Things' 'Rosalyn', Pink Floyd's 'See Emily Play', The Merseys' 'Sorrow' and, perhaps most relevantly, The Kinks' B-side 'Where Have All The Good Times Gone', he got to feel like a fan again. It was therapy.

For three weeks in July at the Château, with his personal chef in attendance, Bowie – still the Ziggy doppelganger – threw himself back into the London club scene of 1964-67. His versions, excepting 'Sorrow', were routine and mostly inferior, but perhaps that was the point; he was all out of ideas.

ABOVE: Bowie's first post-*Ziggy* set, *Pin Ups*, was a covers collection focused on songs popular in and around mid-sixties London clubland. The inclusion of 1965 Kinks B-side 'Where Have All The Good Times Gone' chimed with Bowie's sense of fatigue after an enormously busy and successful year.

ABOVE RIGHT: A plan to take *The Ziggy Stardust Show* to Broadway faltered. Bowie's next idea, to star in a stage production of George Orwell's dystopian novel *1984*, was stymied by a rights issue.

RIGHT: Bowie bids farewell to the Ziggy era at the Hammersmith Odeon, July 3, 1973. Bodyguard Stuey George keeps a watchful eye from behind the speakers.

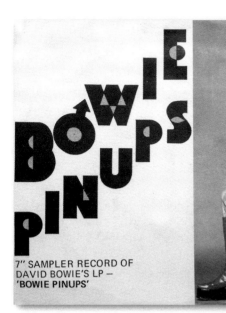

7" SAMPLER RECORD OF DAVID BOWIE'S LP – 'BOWIE PINUPS'

Bowie sat down with a pile of cherished mid-sixties singles and felt like a fan.

During the sessions, *NME*'s Charles Shaar Murray was invited over for the big interview. 'I had a certain idea of what I wanted my rock'n'roll star to be like,' said Bowie of the previous two years. 'The star was created; he worked, and that's all I wanted him to do. Anything he did now would just be repetition.'

Bryan Ferry's own standards collection was more radical. It rewrote the rulebook by giving equal weight to songs across different genres (and, in the case of the title track, across the decades), ranging from Dylan's 'A Hard Rain's A-Gonna Fall' to Erma Franklin's 'Piece Of My Heart'.

Further still, unlike Bowie's faithful endeavour, Ferry remade the songs in his own image: replacing rebellion with some cackling supper-club Satanism on the Stones cover, channelling Dylan's ire into a

foot-tapper and mischievously retaining the jilted-girl perspective of 'It's My Party'. (In a further twist, original singer Lesley Gore was a lesbian.)

Quizzed about his Dylan cover by *NME*'s Ian MacDonald, Ferry replied: 'I think it's a beautiful song, although I can't be bothered with all that Cuba [missile] crisis stuff. I like the images.'

The vocalist had no doubts about the emotional honesty of his interpretations. Back in his native northeast, he'd once sung Frank Sinatra's 1966 hit, 'Strangers In The Night', at a talent contest in a working men's club. He didn't win – and never forgot it. Given that Ferry's vocal style was becoming a regular target for caricature, *These Foolish Things* was as much about proving his worth as a singer.

Both released in October 1973, Ferry's album and Bowie's *Pin Ups* marked a turning point of sorts, re-emphasising the idea of the pop soloist and lending at least some credibility to the idea of the cover version. On November 3, *Pin Ups* entered the chart at No. 1 and *These Foolish Things* at No. 5.

When Bryan was asked at the time whether his band might now be renamed Bryan Ferry & Roxy Music, Ferry's PR man butted in and told him, 'You don't have to answer that!'

LEFT: After Bowie namechecked sixties model Twiggy on 'Drive-In Saturday', her partner, photographer Justin de Villeneuve, approached him with a view to shooting the pair for *Vogue*. Bowie agreed to the session but used the key image for the *Pin Ups* cover. This outtake emphasises Bowie's distinctive non-matching eyes.

ABOVE: A 7" *Pin Ups* sampler made for the New Zealand market. Single 'Sorrow', a top-five hit for The Merseys in 1966, peaked at three in late November.

Chapter 21
Send in the Clowns

In April 1973, an 18-year-old sometime actor, Simon Turner, was promoted as Britain's answer to David Cassidy. 'A five foot five, blond bundle of unsure, good-looking talent,' ran the press release, though blue-eyed Turner was more in the mould of a young Bowie or Peter Frampton, 1968 vintage. His new debut album even included a version of Bowie's 'The Prettiest Star'.

Turner was the protégé of Jonathan King, who was also looking after 'the new Donny', Ricky (son of fifties rocker Marty) Wilde. King had his own label, UK Records, and his own limo. He'd also launched the careers of Genesis and, more recently, 10cc.

Now Turner became a regular face in *Record Mirror*, a columnist for the *Diana* girls' mag and a popular draw in record shops around the country, to which he was packed off for signing sessions.

But Simon Turner hated pop. He preferred US

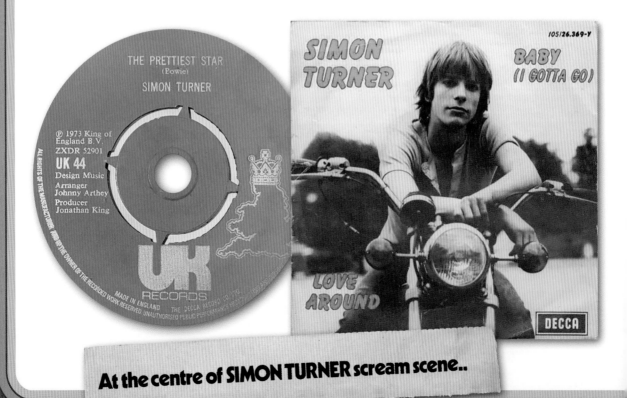

At the centre of SIMON TURNER scream scene..

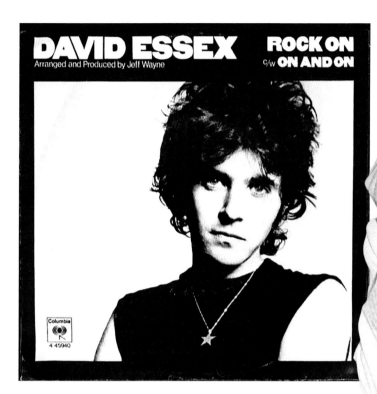

hard-rock bands such as Mountain and Steppenwolf. Most remarkably, like Eno he was part of the Portsmouth Sinfonia – an orchestra comprising music students and enthusiasts with no musical training. His favourite album of 1973 was *Journey*, a pioneering electronic work by Arthur Brown's Kingdom Come.

In terms of magazine publicity, Turner was a star. But not one of his eight singles for UK Records would ever sell enough to dent the chart.

(Later, after spells spent house-sitting for David Bowie and driving for Adam Ant, Simon Fisher Turner would re-emerge in the 1980s as a soundtrack composer for Derek Jarman's art films.)

Still, Jonathan King had astutely spotted a gap in the market for a homegrown heartthrob. Much of what had happened in pop since early 1971 had been propelled by the face of Marc Bolan. Rod and Bowie may have played supporting roles, but Bolan, with his poet-mystic persona, had represented a new, near-supernatural kind of pop star.

By May 1973, the T. Rex frontman was still capable of pulling off a *Jackie* cover story, but overfamiliarity had dimmed his allure. The pin-up culture he'd once dominated had been largely surrendered to David Cassidy, Donny Osmond, Michael Jackson and, mostly for their sartorial excesses, to Gary Glitter, The Sweet and Slade.

He sang the bare bones of the song while playing percussion on a rubbish bin.

LEFT: Tipped as the British David Cassidy, young actor Simon Turner released a version of Bowie's 'The Prettiest Star'. He soon walked away from pop.

ABOVE: David Essex's 'Rock On', all fragmented bass, reverb and sonic disorientation, took the brave option in launching a new star.

London – was 25 and had set out on a career in music at the same time as Bowie and Bolan. The Fontana, Pye and Decca labels all tried to launch his career, with no success.

David Essex's big break came in 1971, when he was chosen to play Jesus in the rock musical *Godspell*. Soon afterwards, *Sunday Times* critic Harold Hobson was comparing Essex's portrayal to El Greco's tormented Christ and Murillo's benign shepherd. The production was a huge success – with Essex's twinkly eyes and compassionate expression entrancing audiences. He was also heavily featured on the Original London Cast album, which peaked at No. 11 in April 1972, just behind *Electric Warrior* and *Slade Alive!*.

In July 1973, Essex announced he would be leaving the production in September. The catalyst was *That'll Be The Day*, a gritty take on rock'n'roll nostalgia that had become the big summer hit in British cinemas. Having played lovable rogue and aspiring pop star Jim MacLaine, Essex wanted another crack at pop stardom himself.

The double LP soundtrack album, advertised on TV by budget label Ronco Records, topped the album chart all summer. Included amidst a vast selection of original fifties and early-sixties hits was Essex's 'Rock On', tucked away on side four. The song didn't feature in the film, though it was used later in the US print for the end credits.

In August, 'Rock On' was issued on 45 via the actor-singer's new solo deal with CBS. The title suggested a cynical cash-in on the continuing rock'n'roll revival. But Essex – who once let it be known that he admired rock's furthest-out adventurer, Captain Beefheart – was now taking his music seriously. 'Rock On' was the most original-sounding single to crash the chart since

During the summer, *Jackie* reverted to putting more young women modelling hats, hairstyles and lipstick on the cover. But the magazine was still on the hunt for new heartthrobs. Over two weeks that same month, the biggest selling teenage weekly offered a poster of David Essex – one of its regular poster-in-instalments offerings.

Like Simon Turner, Essex was an actor with pop-star looks, but he wasn't 18. While his angelic, heart-shaped face made him look younger, Essex – originally David Cook from Canning Town, east

Essex's portrayal had been compared to El Greco's tormented Christ.

Roxy's 'Virginia Plain' or the first Glitter 45 – possibly even more so.

Nothing had sounded this sparse since Timmy Thomas's 1972 hit, 'Why Can't We Live Together'. That was socially conscious, lo-fi soul in mono, set to a primitive drum machine. Essex's song was all reverb and sonic disorientation, featuring twangy, double-tracked bass parts (courtesy of Herbie Flowers, who'd performed similarly singular sessions for Bowie and Lou Reed) and swooping strings – an inspired cubist framework for Essex's hollowed-out vocals.

The production whizz behind this dub-style pop masterpiece was Jeff Wayne. Essex had sung the bare bones of the song to the producer whilst playing percussive accompaniment on a rubbish bin. It gave Wayne – later known for adapting *The War Of The Worlds* into a musical extravaganza – the idea to use echo, rather than chords, as the song's building block.

Both were convinced that 'Rock On', essentially a piece of mood music, was a riskier but more distinctive way to launch Essex than taking the usual actor-as-balladeer route. But the rock press was wary. 'Very much a manufactured article,' insisted

Michael Watts in *Melody Maker*. The full-page ad for the *Rock On* album, released in November and not half as adventurous as the single, didn't help with its prominent 'Produced, arranged and conducted by Jeff Wayne for Jeff Wayne Music' credit.

The follow-up 45, 'Lamplight', issued like the album in November, sounded much like a Jazz Age 'Rock On'. Despite the pleasant surprise of his initial No. 3 hit, many shared Watts' view of Essex's transition from screen to recording studio: 'He sounds, in short, what he is: a guy of large theatrical talent muscling in on the pop biz.'

David Essex didn't stay away from acting for long. In September 1973 came news of a sequel to *That'll Be The Day*. Its title had a familiar ring: *Stardust*.

The storyline would chronicle the many perils of fame, that age-old *A Star Is Born* routine reworked for the rock scene: compromises made on the way up; fallouts between band and frontman; ruinous visits to the States; suggestions of bisexuality; a lofty rock opera – followed by the inevitable slide into drugs, creative stasis and taking flight to live a hermit's existence in the wilds of Spain, before OD'ing on the cusp of a comeback.

LEFT: Essex was singled out for praise from the start of *Godspell*'s long theatre run. 'An excellent choice for Jesus,' wrote one critic in 1971. '*Godspell* will do him no harm.' He bowed out of the production on September 15, 1973.

ABOVE LEFT: Follow-up 45 'Lamplight' sounded like a Jazz Age 'Rock On'. Essex's lead role in *Stardust* followed the well-worn *A Star Is Born* trajectory, ending in disillusionment and disintegration.

OVER PAGE: 'SLADISM!' Slade fans congregate outside Earls Court, London, July 1, 1973. At Slade gigs, fans would hold their scarves high and sing football anthem 'You'll Never Walk Alone'.

Stardust had been in the works before Bowie cut Ziggy off in his prime at the Hammersmith Odeon. But the tale of disillusionment and disintegration – eventually released in autumn 1974 – anticipated the mood: Alice Cooper, The Faces, Bolan, Roxy Music, even Slade were all experiencing similar convulsions.

On July 1, 1973, less than two months after Bowie's Earls Court disaster, Slade packed the venue with 17,000 boisterous fans, many dressed in silver, tartan, top hats, platform shoes and hooped socks. Noting the pitfalls that ruined Bowie's show, manager Chas Chandler made sure there would be no repeat performance: a raised stage was constructed with giant screens on either side and an 11,000-watt PA system installed. 'It will be like watching monster colour TV,' predicted a Polydor Records spokesman.

As usual, there was a strong support act: The Sensational Alex Harvey Band. But despite their reputation as tough rock'n'rollers, the SAHB had been plagued by 'We want Slade!' chants on the May and June dates. At Earls Court, the crowd were no less impatient but more gracious.

Slade were hitting a peak. A tricky six-week US tour during April and May – pairing them variously with The Eagles, Lou Reed and Steely Dan – was now behind them. When, on May 31, they played Glasgow for the first night of the next British tour, Holder responded to the 'Nice one, Noddy' chants – based on football anthem hit 'Nice One, Cyril' – with a relieved, 'It's great to hear the roar of a home crowd'.

By the time Slade hit Earls Court, 'Skweeze Me, Pleeze Me', their latest, most histrionic hit yet, was just into its second week at No. 1. The band were in great form visually, too: Don Powell all in white; Jim Lea in his favoured red lurex suit; Noddy Holder wearing his mirrored top-hat and chequered waistcoat; Dave Hill in silver boots and a long embroidered coat, with silver glitter on his face.

'It would be difficult to imagine any group emulating the barrage of fanatical acclaim that Slade won for themselves at Earls Court,' wrote Chris Charlesworth in *Melody Maker* the following week. 'It was more of a convention than a concert, a gathering of the converted that rivalled political assemblies, royal weddings and sporting crowds in both size and fervour. It was bluddy wonderful.'

At one point, the house lights went up and everyone sang that most famous terrace chant: 'You'll

Never Walk Alone'. Many waved scarves above their head; some fainted.

Holder didn't let the size of the venue curtail his ribald humour. Calling for a minute's silence, he added a forfeit to anyone who dared make a noise: 'If it's a bloke, he's got to come up on stage and take his trousers down. If it's a young lady, she's got to come up here and take her knickers off.' Earls Court erupted.

The evening ended with a mass singalong of 'Mama Weer All Crazy Now'. One of the many headlines that followed hailed the event – which was filmed – as 'Slade's Finest Hour'.

The band had been on the road almost continuously since late March. On June 8, a homecoming gig at Birmingham Town Hall had been cut short after drummer Powell collapsed. He was exhausted. After Earls Court the band prepared for a well-earned break, with Wolverhampton as the first stop so that they could be with their families.

Don Powell and Dave Hill – now restyled as 'Super Yob', complete with customised guitar – had even more reason to welcome some time off. They'd booked a double trip to Mexico, where Dave and his girlfriend planned to marry – with a suggestion that Don and his partner might get hitched too. But only one couple would make the journey.

Two nights after Earls Court, in the early hours of July 4, Don picked up his girlfriend, Angela Morris, from the club where she worked. Minutes later, the pair were thrown through the windscreen of the drummer's white Bentley, after it veered off the road into a brick wall.

Angela was killed instantly. Don was rushed into intensive care. His father called the rest of the band to tell them his son was in a coma, and to expect the worst.

After five days, Don Powell regained consciousness. His skull was held together with clamps. He had no memory of Angela or the crash. His sense of smell and taste were gone forever.

But he was out of danger and on the start of a long road to recovery. It soon became apparent that even his memory of Slade's repertoire had mostly been erased. 'The only thing I remembered was who I was and that I played drums,' he'd later admit in his autobiography.

Meanwhile, Dave Hill married his girlfriend in Tijuana in a $35 ceremony, which they celebrated with a bottle of sparkling red wine.

By mid-September, Don Powell was flying out with Slade for their delayed US tour. His early return was

advised by his specialist. The man known as 'The Powerhouse' was back at his kit but had to be helped onto the stool each night. Despite the exertions, he began putting on weight because he'd forget that he'd already eaten.

Slade's uncomplicated attitude to life helped Don's healing. Now affectionately known as 'Mr Memory Man', the drummer acquired a new catchphrase: 'How does it go?' But the laughs only took him so far.

Always Mr Reliable, Powell was haunted by the idea that he'd let the band down – to the point where he'd regularly tell friends he was leaving. But one thing stayed the same.

While Don was laid up, fans inundated the Wolverhampton Royal Hospital with packs of the era's great unsung accessory – the stuff he inadvertently advertised every time Slade appeared on *Top Of The Pops*. 'Five tons of it,' joked Jim Lea at the time. 'He won't have to buy any chewing gum for a few years.'

LEFT: Dave Hill as 'Super Yob' was one of the era's most spectacular creations.

ABOVE: July 31, 1973. Don Powell reading 'get well' cards at his parents' home in Bilston, Staffs, after his accident.

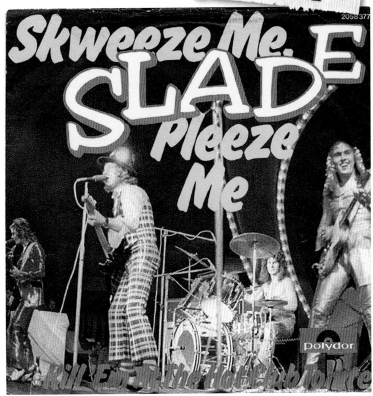

THANKS EVERYBODY
FOR
VOTING ME

1st TOP MUSICIAN

2nd TOP SINGLE –"See My Baby Jive"

6th TOP SINGER/SONGWRITER

ROY WOOD

HOPE TO SEE YOU ON THE FORTHCOMING WIZZARD TOUR

★

During the 1973 summer holidays, with Ziggy gone but Glitter's 'I'm The Leader Of The Gang (I Am!)' firmly installed at No. 1, glam was at its most contested. 'Glam Rock? It Went Out Years Ago' ran a headline in the July 21 issue of *Record Mirror*. It wasn't Bolan stating his opinion again, nor was it Bowie, who tended to stay out of the 'glitter/glam' debate. Instead, it was ex-Love Affair singer Steve Ellis, one of the magazine's cover stars back in January 1970 when he'd announced the end of teenybop.

'Boley talks as though he invented Glam Rock,' Ellis told Peter Harvey, 'but I was wearing frilly-fronted shirts when I was 16.

'If anybody did start the current trend, though, it was Roy Wood not Bolan. He can get away with it.'

But Wood never had much desire to compete with Marc, Rod, Elton, Alice or any other early seventies pop superstar. Despite his passion for dressing up and (from 1970 onward) face makeup, Wood was a reluctant frontman, almost embarrassed by success and inadvertently prone to sabotaging his career.

LEFT: Roy Wood never once disappointed a Thursday evening *Top Of The Pops* audience.

Certainly, Wizzard had failed to fully satisfy with their *Wizzard Brew* album. Their gigs could be hit-or-miss – one reviewer likened the atmosphere at a Wizzard gig to that of a morgue. However, having perfected a 'glam Spector' sound on 'See My Baby Jive' back in the spring, Wood was now ready to run with it.

'Angel Fingers' was very much the full-on rocked-up Spector – filthy saxes, angelic bells, siren voices, joyous layers of sound. On September 1, 1973, the single went in at No. 12 and the vast ensemble – like hairy Teds from Pluto – were back on *Top Of The Pops*. With his hair in a ponytail, his beard tapered into two points and brightly coloured stars around his eyes, Wizzard's master of ceremonies was in his element. Around him, the rest of the band wore an assortment of drape jackets, heavenly robes and outsize angel wings.

On September 22 'Angel Fingers' hit No. 1, repeating the feat of 'See My Baby Jive'.

While Roy Wood's one-man rock'n'roll hit machine was hitting its cheery stride, Nicky Chinn and Mike Chapman were expanding their own hit factory. Having toughened up The Sweet's sound from light bubblegum to hard pop, Chinnichap effected a similar transformation on two Mickie Most protégés, Suzi Quatro and Mud, during 1973. Quatro – with two hits behind her – was already a hot prospect.

But Suzi was still Most's act. Despite their demand for more control over their work, The Sweet remained Chinnichap's priority with first choice on any new material. The creative tension between band and management had already raised their collective game, as evidenced by the enormous success of 'Blockbuster!' and 'Hell Raiser'.

Filthy saxes, angelic bells, siren voices, joyous layers of sound.

THE SWEET
THE BALLROOM BLITZ

NEW SINGLE RCA 2403

THE
BALLROOM BLITZ
THE SWEET

RCA
LPBO-9060 ST
VICTOR

N.° 1 en
Inglaterra

Sweet
LIVE
official programme 25p

No.54
DISCO
45
Songbook

SPECIAL PRICE!
KENNY
T-SHIRT OFFER
INSIDE...

September 1973's 'The Ballroom Blitz' was even more hard-hitting – befitting the song's origins in a nasty face-off between band and audience at the Grand Hall, Kilmarnock that involved bottles and running battles among the crowd.

As usual, Mike Chapman presented the band with his raw, sketched-out demo. 'It sounded like a watered-down Marc Bolan song,' said Steve Priest. 'We thought, "What the fuck are we going to do with this?" Then [producer] Phil Wainman arrived and said, "Why don't we do a [surf-era legend] Sandy Nelson drum thing?" Suddenly, it came to life.'

'The Ballroom Blitz' riffed hard, like an old Pink Fairies rocker in Lurex. Brian Connolly deadpanned his verses in rigid, tonged-and-blow-dried fashion; the choruses showed off the band's skilled harmonies. Chapman, whose dry run for the song was far more accomplished – and suitably maniacal – than Priest remembered, had already sketched out the Shangri-Las style 'Are you ready, Steve?' intro.

Under the headline 'Rock band with a Sweet tooth,' Connolly told *Record Mirror*'s Sue James: 'Chinn and

Chapman are brilliant songwriters. But there's no point in putting their songs on the album because they make good singles.' Yet despite all the talk of writing their own material, there was still no Sweet album on the horizon.

Suzi Quatro was quicker off the mark, releasing a self-titled album in October 1973. Chinn and Chapman produced, and also provided the drum- and chant-heavy 'Primitive Love', as well as '48 Crash' which kicked off the set. Quatro and Len Tuckey wrote most of the material, including the swaggering 'Glycerine Queen', and there were also three covers: the old Stones hit 'I Wanna Be Your Man' (gender role left unchanged), Presley's 'All Shook Up' and Johnny Kidd & The Pirates' 'Shakin' All Over'.

While The Sweet embraced rock, pop and panto, Quatro was a down-the-line rock'n'roller. The *Suzi Quatro* album hit No. 32 for one week in October, then disappeared. Of more concern was how her third hit, 'Daytona Demon', stalled at No. 14 that same month. Perhaps its tough, harbinger-of-punk hookline was just too knuckle-dragging for these spotlit times.

Even Slade had a minor setback that same month, when 'My Friend Stan' failed to make their third No. 1 in a row – though any No. 2 single that sounded like John Lennon gatecrashing a Mrs Mills singalong could hardly be described as a failure. It was their first hit single since summer '71 with a correctly spelled title, and the first since Don Powell's accident.

That autumn, pop seemed to enter another one of its periods of drift and uncertainty. *Top Of The Pops* celebrated its 500th episode on October 4. The launch issue of *Story Of Pop* ('The First Encyclopaedia Of Pop In 26 Weekly Parts') hit the newsstands, with Elvis

and Bowie sharing the cover. Another chapter seemed to be closing.

Meanwhile, despite Peters & Lee's massive MoR hit 'Welcome Home' finally dropping down the charts, hits by Perry Como, Max Bygraves, Al Martino and the chart-topping 'Eye Level' (theme to TV drama series *Van Der Valk*) all suggested that BBC Radio 2 listeners were reclaiming the pop 45.

Middle-of-the-road tastes received a further boost on September 29, with the arrival of talent show *New Faces*. It was an update of the old *Opportunity Knocks* format, but with celebrity-panel judges instead of viewers voting from home. Roy Wood's old Move colleague Carl Wayne sang the theme song; its refrain was 'You're a star, superstar.'

One of the regulars on the panel was Mickie Most. On the November 17 edition, he made a strong case for an eight-piece rock'n'roll revival act from Leicester called Showaddywaddy. Winning the heat, the ensemble progressed to the grand final in December but lost out to Cardiff club singer Tom Waite. Their success earned them an audition for Polydor, but it was the astute Bell Records who launched them the following spring with the unashamedly retro 'Hey Rock'N'Roll'.

It sounded like John Lennon gatecrashing a Mrs Mills singalong.

Mickie Most took note. RAK label band Mud – who'd been together since 1967, when they released debut single 'Flower Power' – had come up through the clubs and were still playing 'Jailhouse Rock', 'Blue Moon', 'All Shook Up' and 'Teddy Bear' in their live set.

(Mud were more versatile than their popular image suggested. Their autumn 1973 repertoire also included T. Rex's 'Hot Love', Chicory Tip's 'Son Of My Father' the Stones' 'Honky Tonk Women', Sly & The Family Stone's 'Dance To The Music', Steppenwolf's 'Born To Be Wild' and music-hall staple 'Knees Up Mother Brown'. They'd also released two hits by this point, 'Crazy' and the Bolanish 'Hypnosis'.)

For October's 'Dyna-Mite', their third single of 1973, Mud dressed in matching red drape suits and black shirts, and wore highly visible socks Teddy Boy-style. It was a quiff-free, faux-fifties, glam-pop image also favoured by Showaddywaddy.

The song, already rejected by The Sweet, was based on the Glitter beat. Guitarist Rod Davis was the band's Steve Priest, with long sparkling earrings and flapping culotte trousers. To widen the appeal further, singer Les Gray and bassist Ray Stiles doubled up for a dance routine that had taken off among audiences during Status Quo's spring tour (face to face, fingers in belt hooks, heads down alternately left and right).

'Dyna-Mite' hit No. 4 in November. That made nine out of nine hits for Chinn and Chapman during 1973 – three apiece for The Sweet, Suzi and Mud.

From *That'll Be The Day* to Mud and Wizzard in drapes, rock'n'roll revivalism had moved centre stage since the summer. Then, in November, one man emerged as if he'd been in splendid hibernation since 1959.

Shane Fenton was, like Paul Raven had been, long in the tooth and desperate for a change in fortune. Rock'n'roll was in his bones. As a teenage enthusiast in the late fifties, young Bernard Jewry from Mansfield would take his acoustic guitar – which he named Peggy Sue – to all the package tours. Everyone autographed it: first Buddy Holly, then Bill Haley, Eddie Cochran, Gene Vincent, Billy Fury, Chuck Berry – a veritable who's who of rock'n'roll's golden age.

By 1961 Jewry had joined The Fentones, inheriting the name from original frontman Shane Fenton, who'd died suddenly from rheumatic fever. The band's first record was 'I'm A Moody Guy' and the new Fenton played his role well.

Everything changed with The Beatles. George Martin offered the artist now known as Shane Fenton 'Love Me Do'; Brian Epstein suggested he record 'Do You Want To Know A Secret?'. The singer turned both down, moving instead to cabaret where the pay was better. By the end of the 1960s, with fifties nostalgia in the air, he was back fronting The Shane Fenton Rock'n'Roll Trio.

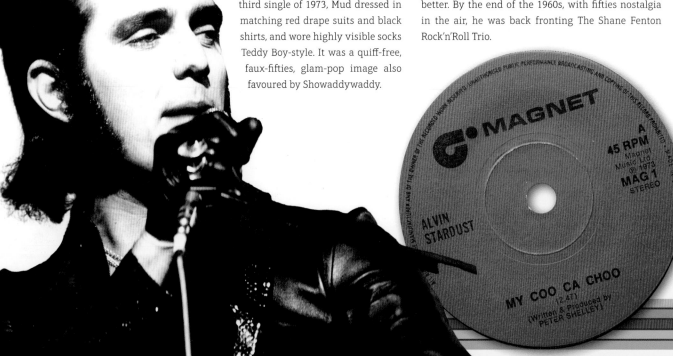

In late summer 1973, songwriter and ex-Decca A&R man Peter Shelley decided to join pop's latest gold rush. He had the song, which he'd written, produced and sung himself, but it needed a fashionable name to sell it. An early consideration was 'Al Star', before Shelley too succumbed to the magic of Stardust – in his case, 'Alvin Stardust'. To launch his creation, Shelley co-founded a record label, Magnet.

The song, 'My Coo Ca Choo', was built on the same classic boogie riff that drove Norman Greenbaum's 'Spirit In The Sky' all the way to No. 1 in 1970. Only this time it was frosted with a Glitter-ish handclap 'n' stomp routine. Shelley's voice quivered and cooed like pre-army Elvis, while Terry Britten's guitar break – decidedly more Alvin Lee than Alvin Stardust – was there to impress the rock crowd.

When the single took off in October and TV pop show *Lift Off With Ayshea* came calling, Shelley was obliged to step into the role, opting for a white-faced clown look. But he was unconvinced, both by the prospect of becoming Alvin Stardust and his own abilities to sell the record. Late fifties veterans Marty Wilde and Joe Brown both turned the project down; Shane Fenton, who already had form as a singing ghost, seized the opportunity.

Booked for the November 15, 1973 edition of *Top Of The Pops*, the rechristened Alvin bought black hair dye from Woolworths, a pair of outsize 'sideboards' from theatrical outfitters Wig Creations and black leather gloves from a ladies' shop. The gloves, he said, had been inspired by actor Jack Palance, famed for his big-screen villains. The effect was intensified by slipping one or two huge rings over the fingers.

In his *TOTP* debut, Alvin Stardust was no space-invader starman. Wearing a Gene Vincent-style, black leather two-piece and sporting a suspiciously high-rise, jet-black quiff, he fixed the camera like a pro, flashing his preposterously outsize ring at every opportunity. Alvin was the man in black, the dark prince to Gary Glitter's kingly sparkle. By early December, 'My Coo Ca Choo' had hit No. 2. It would spend more than two months in the top ten.

Initially, Alvin Stardust was a man of mystery. It didn't last long. *TOTP* presenter Tony Blackburn recognised him as Shane Fenton, as did the elders of the pop press, but the outing did little to dent his reputation as a 'mean and moody' newcomer in *Jackie* and *Popswop* magazines.

Peter Shelley quickly crafted a follow-up utilising the same materials. By early March 1974, 'Jealous Mind' put Alvin Stardust at No. 1.

The song was a plea to break free from the cigar men, the crowd, the ridicule.

ABOVE: Poplife in 1973 sounded like one never-ending party. No surprise then when Slade and Wizzard crowned the year with Christmas songs. 'Never again,' said Slade's Jim Lea. 'It'll probably come up every Christmas now.'

RIGHT: Leo Sayer's winter hit, 'The Show Must Go On', was a plea for the masquerade to end.

Recent pop Christmases had been dominated by novelty songs – 'Two Little Boys' by Rolf Harris (1969), 'Grandad' by Clive Dunn (1970 – written by the ubiquitous Herbie Flowers), Benny Hill's 'Ernie (The Fastest Milkman In The West)' (1971) and, in 1972, a double dose of Little Jimmy Osmond's 'Long Haired Lover From Liverpool' and Chuck Berry's 'My Ding-A-Ling'.

1973 would be different. It was the year glitter had gone 'glam'; the year the superstars went missing and the super-hams stepped up to fill the vacuum; the year when songs sounded more like parties and the costumes were more fancy dress than ever. To *Top Of The Pops* viewers and *Popswop* readers alike, the year had been one long Christmas.

This wasn't lost on Slade or Wizzard, who'd both lined up seasonal songs during the summer. By Christmas Day 1973, Slade's 'Merry Xmas Everybody' was at No. 1, with Wizzard's 'I Wish It Could Be Christmas Every Day' close behind at No. 4.

Gary Glitter's contribution to the Christmas singles chart was a big old sentimental singalong, 'I Love You Love Me Love'. Meanwhile, tucked in at No. 7, was a song with a more pertinent message: 'The Show Must Go On' by newcomer Leo Sayer.

Its sudden rise was due to Sayer's appearance on the previous week's *TOTP* dressed in a Pierrot outfit, his face made up like a sad circus clown. While Alvin Stardust – still in the top five – had lifted only a part of his name from Bowie's character creation, Sayer came on like yet another renegade from Lindsay Kemp's mime troupe. 'The Show Must Go On', featuring a distinctive, cabaret-style banjo part, even shared something of Bowie's *Hunky Dory*-era songcraft.

The image – which Sayer debuted on a nationwide tour supporting Roxy Music in late autumn – helped sell the record. By mid-January it hit No. 2. Yet the song itself neatly undermined the title: it was a plea to break free from the industry's 'big cigar' men, the crowd baying for blood, the ridicule. All that mattered was liberation, a release from 'this masquerade'. The truth was in the refrain: 'I wo*n't* let the show go on.'

Writing in the December 15 issue of *Record Mirror*, journalist Roger Greenaway also sensed the passing of an era: 'Glam rock may have died that warm spring evening when David Bowie whet a hundred eyes, and umpteen thousands of knickers, with his farewell scene… His "quit" night left pop without a totally demanding stage personality.'

As further evidence, he cited Bolan's 'self-imposed exile', Slade's loss of momentum after their drummer's car crash and Gary Glitter's lack of a 'proper stage presence'. 'Yes folks,' Greenaway continued, 'as 1973 drew to a close your scribe drew in breath to exclaim: "The scene's dead."'

Bowie himself, who had cleaned up at the readers' polls for the second year running, may have concurred. 'I'm sure there is a new era coming,' he said. 'There's this resurgence of spirit in entertaining.' But he wasn't sure whether that meant the return of old-style entertainers, such as Doris Day or Engelbert Humperdinck, or those with 'some kind of redeeming social value'.

'I don't even know which category I fit into,' he concluded. 'I have no stability as an artist.'

Chapter 22
Teenage Nightmare

On October 6, 1973, *Sladest*, Slade's hits collection, made its UK chart debut at No. 1 and hung around the top ten until the new year. The following month, T. Rex's *Great Hits* charted at No. 32 and was gone from the top fifty three weeks later. Full-page ads for the T. Rex collection had stated: 'By Public Demand.'

Marc Bolan cared deeply about record sales and chart placings. Even when T. Rex were huge, during 1971-72, he'd always talk the figures up higher still.

In terms of singles, Rex still enjoyed a good 1973 – both '20th Century Boy' and 'The Groover' had gone top five, with only November's 'Truck On (Tyke)' stalling outside the ten. By now, though, he was gripped by another obsession – unlocking the door to his creative renaissance.

To that end, Bolan had been taking dramatic new steps to resurrect his muse. Adding second guitarist Jack Green in time for the eleven-week summer US tour gave him free rein to play the front man – and parade his skills as a lead guitarist.

'He really tried hard to break the States,' says Green, who insists gigs were better received than critics would claim. But Bolan's showmanship and long instrumental workouts seemed unlikely to impress audiences who'd come to see headliners Three Dog Night. Cocaine, now the staple diet of the touring rock musician, played its part in keeping Bolan high on his pedestal. 'We had so much our faces would freeze into a smile,' says Green.

During the trip, in late August, Bolan paid homage to Jimi Hendrix by recording at Electric Lady Studios in New York. By then, he'd also struck up a relationship with backing singer Gloria Jones. 'He didn't have to tell me,' said Mickey Finn. 'I knew. The road's a lonely place.'

On a tip-off, June Bolan flew out to Seattle in mid-August to confront him. She had staged a similar showdown back in 1969, after Marc's brief romance with US singer/*Hair* actress Marsha Hunt.

By Public Demand
T. REX
GREAT HITS
BLN 5003   OUT NOW

The night before June's arrival, Bolan momentarily fired his rhythm section, Steve Currie and Bill Legend, on stage in Portland after falling to his knees mid-song. He was frustrated – creatively, in his personal life, and with his inability to take his limited American success to the next level.

June had been his protector. She championed his work, organised his life, even corrected his awful spelling. Gloria Jones was a singer, pianist and songwriter with deep roots in gospel and a track record at Motown. Bolan had come from the streets of northeast London, Gloria from the churches of LA. He'd grown up on US R&B and had been fired up the contemporary soul sounds he'd heard in the States. That was Gloria's world.

Bolan could sense his world was collapsing. He had to trust his spirit animal, become a voodoo child. Glam was dead. Ziggy too. Marc Bolan was ready to rise again. But first he had an important story to tell.

He'd put it all down in a song: 'Teenage Dream'.

On a plane journey out of New York, early in August, Gloria Jones had spotted Lonnie Jordan, an old friend now leading LA funk band War. It was a fortuitous meeting. While out on the West Coast, Bolan was keen to record the new song. Invited to the session, Jordan set the tone with a distinctive piano part, alternately nubbly and ornate – much like Bolan himself.

'Lyrically, it's pretty important,' Bolan later told *Melody Maker*'s Chris Welch, prior to its release in February 1974. Initially, in an echo of mid-sixties Dylan, Bolan had written 'Teenage Dream' as a nine-verse song before trimming it down to six. 'I thought of everything that day that had influenced me, and I very rarely do that,' he told Welch. 'The song is about growing up.' Growing up and moving on.

The repeated 'Whatever happened to the teenage dream?' hookline suggested the song was intended

LEFT: T. Rex's *Great Hits* flopped. Slade's hits collection topped the charts and hung around for months. But Bolan had spent long periods out of the country attempting once again to break the US market.

ABOVE: December 12, 1973: back on the streets of London with minder and rickshaw-puller for the day Alfie O'Leary. Without his long curls, Bolan looked more like Lou Reed than the flashy pop star who delivered '20th Century Boy' a few months earlier.

as a lament – both to the passing of his youthful fantasies and his period of pop supremacy. Such was Bolan's state of mind at the time of its recording, it came out more like a taunt, his intoxicated delivery revelling gleefully in the Promethean chaos of his spinning-wheel life.

The lyrics speak of 'a broken god from a rusty world', trapped in a prison of his own making. But in front of the mike, his mouthpiece to the world, Bolan snatched a kind of victory from the jaws of defeat. The song ends in an unholy, fuck-it mess, as he crashes into the microphone with one last defiant cackle.

Back in London, Tony Visconti matched Bolan's unhinged performance with a suitably bigger-than-life arrangement – all swooping, cinematic strings and sky-high backing vocals – raising the drama to almost tragicomic levels. Bolan was uncontainable. 'The day we put the strings on "Teenage Dream",' says Tony Visconti, 'my parents visited Marquee Studios in London. [Marc] ran up to my mum and yelled in her ear, "MONEY!"'

'He had a nice attitude until he believed his own publicity,' said Mickey Finn. 'That's not a put-down, that's just the music scene. He used to ring up [manager] Tony [Howard] and say, "You've got to talk to the director of *Top Of The Pops*, they've shot me from the wrong angle." He got a little bit OTT.'

Visconti had seen it coming. '"Truck On (Tyke)" has an oboe on it,' he says. 'It's known as the ill wind in the orchestra. After that, I saw the writing was on the wall. The last straw was the *Zinc Alloy* album.

ABOVE: On February 1974's 'Teenage Dream', newly cropped Bolan revelled gleefully in the Promethean chaos of his spinning-wheel life.

LEFT AND BELOW: *Zinc Alloy* was a brave 'superfunk' album. The 'Truck Off' tambourine was manufactured for the tie-in tour.

'Truck On (Tyke)' has an oboe on it. It's known as the ill wind in the orchestra.

Bolan performing guitar heroics at the Glasgow Apollo on the opening night of T. Rex's February 1974 tour. Midway through the set, he tripped on the star-shaped dais that had raised him up at the start of the show. Mickey Finn was there to catch the falling star.

ABOVE LEFT: A Deborah Loads audience shot of Rex's gig at Manchester's Free Trade Hall

ABOVE: Kath Andryszewski's ticket for the Newcastle City Hall show. 'Two lads lifted me on stage, and I ran and got a cuddle off Marc,' she recalls.

'I'd told Marc many times, "You've proved yourself as a pop icon. Now take a year off and make something like *Tommy* or *Sgt Pepper*." He'd say, "No, I've gotta make one more for the kids."

'*Zinc Alloy* was the one for the kids that I couldn't handle. It was too disjointed, too druggy.'

Bolan was a true believer in the power of *Zinc Alloy* – or *Zinc Alloy And The Hidden Riders Of Tomorrow Or A Creamed Cage In August*, to give its full title. It would be more Marc Bolan than T. Rex (hence the eventual shared billing), more future soul than old gold. At the summer '73 sessions in Munich, Marc had scrawled his intentions on paper: 'spaceage funk/interstellar supersoul'.

Despite the difficult circumstances of its recording, Bolan achieved his ambition to break new ground, incorporating James Brown's deep funk, Hendrix's intergalactic soul, a loud, sanctified 'Cosmic Choir' and, on keynote song 'Change', an echo of the wise young Tyrannosaurus mystic.

But on its release early in March 1974, *Zinc Alloy* pleased virtually no one. Having peaked at No. 12, it was gone from the top fifty just three weeks later. Bolan's optimism had been misplaced. The kids were no longer there. Some even chided Bolan for adopting a *Ziggy*-like album title, even though he'd first mentioned Zinc Alloy as an alter-ego back in summer 1968.

'Teenage Dream' fared better, hitting No. 13 in mid-February during a five-week run in the top thirty. 'There's a touch of the 'Whiter Shade Of Pale's' about it,' Bolan boasted, claiming that EMI were rush-releasing the single.

'The worst yet,' demurred one *Record Mirror* reader. 'It sounded more like someone on DRUGS.'

Bolan had changed. But in contrast to butterfly Bowie, his character was regarded as so unambiguous and naturally defined that any change felt like treachery. Bolan revelled in his new self, even chopping off the long curls integral to his appeal since 1968. It was a statement haircut, but it also begged the question: had Samson surrendered the source of his strength?

On a short British tour in February, even the band had changed beyond recognition. Now T. Rex were a ten-piece, including a Glitter-inspired two-sax/two-drum format plus the Cosmic Choir of Gloria Jones and Pat Hall.

As the T. Rex name flashed up in lights, Bolan flipped back into showbiz mode, churning out the hits while drawing out the songs to allow for his guitar heroics. At the Glasgow Apollo on January 22, the star-shaped dais that had raised him into action at the start of the show felled him midway through the set. Mickey Finn rushed to catch the falling star. Reviewing the gig in *NME*, Julie Webb noted another change in Marc, describing him as a 'Porky Pixie' and 'a glittering chipolata sausage'.

The six-date tour – with a conspicuous absence of a London gig – pleased his vastly diminished fanbase, but it seemed a significant misstep. The set included just one number from the new album, 'Teenage Dream'. 'It felt like we were just doing the same old thing,' said Mickey Finn. 'I mean, even if we did do new songs, all everybody wants were the hits. But you can't keep selling something you've already sold.'

'I don't want to be a plastic idol,' Bolan had told *Disc*'s Michael Benton back in December. 'I want respect as a musician. I've spent four crazy years and now I've got the bread to disappear into the sunset anytime I like.'

In mid-April 1974, Marc and Gloria took off for a holiday in Spain before moving on to the States. The pair spent virtually the rest of the year out of the UK.

In November 1973, British music critic Simon Frith described The Sweet in *Creem* as the seventies answer to Dave Dee, Dozy, Beaky, Mick & Tich: 'Lots of hits, lots

of money, lots of women, but nothing to write about.'

The Sweet were a pin-up band. But unlike Slade, who presented four individual personalities from the moment they broke big, much of The Sweet's early appeal had centred on Brian Connolly.

'Brian was the pretty boy at the front,' said bassist Steve Priest, 'and that was resented by the rest of us. He was doing the brunt of the work – though he did have a car to pick him up…'

Their 1973 No. 1, 'Blockbuster!', marked a shift in musical style; it also gave more focus to the instrumentalists. According to Priest, the big change came after Mike Chapman decided to introduce the rest of the band on 'The Ballroom Blitz' intro. 'That's when the magazines started taking pictures of the rest of us.'

But the three musicians weren't from the same charm school as Connolly. The Sweet's reputation for ribald humour on stage could have put Noddy Holder to shame. In the introduction to *The Sweet Folio*, a collection of sheet music published late in the year, Priest remarked: 'We don't want to be put down as an airy-fairy group. People call us puffs, but we're not. If

ABOVE: March 1975: Marc Bolan and Gloria Jones visit AIR Studios, where Mick Ronson was co-producing Ian Hunter's first solo album. 'We were just two musicians in the world of rock'n'roll and very blessed to have found one another,' says Gloria. 'It was a new lease of life for both of us.'

RIGHT: When Steve Priest stepped up to sing his cameo for 'Teenage Rampage', he remembered Mike Chapman telling him, 'Think of yourself as Dr Doolittle talking to the animals.'

I hear any taunts, people saying "He's queer," then I really start overdoing it.'

Late in 1973, Mike Chapman decided to steer The Sweet in another direction. With *The Rocky Horror Show* now a theatrical hit on the King's Road and Alice Cooper in partial retreat after a world tour, he envisaged The Sweet shifting to the dark side. To that end, he wrote and demoed 'Moonlight In Baskerville', a Sweet-like song with added Screaming Lord Sutch howls. As they'd already done with 'Dyna-Mite', the now assertive Sweet rejected it.

Days later, Chapman returned with another potential single. This time there was no hesitancy. 'Teenage Rampage' had it all: a magnificently high-camp 'We Want Sweet!' intro chant – reminiscent, some noted, of a Nuremberg rally – and a well-paced build-up towards a hysteria-driven chorus of voices in unison on the irresistible 'revolution'/'constitution' couplet.

'We did the vocal arrangements,' says Steve Priest. 'We didn't have to sit down and rehearse them. We knew exactly what we were singing.'

The incitement to riot was all meaningless fun – The Sweet were hardly the Angry Brigade – but the dynamics that roared from the 45 came from an increasingly fractious place. 'At one point when we were doing "Teenage Rampage",' said Priest, 'I had to sing "imagine the sensation of teenage occupation".

Mike Chapman said, "Think of yourself as Dr Doolittle talking to the animals." I looked at them all sitting behind the desk and said, "I thought I was." That didn't go down too well.'

'There was a certain bitterness involved in the relationship,' Chapman told John Tobler and Stuart Grundy for their 1982 book, *The Record Producers*. 'And I think the aggression that existed between Nicky [Chinn], myself, the band and [producer] Phil Wainman came out in those songs.

'Apart from Brian Connolly… with the others, it was a very aggressive relationship, especially with me. Towards the end, it was almost down to fights, but that came out on the records.'

All the pent-up frustration of The Sweet's early years was vented in an extraordinary twelve months of hit singles. 'Blockbuster!' had seen off Bowie; 'Hell Raiser', 'The Ballroom Blitz' and 'Teenage Rampage' all clocked in at No. 2.

But there was a twist in the tail. The song that kept 'Teenage Rampage' off the top was Mud's 'Tiger Feet', another intense Chinn and Chapman number for a promising, far less troublesome band. As for the single that replaced 'Tiger Feet' at the top,

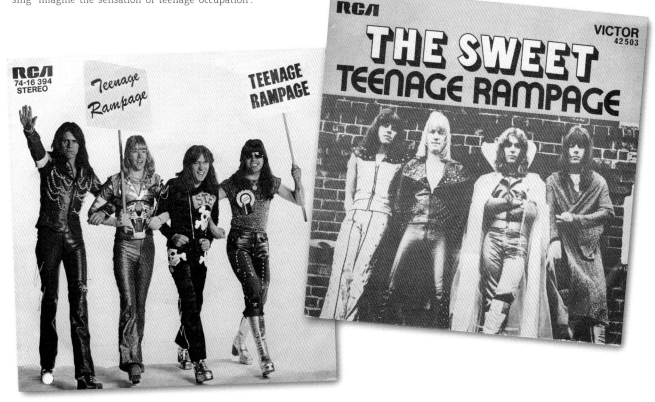

SWEET ON THE RAMPAGE

Rampant, riproaring, rousing, rocking, raging, ranting, rebellious, running riot over the airwaves and in concert halls even [...] the [...]

We Want The Sweet

Andy, Minister for Energy. No power cuts here —electric excitement all the way!

Party leader Comrade Brian, in fine form, shows how it should be done.

A meeting of the entire Cabinet giving a Party broadcast at a mass rally.

Steve, Minister for High Decibels, gets down to bass-ics.

SWEET
SWEET FANNY ADAMS
RCA
Records and Tapes

it was Suzi Quatro's 'Devil Gate Drive' – another Chinnichap production.

The Sweet may have felt usurped and aggrieved, but they had other priorities now. On stage, they were now performing 90-minute sets worthy of the hardest rock band, with big-screen backdrops, virtuoso displays and plenty of volume. They had a US tour lined up for June. But first, having secured a new three-year deal with RCA in December, they would deliver an album worthy of their talents.

Determined, as 'Teenage Rampage' put it, to 'turn another page', Sweet – who'd dropped the definite article for the album – lined up just two Chinn and Chapman songs for *Sweet Fanny Adams*. Aside from a cover of 1962 Joey Dee & The Starliters hit 'Peppermint Twist', the rest were band compositions. Andy Scott volunteered two of his own.

The album title, based on a popular slang phrase ('sweet FA' – 'fuck all', a sum total of nothing), demonstrated a desire to reach beyond their younger fans. Musically, it was a ballsy-sounding affair with far less production gloss. When *Sweet Fanny Adams* appeared, in April 1974, a more democratic approach in the vocal department was also noted. Scott sang his own 'Into The Night' while Steve Priest took two vocal leads.

The reason, unreported at the time, had little to do with band democracy. With 'Teenage Rampage' enjoying a three-week run at No. 2 during February, Brian Connolly was violently attacked outside a pub in Staines, a west London suburb. He was hospitalised and specialists doubted whether he would sing again.

In the March 9, 1974 edition of *Record Mirror*, Andy Scott told Genny Hall: 'We're having trouble finishing the album 'cos Brian's lost his voice. Brian needs to put another four vocal tracks down and his voice isn't ready yet.' No mention was made of Connolly's duffing-up for fear of jeopardising future bookings.

'It was definitely something dodgy,' insisted Steve Priest. 'There are two versions of the story. One, that Brian was in a pub with one of the roadies eyeing up some girls. The lads got jealous, followed him out and gave him a kicking. The other is that he stopped off at a pub to buy some cigarettes and [the attackers] had already been following him.'

'It makes a great story to say it was done on purpose,' counters Andy Scott. 'But something happened [in the pub]. Then he goes into a car park, there's a couple of local lads jumping on the bonnet of his Mercedes, and he gets hit from behind. When he's on the floor he gets kicked in the throat.'

BELOW: First, Mud's 'Tiger Feet' kept 'Teenage Rampage' off the top. Then along came Suzi Quatro's 'Devil Gate Drive' to do the same. All three were massive early 1974 hits for Chinnichap.

SWEET IN CHARLTON LINE-UP

THE SWEET have been added to the Who's "Summer Of '74" rock extravaganza at Charlton Athletic football ground in South-East London on Saturday, May 18 — for which, as reported last week, other bookings include Humble Pie, Lou Reed, Lindisfarne, Bad Company and Dave Mason. But the event will NOT now be repeated in Scotland the following weekend, as originally planned, although a Scottish date will take place later in the summer.

Pete Townshend told NME this week: "We are really delight-ed and happy that the Sweet are in the show. There may be a few rock snobs who will be surprised by the Sweet's inclusion — but we have seen them live, and they are a very different proposition from what you might think from those brief flamboyant appearances on 'Top Of The Pops'. I think it speaks for itself that they have the confidence to compete with some of the heavy metal groups, who are already on the bill."

Promoter Michael Alfandary commented: "I can now say that there will definitely be no more Who shows in the near future. It is true we were planning an event for Glasgow Shawfield Stadium on May 25, but this has been dropped for reasons beyond our control. However, there could well be other similar shows later

There's no disputing what happened next. Brian Connolly was having throat injections from a specialist in Harley Street in the hope of saving his voice. In May, with his injuries still prohibiting him from singing, Sweet went public with the news, cancelling a spring tour and the prestigious Summer Of '74 one-day festival at Charlton Athletic's football ground on May 18, where they'd been invited as special guests by The Who.

'Everyone was claiming we were cowards,' said Priest, 'that we wouldn't go on with The Who. It was a load of old codswallop; we were raring to do it. It would have put us on the map as a real band.'

Andy Scott was more than convinced of Sweet's capabilities as a real band: 'Steve's playing on the album reminds me of [Yes's] Chris Squire, [The Who's] John Entwistle and Jack Bruce. It was that good. Mick used to idolise [Deep Purple's] Ian Paice. I'd tell him, "No idolisation needed there, mate."'

With Connolly still in recovery, there was even some loose talk of separating the band from the singer. 'Mike Chapman raised the possibility,' says Scott. 'Let's keep him in the box he's happy in and get in a keyboard player who can sing and move the band on.' The musicians rejected the idea.

'It was one for all, all for one,' says Scott. 'The next things Mike wrote for us were "The Six Teens" and "Turn It Down". He realised things needed to change.'

Brian Connolly was back on stage with Sweet for a few gigs in August. 'But he was never the same after that incident,' says Scott.

ABOVE: Sweet were invited by The Who to join them for the Charlton Festival on May 18, 1974. But a savage beating that put Brian Connolly in hospital and his singing career in jeopardy forced the band to pull out. 'That half-ruined our career,' said Steve Priest, 'because people said, "Ah, they're chickening out." We were looking forward to it. We loved The Who. We even did a Who medley on stage. It would have put us on the map.'

'Teenage Dream', 'Teenage Rampage' – it was widely noted that songs with 'teenage' in the title hadn't been this fashionable since the late fifties. A resurgence in the States at the start of the seventies had offered a glimpse of what was to come: MC5's 'Teenage Lust', Flamin' Groovies' *Teenage Head* and, notably, Alice Cooper's spring '71 breakthrough 'I'm Eighteen'.

Three years on, Cooper was back on similar territory. But whereas 'I'm Eighteen' had seen the band stride confidently into the spotlight, tapping into the frustration of the neglected post-hippie generation, 'Teenage Lament '74' – which hit No. 12 in the UK in mid-February – sounded indifferent, almost like freeway-riding soft rock. 'What are you gonna do?' the song asked; but its target teenage audience was already moving on, looking elsewhere for kicks.

Alice Cooper had once been the collective name for an act commonly lampooned as the runt of the psychedelic litter. Then Alice Cooper the band became synonymous with its frontman. By spring 1974, it was superstar Alice Cooper backed by a band augmented by hired hands.

In March, Alice – the man, not band – joined presenter Bob Harris for one of his cosy *Old Grey Whistle Test* chats. Cooper gave his usual spiel: 'Violence is theatrical. If Shakespeare can do it why

can't Alice Cooper?' But he also had some personal news to impart to UK viewers.

Alice would soon be appearing in an episode of *The Snoop Sisters* ('The Devil Made Me Do It!') starring veteran actresses Helen Hayes and Mildred Natwick. But first he was hoping to get in a round of golf with Bob Hope, famously one of the biggest reactionaries in Hollywood.

It was as if the truth of the band's current predicament had been laid bare on the single – key line: 'Why don't you get away?' – as co-written with Neal Smith. Cooper's voice, wrapped in echo, was more isolated. The backing was polished and textured, with a country-ish twang discernible in the guitar playing. A chorus of female backing voices grew louder as the song progressed. By the end, the Cooper band had been engulfed and erased.

Producer Bob Ezrin, the great enabler in Alice Cooper's transformation from rank outsiders to the great all-American freakshow, had seen it coming. 'I'd just done *Berlin* with Lou Reed,' he says, 'one of the most difficult experiences of my life. I came back relieved I was gonna be back with my buddies and it would be a party again. Instead, I walked into a shit storm.

'They came back after the [*Billion Dollar Babies*] tour a different band,' Ezrin continues. 'The pressures of wild success, and the focus on Alice over and above the members of the band began to bear on them.'

'It wasn't that we didn't like each other,' says Alice. 'We'd got so big and I was the only one who'd get up and do the interviews, who'd stay late and do the interviews while the guys got the girls.'

The pop superstar, that new creation which had defined the early seventies, was now ripping apart old loyalties. It had happened with Bowie and the Spiders, and with Bolan and T. Rex. It was even corrupting the 'all join in' spirit of inclusiveness that had fired up pop's rebirth in the first place: Ian Hunter was now the personification of Mott The Hoople, while Rod Stewart was in a different league to The Faces.

The Alice Cooper band fought back. 'When we started rehearsals for *Muscle Of Love*,' says Ezrin, 'they played me the first song and I stopped them to talk about the drum beat – which is where I'd normally start. And they resisted me! "We like it like this." They wanted to take some control over their lives.'

Alice stayed out of it. 'I was a bit disappointed he didn't step up and say, "This is our producer, the guy who made us all these great records,"' continues Ezrin. 'But I understood later: it's not in Alice's nature. He's not a fighter, he's a very gentle soul and never one for confrontation.

'These are guys he'd lived and starved with, worked with from zero to where they were now, one of the biggest bands in the world. I think he was a bit taken aback.'

Bob Ezrin quit the sessions. '[Ezrin's boss] Jack Richardson came in with Jack Douglas [as co-producers],' says drummer Neal Smith. 'But when you change the chemistry, it changes the whole outcome of the project.'

Star power and studio wrangling played their part in the collapse of the Cooper band. So too did the slow, sad decline of lead guitarist Glen Buxton. Before the *Billion Dollar Babies* tour, he'd apparently undergone some surgery. But he was still left with his boozing habit.

'He didn't play a note on *Muscle Of Love*,' says Smith. 'His health kept him out of the studio.

'It was a big dilemma for us. He was a huge part of our image. He'd basically taught everyone in the band how to play their instrument.'

'Any one of us would have died for Glen,' says Alice. 'He was the heart, the soul and the insanity of Alice Cooper, our Holden Caulfield [from J. D. Salinger's *The Catcher In The Rye*]. He couldn't wait to get away with something. We'd cross a border, and five miles in he'd go, "Look what I've found!"'

By 1974, no one was willing to cross a border to save the Alice Cooper band. The spirit was being sucked out of the music. *Muscle Of Love*, as a title, was all bravado.

Alice devised a plan. 'I said, "Guys, to maintain who we are, the heavyweight champions of the world, we have to make the next show bigger and more theatrical than *Billion Dollar Babies*. But it's gonna cost

FACING PAGE: 'What are you gonna do?' sang Alice on 'Teenage Lament '74'. With their frontman taking time out to appear in an episode of *The Snoop Sisters* between rounds of golf with Bob Hope, the Cooper band began asking themselves the same question.

ABOVE: Bad blood at the *Muscle Of Love* sessions prompted producer Bob Ezrin to walk out. 'I was a bit disappointed that [Alice] didn't step up and say, "This is the guy who made all these great records." But it's not in Alice's nature. He's not a fighter, he's a very gentle soul.'

ATTENTION:
THIS CARTON CONTAINS ONE (1)
ALICE COOPER
MUSCLE OF LOVE

FRAGILE

us." They said, "We don't wanna get more theatrical. We'd rather wear Levis. We'd rather keep the money."

'I said, I can't go backwards now; it's suicide. Bowie's gonna do the biggest show and we're gonna be in the dust."'

'I think he was living the character,' says Michael Bruce. 'Alice Cooper meant that Vince could do what he wanted with no consequences.'

Alice Cooper as a band was at a standstill. *Muscle Of Love* had stalled at No. 10, the worst performing Cooper album in the States since 1972. After a few shows in Brazil in late March/early April 1974, Michael Bruce and Neal Smith began work on solo albums. Alice started hanging around with Liza Minnelli and George Burns.

'I didn't leave the band,' Cooper says. 'I was the only one staying true to what we were doing.

'I said, "I'm gonna take the half-million dollars I have in the bank, and [manager] Shep [Gordon]'s gonna take his half-million and we're gonna produce a show called *Welcome To My Nightmare*. And I'm gonna be Alice Cooper 'cos I'm not gonna change my name."

'Nobody said no. I was a band guy. We always split everything five ways. I never thought of it as my ego getting out of control.'

The rest of the band assumed everyone was taking time off for the first time in six years to rest, play golf or pursue solo projects.

'We had nothing in writing because of the trust between us,' says Neal Smith. 'We had one of the biggest bands in the world called Alice Cooper. But after *Welcome To My Nightmare* he decided he wanted to do another album. I realised that was it. Everybody was pretty upset.'

LEFT: Released in November 1973, *Muscle Of Love* came packaged in a cardboard box that soon fell apart. It was a sign. 'Musically, [the album] was all over the place,' says Alice. 'Conceptually, it was all over the place. We didn't work on it so hard. We thought that whatever we did was gold. And we got that slap in the face that said, "It's not up to your level."'

Chapter 23
Dreams Less Sweet

On December 18, 1973, Roxy Music's two-month tour of the UK and the continent came to an end at Bristol's Colston Hall. That same week their latest single, 'Street Life', was peaking at No. 9. In at 24, on its way to the No. 1 spot, was 'The Show Must Go On' by support act Leo Sayer. It would be a long, strange winter.

FOXY ROXY

In 1972, the readers of all of England's major rock papers voted Roxy Music "The Brightest Hope of the Year." "Stranded" proves they voted properly. Roxy has become known as a band that combines the healthiest strains of electronics, parody, excellent lyrics and musicianship with a pinch of 30-40-50's style.

ROXY MUSIC 'STRANDED'

ROBERT REDFORD   MIA FARROW

THE GREAT GATSBY

GONE IS THE ROMANCE THAT WAS SO DIVINE.

BIBA

New catalogue
Send for your free mail order catalogue now

Roxy, the most daring band of the past eighteen months, were far from crushed by the news. Unlike 'Virginia Plain' and 'Pyjamarama', both separate entities from their first two albums, 'Street Life' – featuring new man Eddie Jobson, scraping up a passably Eno-esque electric violin cacophony midway through – was also the lead-off track on *Stranded*, the band's third set, released in November 1973 and widely acclaimed. 'Roxy's album masterwork,' declared *NME*. Within weeks, it had hit No. 1. Roxy Music now had the album sales to match their carefully styled look. But that, too, was changing.

During Roxy's late autumn tour, the most fashion-conscious fans in pop turned out in their DIY version of haute couture. But Bryan Ferry had moved on. Now dressed in a white dinner jacket, bow-tie and dark trousers, he cut a suave, more classically elegant figure. Nor did his makeover stop at the fitting room. The mannerisms had become less exaggerated, the vocal tremors more enchanting than strange. And there was no Eno to send out fragrant astro-vibes and steal the singer's limelight. Bryan Ferry was now unquestionably Roxy Music's Grand Narrator.

There was nothing remotely 'young teenage' about this slicker, more produced version of the band. Instead, *Stranded* tapped into a more rarefied cultural mood shift. On September 10, 1973, while the band were recording the album at AIR Studios, leading fashion boutique Biba reopened in a seven-floor Art Deco building on Kensington High Street (close to where Ferry lived while writing much of the first Roxy album).

'I can just imagine Ginger Rogers and Fred Astaire dancing over these marble floors,' one eager shopper told a reporter for *The Times* on opening day.

Some analysts felt the expansion was far too ambitious to succeed – which might have reflected the after-the-party comedown of British pop in the aftermath of Ziggy's retirement and Bolan's retreat. Moreover, the Biba aesthetic seemed to yearn for an earlier glamour, the doomed romanticism of the jazz era.

Even Hollywood picked up on the sense of decay surrounding 1973's Beautiful People, investing heavily in a film version of F. Scott Fitzgerald's *The Great Gatsby*. It would rekindle the fad for cloche hats and feather boas on its release the following spring.

In his *Stranded* review, headlined 'Roxy: An Air Of Lush Decay', *Melody Maker*'s Michael Watts noted that one track, 'A Song For Europe', had such an exquisite mood of 'decaying grandeur' that it merited a *Death In Venice* subtitle. Ferry reached further levels of romantic desolation on 'Mother Of Pearl', wrestling with the pantomime of 'powder' parties and the 'search for perfection' in a lyric named after a popular, if now unfashionable, form of jewellery.

But there was more to *Stranded* than the sweetly anachronistic scent of lavender. Ferry, now adopting a more unambiguously hetero image, had sealed the band's future by inviting Andy Mackay and Phil Manzanera to co-write a song each, thus quelling any further rebellion. For the cover, he opted for recent *Playboy* model Marilyn Cole, the magazine's first British Playmate Of The Year. No vintage lingerie or questionable gender this time. The tanned and sultry Cole was laid out provocatively in a faux-jungle setting, looking every inch the visual accompaniment to the album's standout track, the future-funk – with added Eno-style sound bursts – 'Amazona'.

The high-gloss production, Ferry's overtly masculine makeover and a tanned Playmate were all designed to help Roxy overcome a dilemma: how to break the American market. But Warner Brothers had no patience and quietly dropped them. Ferry's quote after the first US tour, that US audiences were 'somehow not as intelligent as British audiences', may not have endeared Roxy Music to US executives.

Early in the new year Atlantic Records subsidiary ATCO picked up *Stranded*, which peaked at No. 186 in

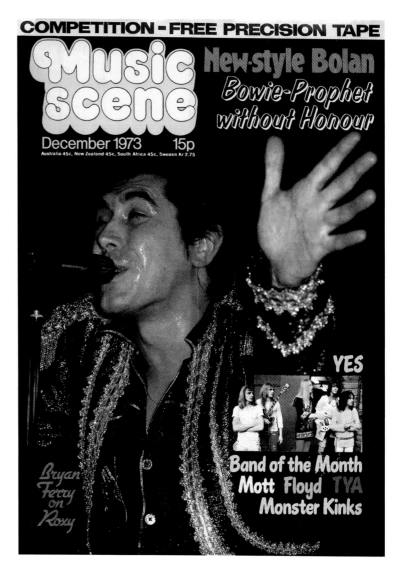

COMPETITION - FREE PRECISION TAPE

Music scene

December 1973   15p
Australia 45c, New Zealand 45c, South Africa 45c, Sweden Kr 2.75

New-style Bolan
Bowie-Prophet without Honour

Bryan Ferry on Roxy

YES

Band of the Month Mott Floyd TYA Monster Kinks

June 1974, on the back of a short US tour. A second Ferry solo album, *Another Time, Another Place*, was more weighted towards US soul and country material, but failed to register in the States. Still, it gave him two top-twenty singles in Britain that summer, both 'The "In" Crowd' and 'Smoke Gets In Your Eyes' feeding into his lounge-lizard persona.

Promoting his own defiantly eclectic *In Search Of Eddie Riff* solo album around the same time, sax player Andy Mackay described *Stranded* as the band's most cautious record thus far. 'I still think of Eno as being part of the greater Roxy,' he added.

Stretched out on the sofa of his Ladbroke Grove living room, a broken rocking-horse in one corner, Eno – 'as wan and wasted as a consumptive 19th

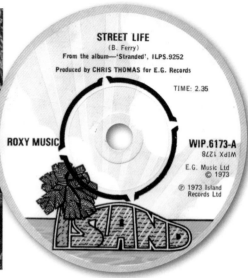

RIGHT: The Italian edition of 'Street Life', Roxy's first single with multi-instrumentalist Eddie Jobson, adapted the *Stranded* cover artwork. Bucking the album's prevailing mood, the image of *Playboy*'s 'Playmate Of The Year' Marilyn Cole was a visualisation of the album's standout song, the future-funk epic 'Amazona'.

FACING PAGE: The 'Non-Musician's Musician' billing for Eno's solo debut, *Here Come The Warm Jets*, flew in the face of all orthodoxy in January 1974. The Roxy renegade couldn't resist a brief Ferry pastiche during 'Dead Finks Don't Talk'.

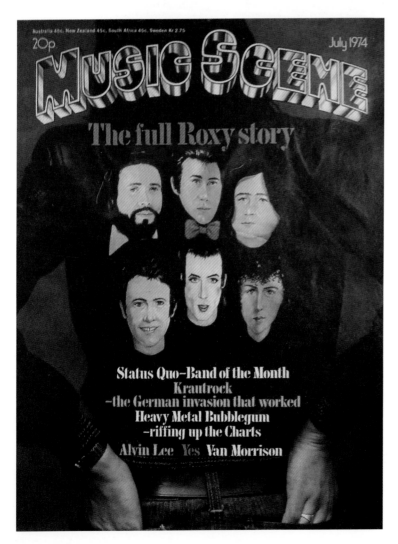

century poet,' wrote *Melody Maker*'s Geoff Brown in November '73 – disagreed. He thought *Stranded* was 'terrific', with one reservation. 'What it lacks is one of the most important elements in my musical life,' he said, 'insanity… The element of clumsiness and grotesqueness that arose from that early [Roxy] thing ceased to be there.'

Roxy Music's renegade walked that thin line between glam exquisite and glam grotesque. But he had no need for theatrical props like Alice Cooper; nor did he don an actor's mask like Bowie. Eno was the benign alien, part-androgyne, part *Doctor Who* extra, the scene-stealer who fiddled about stageside, emitting weird and wonderful noises from his joystick-and-wires contraption.

Eno had given pop a deliciously discordant twist. To many, his departure from Roxy was ruinous to the band, a blow to any forward motion or maverick tendencies that so-called glam rock might possess. It was widely assumed he would simply walk into a telephone box and return from whence he came.

But Eno was made of stronger stuff – and wore his iconoclasm proudly. 'The thing people miss when they do their rock revival rubbish is that early rock music was, in a lot of cases, the product of incompetence,' he told Geoff Brown. 'They were brilliant musicians [only] in the spiritual sense.'

For eighteen months he'd been popular music's most imaginative thinker. Citing pop's raiding of the past, its wardrobe rebellion, disregard for virtuosity and loud embrace of play, he saw potential for a creative revolution that would go way beyond

Alice's 'third-generation rock' or Bowie's 'pantomime rock'. Post-Roxy, he was now free to indulge his own personal imp of the perverse.

Bored with the synthesizer, exasperated by inflated egos, Eno worked up a wide-ranging collection of unlikely pop songs titled *Here Come The Warm Jets*. It included contributions from everyone in Roxy Music except Bryan Ferry, who he briefly lampooned during 'Dead Finks Don't Talk'. Virtuosos such as King Crimson guitarist Robert Fripp and funk bassist Busta Jones were recruited; styles were juxtaposed; lyrics incorporated plenty of free association.

After its release in January 1974, Eno toured with a pub-rock backing band, The Winkies. *Record Mirror*'s Chris Poole was unimpressed, accusing him of poor timing, lack of stagecraft (without 'an ounce of charisma') and padding out the set with covers. He recommended that fans stay home and listen to the album instead.

The tour was soon curtailed after Eno was hospitalised with a collapsed lung. Having re-evaluated what he was doing, he chopped off his hair, dropped his feathery apparel, gave up live appearances and after a second album, November 1974's *Taking Tiger Mountain (By Strategy)*, shifted towards studio-based mood ('ambient') music. Eno wished to explore 'the idea of removing the narrator as the centre of the music', as he told *Creem*'s Lester Bangs later.

By 1975, he was venturing into pure sound – no superstars required. 'I released *Discreet Music* the same week [actually the same year] that Lou Reed released *Metal Machine Music*,' notes the man whose transformation from playful art-rocker to conceptual composer Brian Eno occurred during this period. 'In a way both were brackets around the world of pop music at the time. [Lou] was saying, "It can be a lot nastier than it is." There was a sort of, "You wanna go to extremes? I'll show you…"

'And in a quieter, more English way, that's what I was saying too. "What about a piece of music that would sit still for as long as I can make it?"'

Both Eno and Reed had been androgynous rock anti-heroes of sorts: Eno fragrant and English; Lou hissy, butch, streetwise New York. According to *NME*'s Nick Kent in March 1974, in a piece titled 'Farewell Androgyny', that time had now passed. 'Asexual rock,' Kent declared, 'was Last Year's Thrill.'

The writer – like Bowie, Ferry or, indeed, Reed and Eno – had been swept along by the desire to inject a bit of fantasy, invention, even stupidity, into pop. But

aside from the ever-incongruous Reed, still yet to escape the 'rock'n'roll animal' cliché, they'd all grown frustrated by its collapse into cheap parody, what Kent called – perhaps harshly – the 'whole bloated AC/DC burlesque'.

At first, the superstars of glitter, glam and rock theatre had offered an alternative to what Kent described as the 'overbearing' macho aesthetic at the start of the decade – what feminists and other critics were now belittling as 'cock rockers'. But glam's exaggerated twist on gender blur had descended into a tasteless sideshow, erasing what the writer called the 'truly androgynous aspects of early Presley, [Jim] Morrison – and, of course, Jagger'.

Weeks later, Nick Kent – who cut a cooler figure than most rock stars – followed up with 'The Politics Of Flash', a piece charting the rise and fall of the satin jacket. Now that the public had access to cut-price versions of superstar outfits, the major stars were, he explained, keeping a distance by employing their own designers: Jagger's spangly jump suits were Ossie Clark creations; Ferry was being dressed by 'designer's designer' Anthony Price; even new boys Queen had teamed up with one-time Bolan outfitter Zandra Rhodes.

Chapter 24
New Faces

T he centre was no longer holding. The glam racket, once as vast and as wide-ranging as its wardrobe, had now been reduced to two dominant strands: the Chinnichap pop of The Sweet, Suzi Quatro and Mud – and Mike Leander's Gary Glitter with his backing band, The Glitter Men, now restyled as The Glitter Band and launched as a separate act.

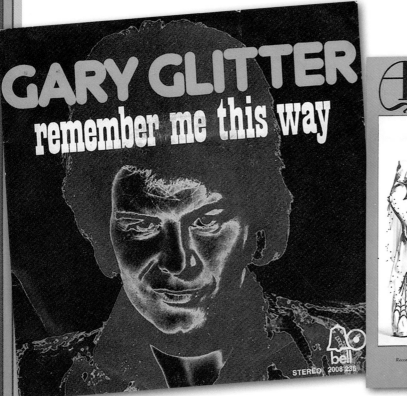

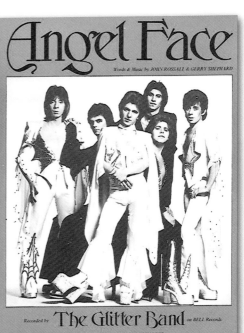

Early in 1974, producer Leander had told *Disc*, 'I can only compare [Gary's] career to Elvis Presley's.' Citing his protégé's larger-than-life personality and all-round appeal, Leander insisted Glitter was destined to follow Presley into feature films. 'The only other thing left to him to do now is to conquer America.'

A documentary film, chronicling the Glitter phenomenon with fantasy sequences and footage shot at London's Rainbow Theatre in November 1973, was already in the bag. By April 1974, it had a title: *Remember Me This Way*. Given Gary Glitter's status since early '73 as the new first man of glam, its

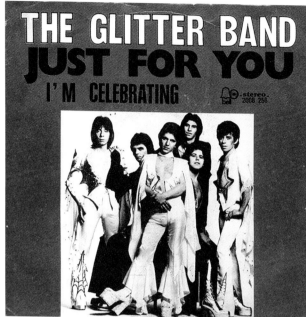

murkily produced theme song sounded like a misstep, more akin to a ghostly self-obituary – there were even echoes of 'Old Shep', Presley's sorrowful ode to a dead dog. The single peaked at No. 3 in mid-April, though the absence of the trademark Glitter sound served The Glitter Band's own debut well, with 'Angel Face' coming in right behind at No. 4.

Gary Glitter visited the States in the spring, talking up the new film and assessing his potential to become the latest Elton John-style showstopper. Back home, Leander atoned for the low-key spring hit with 'Always Yours', a remarkable late-glam return to form, rich in all that 'clumsiness and grotesqueness' Eno felt had gone missing from pop.

By June 22, Glitter was back at No. 1 – although, as had happened with Bolan, his success was now increasingly reliant on hardcore fans, as evidenced by shorter chart runs.

The Glitter Band's second single, 'Just For You', though less maniacal than their circus ringmaster's usual style, was four-square glam distilled to its magnificent essence: regimented beat; handclaps; a terrace-style chant; it even had that old pop trick, a key change towards the end. And there was something else: in the intro chording, which reappeared during the song, there was a glimpse of the punk-rock sound that would explode two years later.

'Glitter Mania Rocks Britain' declared *Record Mirror* on its June 22, 1974 cover. Behind the headline, the recent death of a fan in a crush at a David Cassidy concert at White City Stadium on May 26 had reportedly cast a pall over the latest tour, knocking ticket sales and sapping the appetite for hysteria-driven gigs.

The Glitter Band played their own material during the frontman's costume changes. 'They know who the guv'nor is,' Glitter said at the time. But fans were starting to see cracks in the old façade. Back at the Rainbow on June 15, Glitter flattered the crowd with a chorus of 'You're beautiful!', as a prelude to his forthcoming single. When he followed up by asking, 'What am I?', a small group of lads called back, 'Yer a poof.'

Bolan and Bowie had done much to dismantle old prejudices towards sexuality and gender. By 1974, 'unisex' was not just a trendy slogan but something that had entered the national conversation. Still, it baffled at least as many as it inspired.

The fight for sexual liberation had emerged during the early 1970s. Back then, it wasn't about gender fluidity but part of a more focused, politicised struggle for gay rights. Some activists were even disparaging of pop's 'gender tourists', those largely heterosexual performers, including Bowie and Bolan, for whom a sexually ambivalent identity was more a theatrical conceit than a genuine battle for personal liberation.

Given the environment, perhaps it was to be expected that Suzi Quatro, with her girl-on-a-motorcycle image, would become embroiled in a controversy.

On May 26, 1974, 14-year-old David Cassidy fan Bernadette Whelan died after fans surged towards the stage at the singer's 'farewell' gig at White City Stadium, west London. Hundreds of fans were injured in the crush. 'The place was like a battlefield,' said a spokesman afterwards. The tragedy dampened both enthusiasm and ticket sales for concerts that summer.

A fan's death at a David Cassidy show sapped the appetite for hysteria-driven gigs.

Suzi Quatro shot from the hip and had little time for men in tights.

SUZI
With A Sizzling New Chart Single!

SUZI QUATRO "ALL SHOOK UP"

BULLETING AT 74

ON
BELL RECORDS

GET READY!
SUZI WILL BE SHAKING UP THE
WHOLE COUNTRY DURING HER
AMERICAN INVASION
OF MAJOR CITIES
AUGUST-SEPTEMBER
WITH
URIAH HEEP!

THIS PAGE AND RIGHT: Suzi Quatro returned to her native USA in spring 1974, supporting the New York Dolls at The Bottom Line and opening for Grand Funk Railroad at Madison Square Garden. Like many before her, she would struggle to find major success in the States.

On May 17, 1974, fragrant pop singer/pianist Lynsey de Paul picked up an Ivor Novello award for her November '73 hit, 'Won't Somebody Dance With Me'. But she wasn't feeling particularly sanguine about it. 'That song wasn't good enough for me,' she told *Record Mirror*'s John Beattie, 'not when Sweet, Quatro and Mud get the number ones and they're crap.'

De Paul didn't leave it there. 'She's not feminine is she?' she continued, turning her attention to Suzi Q. 'She's much more butch. In fact, I think she looks like a lesbian and [cue haughty tone] I say that quite candidly.' When pressed on the remarks, Suzi Quatro admitted she was 'hurt' but regarded the matter as too 'silly' to discuss.

At the same Novello Awards ceremony, Mike Leander had won Best Selling British Record for Glitter's 'I Love You Love Me Love'. But it was Mike Chapman and Nicky Chinn who walked off with the Songwriters Of The Year statuette.

Unsurprisingly, there was no special mention for 'AC-DC', the Chinn-Chapman song that closed The Sweet's recent *Sweet Fanny Adams* album. A down-the-line rock number written for laughs, with a rotten 'let's be in it together' line, it concerned a man whose girlfriend was two-timing him with another woman. 'You ought to see her ding-a-ling,' growled Brian Connolly, piling on the sexual ambiguity.

The Sweet had recently signed with manager Ed Leffler, the man who sold The Osmonds to the world. Chinn and Chapman had just gifted them 'The Six Teens', their most sophisticated single yet, with dramatic changes of pace and an undercurrent of gloom. It stalled at No. 9.

The Sweet, wearing their now customary leather, were once again growing frustrated. They complained about being lumped in with Mud and Suzi Quatro. They demanded even tougher, classier material from Chinn and Chapman – who responded with the ballsy 'Turn It Down', which flopped miserably in November. But mostly they banked on Leffler finding them a new deal in the US where, since the surprise top-three success of 'Little Willy' in May 1973, few of their singles were even granted a release.

Having stolen a march on The Sweet back in February, when 'Devil Gate Drive' pipped 'Teenage Rampage' to the top spot, Suzi Quatro also beat them to the States. For her, it was less a speculative venture, more an opportunity for a glorious homecoming.

Quatro was especially keen to get back to Detroit, aka 'Kill City', in whose honour she'd recorded 'Devil Gate Drive'. '"Devil Gate Drive" was a fictitious place,' she says, 'where, when you're kids, there's a street where it all happens, where your parents say, "Don't go there." And of course, you do.'

Suzi, who'd later play Wild West sharpshooter Annie Oakley in a stage musical, seemed far more potentially poised for success in the States than The Sweet. She shot from the hip and had little time for men in tights.

'The guys in my band don't wear glitter on their cheeks, or stardust in their eyes,' she told an uncredited interviewer in spring 1974. 'My guys are real men, in every way – including not having the sort of ego that would stop them taking orders from a girl. That's why we all work together.'

In the spring Quatro visited the US, supporting the New York Dolls at The Bottom Line in New York one night, then opening for Grand Funk Railroad at Madison Square Garden the next. She was back again in September, supporting Uriah Heep – but the tie-in

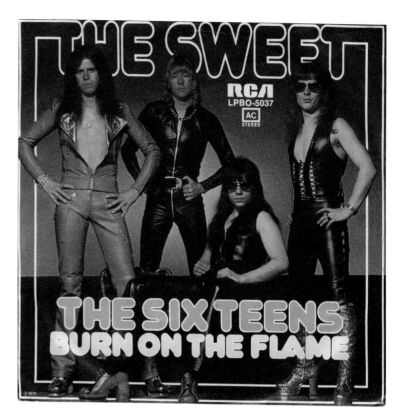

ABOVE: July 1974's 'The Six Teens' was Chinn and Chapman's most sophisticated song yet, all dramatic changes in pace and a whiff of self-importance. It was The Sweet's last single recorded with long-time producer Phil Wainman.

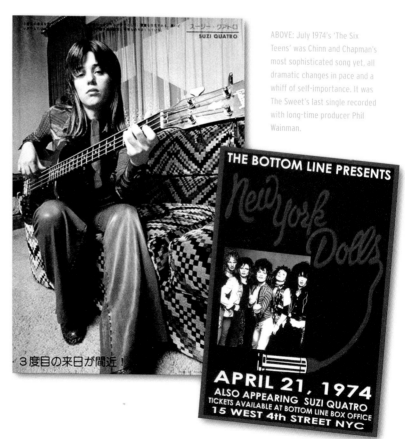

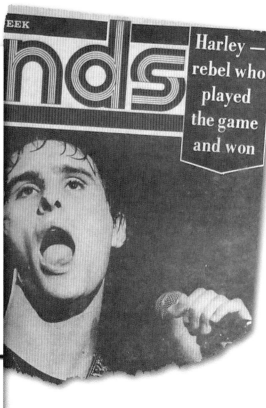

Harley —
rebel who
played
the game
and won

album *Quatro*, liberally spiced with rock'n'roll covers, failed to resonate. It took real business muscle to crack the US market. And besides, 'I can't write commercial music,' Quatro admitted on her return to Britain.

'I was never ever glam rock,' Suzi Quatro now says. 'The only reason I got lumped in was because my first hits came in 1973 when glam rock was exploding. I had no makeup on and wore a plain black jump suit while everyone else was glittered up. I was the odd one out. I've always been just rock'n'roll.'

By 1974, pop music was looking for a bit more than that.

'He's bigoted, single–minded and sure to be a star,' *Record Mirror* had teased in its January 5, 1974 issue. He was Cockney Rebel's Steve Harley, a bright-looking, opinionated guy in tinted specs with a smoothed-out Ziggy cut and an artful pose.

'We are the leaders of Third Generation Rock,' Harley told the magazine's Peter Harvey. When Alice Cooper used the phrase back in 1971, it referred to the passing of both the rock'n'roll decade and the hippie

era. It was Harley's belief that the second generation had continued right up until July 1973, when Bowie killed it off.

'He knew he was at an end, and he did it right,' said the man jostling for position as the new saviour of generation number three.

There were other contenders for 'The Face of '74' – which was the cover headline for the following week's *RM*, whose star was The Sensational Alex Harvey Band's Pierrot-faced guitarist, Zal Cleminson. But while most mid-ranking British acts suffered during the continuing oil crisis, with labels playing it safe and backing the big hitters, EMI persevered with its two major signings of 1973 – Queen, aimed at the rock market, and Cockney Rebel, seemingly tailored for the Roxy Music milieu.

Harley disputed any such comparison. 'People talk about Roxy Music being new, but their music is from the past,' he told *RM*. 'We are the originators.'

Steve Harley believed in Cockney Rebel because he, like Bolan, had grown up marvelling at the self-belief and arrogance of mid-sixties Dylan. It seemed to be working. By turning down an advance from Mickie Most, Harley had secured a better deal with

LEFT: EMI expected great things from Cockney Rebel in 1973. But despite good material, a big budget and main man Steve Harley, pop's biggest self-publicist since Bolan, debut set *The Human Menagerie* wasn't the commercial breakthrough they'd hoped for.

ABOVE: Steve Harley was undeterred. 'I'm going to be a huge star,' he said. 'I know I am.'

Cockney Rebel

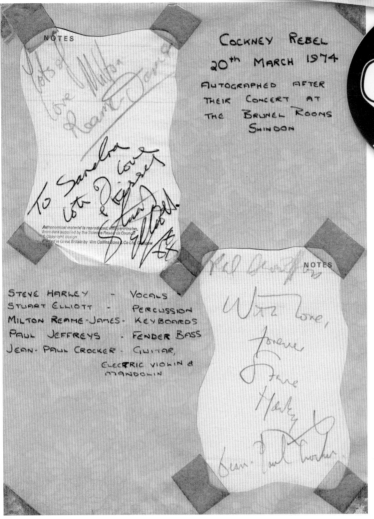

COCKNEY REBEL
20th MARCH 1974
AUTOGRAPHED AFTER
THEIR CONCERT AT
THE BRUNEL ROOMS
SWINDON

STEVE HARLEY — VOCALS
STUART ELLIOTT — PERCUSSION
MILTON REAME-JAMES — KEYBOARDS
PAUL JEFFREYS — FENDER BASS
JEAN-PAUL CROCKER — GUITAR,
ELECTRIC VIOLIN &
MANDOLIN

dressed in bowties and waistcoats, scattered around him. Harley may have sneered at Roxy, but Cockney Rebel's glamour was similarly refined and nostalgic.

The Human Menagerie had been recorded at AIR Studios with seemingly no expense spared. A single from the album, 'Sebastian', featured a 50-piece orchestra and chorus. Suspicions were immediately raised. *NME*'s Roy Carr, for one, wasn't convinced. 'The ultimate poseurs' party band with neither the perception nor the style to pull it off,' he sniffed. 'Just Kings Road Cafe Society muzak.'

Despite – or perhaps because of – the publicity, the album failed to chart. But 'Sebastian' had gone top five in Belgium and Holland. EMI was seemingly undeterred, re-promoting both album and single in January 1974.

Harley continued his press assault. 'I'm going to happen,' he told *Record Mirror*, in an echo of Bolan and Bowie's earlier braggadocio. 'I'm going to be a huge star. I know I am. No way will you stop me. I know how to get it and it's carefully contrived.'

On January 29, Cockney Rebel hosted a mixed media evening at Biba's Rainbow Room. Titled *The Human Menagerie*, it featured a string quartet, a mime artist and vocal group Thunder Thighs – who'd sung on Lou Reed's 'Walk On The Wild Side' and, more recently, Mott The Hoople's 'Roll Away The Stone'.

Appearances on Radio 1's *In Concert* and *The Old Grey Whistle Test* followed, but nothing seemed to translate into significant sales. Then the indefatigable Harley dug deep into a stash of songs that dated back to his days as a busker and found 'Judy Teen'. Charming, clever and quirkily commercial, it owed as much to the wry, music-hall theatricality of Kinks frontman Ray Davies as to anything contemporary.

By May, 'Judy Teen' had hit No. 5. By June, Cockney Rebel audiences were chanting the chorus of Bowie's 'Rebel Rebel' – a hit earlier in the year – in tribute

EMI – compelling the label to put serious money behind its investment.

The son of a south London milkman, Harley shared Marc Bolan's background and fighting spirit. He'd followed Tyrannosaurus Rex as a teenager and used Bolan as inspiration for 'Mirror Freak' on Cockney Rebel's November 1973 debut, *The Human Menagerie*: 'Exhibition yourself / We'll hold a show on the shelf' – for 'Marc was always on show, "always on", as they say in showbiz.'

Harley's haughty manner was proudly exhibited on the debut album cover. He sat in a fashionable, throne-like rattan peacock chair with the band,

the psychomodo

EMC 3033

Also available on cassette and cartridge

and behaving like boisterous Faces fans. Steve Harley had arrived.

Witnessing a gig at the Croydon Greyhound on July 7, *RM*'s Peter Harvey wrote of the evening's circus-like atmosphere, casting Cockney Rebel as 'the People's Band' and the frontman as 'Steve Garland, Judy Harley'.

'It's not a Slade phenomenon,' Harley told Harvey during the tour. 'It's not a David Bowie phenomenon, or a Beatles phenomenon. I don't know what it is, but there's a respect they're showing me that almost frightens me.'

To Harley's chagrin, that respect was rarely observed by flagship rock weekly *NME*. 'Cocky Rabble,' jested Charles Shaar Murray in June. 'One thing you gotta admit about Steve Harley… he does the funniest interviews since Marc Bolan.'

Nevertheless, Harley roared into overdrive. At the end of the two-month tour, at the Manchester Hardrock on July 22, he suddenly announced that Cockney Rebel were splitting.

The timing seemed off. *The Psychomodo*, the band's gutsier, more ambitious second album, had just made the top ten; its twitchy, circus-like 45, 'Mr Soft', was on its way to No. 8. The musicians had, it transpired, been pushing for more involvement.

But Harley, who'd been telling interviewers that the third album should have 'more ego… I want the spotlight on me,' begged to differ. So the avowed man of action decided to pull off his own 'Ziggy at Hammersmith' moment.

He even wrote a song – 'a finger-pointing piece of vengeful poetry', he later admitted – about the break-up. In February 1975, that song, the acerbic and irresistible 'Make Me Smile (Come Up And See Me)' gave Harley – now going out as Steve Harley & Cockney Rebel – his first and only No. 1 hit. He'd made it.

On May 9, 1974, two little-known brothers from a Los Angeles suburb burst into instant *Top Of The Pops* immortality with a performance as potty as anything Bolan, Bowie, Glitter or The Sweet had ever delivered.

Promoting their launch single, 'This Town Ain't Big Enough For Both Of Us', Ron and Russell Mael made the most improbable double act. Singer Russell was an angel-faced mop-head in the Bolan mould, hyperactive, with a distinctive chipped tooth.

Brother Ron – who'd recently told *Melody Maker*'s Chris Welch 'the secret of English bands is having

BELOW: From the start, critics noted the Mael brothers' fascination for all things British. It was something they shared with Todd Rundgren, who found them a deal and produced their 1971 debut album and tie-in single, 'Wonder Girl'.

RIGHT: Brothers Ron (right) and Russell (left) had trouble convincing British critics at first. One dismissed them as a poor man's Dave Dee, Dozy, Beaky, Mick & Tich. 'Too many groups we know are into music,' said those mischievous Maels.

Wonder Girl

A Smashing Hit Single by Sparks on Bearsville

Special Thanks to John Parker, WHHY, Montgomery, Alabama

BSV 0004

Manufactured by Warner Bros. Records

It was as potty as anything Bolan, Bowie, Glitter or The Sweet had done.

rotten teeth' – sat rigid and unsmiling at a keyboard, occasionally angling his neck like a showroom dummy. The finishing touch was a toothbrush moustache, synonymous both with Charlie Chaplin and Adolf Hitler. Ron's robotic moves and slicked-back hair were also oddly reminiscent of silent cinema and the Nazi era.

John Lennon is said to have thought so, reputedly calling up Ringo Starr after seeing the performance and exclaiming, 'Christ, they've got Hitler on the telly!' (Though how he would have seen an episode of *TOTP* in spring 1974, while living in New York, has never been explained.)

On *Top Of The Pops*, there was little concern that Sparks were advocating anything other than the right to startle and to ensure no one would forget them. It worked. Two weeks later, 'This Town Ain't Big Enough For Both Of Us' was at No. 3 and Sparks were back in the *TOTP* studio. By June 1, only The Rubettes' 'Sugar Baby Love' kept it off the top spot.

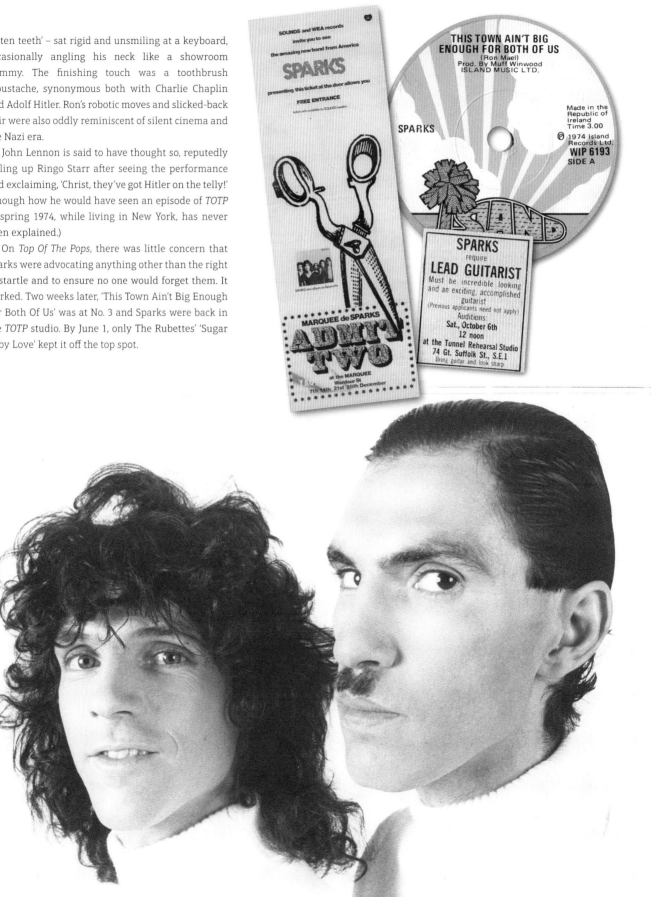

"This Town Ain't Big Enough for Both of Us."

The Smash Single by

Single No. IS OO1

SPARKS

England's Hottest New American Group.

KIMONO MY HOUSE
Includes the Hit:
'This Town Ain't Big Enough for Both of Us.'

ILPS 9274

The song was every bit as extraordinary as its writer, Ron Mael: the complex structure and staccato style; Russell Mael's swooping falsetto; its glinting phrases ('Heartbeat! Increasing heartbeat!'); Spaghetti Western gunshots; the instrumental breakouts that flirted with hard rock. It was, insisted *MM*'s Chris Welch, 'probably the most original single heard in several celestial rotations'.

For sheer artfulness – and the absence of a traditional chorus – the closest thing to an antecedent had been Roxy Music's 'Virginia Plain'. But there was also a suggestion of the Alice Cooper band's iconoclastic, underbelly-of-LA attitude.

'Too many groups we know are into music,' the Maels had advised *Disc*'s Andrew Tyler in November 1972, during Sparks' first visit to Europe. It was oddly reminiscent of what led Frank Zappa to sign Alice in the first place – and a dry run for the Sex Pistols' 'We're not into music, we're into chaos' stance four years later. In fact, Sparks had played Alice Cooper haunt the Whisky A Go Go on several occasions, including in their early incarnation as Halfnelson.

That's where they likely first encountered The GTOs' Miss Christine, whose affection for the band – and especially for Russell, with whom she had a brief fling – sparked the interest of her then-boyfriend, Todd Rundgren. The artist/producer in turn found them a deal with ex-Dylan manager Albert Grossman's Bearsville label.

Grossman liked the Maels because they were funny. The Maels liked Rundgren because he wore satin trousers and gave them freedom to be themselves in the studio. 'Sparks make you feel stupid because you can't pin them down,' Rundgren recalled admiringly. That didn't stop *NME*'s Andrew Tyler from having a try, describing them as possessing a Mothers Of Invention-like 'air of latent insanity [yet being] pretty and tuneful enough to stand in line with David Cassidy'.

Like Alice Cooper, the brothers shared a fascination for Hollywood, sometimes even passing themselves off as Doris Day's sons. Years before Cooper reprised the title, they had a song called '(No More) Mr Nice Guys'. Russell sometimes messed around with a sledgehammer while they performed it.

But the Maels, both arts graduates from UCLA, had little interest in creating a rocky horror show. The thrill of an awkward juxtaposition was their thing, which manifested itself in startling wordplay and quirky songs. Playing support to trad-rock acts like Little Feat did them few favours.

Neither did Halfnelson, a name derived from a wrestling clinch. Grossman had a better idea: noting a similarity to Hollywood comic aces the Marx Brothers, he suggested they go out as The Sparks Brothers. The Maels volunteered Sparks as a compromise…

US reviewers also noted the band's 'Englishness' – like Rundgren, the brothers were huge Anglophiles, with a particular interest in The Kinks and – 'when they still dressed well' – The Who. However, *Melody Maker*'s Roy Hollingworth, in New York in October '72 to suss out the city's thriving club scene, dismissed Sparks as a poor man's Dave Dee, Dozy, Beaky, Mick & Tich after catching them at Max's Kansas City. Another example of a cash-rich label investing in 'pointless bands', he added. 'Forgettable.'

Right afterwards, Sparks spent several weeks

ABOVE: At a time of enormous theatricality in pop, 'This Town Ain't Big Enough For Both Of Us' had it all. It was an exemplary three-minute pop opera fronted by the most compelling duo since Laurel & Hardy.

RIGHT: The 'Kimono My House' sleeve was the work of the team responsible for the Roxy Music covers. The title was a play on Rosemary Clooney's 1951 hit, 'Come On-A My House'.

in Britain during November and December '72. The band secured a short residency at the Marquee where, on December 20, they were supported by new EMI signings Queen. Sparks also appeared on *The Old Grey Whistle Test*, where Bob Harris paid them a backhanded compliment by comparing them with both The Mothers Of Invention and late-fifties teen idol Bobby Vee.

Looking after Sparks during the visit was John Hewlett, one-time bandmate of Marc Bolan in John's Children. Hewlett kept in touch after their return to the States, where their second album, *A Woofer In Tweeter's Clothing*, created nothing like the ripples of enthusiasm they'd aroused in Britain.

Eventually, he convinced Island Records A&R Muff Winwood to take a gamble. By summer '73, the Mael brothers were back in London, their left-behind backing musicians replaced by two members of Mod-inspired glam hopefuls Jook (also managed by Hewlett). A speculative 'Musicians Wanted' ad in *Melody Maker* had been specific in its requirements: 'Must be beard-free and exciting.'

Winwood demanded a tougher sound, with more prominent guitar. High on the newly charged scenario, Ron got himself a haircut and speed-wrote a set of new songs. By December, with Winwood producing after apparent first choice Roy Wood was unavailable, *Kimono My House* was well underway.

The title was a play on Rosemary Clooney's 1951 hit, 'Come On-A My House'; the glossy cover an exotic twist on the Roxy Music pin-up, executed by the same team of Nick De Ville and Karl Stoecker. It featured two Japanese dancers in geisha costumes and subversively smudged makeup, with no sign of the band (or even the Sparks name) anywhere.

The songs – fast, compact, each one a potential single – were similarly stylised. There was a deranged grandeur about it all, exemplified by 'Here In Heaven', delivered by a dead lover to the girlfriend who failed to honour their suicide pact.

Sparks were caught in the nether regions between pop and rock, between artfulness and naivete. 'These days nobody's primitive and I don't think you can pretend you are,' Ron Mael told *NME*'s James Johnson close to the album's release in April 1974. 'Once you've lost your innocence, you can't go back. If we tried a naive approach, it would come off really contrived, so we really make contrived songs so it's eventually less contrived.'

The album hit No. 4 in late June. The follow-up single, 'Amateur Hour', a rowdy celebration of sexual fumbling that thudded like punk rock, hit the top

The Mael brothers sometimes passed themselves off as Doris Day's sons.

SPARKS' NEW ALBUM KIMONO MY HOUSE

Muff Winwood produced their first British album including the single "This Town Ain't Big Enough For Both of Us."

ILPS 9272

ten in August. The hastily released follow-up album, *Propaganda* – its cover featuring the brothers bound and gagged on the back of a speedboat – gave Sparks another top-ten success before the year's end. Hysteria greeted their first two British tours. Russell even got to write a weekly column for *Mirabelle* magazine.

By the autumn, Sparks were back in the States, where 'This Town Ain't Big Enough For Both Of Us' was said to have stalled at No. 256 – way outside of the *Billboard* Hot 100. But US journalists were intrigued by the band's success abroad. Talking to *Rolling Stone*'s Richard Cromelin in January 1975, Ron Mael explained of the British: 'Their heroes aren't… legendary figures like Dylan and Clapton and Crosby, Stills & Nash. It's all new people who probably only get heard for a couple of months and then fade away. That makes it really silly in a certain way, but exciting too.'

Meanwhile, towards the end of 1974, Roxy Music finally earned their US breakthrough when *Country Life* – already a top-three album in Britain – broke into the US top forty. The title traded on the aristocratic lifestyle back home; the cover – two women in fancy underwear, strategically airbrushed for the US market – tapped more obviously into the irrepressible male

gaze of US rock. The album even concluded with 'Prairie Rose', a paean to Ferry's Texan-born girlfriend, Jerry Hall.

When Roxy returned for a British tour, Steve Harley caught up with them at the Rainbow. 'A most disappointing evening,' he complained afterwards, adding that the band were beginning to look like roadies. Harley's attendance was not entirely wasted though. 'I did get to sign around a hundred autographs,' he teased.

NME writer Nick Kent had no time for such conceit. In his 'Farewell Androgyny' piece back in March, he'd reserved a special contempt for the latest wave of theatrically minded acts hyped up by EMI. 'Dear old Queen and Cockney Rebel,' he sniffed, 'the definitive music machine for redundant poseurs, worked by redundant poseurs…'

★

At the Hammersmith Odeon on December 14, 1973, new best friends Jagger and Bowie danced in the aisles at the climax of Mott The Hoople's latest tour. But they, like some other members of the audience, had also come along to check out the support act.

Together since 1971, Queen had the hunger of The Who and the panache of Led Zeppelin. They were aimed squarely at the rock market with, as their very British name suggested, the States foremost in mind.

But frontman Freddie Mercury messed with the formula. Shy, buck-toothed and of Indian heritage, Farrokh Bulsara had learned to overcome his outsider status by cultivating a sense of comic outrage.

His big inspiration was Jimi Hendrix, whom he'd first seen perform at the Bag O'Nails in January 1967 and would witness several times more. Of mixed race and culturally nomadic, Hendrix remained musically open to everything. But while the guitarist found himself in sound, Freddie – famed for his Hendrix

His inspiration was Jimi Hendrix. He'd seen him several times in concert.

RIGHT: Queen turned heads during a November/December 1973 British tour supporting Mott The Hoople. 'They're a good group to have on tour,' said Mott's Ian Hunter. 'We don't take crap with us.' The following March, with *Queen II* fresh in the racks, Queen went out as headliners.

SHOW SOUVENIR

THIS BOOK IS DESIGNED FOR YOUR FURTHER ENJOYMENT OF THE SHOW

QUEEN
IN CONCERT

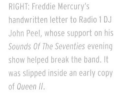

impersonations at Ealing Art College – would find freedom through the act of performance.

Hendrix had struggled with his boas and burning guitar public image. Mercury, who'd adopted his stage-name around April 1970 when he joined Brian May and Roger Taylor in Smile, wore his extended character like an ermine cloak. By 1971, he was already immortalising himself in song: 'Mother Mercury, look what they've done to me,' he wrote in an early lyric, 'My Fairy King'.

It was Mercury who had suggested the band change its name from Smile to Queen. He loved the regal connotations, he said later, though he was also keenly aware of its meaning in the gay community.

RIGHT: Freddie Mercury's handwritten letter to Radio 1 DJ John Peel, whose support on his *Sounds Of The Seventies* evening show helped break the band. It was slipped inside an early copy of *Queen II*.

On 'Keep Yourself Alive', Queen's first single, guitarist Brian May immortalised Mercury's time spent manning a stall on Kensington Market – where customers included Hendrix and Bolan. 'I sold a million mirrors in a shopping alleyway,' wrote May. It was a cautionary tale of sorts, though Mercury cherished the 'Be a superstar' line.

When he first joined May and drummer Roger Taylor, Mercury sometimes sang with a Bolanish bleat in his voice. By the time the newly named Queen made their official London debut at Imperial College on July 18, 1970, it was his stage presence that everyone noticed. John Anthony, whose nose for idiosyncratic talent had already led him to prog mavericks Van Der Graaf Generator, later described Mercury as a latter-day Nijinsky. It was Anthony – coincidentally an A&R man for the Mercury label – who teamed the band up with Trident Studios and eventually co-produced Queen's debut album.

A tiny dancer turned enormous presence, Freddie Mercury soon came to define the band. He drew on his graphic-design studies – and love for *fin de siècle* illustrator Aubrey Beardsley – to devise the band's crest and logo. He was also Queen's unofficial costumier until Zandra Rhodes came on board in 1974.

Mercury released a solo single just prior to the debut album, comprising covers of The Beach Boys' 'I Can Hear Music' and Goffin-King's 'Goin' Back'. Released in late June 1973, it was credited to Larry Lurex. But for all his credentials as a high-class challenger to Gary Glitter, it was done purely as a favour to Trident producer Robin Cable, who was testing out his capabilities as a Spector *pasticheur*.

No one even imagined Mercury would be tempted away. He was entirely wrapped up in Queen, having written half the first album and been at the centre of all the band's meticulous discussions about their

Mel Bush presents

MOTT ON TOUR

with supporting act

Queen

NOVEMBER
12 Leeds, Town Hall
13 Blackburn, St. George's Hall
15 Worcester, Gaumont
16 Lancaster University
17 Liverpool, Stadium
18 Hanley, Victoria Hall
19 Wolverhampton, Civic Hall

20 Oxford, New Theatre
21 Preston, Guild Hall
22 Newcastle, City Hall
23 Glasgow, Apollo Theatre
25 Edinburgh, Caley Cinema
26 Manchester, Opera House
27 Birmingham, Town Hall

28 Swansea, Branglyn Hall
29 Bristol, Colston Hall
30 Bournemouth, Winter Gardens
DECEMBER
1 Southend, Kursaal
2 Chatham, Central Hall
14 London, Odeon, Hammersmith

NEW MOTT SINGLE
RELEASED NOVEMBER 9th
"ROLL AWAY THE STONE"

Queen

Dear John,
    Thanks very much
for all the wonderful things
you've been saying about us —
    After six solid months of
constant posing and poovery we've
finally come up with Queen II.
Hope it's mad enough
for you.
            Love,
            Freddie Mercury

INTERNATIONAL
QUEEN
FAN CLUB

LEFT: The highlight of the *Queen II* tour was a performance at the Rainbow on March 31, 1974. But like Cockney Rebel, Queen's hyped-up theatricality didn't always sit well with critics, many of whom were calling time on pop and rock's obsession with 'flash'.

work and its presentation. 'Keep Yourself Alive', with its layers of voices and guitars, had been the sonic template. They just needed the right visual hook.

Invited to photograph the band in December 1973, Mick Rock shot them shirtless; 'looking as queer as clockwork oranges,' he remembered. Two months later, the band played him an advance copy of *Queen II*. He told them it sounded like Ziggy Stardust playing Led Zeppelin. There were grins of approval all round.

Tasked with shooting the cover, Rock dug out a classic portrait of Marlene Dietrich, lit from above on the set of the 1932 film *Shanghai Express*. It was the inspiration he needed. He bunched all four band members together; Freddie Mercury crossed his hands and raised his head slightly. Queen now had their admittance card to rock theatre's top table.

'It scared the other members of the band,' says Mick Rock, 'because they looked like a classically established act. But it didn't scare Freddie.'

Ironically perhaps, as glam rock had gained currency during 1973, the band briefly toyed with the idea of a name change. 'Because of dubious connotations,' Roger Taylor told *Record Mirror*'s Genevieve Hall the following February. The drummer was keen to stress that stage makeup was used strictly for theatrical purposes: 'in no way is there any glitter.'

'Contrary to general opinion,' Taylor concluded, 'we're straight!'

Nick Kent wasn't alone in harbouring deep suspicions of the Queen juggernaut. In his March 16, 1974 review of *Queen II* in *Record Mirror*, Chris Poole wrote: 'This is it, the dregs of glam rock. The band with the worst name have capped that dubious achievement by bringing out the worst album for some time.' Describing the material as 'weak and overproduced', Poole dismissed Mercury's voice as 'poor… dressed up with multitracking'.

Queen, like Cockney Rebel, had fallen victim to the press backlash against hype. One of its focal points was the enigma that was Freddie Mercury, a man whose confidence, wrote Genevieve Hall, 'can sometimes be mistaken for arrogance', who 'commands attention rather than demands it'.

That same month, however, Nick Kent underscored the general fatigue with superstars and their flamboyant ways. 'The only way this whole rock'n'roll mess can be salvaged,' he wrote, 'is if, as will happen, the whole schism blows itself up… [Then] a whole new breed of teenage bands will sprout up slowly who will write songs about… all the hideous things young teenage kids really have to go through.

'Consequently, rock music will start to have some true relevance again, beyond existing as some exotic musical broadsheet for other people's bloated fantasies.'

Chapter 25
Far, Far Away

Three years on from his conquest of the Laurel Canyon rock crowd at the Troubadour, Elton John was back in LA in September '73 for two nights at the Hollywood Bowl. This time, half of the world's entertainment elite showed up.

ABOVE: The highlight of Elton John's autumn 1973 US tour, his biggest yet, was a September 7 show at the Hollywood Bowl in Los Angeles. Elton made a dramatic entrance down an illuminated staircase in an outfit outlined in white feathers.

Elton rewarded them with a spectacular not seen since the days of Busby Berkeley. Linda 'Deep Throat' Lovelace emceed the shows. Lookalikes of Mae West, Groucho Marx and The Beatles entered the stage via an illuminated staircase, followed by Elton himself, resplendent in a gown of white feathers and a matching hat. Doves flew from inside five piano lids that spelled out his name.

It was the high point in Elton John's biggest US tour yet – forty-two cities, gates of between fifteen to twenty thousand in a mix of auditoria and stadia. This was not so much glam rock as classic showbiz glamour.

Four months later, in January 1974, Elton was nine thousand feet up in Colorado's Rocky Mountains, on an old stud farm recently converted into a hi-tech recording studio.

Opting to record his eighth studio album at Caribou Ranch was the latest stage in what *Creem*'s Wayne Robbins described as 'The Americanisation of Elton John'. Its predecessor, the two-disc set *Goodbye Yellow Brick Road*, had been a farewell of sorts to Hollywood-driven fantasy. Its flagship song 'Candle In The Wind', was a downbeat rumination on fame inspired by the premature death of Marilyn Monroe.

'We've gone as far as we can with this type of sound,' Elton told *Record Mirror*'s Michael Beattie in November. He aspired to create a funkier, more American vibe.

Joining him for the Caribou sessions was a contingent of notable Americans: The Beach Boys' Bruce Johnston and Carl Wilson; Chester Thompson, drummer of top soul/funk band Tower of Power;

*Stick Around
You're Gonna Hear Electric Music,
Solid Walls of Sound

"BENNIE AND THE JETS" MCA-40198

The new ELTON JOHN Single
from the Platinum Album
"GOODBYE YELLOW BRICK ROAD"
MCA 2-10003

P.S. Elton says "Many Thanks"
for the great R and B Airplay!

MCA RECORDS

Captain & Tennille; and the teenage Elton's poster girl Dusty Springfield, now living in California.

The air was thin, but the lines of cocaine were satisfyingly thick during the sessions. (Elton later admitted to a keen appetite for the stuff.) The studio atmosphere was tense, stifling the band and upsetting producer Gus Dudgeon, who'd describe the sessions as the worst he'd been involved in. Whilst recording the album's big ballad, 'Don't Let The Sun Go Down On Me', Elton raged that such schmaltz was beneath him.

In his addled state, the song's melancholia may have spoken too loudly to him. Elton John was now Britain's biggest pop success in the States since The Beatles, but perhaps it seemed as if there was now only one way he could go.

Back in London that spring, Elton took some comfort in the recent success of 'Bennie And The Jets'.

Released as a B-side in Britain, it was flipped by MCA in the States, picked up by black radio stations and landed on the *Billboard* R&B chart. A self-professed 'black record fanatic', Elton was delighted.

He was also exhausted. He'd spent virtually four-and-a-half years on the road. A May 1974 European tour was cancelled.

Talking to *NME*'s Charles Shaar Murray in July, Elton described himself as a 'T.O.T. – tired old tart'. His self-image, never his strong point, had taken another battering.

'Bette Midler said my new album should be called *Fat Reg From Pinner*,' he admitted, adding that he preferred *Ol' Pink Eyes Is Back*, but his band wasn't convinced. In an echo of the *Honky Château* days, Elton eventually named it after the recording studio: *Caribou*.

LEFT: A massive US soul and R&B enthusiast, Elton was overjoyed when 'Bennie And The Jets' was picked up by black radio stations across America and landed on the *Billboard* R&B chart.

ABOVE: Elton arriving home from Los Angeles with friend June Bolan, September 11, 1974. June was now estranged from husband Marc. Elton was taking a short break before flying back out for a two-month stadium tour.

Elton's enormous success, especially in the States, dangled like a prize carrot.

In late 1973, Elton John had become vice-president of Watford FC, the football team he'd supported since boyhood. He was mixing with what he called 'ordinary people' again, including his old mucker Rod Stewart, who'd join him on May 5 for a benefit gig for the club – Elton's only major performance that spring. He'd already donated 'Let Me Be Your Car' for Stewart's next album. Rod responded with a bit of advice, that Elton had become 'blimpish'. It was a cue to shed two stone in weight.

Elton hadn't wanted to make the latest album or do another tour. Weeks earlier, he'd told *Melody Maker*'s Chris Welch that his fantasy for 1974 would be to put together an all-star package tour, 'a really bizarre one with Gary Glitter, David Bowie, Cassidy, The Who, and make it really showbiz.'

Elton was tired of his relentless schedule. Above all, he was tired of being 'Elton John'. 'I'll tell you what has ruined pop,' he continued, 'all these fucking PRs and people like that. "You can't do that, it'll ruin your image…"'

The January 1974 issue of *Let It Rock* led with the cover story 'Rod Stewart – The Best Singer In The Best Band?' But the real question was how much longer such an alliance would hold. Previous months had seen Bowie, Bolan, Ferry, even The Who's Roger Daltrey, ditch the band format to various degrees.

There was a far bigger share of the pie to be gained by a solo act, that was obvious. The enormous and continuing success of Elton John, especially in the States, dangled like a prize carrot.

In the run-up to The Faces' headline appearance at the Reading Festival over the 1973 August bank holiday, manager Billy Gaff announced it might well be the band's last in the UK. He cited work permit problems for Tetsu Yamauchi, the ex-Free bassist who'd replaced Ronnie Lane.

The real issue was the one that had dogged the band. Rod Stewart's first greatest hits album, *Sing It Again Rod*, had just topped the British charts. For the first time, the singer had also released a stand-alone, non-album 45, a cover of Maxine Brown's soul-stirring 'Oh! No Not My Baby'.

The song came with a sweet string section; the record came gift-wrapped in a tartan sleeve, a symbol of the north London-born singer's sentimental loyalty to his Scottish heritage. Spending three weeks in the top ten during September 1973, the hit

LEFT: November 7, 1973: about to become vice-president of Watford Football Club, boyhood fan Elton roped in Rod Stewart to join him for a kickaround with the players. The pair returned to Vicarage Road on May 5, 1974, to play a benefit concert for the club. Among the songs they performed was the Taupin/ John original 'Country Comfort', covered by Stewart on 1970's *Gasoline Alley*.

suggested a new seriousness in Stewart's attitude toward a solo career.

Rod gave a typically ambivalent assessment to *Sounds*' Penny Valentine: 'I don't feel either my albums or The Faces albums are as good as they could be. So the next album is the last I'm going to make on my own and next year we start making them together: Rod Stewart/Faces albums.

'I don't mean the band's breaking up,' he continued. 'I just mean I want to think a bit more for myself. I love change. I change everything – my old ladies, cars, everything. I'm never happy with what I've got.'

Speaking in December, during The Faces' biggest tour of Britain, keyboardist Ian McLagan – now wearing a three-piece tartan suit to emphasise his own Scottish roots – admitted that 80 per cent of the band's earnings came from the States. He also reiterated the band's early fears that The Faces 'might end up as Rod's backing group or something'.

The release, in January '74, of the *Coast To Coast: Overture And Beginners* live album was further evidence that The Faces were being relegated to second on the bill. It was the first album to receive the Rod Stewart/Faces credit. It was also a contract-fulfilling set and sounded like it.

That spring, after an Australasian tour, Ronnie Wood continued to work on his solo album; Rod decamped to Frankfurt and Brussels to record his first solo album in two years. There would be no Faces tour of the States in 1974.

On December 14, 1973, Mott The Hoople played two gigs at the Hammersmith Odeon, the climax to the band's successful British tour, with Queen providing robust support. 'Mott Riot!' announced *Melody Maker* the following week. 'Rock'n'Roll is here to stay.'

The band had been catalysed by the arrival, midway through their late summer US tour, of guitarist Ariel Bender. Formerly known as Luther Grosvenor of Spooky Tooth, it was said he acquired his new name after the similarly pseudonymous Lynsey de Paul had seen his predecessor, Mick Ralphs, bending car aerials in rage while both acts were in Germany. The truth was more prosaic – and almost certainly a classic case of transit-van wit: 'a real bender'.

Ralphs, who had since founded Bad Company with ex-Free singer Paul Rodgers, had been uncomfortable with the frivolities of glam rock. The renamed Bender was not. 'His flash dress and superlative guitar playing have re-energised Mott totally,' wrote *Record Mirror*'s John Beattie in December '73.

Hunter agreed. 'I'm really excited,' he told Nick Kent weeks later. 'Ariel has this thing where he *wants* to be a rock'n'roll star and he *wants* to be noticed on stage and prance around and be a guitar hero.' Bender was, Hunter added, 'another frontman. He's going to be great because he's got this ego thing which *is* rock'n'roll more than anything else.'

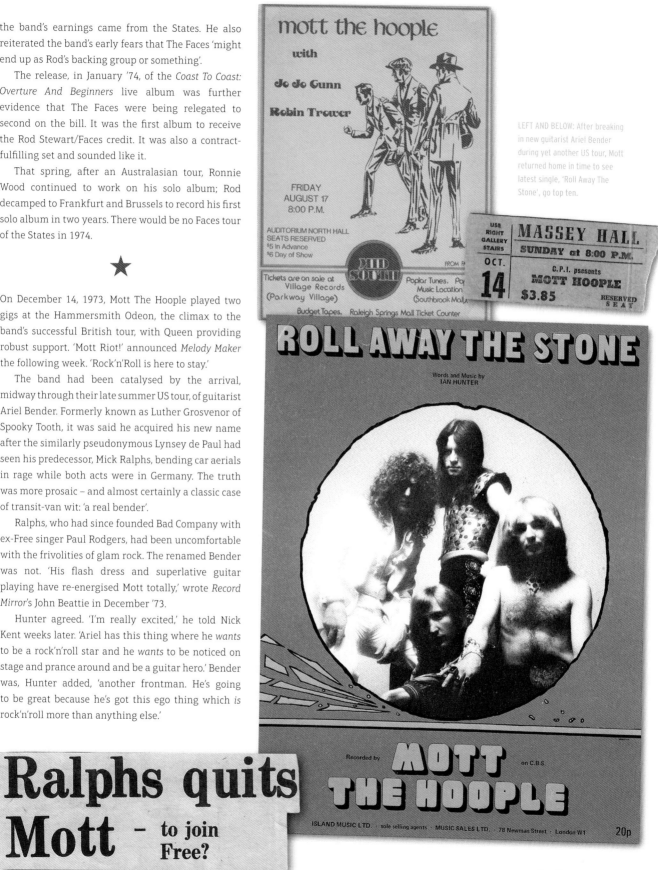

LEFT AND BELOW: After breaking in new guitarist Ariel Bender during yet another US tour, Mott returned home in time to see latest single, 'Roll Away The Stone', go top ten.

RIGHT: March 7, 1974: all the young couples. Ian Hunter with wife Trudi, Ariel Bender with Githa, and Buffin with Paula. The band were working on *Mott*, their first with Bender on board, at the time.

FACING PAGE: The cover of March 1974's *The Hoople* featured Kari-Ann Muller from the first Roxy Music album.

FACING PAGE FAR RIGHT: Mott's five-night run at the Uris Theatre on Broadway was marred when Led Zeppelin's entourage decided they'd join in for 'All The Young Dudes'. Fisticuffs duly ensued.

I HAVE A HEART ON FOR
Mott the Hoople
Blue Oyster Cult

Bender's arrival coincided with Mott The Hoople at a peak. 'All The Way From Memphis' had hit No. 10 in September; 'Roll Away The Stone' spent almost all of December in the top ten. Both had featured Mick Ralphs on guitar.

Despite his archetypal rock-star image and the nonchalance of his Dylan-ish, mid-Atlantic drawl, Hunter was a benevolent worrier. His latest concern, he told Kent, was that bassist Overend Watts and drummer Buffin were not enjoying the financial rewards that came with composer's royalties.

He was also aware that a new Mott album needed to be written. While the band holidayed over the New Year, Hunter wrote feverishly. The result was *The Hoople*, released in March 1974. Kari-Ann Muller, from the first Roxy Music album, graced the cover. Seven of the nine songs were Hunter originals.

'I remember them coming up and saying, "Is this your solo album?"' Hunter says. 'It just seemed as if I'd taken over. In fact, I didn't wanna take over but, you know, Mick Ralphs isn't there; I gotta write all the stuff. It was the beginning of the end, basically.'

A key song was 'Marionette'. Disillusion unfolds in every verse: 'I wanna get out!' sings Hunter. 'They won, I'm done.' It was, he said, the best thing he'd ever written.

By the time *The Hoople* peaked at No. 11 in Britain, in May 1974, the band were midway through another US tour, again with Queen in support. During the previous dates, one or two critics felt Hunter had gone too far with what Barry Taylor of *Record Mirror* called the 'bisexual approach… an almost limp-wristed fey image in [a] white suit'. Outraged, Hunter bit back. 'If he wants to compare me, I'd rather be compared with [Jethro Tull's] Ian Anderson, not Bowie.'

The current single, 'The Golden Age Of Rock'n'Roll', tapped effortlessly into tradition. But Columbia Records were backing Mott big in the US and wanted to cover all bases. A five-night stint at the new Uris Theatre in New York was arranged; it was the first time a rock band played Broadway.

But Mott weren't Bowie or Alice Cooper. Their theatrics involved little more than Hunter yelling 'Rock'n'roll!' to the crowd and the audience singing along to 'All The Young Dudes'. The only props at the Uris were a puppet on a stick and some mannequins for 'Marionette'.

But there was some drama, albeit unscripted. Led Zeppelin, with roadies in tow, turned up on opening night the worse for wear. Having intimidated the band from the start, drummer John Bonham demanded to join Mott for the 'All The Young Dudes' encore. Fisticuffs ensued and Mott's own drummer, Buffin, took a knock on the knee from a Zep roadie which swelled up as he played. (Afterwards, Hunter received a rare apology from Zep manager Peter Grant.)

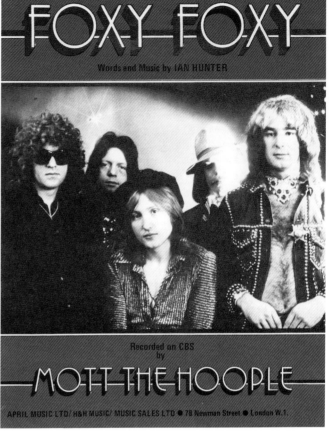

The tour was a success. But by the time *The Hoople* became the first Mott album to hit the *Billboard* chart (at No. 28), the band were home and one man down.

Having played *Top Of The Pops* to promote their latest 45, the Wall of Sound-ish 'Foxy, Foxy', they played with Ariel Bender for the last time at the Palace Lido, Douglas, on the Isle Of Man. Further dates were cancelled at short notice.

Bender's departure was a devastating blow. Hunter regarded the guitarist as 'a lovely man', full of positive energy. But there were the usual 'creative differences' during the making of the album and further tensions had surfaced during the US tour. Bender claimed he wanted to form a new band, with a new singer, expressly aimed at success in America.

In the May issue of *Creem*, Ian Hunter (Mott – Top Group, Top Album) had been pictured on the cover along with other winners of the magazine's Readers' Poll: Elton (Hero, Best Songwriter – with Bernie Taupin), Bowie (Best Male Singer), Led Zep's Jimmy Page (Best Guitarist) and Alice (second Best Live Act – after the apparently less coverworthy Who). Inside, among the many other categories, was 'Fad': in ascending order, Watergate, Homosexuality, The 1950s and, most despised of all, Glitter (the style, not the singer).

Weeks earlier, *Rolling Stone*'s Greg Shaw had written: 'The biggest factor preventing the spread of glitter rock in America is the persistent popularity of blues, particularly in the form of its degenerate offspring, boogie.' He predicted a US rock band would follow Edgar 'Frankenstein' Winter's attempt to bring glitter to the blues, adding 'flash and glamour'. The ingredients cited by Shaw were fairly accurate. He just failed to predict which band.

Formed in Queens, New York, in late 1972, KISS played an animated brand of booglarised riff-rock – as if Grand Funk Railroad had gone glam. An early observer, noted US critic Dave Marsh, filed a report on the still waiting-to-burst New York scene for *Melody Maker* in October 1973. Comparing KISS visually to characters from John Waters' underground film *Pink*

ABOVE: Soon after Mott promoted new single 'Foxy, Foxy' on *Top Of The Pops*, Ariel Bender sensationally quit on July 6 after a gig in Douglas on the Isle of Man.

RIGHT: KISS around the time of their debut album, February 1974. L–R: Ace Frehley (The Spaceman), Paul Stanley (The Starchild), Peter Criss (The Catman) and Gene Simmons (The Demon). By masquerading as superhero characters, KISS appealed to a much wider section of the US public than fragrant English stars like Bolan and Bowie ever could.

Flamingos, he wrote: 'I was right all along in thinking that the glitter craze was an ugliness contest.'

But he was by no means dismissive: 'Kiss's music sounds as if it's the most thought-out, controlled sound around, and the stage show is just as professional.'

What mattered was the band's attitude. KISS thought *BIG* – that's why they capitalised the band name. When they found themselves a manager, he wasn't a tried-and-tested rock manager but a TV director/producer.

'Bill [Aucoin] sat down with [bassist] Gene [Simmons] and me and said he wasn't interested unless we wanted to become the biggest band in the world,' singer/guitarist Paul Stanley told *MOJO*'s Pete Makowski in 2014.

KISS had a simple but audaciously effective concept. Rather than try to pass off one or more of them as a mere superstar, they would adopt the

guise of four distinct superhero characters: Demon, Starchild, Spaceman and Catman.

With the considerable backing of Neil Bogart's Warner Brothers-funded Casablanca label, KISS followed the route taken by Alice Cooper during 1971 – a relentless gigging schedule that took them way beyond the coasts and deep into the US heartlands, backed by an extensive publicity campaign.

While Alice spent much of 1974 partying with the real Groucho Marx, Fred Astaire and Mae West (no lookalikes) in Hollywood, KISS filled the void with their rock'n'roll spectaculars, exemplified by Gene Simmons' fire-eating routine. The debut album failed to take off, but 1975's *Alive!* delivered KISS to a mass album-buying audience.

KISS thought BIG – that's why they capitalised the band's name.

KISS were glam rock mainstream America-style – no individual egos or, Lord forbid, sexual ambiguity. Nick Kent caught a whiff of them early in 1974: 'And, of course, it absolutely reeks,' he sniffed. 'It's hard to foresee anything beyond failure on all levels. The music is boring, the visual quite repulsive: KISS are nothing more or less than America's very own Chicory Tip.'

Alas, while Tip had ended up wearing some of the most bizarre gear known to glam, the American quartet also had everything else in place to guarantee success. By 1976, KISS would be the biggest band in the States. They wouldn't hit the top ten in Britain until they washed the makeup off for 1983's *Lick It Up*.

On October 11, 1974, LA's Hollywood Palladium hosted The First Annual Hollywood Street Revival & Trash Dance. A partially revived GTOs sang a few songs, before backing Silverhead frontman – and Miss Pamela's new beau and future husband – Michael Des Barres on some Elvis covers.

A platinum-haired Iggy Pop ignored all calls for Stooges classics, instead playing a set of Stones covers. The New York Dolls – soon to be dropped by

Mercury after disappointing sales for their aptly titled second album, *Too Much Too Soon* – headlined with a set heavily weighted to mid-sixties R&B favourites. Afterwards, it was all back to Rodney Bingenheimer's English Disco club for a stomping, Anglophilic after-show. Except that almost no one came. The event soon became known as 'The Death Of Glitter'.

There was no such singular moment in Britain. The scene that had emerged during 1971-72, from a desire for new stars and a renewed sense of youthful energy and showmanship, dissolved in similarly haphazard fashion.

When Mott The Hoople replaced Ariel Bender with ex-Spiders From Mars guitarist Mick Ronson in September, it seemed like a masterstroke. But Hunter remained unsettled and Ronson was recovering from a stalled solo career.

It had begun well, with February 1974's solo debut, *Slaughter On 10th Avenue*, going top ten. But despite Ronson's reputation and a big promotional campaign, it soon became clear that Bowie's gifted ex-lieutenant was not going to be the saviour of '74 some were predicting. The choice of an old Presley ballad, 'Love Me Tender', as the first single did him no favours; a series of gigs in the spring revealed further

ABOVE: Ian Hunter was convinced that Mott's October 1974 single, 'Saturday Gigs', was top-ten material. It flopped miserably.

ABOVE RIGHT: After launching his solo career in February 1974 with *Slaughter On 10th Avenue* to a mixed reception, Mick Ronson accepted the invite to join Mott after Bender's departure. 'Mick was one of the best sidemen ever,' says Hunter, 'but he wasn't a frontman'. It seemed a perfect fit.

Der heisseste Live Act der Welt

MOTT THE HOOPLE

MOTT 'THE HOOPLE'

Guest Star: TITANIC

Auf Deutschland Tournee

Saarbrücken	16.10.	TASV-Halle
Stgt.-Sindelfingen	17.10.	Ausstellungshalle
München	21.10.	Theater in der Brienner Straße
Ffm.-Offenbach	25.10.	Stadthalle
Heidelberg	26.10.	Stadthalle
Hannover	28.10.	Niedersachsenhalle
Rendsburg	29.10.	Nordmarkhalle
Hamburg	30.10.	Musikhalle

CBS The Family of Music

The golden age of Rock'n Roll:

MOTT THE HOOPLE

in Concert!   u. Guests

Samstag, 26. Oktober 1974 20 Uhr
Stadthalle Heidelberg

1769 *

DM 1?
zuzügl. Vor...

MOTT THE HOOPLE

Mott split?

First news of the break-up in last week's NME

NOW IT'S OFFICIAL

IAN HUNTER and Mick Ronson have definitely broken a... ...Mott The Hoopl... now offic... ...pursue a ... for reco... work, wit... second-in-... musical di... This com... ...assess...

Rather surprisingly, they have decided to retain the name o... Mott The Hoople. Spokesma... ...ly said this week

Hunter, Ronson split Hoople

mm 74.12.2?

MOTT THE Hoople have split up. After week? mounting speculation and rumour it was offici? confirmed this week that the band are no mor?
Ian Hunter, whose recent illness led to the cancell? of Mott's British tour, is now working on a new ?lbum — to be produced by Mick Ronson, who jo? Mott as replacement for Ariel Bender in Septe? Hunter and Ronson are now planning to form a ?and which, after the completion of an album, wi? going on the road.
The split comes as the ?...

shortcomings. 'Just a little too laid back,' wrote *RM*'s Peter Harvey, who also noted a certain nervousness on Ronno's part.

'Mick was one of the best sidemen ever,' says Hunter, 'but he wasn't a frontman.'

As a team, Hunter and Ronson gelled. But now, with two big names, Mott grew even more lopsided. They were dispirited too, forever trying to reconcile their rock and pop faces. Ian Hunter was convinced October 1974's thumper, 'Saturday Gigs', was a top-ten hit. It failed to make the top forty.

Out in New Jersey in October, Hunter broke down. Mott's sell-out British tour was cancelled. In December, he announced he was leaving the band, though he'd re-emerge in April 1975 with a top-twenty hit, 'Once Bitten Twice Shy', co-produced with Mick Ronson. But

ABOVE: After the Ronson-powered Mott toured Germany in October, Hunter took off to New Jersey where he was taken ill, suffering from exhaustion. A forthcoming British tour was cancelled, and in December it was announced that both Hunter and Ronson had left the band.

the record business would get in the way of the short-lived Hunter Ronson Band: Hunter was signed to CBS, Ronson to RCA.

On July 13/14, 1974, Ron Wood played two solo gigs at the Kilburn Gaumont State Cinema. Among the invited guests on stage were Faces Ian McLagan and Rod Stewart – and Rolling Stones guitarist Keith Richards. The Faces returned to the venue in December, crowning a five-week British tour. Once again, the Stones guitarist sat in, though Stewart wasn't best pleased. He was even less impressed afterwards when he was told Ron would be joining the Stones.

It wasn't strictly true – but in April 1975, the Stones did announce Wood as their temporary replacement guitarist for a summer US tour. Stewart, who'd already told *Penthouse* magazine in January he was going to do 'something completely different', had been making alternative arrangements.

ABOVE: Bassist Tetsu Yamauchi joined The Faces in time for the band's appearance at the 1973 Reading Festival at the end of August. But with Lane's departure, the soul of the band had gone. Ron Wood started playing solo gigs and getting chummy with the Stones. Rod took up with actress Britt Ekland and prepared to make an Atlantic crossing that would finish off The Faces.

He announced his departure from Britain and took off to the States – with his new celebrity girlfriend, actress Britt Ekland – where he teamed up with ace producer Tom Dowd and the Muscle Shoals studio musicians. He'd re-emerge in August 1975 with *Atlantic Crossing*. The title said it all: this was an all-new Rod Stewart, freed from rock'n'roll and embracing a polished, impeccably crafted AOR sound. He was following his old mate Elton with a serious assault on the fast-changing, mid-seventies US market.

In the spring of 1974, Slade still had their eye on the States. As drummer Don Powell would note in his memoir, 'the glam era was coming to an end, and we wanted to change.'

The band toured Britain in the spring supported by visiting US rockers Brownsville Station, who'd had a not entirely dissimilar sounding hit in '73 with 'Smokin' In The Boys Room'. During the tour, it was

announced that Slade would soon be making their own film. The initial concept was comedy, perhaps with a silvery sci-fi touch: but *The Quite A Mess Experiment*, inspired by 1953 TV science fiction series *The Quatermass Experiment*, was dropped in favour of a script based more closely on the band itself.

A screenwriter, Andrew Birkin (brother of singer/actress Jane), joined the band for their June US tour. What he observed wasn't exactly *A Hard Day's Night*. That the band were still correcting journalists who assumed their name was 'Slide' on account of their Brummie accents was potential comedy gold. More seriously, the contrast between the hugely successful British dates and yet another tough slog across the States, often competing with Aerosmith and the James Gang, was taking its toll.

TOP LEFT: So convincing was Slade's on-screen portrayal of fictional band Flame that many fans assumed, as per the script, that Slade were no more.

ABOVE: The Serpentine, Hyde Park, 1974: the original idea was to call the film *The Quite A Mess Experiment*. It's likely that Slade would have made a success of that too.

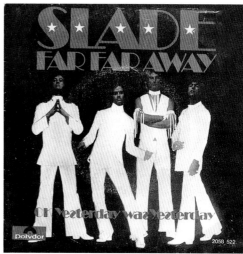

Slade had been Britain's most successful band of the era – six No. 1s since late 1971, plus another four top-five hits and three chart-topping albums. But Birkin's script – which was based on long conversations with the band – turned all that on its head. This was an archetypal study of the souring of pop dreams, closer in spirit to a kitchen-sink drama than to some *Glam Crazee!* celebration.

So convincing were Noddy, Dave, Jim and Don in their eventual roles as fictional band Flame that those who made it to the cinema on its release, in February 1975, left with the impression that Slade were finished.

The strongest song on the soundtrack was the homesick 'Far Far Away', sparked by Noddy Holder watching a Mississippi paddle-steamer from a balcony in Memphis. Soon after the release of *Slade In Flame* (as the film was billed), Slade disappeared again, relocating in one last attempt to make it in the USA.

On Chas Chandler's advice, Dave Hill even ditched his platforms. But the flame was flickering out.

LEFT: Glasgow, March 10, 1975: the idea was to promote *Flame*. Hearse driver Jimmy McDonald might have been forgiven for thinking Slade were there to bury a pop era that had just about had its day.

Epilogue
Brothers in Exile

On April 3, 1974, David Bowie stepped onto the *SS France* at Cannes, destination New York. He was on a one-way ticket. Eight days later, he arrived wearing a blue-check jacket, his flame-coloured hair now cut to the collar and mostly obscured by a large fedora.

BOWIE
"REBEL REBEL"
LPBO.5009
A VALENTINE DAY RELEASE
MAINMAN
RCA Records and Tapes

Bowie's work in Britain was done. The Stones-like 'Rebel Rebel', his first single of 1974, peaked at No. 5 in early March then disappeared fast. Lulu's foxy cover of 'The Man Who Sold The World' – which Bowie had co-produced with Mick Ronson during the *Pin Ups* sessions – did better, hitting No. 3 in February.

The domestic hit 45s mattered little. Everything in Bowie's world was geared towards the US tour which began in Montreal on June 14, ending with two nights at New York's Madison Square Garden five weeks later. Ostensibly, the tour was designed to promote Bowie's latest album, *Diamond Dogs*, a vast and compelling set of Doomsday episodes inspired by George Orwell's dystopian novel, *Nineteen Eighty-Four*, the cut-up technique of Beat writer William S. Burroughs ('When you cut into the present, the future leaks out,' Burroughs explained) and, surely, the post-apocalyptic imagery in Harlan Ellison's 1969 novella *A Boy And His Dog*.

LEFT: The motor for Bowie's first single of 1974, 'Rebel Rebel', was the greatest riff never to appear on a Rolling Stones record.

RIGHT: Bowie with his 'Édith Piaf' Lulu, December 27, 1973. Lulu enjoyed a career revival with her Bowie/Ronson-produced cover of 'The Man Who Sold The World'. Bowie wore a Brian Jones T-shirt.

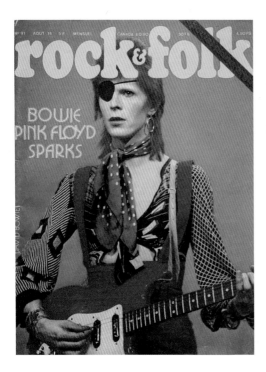

In *NME*, Charles Shaar Murray described *Diamond Dogs* as 'The final nightmare of the glitter apocalypse.' The depth and breadth of the album suggested Bowie was between worlds – and not just in a transatlantic sense.

The cover was designed by Belgian artist Guy Peellaert, whose work Bowie had been introduced to by Mick Jagger the previous winter. The pair featured – alongside Elvis, Lennon and Dylan – on the cover of *Rock Dreams*, a collection of Peellaert's photorealist work published in March.

Diamond Dogs was one of Bowie's most enigmatic and provocative releases – and the tour was every bit its match. Sitting high above the first six rows in a cherry picker, singing Hamlet-like to a theatrical skull in his meticulously constructed, post-apocalyptic Hunger City stage set, Bowie was taking rock theatre – quite literally – to a whole new level.

ABOVE: Bowie promoted 'Rebel Rebel' as Halloween Jack, a short-lived character adopted for just a few weeks early in 1974.

RIGHT: Bowie backstage with girlfriend Ava Cherry and Gary Glitter at The Faces' Madison Square Garden show, February 24, 1975.

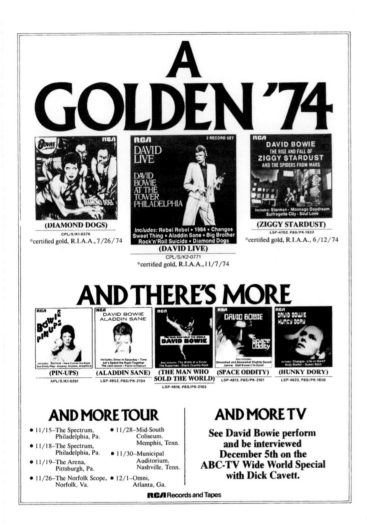

A GOLDEN '74

Bowie
RCA
(DIAMOND DOGS)
CPL/S/K1-0576
*certified gold, R.I.A.A., 7/26/74

RCA 2 RECORD SET
DAVID LIVE
DAVID BOWIE AT THE TOWER PHILADELPHIA
Includes: Rebel Rebel • 1984 • Changes
Sweet Thing • Aladdin Sane • Big Brother
Rock'n'Roll Suicide • Diamond Dogs
(DAVID LIVE)
CPL/S/K2-0771
*certified gold, R.I.A.A., 11/7/74

RCA
DAVID BOWIE
THE RISE AND FALL OF
ZIGGY STARDUST
AND THE SPIDERS FROM MARS
Includes: Starman • Moonage Daydream
Suffragette City • Soul Love
(ZIGGY STARDUST)
LSP-4702, P8S/PK-1932
*certified gold, R.I.A.A., 6/12/74

AND THERE'S MORE

RCA
BOWIE PIN-UPS
Includes: Sorrow • Here Comes the Night
See Emily Play • Anyway, Anyhow, Anywhere
(PIN-UPS)
APL/S/K1-0291

RCA
DAVID BOWIE
ALADDIN SANE
Includes: Drive-In Saturday • Time
Let's Spend the Night Together
The Jean Genie • Panic in Detroit
(ALADDIN SANE)
LSP-4852, P8S/PK-2134

RCA
THE MAN WHO SOLD THE WORLD
DAVID BOWIE
Also includes: The Width of a Circle
The Supermen • Black Country Rock
(THE MAN WHO SOLD THE WORLD)
LSP-4816, P8S/PK-2103

RCA
DAVID BOWIE
Space Oddity
Includes: Unwashed and Somewhat Slightly Dazed
Janine • God Knows I'm Good
(SPACE ODDITY)
LSP-4813, P8S/PK-2101

RCA
DAVID BOWIE
HUNKY DORY
Includes: Changes • Life on Mars?
Andy Warhol • Queen Bitch
(HUNKY DORY)
LSP-4623, P8S/PK-1850

AND MORE TOUR
- 11/15–The Spectrum, Philadelphia, Pa.
- 11/18–The Spectrum, Philadelphia, Pa.
- 11/19–The Arena, Pittsburgh, Pa.
- 11/26–The Norfolk Scope, Norfolk, Va.
- 11/28–Mid-South Coliseum, Memphis, Tenn.
- 11/30–Municipal Auditorium, Nashville, Tenn.
- 12/1–Omni, Atlanta, Ga.

AND MORE TV
See David Bowie perform and be interviewed December 5th on the ABC-TV Wide World Special with Dick Cavett.

RCA Records and Tapes

> This wasn't glam rock or showbiz. This was a man playing for his life.

ABOVE: Bowie spent much of 1974 in the States. Midway through the *Diamond Dogs* tour, in August, he took off to the Sigma Sound Studios, home of Gamble & Huff's 'Philly Sound' for several days' recording. When the tour picked up again in September, Bowie had reinvented his sound to reflect what he'd been hearing in clubs and on R&B radio stations. Out went the elaborate theatrics, too. The so-called 'Philly Dogs' tour had become a dynamic, revue-style presentation.

RIGHT: Like Bowie, Marc Bolan had been a lifelong R&B enthusiast. T. Rex's funky summer '74 hit, 'Light Of Love', had brought Clavinet-playing Gloria Jones to the forefront. 'He was a soul man,' she says.

Away from the stage, he experienced an epiphany of sorts. The slick, club-oriented sounds of contemporary US soul – both on the radio and in Puerto Rican clubs frequented with his new guitarist pal, Carlos Alomar – reacquainted him with his early love of US R&B. The music also suggested another of his abrupt creative turns, as well an alternative route to winning over the American market.

Bowie booked Sigma Sound Studios, the home of ace 'Philly Sound' producers Gamble & Huff – mentors to Billy Paul, Harold Melvin & The Blue Notes and The O'Jays. He called up producer Tony Visconti, back in the fold since *Diamond Dogs*, and brought in the all-American rhythm section of Andy Newmark and Willie Weeks. Alomar also introduced him to relatively unknown R&B singer Luther Vandross – and Bowie's current squeeze and protégé, Ava Cherry, came too.

The bulk of what would become *Young Americans*

was recorded in less than two weeks during early-mid August 1974. Bowie later described his translucent-white embrace of contemporary R&B as 'plastic soul'. Always keen to undermine the platitudes and pomposity that governed rock, he revelled Warhol-like in the perceived insincerity of it all.

Yet his self-deprecation masked a genuine passion for the music of new Black America. In the studio, he'd occasionally throw in a subtle, Al Green-style vocal tic. On the town, he'd dress in the brightly coloured, generously tailored zoot suits favoured by African-American and Latino teenagers during the 1940s, which on him looked simultaneously chic and freaky.

For a final session, in January 1975, Bowie recorded a totally unexpected version of John Lennon's meditative hippie-era anthem, 'Across The Universe'. Whereas Lennon had brought in a couple of sweet-voiced 'Apple scruffs' (young Beatles diehards who hung about outside Abbey Road studios) to sing the idealistic 'Nothing's gonna change my world' chorus, Bowie sang the lyric as if it was diseased, yelling out the chorus with gritted-teeth resolve for the individualistic 1970s. It was at a time when he was about to sever his relationship with his manager of five years, Tony Defries.

Early in September 1974, Bowie had resumed the *Diamond Dogs* tour with a week at the Universal Amphitheatre in Los Angeles. Marc Bolan and Gloria Jones turned up – and left halfway through.

Like Bowie, Bolan had also quit Britain in spring '74 and was determined to advance the strong soul/R&B influence he'd already adopted during 1973 for

the *Zinc Alloy* album. He spent much of the summer in Los Angeles, recording with some of the West Coast's leading session players, and secured a new deal with the go-getting Casablanca label – home of KISS.

On a brief return to Britain, Bolan had remained upbeat about his prospects. 'I haven't slipped,' he told *Record Mirror*'s Tony Norman. 'I'm still number one.

'The only rival I've got is David Bowie, and we're close friends. We sat down… in New York recently and sorted out our future[s] for the next two years,' he claimed.

That summer's single, 'Light Of Love', was freshly upbeat pop, all funky Clavinet and handclaps. It was one in the eye for those who constantly carped about a trademark T. Rex sound. But it stalled at No. 22 on the UK chart. A month later, Casablanca released *Light Of Love*, a US-only set rushed out in time for a long, make-or-break T. Rex autumn tour.

Four songs from an October 8 performance at Long Beach, California were broadcast on *Don Kirshner's Rock Concert*. Clearly overweight and sporting unflattering, Elvis-style shoulder pads, Bolan wrestled manfully

with one song in particular: 'Token Of My Love', from the US album.

'Every day / Every single day / My heart is broken,' he sang, against a leaden, sludgy sound. It was part cabaret soul, part freakshow. Gloria hid behind dark glasses and a headscarf; Bolan underscored each line with T. Rexcessive flurries of overamped guitar; the pair wailed despairingly at regular intervals.

This wasn't glam rock, or even rock'n'roll showbiz – this was a man playing for his life. T. Rex began cancelling dates. Bolan and Gloria returned to LA. Shortly afterwards, Marc had broken down.

'You get involved in this business,' says Gloria Jones, 'and you believe the hype. Then one day you're like, "Where are the fans? They're not hearing the new ideas." That broke his heart.

'He was [also] fighting with himself. Maybe he thought he made the wrong decisions by trying to experience something new. He had to go within himself. After that, we went to the health farm in the south of France.'

In September 1977, Bolan and Bowie shared a public stage for the first time. Bolan was filming the sixth and final episode of his afternoon TV series, *Marc*. Bowie had a new single to promote, '"Heroes"'.

Much had happened since Bolan quit Los Angeles at the end of 1974. He'd returned, via the south of France, to London and become a father in September 1975, naming his son Rolan Bolan in the style of Zowie Bowie.

Bolan had also become a regular on afternoon TV pop shows such as *Supersonic*. From late 1976, he'd nail his colours to the mast of the growing punk-rock movement, touring with The Damned and declaring himself 'Godfather of Punk'.

Bowie, too, had bounced back fitter and happier, after hitting a cocaine and paranoia-induced rock bottom in Los Angeles in late 1975. But unlike Bolan, he'd put his psychological difficulties to better creative use: scoring his first US No. 1, a purgative rumination on 'Fame' with John Lennon, in September '75; acting out his paranoia regarding the mass media and the end of civilisation in Nicolas Roeg's 1976 film, *The Man Who Fell To Earth*; less successfully, he'd tried to warn of the parallels between rock music and fascism ('Hitler was the first rock star').

The pair had crossed paths several times since their glam wars of 1972-73. In early March 1977, while Bowie was in London to perform as a backing musician on an Iggy Pop tour, he visited Bolan and Gloria in their west London home. They plugged in guitars and a keyboard and worked up an intense, ultra-punkish demo, 'Madman'. Then Bowie went off to the States with the revitalised Iggy, before moving on to Berlin to record a new album, *"Heroes"*, in Berlin.

'David's perfect for me to work with,' Bolan told Capital Radio's Maggie Norden on September 4. 'We're hot when we're hot; we're cold when we're cold.' Three days later, Bowie – now defying his aerophobia by taking planes – flew in from Switzerland to join him at the Granada TV studios in Manchester.

LEFT: Bolan invited punk act The Damned to join the spring 1977 T. Rex tour. 'Bolan was well over the top,' remembers Captain Sensible. 'The punk crowd appreciated that.'

RIGHT: September 7, 1977: Bolan and Bowie together on stage and in front of the TV cameras for the first and only time.

FAREWELL TO MARC

Weeping fans mingled with stars on Tuesday (20-9-77) to say goodbye to rock idol Marc Bolan, who was killed in a car crash on Friday (16-9-77). Hundreds of fans - decked out in Bolan T-shirts, scarves and badges - failed to get into the funeral service. But stars such as Rod Stewart and David Bowie joined the singers family inside the chapel at Golders Green crematorium in London.

PS: THE STAR: David Bowie leaves the service.

*DM:77-5074-24A   21st September 1977

See also pictures 77-5074-14A,11C,19C & 28B

Evening News

BIGGEST EVENING SALE

LATE SPECIAL CITY PRICES

Pop star's car smashes into tree

MARC BOLAN KILLED

No one talked about glam, or glitter, or even superstars anymore. Queen's 'Bohemian Rhapsody', No. 1 for nine weeks over winter 1975-76, had been the final word on all that.

Bowie had placed inverted commas around '"Heroes"' for good reason. He'd been through the whole star-making process and come out the other side. What he experienced wasn't always pretty. Yet with all the ambivalence that Bowie excelled in, '"Heroes"' was steeped in a kind of heroic grandeur that both he and Bolan – and even the punks who'd come to destroy their generation – could never quite shake off.

Playing bass that day was Herbie Flowers, whose song 'Grandad' denied 'Ride A White Swan' a No. 1 spot back in winter 1970-71. He'd worked intermittently with Bowie since 1967, even leading a revolt over pay during the *Diamond Dogs* tour that contributed to Bowie coming off the road and recording *Young Americans*. Flowers had also been playing with T. Rex since autumn 1976.

'They [both] stuck to that great tradition of the Shakespearean minstrel,' he reflects, 'the masquerade. They weren't afraid to dress up and get the bird for it. It's theatre. You don't go and hear a band; you go and see a band.'

For the show's big finale, Bolan and Bowie strapped on guitars and started up a standard R&B riff. 'The last time David looked at Marc was when he fell off the stage,' says Herbie Flowers. 'He had a big smile on his face and Marc was hopping about saying, "I think I broke me ankle." We were all laughing.'

Less than two weeks later, Bowie would join Rod Stewart, Tony Visconti and a vast cross-section of musicians and fans to pay his last respects to Bolan at Golders Green Crematorium, in north London. Marc had been killed in a car accident during the early hours of September 16, 1977.

TOP LEFT: Four shots featuring fans Kath Andryszewski [bottom left] and Judith Henderson [top right] taken outside Bolan's New Bond Street office on September 13, 1977. 'Marc was very sweet and happy to pose with us,' says Judith. Three days later, he was dead. 'We took our films in to be developed with tears streaming down our faces,' Kath remembers. 'We begged them not to lose them.'

Bolan's death focused minds on what he'd helped unleash back in 1971 – pop as a kind of soap opera, crammed with scene-stealing characters and a thrilling new theme song every week. It had fallen a long way since then. But his recent championing of punk rock, while partly opportunistic, went right to the core of his unswerving belief that young audiences and young bands were the lifeblood of pop.

In May 1977, Bolan had turned out to see one of the more daring of those new acts, Siouxsie And The Banshees, at the Music Machine in London. The Banshees' prime movers, Siouxsie Sioux and Steven Severin, had met at a Roxy Music show in autumn 1975. Singer Siouxsie had grown up with glam, particularly Bolan, Bowie and Roxy Music. By late summer 1977, they were covering T. Rex's '20th

Century Boy' in concert and eyeing up Marc Bolan as a potential producer.

The Banshees' first drummer, Sid Vicious, had once sported a Bolan perm; he also saw Bowie at the peak of Ziggy and acquired his *nom de guerre* via a song on Lou Reed's *Transformer*. His replacement, Kenny Morris, had mastered and refined the Glitter beat.

Those early years of the 1970s represented 'a brave new world', Siouxsie reflects, 'tearing down old traditions and clichés and social acceptances around role models, male and female. It was a springboard in seeing how you could accentuate your own individuality.'

Back in 1972, T. Rex's hit 'Children Of The Revolution' had prompted much debate: 'What revolution?' critics asked. By 1977, they had their answer.

PREVIOUS PAGE AND ABOVE: Rod Stewart, David Bowie and Tony Visconti headed a large cast of mourners at Bolan's funeral at Golders Green crematorium four days after his death in the early hours of September 16, 1977.

FACING PAGE: At the time of his passing, Bolan – the self-styled 'Godfather of Punk' – was thrilled that a new generation was bringing life back to a moribund rock scene. He'd seen Siouxsie And The Banshees, whose 1977 set included T. Rex's '20th Century Boy', at the Music Machine. There was talk of him producing the band.

The pic you see of me on this page is with a little lady called Siouxsie, who was playing with her group called the Banshees at the London Music Machine a few weeks ago when I went along to listen. She does a version on stage of one of my old hits, 'Twentieth Century Boy', which is really interesting and nothing like mine. I thought she was great and it's always a real compliment for someone to take one of your songs and do something different with it. This lady has er . . . potential!

Postscript
Glam and Me

For this young pop fan during the sixties, it was always the ones with 'The Look' that shone brightest – Brian Jones, Dave Davies, Chris 'Ace' Kefford, Peter Frampton. By 1969, one performer stood head and shoulders above them all – The Move's Roy Wood. He was like a character from my shelf of illustrated history books. There was also a fuzzy awareness of Medusa-haired Marc Bolan, whose Tyrannosaurus Rex LPs were often advertised on the Regal Zonophone sleeves that housed those classic Move 45s. Mick, the hippie-next-door, once played me one on his big, hand-built stereo system painted in psychedelic colours.

By the time Bolan broke big, in late spring 1971, pop now had to compete with football, speedway and the shocking, suit-wearing formality of life at grammar school. I have no recollection of any one song hauling me back wholeheartedly to music – but by 1972 I was taking my weekly copy of *New Musical Express* into class, obsessing over the charts and ending each day in bed with Radio Luxembourg.

(It was there, through the hazy cosmic jive of radio static, that the otherworldly delights of Roxy Music's 'Virginia Plain' first came calling. *What the hell was that?*)

Bolan was Number One – the voice, the face, that hair, the lyrics that raced around the playground like Chinese whispers. Soon enough, there were T. Rex vs Slade glam wars on the school bus. Happily, there were no serious pastings for the outnumbered and reputedly 'sissy' Bolanites.

But something happened to the T. Rex man himself that year. In the first days of May 1972, I'd cycled over to a nice part of town where a friend of a friend had a hot-off-the-press copy of 'Metal Guru'. It was Rex's best yet and we listened to it several times, in he-and-she young teen silence.

Later that summer, my classmate and fellow Rex fan Kevin Fisher cycled over with his brand-new cassette copy of *The Slider*. I had the previous album, *Electric Warrior*, and its poster was probably still up on the wall. Good as it was, I remember thinking there was something just a little too familiar about Rex's latest. (Only later did I come to appreciate its nuances.)

Returning to the original press sources for this book confirmed my suspicions; Bolan was no longer having it all his own way by the summer of '72. The competition came thick and fast. Alice, Mott and Glitter dominated the holidays – with Hawkwind's space-rocker 'Silver Machine' opening up another exciting new musical front.

That autumn everything went Roxy Music. Having seen them on *Top Of The Pops* and discovered that Eno was a visitor from the Planet Xenon (but *of course* he was…), nothing else could compete. Bolan was still releasing cracking 45s, but now there was Bowie, too, whose 'John, I'm Only Dancing' was so irresistibly shrill and fleet-footed. Lieutenant Pigeon served up the laughs; sixties girl group The Shangri-Las – back in the charts with the comic-strip style 'Leader Of The Pack' – intensified the rampant atmosphere of teen-pop hysteria. Ditto the arrival of *Popswop* and *Music Scene* magazines – in colour.

Though nowhere near as prolific as Bolan and

Bowie, everything Roxy did sounded unexpected. Their first album turned out to be nothing like 'Virginia Plain'; the exquisite 'Pyjamarama' was a pop single that sounded nothing like a pop single.

In spring '73, Roxy Music came to town. It didn't seem possible – five magnificent space cadets on a stage in a fading art-deco seaside resort. In the row directly below us, a group of grown-up girls wore sparkling outfits more befitting classic Hollywood than C&A. That evening, I lit up that first Consulate and entered young adulthood.

Under the spotlights, a ravishing Bryan Ferry slid snake-like across the stage, throwing his arms out as if he were some B-movie magician or mesmerist. That fabulous creature Eno lurked mysteriously stage-left, alas too often obscured by equipment and darkness.

When Roxy returned in November, everything had changed – but then a week can seem like a whole season when you're 14. Eno's departure was greeted with much sorrow by us Class 3-12 pop diehards; I passed on the new album, *Stranded*.

Then, at the end of the month, an epiphany of sorts. Mott The Hoople rolled up, supported by a new band, Queen. We'd all heard Queen's debut thanks to classmate Den, whose mum lavished him with new albums *and* bought him a killer stereo with floor speakers.

There was plenty of lively chatter in the stalls after Queen's set, much of it about the band's dynamo frontman. Some of the elders even left during the interval, having seen and heard all that they needed to.

But to be part of 'All The Young Dudes', the anthem of those times, was why most of us were there. It didn't disappoint. Yet, down the front for the epic climax, amidst a heaving, all-singing, all-clapping mass, I found myself in an awkward minority of one, yearning for another time, another place.

Mott may have been singing about classic rock'n'roll, as they often did à la 'All The Way From Memphis'. And I too was now fast flipping back to a previous era, thanks to several competitively priced double-albums: the first two Hendrix LPs packaged as one, a Velvet Underground compilation, Pink Floyd's *A Nice Pair* and those two Tyrannosaurus Rex 'doubleback' sets.

During research for this book, I was surprised to discover just how many critics were calling time on the whole glitter/glam shebang during that long, candlelit winter of 1973/74. (An extraordinary time marked by strikes and blackouts – though the three-day week made perfect sense to me.) Neither had I realised how many of its protagonists were walking away and/or cracking up during that time.

That said, the fashions weren't immediately discarded. Those dark blue 4-inch platform boots – at £14.99 from Faith, the most expensive footwear in town – stood tall for several months afterwards. Only now they were worn with hand-frayed and faded jeans and, it pains me to say, my grandmother's three-quarter-length musquash fur coat.

It was easy to reject 'The Now' by 1974. The fashions had sobered up, and the music? Well, now it was just music: no sense of occasion, nothing to get excited about. The last thing anyone expected two years hence was punk rock. After an initial period of confusion – short hair? a whiff of violence? – it made everything matter again.

As I've noted in these pages, by the time of Bolan's death in September 1977 the Children of the Revolution had grown up. Seduced by Malcolm McLaren's glorious call to insurrection, they set about reinventing 'glam' for a new era of anti-fashion and anti-heroes. And this time, we could all join in.

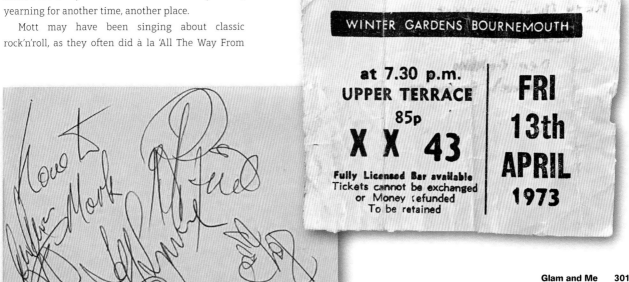

WINTER GARDENS BOURNEMOUTH

at 7.30 p.m.
UPPER TERRACE
85p
X X 43
Fully Licensed Bar available
Tickets cannot be exchanged
or Money refunded
To be retained

FRI
13th
APRIL
1973

Select Bibliography

MAGAZINES AND NEWSPAPERS

Beat Instrumental
Billboard
The Bromley & Kentish Times
Cream
Creem
Daily Express
Daily Mirror
Daily Sketch
Daily Telegraph
Dateline
Disc and Music Echo
Disco 45
Evening Standard
Frendz
Friends
Gay News
International Times
Jackie
Let It Rock
Life
Melody Maker
MOJO
Music Scene
New Musical Express
The New Yorker
The Observer
Penthouse
Popswop
Record Mirror
Rock
Rolling Stone
Sounds
The Sunday Times
Superstar
Town
The Weekly News
Vogue
Zigzag

While drawing on a wide variety of magazine sources, I've paid particular attention to the often overlooked *Record Mirror* archive. The publication prioritised singles-chart artists – especially relevant here – and was quick on the uptake with both Elton John and Rod Stewart.

Once again, online music journalism archive *Rock's Backpages* has proved indispensable, especially in sourcing some of the more obscure material. **www.rocksbackpages.com**

Chart statistics courtesy of the Official Charts Company and *Billboard*.

BOOKS

- Bracewell, Michael – *Re-Make/Re-Model: Art, Pop, Fashion And The Making Of Roxy Music 1953-1972*. Faber & Faber, 2007.
- Bowie, Angie – *Backstage Passes: Life On The Wild Side With David Bowie*. Orion, 1993.
- Bruce, Michael – *No More Mr Nice Guy*. SAF, 1996.
- Des Barres, Pamela – *I'm With The Band*. Omnibus Press, 2018.
- Doyle, Tom – *Captain Fantastic: Elton John's Stellar Trip Through The '70s*. Polygon, 2017.
- Dunaway, Dennis – *Snakes! Guillotines! Electric Chairs!: My Adventures In The Alice Cooper Group*. Omnibus Press, 2015.
- Easlea, Daryl – *Talent Is An Asset: The Story Of Sparks*. Omnibus Press, 2009.
- Gorman, Paul – *The Look: Adventures In Rock And Pop Fashion*. Sanctuary Publishing, 2001.
- Hill, Dave – *So Here It Is: The Autobiography*. Unbound, 2017.
- Hunter, Ian – *Diary of A Rock'n'Roll Star*. Panther, 1974; republished Omnibus Press, 2018.
- John, Elton – *Me: Elton John*. Macmillan, 2019.
- McLagan, Ian 'Mac' – *All The Rage*. Sidgwick & Jackson, 1998.

- McLenehan, Cliff – *Marc Bolan 1947-1977: A Chronology*. Helter Skelter Books, 1995; updated Kindle, 2019.
- Neill, Andy – *The Faces: Had Me A Real Good Time*. Omnibus Press, 2011.
- Pitt, Ken – *Bowie: The Pitt Report*. Omnibus Press, 1983.
- Paytress, Mark – *Bolan: The Rise And Fall Of A 20th Century Superstar*. Omnibus Press, 2005.
- Paytress, Mark – *BowieStyle*. Omnibus Press, 2000.
- Powell, Don with Falkenberg, Lise Lyng – *Look Wot I Dun: My Life In Slade*. Omnibus Press, 2019.
- Quatro, Suzi – *Unzipped*. Hodder & Stoughton, 2008.
- Reynolds, Simon – *Shock And Awe: Glam Rock And Its Legacy*. Faber & Faber, 2017.
- Sontag, Susan – *Notes On 'Camp'*. Penguin Classics, 2018.
- Stewart, Rod – *Rod: The Autobiography*. Arrow, 2013.
- Sylvain, Sylvain – *There's No Bones In Ice Cream: Sylvain Sylvain's Story Of The New York Dolls*. Omnibus Press, 2018.
- Thompson, Dave – *Children Of The Revolution: The Glam Rock Story 1970-75*. Cherry Red Books, 2010.
- Tobler, John and Grundy, Stuart – *The Record Producers*. BBC Books, 1982.
- Tremlett, George – *The Gary Glitter Story*. Futura Publications, 1974.
- Visconti, Tony – *The Autobiography: Bowie, Bolan And The Brooklyn Boy*. HarperCollins, 2007.
- Wale, Michael – *Voxpop: Profiles Of The Pop Process*. Harrap, 1972.
- Wood, Ron – *Ronnie*. Pan, 2008.
- Woodmansey, Mick - *Spider From Mars: My Life With Bowie*. Sidgwick & Jackson, 2016

CREDITS

Pages 5, 7, 21, 29, 37, 41, 41, 63, 68, 69, 71, 73, 75, 85, 88, 90, 96, 101, 103, 104, 128, 129, 133, 135, 143, 149, 152, 159, 160, 162, 163, 172, 179, 180, 182, 185, 187, 188, 190, 203, 215, 219, 221, 222, 226, 227, 231, 233, 234, 252, 273, 274, 276, 278, 279, 284, 285, 286, 289, 291, 294, 296, 298, Mirrorpix; page 9 Shepard Sherbell/CORBIS SABA/Corbis/Getty; pages 10, 57, 115, 140, 191 Shutterstock; page 14 Peter Sanders; page 15 Don McCullin; pages 19, 26, 27, 121 Ray Stevenson; page 34 Dick Barnatt/Redferns/Getty; page 39 Ed Caraeff/Iconic Images/Getty; page 44, 120, 261 Michael Ochs Archives/Getty; page 47 Pamela Des Barres; page 48, 241 Pictorial Press Ltd/Alamy; pages 54, 74, 98, 220 Michael Putland/Getty; page 58 Gems/Redferns/Getty; page 71 Andrew Maclear/Hulton Archive/Getty; pages 82, 118 George Underwood; page 93 Gloria Stavers; page 94 Estate of Keith Morris/Redferns/Getty; pages 98, 154 Ron Howard/Redferns/Getty; page 111 BBC; page 138 Brian Cooke/Redferns/Getty; page 166 Central Press/Hulton Archive/Getty; page 170 Anwar Hussein/Getty; page 174 Kris Needs; page 177 Look-In/Rebellion Publishing Ltd © 1973, 2022; pages 195, 235 Deborah Loads; page 198 Gijsbert Hanekroot/Redferns/Getty; page 201 Michael Warley; page 207 David Warner Ellis/Redferns/Getty; page 210 Jorgen Angel/Redferns/Getty; page 211 Steve Wood/Express/Getty; page 212 Justin de Villeneuve/Getty; page 217 Jackie/DC Thomson & Co Ltd; page 236 Ian Dickson/Redferns/Getty; page 268 Martyn Goddard/Corbis/Getty; page 271 Terry O'Neill/Iconic Images/Getty; page 281 Tom Hill/WireImage/Getty; page 295 London Features/Avalon; page 296 Kath Andryszewski; page 299 Denis O'Regan/Getty.

Grateful thanks to the following fans/collectors/organisations for generously opening their archives, and by doing so, helping make this book the visual feast it needed to be:

Steve Aldred; Kath Andryszewski; Greg Brooks at The Queen Archive; Rob Caiger; Lee Davey at www.alicecooperechive.com; John Dowell; Sue Ford; Michael Green; Jim Jenkins at The Official International Queen Fan Club; Dave Jewell at The Slade Fans Page; Andy Jones at The David Bowie Glamour Fanzine; Brad Jones, author of *The Sweet*; Dave Kemp (Slade fan extraordinaire, RIP; www.davekempandslade.com); Richard Laymon at label/sleeve specialist site www.rockfiles.co.uk; Deborah Loads; Louise Longson; Kris Needs; John O'Brien at www.vivaroxymusic.com; Steve Parkins; The John Peel Archive; Justin Purington at www.justabuzz.com; Ruud Swart at www.fanmael.nl; Michael Warley; and to everyone else who got in touch but whose material we were unable to use.

Acknowledgements

I'd firstly like to thank David Barraclough at Wise Music for commissioning the book – and for extending the deadline as I found myself marooned during these strange times. I'd also like to thank copy editor Paul Woods for his well-judged intervention on several structural issues, and for his sharp and incisive comments on the text; project editor Imogen Gordon Clark for her expert coordination skills and patience; Joe Barnes for his attentive proofreading; Claire Browne for some last-minute fixes; and designers Amazing15 for the superb cover and skillful handling of an enormous pile of visuals.

Eternal love and gratitude to my partner, Cristiana Turchetti, for her support and patience – especially during my many long periods of hibernation whilst researching and writing this book.

I've drawn extensively from my own cache of interviews, conducted over four decades. So thanks for the memories – and the wisdom shared – to: Bev Bevan; Michael Bruce; Alice Cooper; Robert Davidson; Jeff Dexter; Dennis Dunaway; Brian Eno; David Enthoven; Bob Ezrin; BP Fallon; Bill 'Legend' Fifield; Mickey Finn; Peter Frampton; Gary Glitter; Jack Green; Bob Harris; Dave Hill; Noddy Holder; Ian Hunter; Gloria Jones; Kenney Jones; Jim Lea; Phil Manzanera; Ian 'Mac' McLagan; Mike Leander; Tony Norman; Iggy Pop; Don Powell; Steve Priest; Suzi Quatro; Mick Ralphs; Lou Reed; Mick Rock; Andy Scott; Ken Scott; Tony Secunda; Siouxsie Sioux; Cindy Smith; Neal Smith; Sylvain Sylvain; Tony Visconti; Roy Wood; and Mick 'Woody' Woodmansey.

To avoid confusion, I've used the present tense for all interviews conducted by me, unless the person is no longer living or, in Glitter's case, *persona non grata*. Interview quotes from all other sources have been placed in the past tense.

I'm especially grateful to those journalists and commentators who were there to chronicle the era at first hand: Keith Altham; Lester Bangs; John Beattie; Michael 'Mike' Beatty; Michael Benton; Caroline Boucher; Geoff Brown; Roy Carr; Chris Charlesworth; Robert Christgau; John Coleman; Ray Coleman; Richard Cromelin; Bob Dawbarn; Robin Denselow; Barry Dillon; Royston Eldridge; Bernard Falk; Timothy Ferris; Danny Fields; Pete Frame; Simon Frith; Roger Greenaway; Albert Grossman; Genevieve 'Genny' Hall; Russell Harty; Peter Harvey, Martin Hayman; Robert Hilburn; Harold Hobson; Roy Hollingworth; Peter Holmes; Sue James; James Johnson; Peter Jones; Nick Kent; Mike Ledgerwood; Nick Logan; Valerie 'Val' Mabbs; Ian MacDonald; Steve Mann; Dave Marsh; Lisa Mehlman; Bill McAllister; John Mendelsohn; John Morthland; Charles Shaar Murray; Anne Nightingale; Tony Norman; Rory O'Toole; Tony Palmer; Steve Peacock; Chris Poole; Simon Puxley; Wayne Robbins; Jean Rook; Lillian Roxon; Rosalind Russell; Rick Sanders; Barry Taylor; Nick Tosches; George Tremlett; Steve Turner; Andrew Tyler; George Underwood; Penny Valentine; Michael Watts; Julie Webb; Charles Webster; Chris Welch; Richard Williams; and Ellen Willis.

Thanks also to subsequent chroniclers Danny Baker, Paul Du Noyer, Pete Makowski and especially to Kris Needs, who was just the right age to get close to the action. Further thanks to Chris Fraser and Trevor King, for sharing a few glam-racket theories; to my sister, Julie-Anne Fraser, who howled when I told her that Donny Osmond had 'broken' his voice; to Martin Barden, who since 1994 has joined me in working up the T. Rex catalogue; and to Cliff McLenehan, whose day-by-day Bolan chronicle (see bibliography) makes a fine companion to my own Bolan biography.

In memory of Norman Paytress, my Radio 2-loving father who had an uncanny gift of predicting future No. 1 hits – including Edison Lighthouse's 'Love Grows (Where My Rosemary Goes)', an early riser in this book.